W9-BSM-227

GAMING
HACKS™

Other resources from O'Reilly

Related titles

Physics for Game Developers

AI for Game Developers

TiVo Hacks™

Mac OS X Panther Hacks™

Building the Perfect PC

PC Hacks™

Games, Diversions, and Perl Culture: The Best of the Perl Journal

Digital Photography Hacks™

iPod and iTunes Hacks™

Hacks Series Home

hacks.oreilly.com is a community site for developers and power users of all stripes. Readers learn from each other as they share their favorite tips and tools for Mac OS X, Linux, Google, Windows XP, and more.

oreilly.com

oreilly.com is more than a complete catalog of O'Reilly books. You'll also find links to news, events, articles, weblogs, sample chapters, and code examples.

oreillynet.com is the essential portal for developers interested in open and emerging technologies, including new platforms, programming languages, and operating systems.

Conferences

O'Reilly brings diverse innovators together to nurture the ideas that spark revolutionary industries. We specialize in documenting the latest tools and systems, translating the innovator's knowledge into useful skills for those in the trenches. Visit *conferences.oreilly.com* for our upcoming events.

Safari Bookshelf (*safari.oreilly.com*) is the premier online reference library for programmers and IT professionals. Conduct searches across more than 1,000 books. Subscribers can zero in on answers to time-critical questions in a matter of seconds. Read the books on your Bookshelf from cover to cover or simply flip to the page you need. Try it today with a free trial.

GAMING
HACKS™

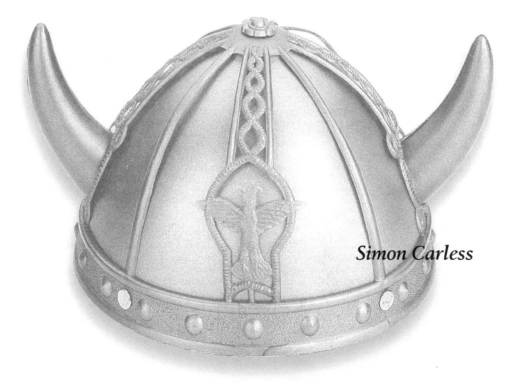

Simon Carless

O'REILLY®

Beijing · Cambridge · Farnham · Köln · Paris · Sebastopol · Taipei · Tokyo

Gaming Hacks™
by Simon Carless

Copyright © 2005 O'Reilly Media, Inc. All rights reserved.
Printed in the United States of America.

Published by O'Reilly Media, Inc., 1005 Gravenstein Highway North,
Sebastopol, CA 95472.

O'Reilly books may be purchased for educational, business, or sales promotional use. Online editions are also available for most titles (*safari.oreilly.com*). For more information, contact our corporate/institutional sales department: (800) 998-9938 or *corporate@oreilly.com*.

Editor:	chromatic	**Production Editor:**	Mary Anne Weeks Mayo
Series Editor:	Rael Dornfest	**Cover Designer:**	Hanna Dyer
Executive Editor:	Dale Dougherty	**Interior Designer:**	David Futato

Printing History:

October 2004:	First Edition.

Nutshell Handbook, the Nutshell Handbook logo, and the O'Reilly logo are registered trademarks of O'Reilly Media, Inc. The *Hacks* series designations, *Gaming Hacks*, the image of a Viking helmet, "Hacks 100 Industrial-Strength Tips and Tools," and related trade dress are trademarks of O'Reilly Media, Inc.

Many of the designations used by manufacturers and sellers to distinguish their products are claimed as trademarks. Where those designations appear in this book, and O'Reilly Media, Inc. was aware of a trademark claim, the designations have been printed in caps or initial caps.

While every precaution has been taken in the preparation of this book, the publisher and author assume no responsibility for errors or omissions, or for damages resulting from the use of the information contained herein.

Small print: The technologies discussed in this publication, the limitations on these technologies that technology and content owners seek to impose, and the laws actually limiting the use of these technologies are constantly changing. Thus, some of the hacks described in this publication may not work, may cause unintended harm to systems on which they are used, or may not be consistent with applicable user agreements. Your use of these hacks is at your own risk, and O'Reilly Media, Inc. disclaims responsibility for any damage or expense resulting from their use. In any event, you should take care that your use of these hacks does not violate any applicable laws, including copyright laws.

OTABIND®
INTERNATIONAL

This book uses Otabind,® a durable and flexible lay-flat binding.

ISBN: 0-596-00714-0
[I]

Contents

Credits

About the Author

Simon Carless (*http://www.mono211.com/ffwd*) is an editor, writer, and former game designer who originally hails from London, England, but now lives and works in the Bay area. He currently works as Managing Editor for the online arm of *Game Developer Magazine*, Gamasutra.com, and was formerly an editor at the techgeek site Slashdot, concentrating on the Slashdot Games pages (*http://games.slashdot.org/*).

Simon also works on multiple digital archiving projects at the nonprofit Internet Archive (*http://archive.org/*) in San Francisco, including several video game-related projects. Formerly, he was a lead game designer at companies such as Eidos Interactive and Atari, where he worked on a diverse set of titles for both console and PC platforms.

Contributors

The following people contributed their hacks, writing, and inspiration to this book:

- Adam Cadre (*http://adamcadre.ac*) is the author of the novel *Ready, Okay!* and the web comic *ACX*. He has also written several computer programs, most of which prominently feature the line 20 GOTO 10. Among those that don't are the interactive fiction works *Photopia*, *Varicella*, and *Narcolepsy*.

  [Hacks #88 and #89]

- chromatic cut his teeth programming games for the Commodore 64 before growing up to become Technical Editor of the O'Reilly Network. In practice, that means he edits *ONLamp.com* (open source administration and development), *Perl.com*, and, occasionally, books like this one. Outside of work, he enjoys cooking and producing weird software hacks such as SDL Parrot. Wade through the disarray of his web site at *http://wgz.org/chromatic/*.

[Hacks #2, #3, #81, #91– #93]

- Frank Dellario cofounded the award-winning Machinima animation company, the ILL Clan in 1998 and is its current president. He has served as the producer, production manager, assistant director, and cinematographer on numerous ILL Clan productions, bringing over 15 years of experience in film production to great use. He recently produced a series of vignettes for Spike TV's Video Game Awards. Frank also cofounded, published, and edited *FilmCrew* magazine, a trade journal for the film industry business, for over eight years, and has been a multimedia producer as well. Prior to all this, he spent six years in the U.S. Navy as a nuclear technician on a fast attack submarine.

[Hack #66]

- Hugh Hancock founded Strange Company (*http://www.strangecompany. org/*), the world's first professional Machinima production company, making films in computer game engines, in 1997. Since then, he has produced or directed more than 10 Machinima films, been praised by Roger Ebert, been described as the "guru of the Machinima movement," and worn PVC trousers on some seriously inappropriate occasions. He currently divides his time between running Machinima.com (*http://www.machinima.com/*) and working on Strange Company's first Machinima feature film, *Bloodspell*.

[Hacks #63– #66]

- Jeremiah Johnson is a graduate of the Columbia University School of Engineering and Applied Science, where he spent most of his time skipping classes on Java programming and database management and instead hacking old video game consoles. In 1999, together with friend Mike Hanlon from Detroit, he cofounded the 8bitpeoples, a artist collective interested in the audio/video aesthetics of early video game consoles and home computers, and has released several recordings through 8bitpeoples under the name Nullsleep. His most recent work has focused on the Nintendo Entertainment System and Game Boy, in areas such as music programming and graphics data hacking. He has written several online guides to music programming for Nintendo hardware.

[Hack #62]

- Chris Kohler has written about Japanese video games since 1996. His work has appeared in magazines such as *Wired*, *Animerica*, and *Nintendo Official Magazine UK*, and on web sites including Wired News, Gamespy, and Games Domain. He has contributed research, pictures, and text to books such as *High Score!: The Illustrated History of Electronic Games, Second Edition*, and *Phoenix: The Fall and Rise of*

Videogames, Third Edition. He spent the 2002–03 academic year living in Kyoto, Japan, on a Fulbright scholarship, researching his book *Super Mario Nation: The Cinematic Japanese Video Game*, which Brady Games will publish in late 2004. He graduated summa cum laude from Tufts University in 2002 with a B.A. in Japanese and highest thesis honors. Visit him online at *http://kobunheat.pitas.com/*.

[Hacks #49 and #97]

- Johan Kotlinski is currently working on his Media Engineering masters project at the Royal Institute of Technology, Stockholm. During his education, he had time to program the Little Sound Dj music editor for the Game Boy, maintain the Bleep Street/Rebel Pet Set record label, organize Microdisko club evenings, and helped kick off a new genre of music recognized by the likes of Sven Väth and Malcolm McLaren. Besides being an all-round music superstar, Johan also keeps busy programming the Commodore 64 as a proud member of the Hack'n'Trade demo group; check out the Kid Grid 2 release for an example of a truly hardcore hack.

[Hack #22]

- Joshua "Storm Shadow" LaTendresse writes the audiovisual column "The Hook Up" (*http://www.penny-arcade.com/hookupmain.php3*) for popular web comic *Penny Arcade* (*http://www.penny-arcade.com*). He is active as an instructor and student practicing Tae Kwon Do at UC Berkeley, and resides in the Presidio of San Francisco in California. His narcissism knows no bounds. Through this deeply passionate and profound self-love affair, he has purchased for himself nearly every electronic toy imaginable. Stormy (as his friends call him) will guide you through the constant bickering and irreconcilable differences between consoles and A/V equipment to the hot and steamy three-way action that can coexist between you, your gaming gear, and a great Home Theater.

[Hacks #35,#38–#45]

- Christopher Linder cofounded the independent game house Demiurge Studios (*http://www.demiurgestudios.com/*) along with two fellow Carnegie Mellon alumni. He is a significant contributor to the Unreal Developers Network, where many of his technical documents can be found. Besides programming and writing at work, Chris can be found creating particle systems, monkeying around in UnrealEd, and fiddling with sound effects. One day Chris hopes to outfit his station wagon with roof-mounted auto-targeting rave lasers. While he thinks this will be cool, other people are dubious.

[Hacks #82–#84]

- David J. Long is a father of three little boys six and under and resides in Reading, Pennsylvania. Yup, just like the railroad. He regularly appears in the pages of *Computer Games Magazine* and offers a weekly column, reviews, and his unique insight into playing games and the business of games at GamerDad (*http://www.gamerdad.com/*), the web site of choice for parents looking for information about video games. [Hack #8]

- Chris Sturgill has been a video game artist for the better part of a decade, plying his trade at Atari Games, Midway, and Demiurge Studios on all manner of games from the arcade to home consoles. His content-related documentation can be found on the Unreal Developers Network. His doodles can be found on scraps of paper just about anywhere he's been. [Hacks #82–#84]

- Al Reed is cofounder and Director of Development of Demiurge Studios, Inc., an independent game-development studio located in Boston. Prior to his time at Demiurge, he served in various roles at CogniToy and Iron Lore Entertainment. He is also an adjunct lecturer for a game-programming class at Carnegie Mellon University. [Hacks #82–#84]

- Spenser "Redef" Norrish is an university student who has run and written for GameSpy's PlanetUnreal and PlanetHalfLife fan sites for the past three years, even while playing Counter-Strike competitively and playing in a season of the Cyberathlete Professional League. [Hacks #34, #35, and #94]

- Roger Post hails from southern New Jersey. He has played video games since the Atari 2600 era and tends to gravitate towards shmups, while still enjoying the occasional racer or RPG. Roger, who also goes by the name Postman, enjoys the creative side of gaming, producing the occasional article on just about anything shoot-em-up related, or tracking down fan art on some obscure Japanese web site. While some may accuse him of living in the past, he is still hopeful for the day that 2D shoot-em-ups will make a huge comeback. His web site is *http://www. shootthecore.com/*. [Hack #95]

- Nolan "Radix" Pflug has always got the most out of the games he plays. He started to go for fast completion times with Super Metroid, and in 1997, started a web site to keep track of fast times for the id Software classic Quake. After over 6,000 demos and 6 years, he expanded the site to include console games with his run of Metroid Prime 100% in 1:37. The skill of speed running gets more popular as the site continues to grow. Visit his personal site at *http://planetquake.com/sda/other/*. [Hacks #68 and #69]

- Richard Skidmore, a.k.a. Morfans, has been a game addict for over 20 years, ever since he purchased his first computer (a ZX81) at the tender age of 11. In recent years, time restrictions and his innate lack of any actual gaming talent have meant that he spends more time watching other people play than playing himself, a situation that suits him just fine as an admin at the Speed Demos Archive (*http://planetquake.com/sda*). He lives in the Highlands of Scotland with his family, an assortment of animals, and a very slow Internet connection.
  [Hacks #68 and #69]
- Andrew Plotkin has moved away from Pittsburgh three times and now lives in Pittsburgh. He is interested in making tools that let people make art; he studies what draws people into complicity with virtual worlds. (He suspects the answer is how the interactions are shaped.) He has several Macs and lots of very cool books. He can also cook and enjoys long walks. He would like to get together with a nice geek girl. Email for info (see *http://eblong.com/zarf/home.html* for address).
  [Hacks #85–#87]
- Michael Zenke (*http://www.randomdialogue.net*) writes and consumes oxygen in what is undoubtedly the best city in the world, Madison, Wisconsin. Michael lives with his fiancée Katie. This is his first contribution to a published book. Michael is a sectional editor for Slashdot Games (*http://games.slashdot.org/*) and posts content on a regular basis to his own web site, Random Dialogue. When he's not writing about games, he's usually playing them or running pen and paper games for his friends. There is no truth to the rumor that he once ran over a woman with her own car.
  [Hacks #28–#33]

Acknowledgments

I'd like to profusely thank everybody who took their valuable time and effort to contribute to *Gaming Hacks*. You guys rock.

This book is for Holly, who puts up with a lot, makes me happy in a multitude of sassy ways, and is quite often literally awed by my geekiness. You rock, dear, possibly more than anyone has rocked before, and I love you.

Otherwise, I need to give many thanks out to chromatic (editor extraordinaire), the technical reviewers of this book (Jiji, Loonyboi, NFGMan, and others!), Brewster and the Internet Archive crew (saving the world, a floppy disk at a time?), Rob and the Slashdot crew (commencing the flamewars... now?), all of my family for supporting me so wonderfully, and... anyone else who knows me. That's all of you.

Foreword

I'll let you in on a secret: the best way to make games for a living is ... to make them.

This is like saying that if you want to be a writer, you should write. If you want to be a singer, then sing. If you really want to be an artist, then paint or sculpt or just put a lump of driftwood on eBay and call yourself an "Outsider." If you want to try your hand at any endeavor, it makes perfect sense that you should just dig in, get dirty, and see how it suits you. Mucking around is fun; taking things apart to see how they work is an indispensable part of any craft.

But games are such complicated things. How far can one person go in a field in which, more and more, the hit games are products that take years, and teams of people, to create?

The answer is: farther than you might think.

While you won't necessarily be able to make the next Grand Theft Auto-killer singlehandedly, there is a great deal you can learn by getting into the guts of the games you love: dissecting them, naming the parts, playing Dr. Frankenstein or Moreau as you build new things out of bits and pieces of the old. Even if you don't have any desire to make games for a living, there is a great deal of fun to be had, and a lot you can learn, tinkering with the pieces. Not everyone who takes apart a watch wants to make Rolexes for a living; sometimes it's enough just to find out what makes those things tick.

When I was just starting out doing the thing I most wanted to do with my life—write fantasy, horror, and science fiction—I didn't know what to do other than imitate the stuff I loved. I wrote endless imitations of H.P. Lovecraft's Cthulhu Mythos tales and Fritz Leiber's adventures of Fafhrd & the Grey Mouser, trying to find my own way. I read my favorite stories over and over, hoping to see how they were put together, making my own versions in the desperate hope that eventually some of the magic would rub off on me. It was a humiliating way to proceed, but eventually it worked. The odd thing is, it works for lots and lots of writers. You start by copying, aping, the thing you love. You speak in borrowed accents while you learn to tell your own tales, and eventually, the mannerisms fall away, and you're speaking in your own voice. You go from reading pages to filling them. This is how fans become professionals. The field of fantastic literature feeds itself.

It is much the same, I have found, in the game industry. There is only the slightest separation between gamer and designer. It's all a matter of perspective, a mental shift, really. This is one of gaming's great strengths. In the case of PC games, the technology you use to play the game is indistinguishable from the tools used to build it. You have complete access to the whole mad scientist's laboratory, with the beakers bubbling and Tesla coils snapping and the crazy professor himself having just stepped away from the workbench for a few moments.

I still remember the first time I opened a Quake .*pak* file and got a glimpse of how the gory guts of that game were put together: sounds here, textures there, some mysterious terrifying programmer stuff over there, which, hm, sort of had its own kind of logic. A few lines specified what kind of sound to play whenever the attack dogs barked. Hm. And one line seemed to determine what kind of sound the pistol played when you fired it. And, hum, even though I am about the least technical person around, I am handy with a word processor. Even I could copy and paste a bit of code, switching the dog's bark with the gunshot. And behold, a gun that barked! A dog that gave out ringing shots!

I remember thinking, "You can do that?"

My next real game-hacker buzz came from a very feeble attempt to make a Quake level, using some 3D editing tools that were freely available on the net: a hollow cube, a couple of greenish boulders floating inexplicably in midair, bathed in eerie sourceless light. My first Quake map was a piece of crap, but I will never forget it. It still feels like a real place to me—a tiny world I made by hand, in less than an hour.

Of course, real world-building is not quite that easy. Not if you want to make a reality convincing and alluring enough to attract millions of gamers and keep them busy for hours and hours. But still, that little room of floating boulders was a start. I made bigger levels. They weren't much prettier, but they were more elaborate, more experimental. I mailed these maps to other people, and listened and learned from their comments. Amazing. They were playing my levels! People were actually able to enter the little worlds I had made. Every time I tinkered, every time I listened to the feedback of friends, I learned more.

One thing I learned was how the game community comes together. This was exactly how teams self-assembled to devise their own games. Like-minded tinkerers moved from independence and isolation to form small teams. These teams converted existing games, such as Quake, and came up with games of their own devising. Some were not even games—just odd experiments, hybrids that wouldn't have lasted long off Dr. Moreau's island.

One of my favorite experiments was a bizarre little Quake modification, or "mod," called "Club Shubb." It was a big echoey cave of a nightclub where a techno tune thudded endlessly, and shaggy Shamblers gathered to throw themselves off a stage into a churning pit of fellow monsters. Hilarious, weird, pointless. Um ... really? Hilarious, yes; weird, sure. But I would take exception with the pointless part. Its creators, Steve Bond and John Guthrie, used that little club as their resume, and were among the first employees at Valve Software.

There is a direct correlation between stage-diving Shamblers and the inventive scripted sequences and scenarios of Half-Life.

Reinventing the rules of the game is a legitimate first step toward discovering new types of gameplay.

"You can do that?"

Yes. In the words of six-year-old Amber Riller, explaining how she managed to kick my butt at Mario Kart: "You can do anything the game lets you do!"

Here's another open secret. When you have your own company, and you've developed your own cutting-edge technology, and you are finally making your own game for a world waiting in breathless anticipation, no one will be able to tell you what to do or how to do it. You will still be doing exactly what you did when you started out: hacking the game. It may be your own game, but you'll still be hacking away at it. You will still be switching out pieces, making guns bark, taking apart and reassembling your engine to see what it can do, and breaking down what doesn't work, and stripping it for parts. This process not only never stops, but it's an essential part of game design. This is why games like Counter-Strike and Team Fortress go through version after version, release after release, in pursuit of perfection. To make a good game, it helps to be a bit restless, to chafe at things the way they are. No game is ever done until it ships, and maybe even then…

Counter-Strike started as a mod. A handful of guys had some ideas for a game and weren't about to be stopped by the fact that they didn't have a corporate logo or a diploma from Game Design U.

Team Fortress started as a mod, an ongoing experiment in team-based game design by some inventive young Australians who worked out their ideas about games the best way possible—by actually putting them into practice, using technology that was freely available to them. Strangely enough, the experience of actually playing your game, instead of merely thinking about what it might be like to play your game, allows you to gradually turn it from a pipe dream into something worth playing.

I have talked mostly about games with their roots in Quake and Half-Life, because this is my own background. But there are Zelda hackers, Myst imitators, role-playing-game fans making their own RPGs with such cool tools as RPG Maker. Most of these passionate gamehackers are hobbyists, tinkerers, messing around in order to amuse themselves and their friends, enjoying the process of actively adding to the worlds they love. It's no wonder the game industry is thriving, when it offers such a creative outlet for its fans.

One of my favorite game worlds, the Thief series, continues to feed a large community of Fan Mission creators. Some of these missions are astonishing, on a par with levels that shipped in retail products. But first and foremost, they are labors of love. They are the work of passionate individuals so in love with gaming that they are plowing their passion back into the field from which those games grew.

To the extent the game industry encourages and rewards these passionate fans, by providing them with tools and advice and even the occasional cash infusion, the gaming community—by which I mean fans and professionals alike—can only benefit.

That's why whenever young wannabe designers ask me how to break into the industry, I always tell them the same thing: get some friends together, learn how to work as a team, and make a mod. An inventive mod, an innovative hack of an existing game, can tell a prospective employer more about you than a degree in game design from a prestigious university.

I know without a doubt that today's enthusiastic young gamer is tomorrow's seasoned game designer. So, whether you want to see if you have what it takes to make games for a living, or you just want to hack for the joy of hacking …

What are you waiting for?

—Marc Laidlaw
Writer, Half-Life Series
Valve Software

Preface

We've come a long way since the first digital computers. Our machines now can modify genetic data, monitor nuclear reactions, and guide hundreds and thousands of planes to safe landings across the world.

It's much more fun to play games on them, though.

If you grew up in a world with video games, you know their appeal: deceptively simple rules, colorful characters, and the chance that you might finally win with one more try. In a few short decades, video games have changed from simple sprites shooting each other to massively multiplayer fragfests with players shooting each other from different continents. Could Space Invaders be a quarter-century old? Did DOOM really come out a decade ago? Certainly *something* has matured.

Through all of this, games and publishers, machines and platforms have all come and gone. Some live on in arcades and collections, and some stay buried, better forgotten. This isn't a book about any particular era, though. Instead, it explores and celebrates a few of the most interesting nooks and crannies of the gaming world, whether new, old, or positively ancient.

We've collected a hundred hacks for gamers from game developers, expert players, and fans, representing dozens of rabbit holes related to playing, collecting, modifying, and enjoying the world of video games. Some talk about classic games. Others explore modern consoles. Still more cover PC games. There's something for everyone—from an old idea in a new dress to an unknown concept or wacky idea you'd *never* have considered... until now.

After all, the goal is to have fun.

Why Gaming Hacks?

The term *hacking* has an unfortunate reputation in the popular press, where it often refers to someone who breaks into systems or wreaks havoc with computers. Among enthusiasts, on the other hand, the term *hack* refers to a "quick and dirty" solution to a problem or a clever way to do something. The term *hacker* is very much a compliment, praising someone for being *creative* and having the technical chops to get things done. O'Reilly's Hacks series is an attempt to reclaim the word, document the ways people are hacking (in a good way), and pass on the hacker ethic of creative participation to a new generation of hackers. Seeing how others approach systems and problems is often the quickest way to learn about a new technology.

It's also fun.

How to Use This Book

We've divided this book along various topics, not according to any sense of relative difficulty. Skip around and flip through the book; if you see an interesting title or some paragraph catches your eye, read it! Where possible, we've added cross references to related hacks in the text themselves. For example, if you're feeling nostalgic for Wizardry VII, you might like "Play Old Games Through DOSBox" **[Hack #8]**.

How This Book Is Organized

Chapter 1, *Playing Classic Games*
> If you grew up with video games, you probably have fond memories of Atari consoles, the Commodore 64, and greasy-joysticked arcade cabinets in the local pizza parlor. Those days may be gone, but this chapter can help you relive those glorious games on modern hardware—or play new games on that classic hardware.

Chapter 2, *Playing Portably*
> Before the Game Boy, who could have predicted the market for portable game playing? These days, who can ignore it? Instead of explaining how to complete Tetris on level 9-5 using telekinesis, this chapter explores different ways to take your games with you, including ways to have fun with portable game machines you might not have considered.

Chapter 3, *Playing Well with Others*
> Is there a sweeter word in a game studio's press release than "MMORPG?" Probably, but there are hundreds of thousands of players in dozens of persistent worlds. This chapter demonstrates how to enter this world, find friends and money, and even make a name for yourself.

Chapter 4, *Playing with Hardware*

Are there serious PC gamers who don't worry about having the latest and greatest gear? Perhaps a few. There are so many ways to improve your gaming experience; from quieting your PC to connecting your console or computer to your home stereo system, there is something for everyone in this chapter.

Chapter 5, *Playing with Console and Arcade Hardware*

If you've ever dreamed about having your very own arcade machine, this chapter will show you everything you need to know to start. Alternately, it proves why the $50-or-less Dreamcast is a hacker's delight.

Chapter 6, *Playing Around the Game Engine*

What happens when you break a game's rules? What happens when you ignore the goal and strike out on your own? According to speedrunners, sequence breakers, save hackers, level builders, and machinimaniacs, fun happens. This chapter explains why the fun starts after you've rescued the princess.

Chapter 7, *Playing Your Own Games*

As computers increase in power, consoles become more like computers, and the Internet connects everything, *making* games grows ever easier. Maybe you have a killer story to tell. Maybe you'd like to tweak an existing game. Whatever the case, this chapter will guide you to the point of playing your own creations.

Chapter 8, *Playing Everything Else*

Everything else cool that didn't fit in the other chapters ended up here. This chapter isn't discarded remains, though—not with such hacks as learning just enough Japanese to play imported games or overclocking your Sega Genesis.

Conventions Used in This Book

This book uses the following typographical conventions:

Plain text
  Indicates menu titles, menu options, and menu buttons.

Italic
  Indicates new terms, URLs, email addresses, filenames, pathnames, and directories.

`Constant width`
  Indicates commands, options, switches, variables, attributes, keys, functions, file extensions, utilities, the contents of files, and the output from commands.

Constant width bold
>   Shows commands or other text that you should type literally.

Constant width italic
>   Shows text that you should replace with user-supplied values.

Color
>   The second color indicates a cross reference within the text.

 This icon signifies a tip, suggestion, or general note.

 This icon indicates a warning or caution.

The thermometer icons, found next to each hack, indicate the relative complexity of the hack:

 beginner   moderate   expert

Using Code Examples

This book is here to help you get your job done. In general, you may use the code in this book in your programs and documentation. You do not need to contact us for permission unless you're reproducing a significant portion of the code. For example, writing a program that uses several chunks of code from this book does not require permission. Selling or distributing a CD-ROM of examples from O'Reilly books does require permission. Answering a question by citing this book and quoting example code does not require permission. Incorporating a significant amount of example code from this book into your product's documentation does require permission.

We appreciate, but do not require, attribution. An attribution usually includes the title, author, publisher, and ISBN. For example: "*Gaming Hacks* by Simon Carless. Copyright 2004 O'Reilly Media, Inc., 0-596-00714-0."

If you feel your use of code examples falls outside fair use or the permission given above, feel free to contact us at *permissions@oreilly.com*.

Comments and Questions

Please address any comments and questions concerning this book to the publisher:

O'Reilly Media, Inc.
1005 Gravenstein Highway
North Sebastopol, CA 95472
(800) 998-9938 (in the United States or Canada)
(707) 829-0515 (international or local)
(707) 829-0104 (fax)

There is a web page for this book that lists errata, examples, and any additional information. You can access this page at:

http://www.oreilly.com/catalog/gaminghks

To comment or ask technical questions about this book, send email to:

bookquestions@oreilly.com

For more information about books, conferences, Resource Centers, and the O'Reilly Network, see the O'Reilly web site at:

http://www.oreilly.com/

Got a Hack?

To explore Hacks books online or to contribute a hack for future titles, visit:

http://hacks.oreilly.com

Playing Classic Games
Hacks 1-18

With 25 years of game history under our belts, it's difficult to keep track of all of the games and hardware that've come and gone. With the ever-increasing cost and complexity of making new games for current and new hardware, it's difficult for hobbyist gamers to keep up.

With emulation and emulators, the two problems are solving each other. Who could have foreseen in 1980 that the Atari 2600 would see a renaissance of new homebrew development 25 years later? Now emulation has made this possible.

If you grew up with games in the '80s, you don't have to dig your Atari, NES, or Commodore 64 out of the closet to enjoy a bit of nostalgia. Here are a few of our favorite ways to emulate old hardware and games.

HACK #1 Legal Emulation
How to work within the law when you play emulators.

The whole issue of emulation is very thorny, not least because a great deal of the work done under emulation is somewhat less than legal, if sometimes tolerated. The user may not own the ROMs he is playing. Even if he does own them, it's unclear whether he can legally transfer them between media to play them.

I won't point a finger and disclaim loudly that you're bad for using emulators and must go to jail without passing Go or collecting 200 dollars. I also won't pass definitive judgments on legality, either. I *will* point to a few resources I believe *are* legal with regard to emulation.

Homebrew and Freely Distributable Games

You'll find constant references to homebrew games in this book, sometimes running on the hardware themselves. As a rule of thumb, if someone has gone to the trouble of creating homebrew games that work on a specific console, PC variant, or handheld, they will work on the emulated version of that system as well. In that case, you need to find the correct emulator and then download the homebrew ROM to play.

If you're looking for a general source for freely distributable games for multiple systems, even those not covered in detail in this book, the best console source is the PDRoms (*http://www.pdroms.de/*) site. It features over 1,700 ROMs of various kinds for over 20 different computers and consoles.

Often, hackers with particularly detailed knowledge of an individual computer host specific pages showcasing their wares. For example, The Amiga Legal Emulation (ALE) page at *http://ale.emuunlim.com/* has good information and ROM downloads for the Commodore Amiga in particular. Other sites cover their own specialized subjects similarly. Unfortunately, with much of the more obscure abandonware* flying under the radar of copyright holders, it's sometimes difficult to find a page that has really made an effort to separate completely legal disc images from the disc images nobody cares about anymore (but still may be less than legal). Hopefully, this will change as the emulation scene grows and matures.

The only caveat with these public-domain ROMs is that some homebrew or homemade ROMs may reappropriate intellectual property from other famous games. Consider, for example, a homebrew version of Pac-Man with one letter in the name changed "for parody purposes." It's not clear how legitimate this is, so be careful when looking into homebrew games that may lack proper permissions.

Officially Permitted Abandonware Titles

Most abandonware has a tenuous relationship with legality. The presumption is that if nobody cares about it, it must be okay to distribute it. This concept, while laudable in practical terms of preserving and recognizing relatively unknown classics, doesn't necessarily justify copyright infringement and definitely flies in the face of copyright law.

Sites such as Home of the Underdogs (*http://www.the-underdogs.org/*) have major copyright issues but can provide valuable resources, for example, for

---

* "Abandonware" refers to software that is no longer being maintained by its publisher.

people who've lost legitimate copies of the manuals. The rule is a little fuzzier if you purchased the C-64 version of Skate or Die in the '80s but can't find the actual hardware and want to play the game on an emulator.

However, there is another way, and that's to ask the rights holders for permission to republish their classic material. Many do so to reignite fan interest in certain classic titles, because it may spark them to buy a new title featuring the same characters or otherwise raise the profile of the company. In some cases, companies will give away their classic titles for free. In other cases, they may look for some kind of payment. Either way, you can end up with an emulator-compatible game that's completely legit.

Examples of the former include Revolution's wonderful donation of its classic adventure game Beneath A Steel Sky, which runs on the ScummVM adventure game emulator (*http://scummvm.org/*), or the resurrected Cinemaware's habit of putting disc images of their classic titles, including Defender Of The Crown and It Came From The Desert (plus rare versions of an It Came From The Desert sequel!) on its web site (*http://www. cinemaware.com/*).

What happens when the copyright holder has gone out of business, or no one can find the right contact? It's a shame, but even if no one's left to pursue a copyright infringement case or even care, the law still frowns on trading these games.

The small but burgeoning market for legitimately sold ROM and disk sets centers around the company StarROMs (*http://www.starroms.com/*), as shown in Figure 1-1. StarROMs has signed a deal with Atari to sell its classic arcade ROMs for between $2 and $8 apiece. Unfortunately, the company is missing many extras that might sweeten the deal, such as instruction manuals and game-related adverts, but having Multiple Arcade Machine Emulator (MAME)-compatible ROMs officially available helps to legitimize the cause of emulation (see "Play Arcade Games Without the Arcade" [Hack #10]).

Various other deals have actually allowed raw ROMs. A small U.K. company did a deal with Gremlin Graphics, now part of Atari, to sell around 50 of its old Amiga releases on CD. This area is still developing slowly because, instead of selling the ROMs of obscure old games individually, companies often like to package their famous old games as entire products. In some ways, this is a shame, because a ROM is often more portable than a single-platform fixed product.

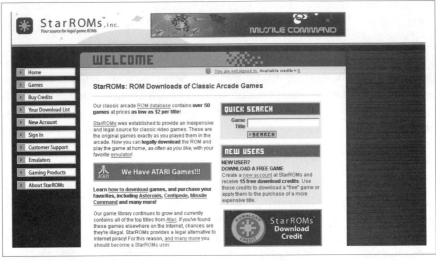

Figure 1-1. The StarROMs legal ROM site

Officially Distributed Emulators

Even if playing freeware or homebrew games, some argue that the very act of running an emulator is less than legal, because the emulator likely uses system ROMs or other proprietary information. Fortunately, officially condoned emulators have started to appear, starting with Cloanto's Amiga Forever emulator (*http://www.amigaforever.com/*), of which they indicate:

> For Amiga Forever, Cloanto has officially licensed from Amiga International the necessary portfolio of Amiga patents, copyrights and trademarks. Amiga Forever is an official member of the "Powered by Amiga" family!

By buying this completely legal emulator for around $30, you can show your willingness to support emulation of noncopyrighted material (such as public-domain demos and games) and still be completely within the law.

Similar things have occurred in Japan with ASCII Corporation and their official release of the MSX Player MSX emulator, with all the rights issues squared away. This hasn't yet come to the West, however, largely because the MSX was much less popular outside of Japan.

These more open emulators, which can play any ROM or disc image you plug into them, are less common, however, but game companies have been quite happy to use emulator authors to provide code for some of their official rereleases that have a limited, fixed ROM-set. For example, the PC version of the Sega Smash Pack compilation used an enhanced version of the KGEN98 homebrew Genesis emulator to allow good quality emulation when they didn't want to duplicate emulators with in-house resources. In a similar vein, LucasArts used Aaron Giles's Scumm adventure game engine emulator when it distributed the classic Sam & Max Hit The Road as a pre-order bonus (though they couldn't be bothered to finish the sequel, damn their britches).

Balancing Copyright with Fair Use

Hopefully, you'll be able to explore some of the more interesting emulation-based hacks without needing to walk anywhere near the slippery plank of copyright infringement. As the emulator scene continues to mature, perhaps a situation will arise in which you can reimburse the rights holders and content creators for their work without having to pay continually for media-shifted versions of rights you already own.

Play Commodore 64 Games Without the C-64
HACK #2

Relive the glory days of Commodore's long-lived personal computers.

Commodore's unassuming C-64 had a surprisingly long run as the king of computer games. The inexpensive machine had powerful sound, colorful graphics, and just enough hackability that clever developers could squeeze every last bit of performance out of its 1-MHz processor and specialized graphics and sound chips.

Although Commodore's Amiga surpassed the C-64 (and the improved, though relatively ignored, C-128), the PC finally took over the reign of computer games in the early '90s. Commodore's 1992 bankruptcy didn't help, either. *

A decade later, the C-64 lives on, sometimes in hardware, but more often in emulators. If you're feeling nostalgic for Commodore BASIC—a simple, easy to use, and, in retrospect, fairly awful programming language—or the thousands of games produced in that heady decade, you're in luck.

Installing VICE

Two emulators vie for the top spot in C-64 emulation, VICE, available from *http://www.viceteam.org/*, and CCS64, available from *http://www.computerbrains.com/ccs64/*. CCS64 is shareware, and the current version runs only on Windows, while the GPLd VICE runs on several platforms. Both work well, but we'll concentrate on VICE.

---

* For more on C-64 history, see *http://commodore.ca/products/c64/commodore_64.htm*.

Download the current version for your platform from the VICE homepage. Windows users: unzip the *WinVICE-1.14.zip* file to its own directory (perhaps *C:\WinVice-1.14*). Mac OS X users: mount and install the *VICE1.14-macosx.dmg* image as usual. Unix users should know what to do already.

> The archive contains a HTML version of the documentation, found in the *html/* subdirectory. See *html/vice_toc.html* for a good starting point.

Run the C-64 emulator as x64. There are also C-128, VIC-20, PET, and CBM-II emulators, if you're feeling really retro.

Loading Disk Images

We'll use Richard Bayliss's public-domain Balloonacy (see *http://web.ukonline.co.uk/tnd64/download_library.html*) as the example game. This cute little action game has you guiding a helium-filled balloon through a dangerous maze of lasers, walls, and sharp corners everywhere.

Launching the game is easy. From the command line, launch the emulator (x64 for the C-64, x128 for the C-128, and so on), passing the name of the disk image to launch as the *final* command parameter. One nice feature of VICE is that it can extract a disk image from inside a compressed file.

```
$ x64 balloonacy.zip
```

This loads the disk image and launches it. Alternately, you can boot the emulator and load the image manually:

```
$ x64
```

When the familiar blue-on-blue screen appears (see Figure 1-2), click the left mouse button and select "Attach a disk image." Choose the drive number to use—remember, the first 1541 or 1571 starts as device number 8—and browse to the disk image to load. Hit the Select button, and then press OK. In effect, you've just put a floppy disk in the drive.

If you don't see the files you want to load, be sure to check the filter expression in the Show box. By default, it shows only files with extensions starting with the letters g, d, or x, regardless of case. To see all files, change the expression to *.*.

Now reach back a decade or more into long-forgotten BASIC commands. To read the directory of the disk, load the special directory file ($), then list it. Figure 1-3 shows the results.

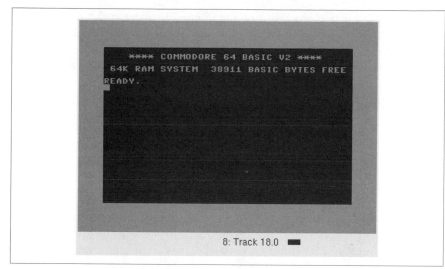

Figure 1-2. The familiar C-64 prompt

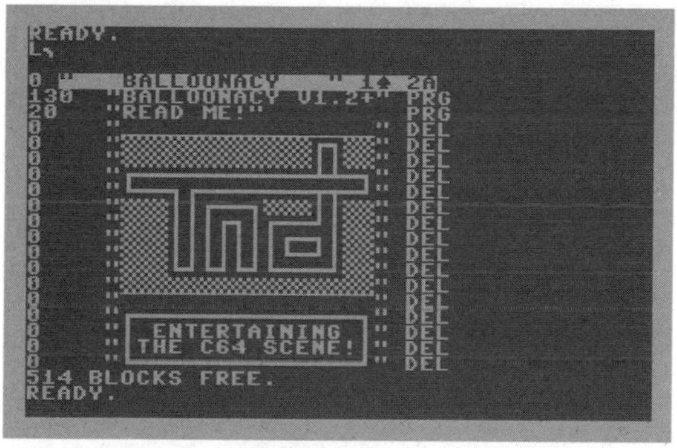

Figure 1-3. The Balloonacy disk directory listing

```
LOAD "$",8
SEARCHING FOR $
LOADING
READY.
LIST
```

If you just want to run the program, use the special "load into memory" command, then run the program (some programs run automatically):

```
LOAD "*",8,1

SEARCHING FOR *
LOADING
READY.
RUN
```

It's been a decade, so how do you remember all of these commands? Unless you spent your childhood writing games on the C-64, you might prefer to consult the Commodore 64 Online User Manual (*http://www.lemon64.com/manual/*). Feel free to snicker over the section on cassette drives.

Configuring Joystick Emulation

Unless you have a joystick plugged into your machine (at the time of writing, this required running VICE on Linux), the number pad is the easiest way to play games. As you'd expect, the number keys correspond to the directions, where 8 is up, 4 is left, 6 is right, and 2 is down. 0 is fire.

Right-click in the VICE window, and select the Joystick settings menu. From here, you can configure joysticks 1 and 2. Many C-64 games contrarily used joystick 2 for player one, and vice versa. Select Joystick device in port 2, then the Numpad option. Be sure that joystick 1 has a different setting; none is fine.

Left-click again, and choose Save settings. This saves you from having to reconfigure the joystick every time you launch a new game.

Now that you have joystick emulation configured, hit 0 on the number pad to start the game. Figure 1-4 shows a (paused) screenshot of the first level.*

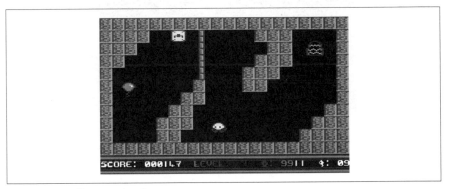

Figure 1-4. Balloonacy level one

There are a few other keys and options worth remembering, as seen in Table 1-1.

---

* To be honest, my arcade skills are rusty enough that in 10 minutes of playing, I couldn't beat this level. That's a good sign.

Table 1-1. VICE key commands

Key	Action
Alt-8	Attach a new image to drive 8.
Alt-1	Load a snapshot.
Alt-s	Save a snapshot.
Alt-F9	Perform a soft reset.
Alt-p	Pause the emulator.

Finding Games

Unless you want to program your own games in Commodore BASIC,* you'll need a disk image. Fortunately, these are easy to find. C64.com (*http://www.c64.com/*) and C64 Unlimited (*http://www.c64unlimited.net/*) have huge collections of downloadable games. If you have a pile of old floppy disks gathering dust in the closet, this is a wonderful resource. If not, or if you're not sure about the legalities of media shifting (see "Legal Emulation" [Hack #1]), it's easy enough to play homebrew games.

It's *exceedingly* difficult to find homebrew games, however. The C-64 had a huge piracy problem, especially considering that it predated the Internet explosion. Though many games are at least a decade old, there are still copyright considerations to keep in mind.

Of course, there's much fun to have in hacking around the games (Chapter 6) and creating games (Chapter 7).

Play Atari ROMs Without the Atari

HACK
#3

Can't find your 20-year-old 2600? Your desktop machine will do.

Chances are, you own a computer with slightly more graphics, CPU, and processor power than an Atari 2600. (Chances are, you can buy a graphics card with better specs for a nickel or so.) Is this a sign of bloat, waste, and the decline of Western civilization into conspicuous consumerism? Perhaps. Of course, it also means that emulating a 2600—imitating the exact hardware of the 2600 to run its games—is practical.

If you have a pile of 2600 cartridges in the closet, perhaps it's time to revisit the nostalgia of the early '80s (though see "Legal Emulation" [Hack #1] for further discussion). If you don't have any cartridges, don't fret. There are still

---

* At least one author started his illustrious career this way.

programmers producing new work for the grandfather of all modern consoles (see "Create Your Own Atari 2600 Homebrew Games" **[Hack #6]**).

Maybe you'll join their ranks someday. Maybe you just want to play Adventure again. First, you need an emulator.

Installing Stella

Bradford Mott's Stella (*http://stella.sourceforge.net/*) is a well-maintained, cross-platform Atari emulator. It runs on Linux, FreeBSD, Unix, Mac OS X, and Windows through DOS, so it's an excellent choice.

At the time of writing, Version 1.3 is the current stable version with 1.4 on the way. From the download link (*http://sourceforge.net/project/showfiles. php?group_id=41847*), grab the appropriate file for your operating system. Windows users: download *st13.zip*. Unix users: fetch a binary package or the source code in *stella-1.3-src.tar.gz*. You may need to install SDL from *http://www.libsdl.org/*.

Follow the installation instructions (*http://stella.sourceforge.net/docs/stella. html#Installation*) in the user's guide. If you're a Windows user, fire up a DOS window, and run an unzip command; that's as complex as it gets.

If you want to play games, make sure that *stella.pro*, the Stella properties file, lives in the right location. For DOS and Windows users, this is the directory containing *stella.exe*. For Unix users, this is either */etc* or *.stella* under your home directory.

Fortunately, the latest versions of Stella include this file; older web sites may tell you to download it from Erik Kovach's site. Unfortunately, it appears that he has disappeared from the Web.

Launching ROMs

Let's assume that you've downloaded Piero Cavina's classic Oystron ("Create Your Own Atari 2600 Homebrew Games" **[Hack #6]**) and want to play it. Using the Linux SDL version, the following command launches the program with the ROM:

```
$ stella.sdl OYSTR29.BIN
```

From DOS, the same command is:

```
C:\stella> stella OYSTR29.BIN
```

Press F2 to start the game.

From there, use the arrow keys to move your spaceship, and use the Tab key or spacebar to fire. When you've had enough abuse, use the Escape key to quit. Again, the user's guide has a full list of keyboard options (*http://stella. sourceforge.net/docs/stella.html#Keyboard*).

> Don't know what's going on? The *OYSTRON.DOC* file included with the download should slightly demurk the story. Shooting the slow asteroid sprites turns them into space pearls, which you can capture and plant on the left side of the screen. Planting eight in a row earns you a bomb. This is one of those games that's much more fun to play than to explain.

See Also

Of course, launching games from the command line isn't for everyone, especially if you want to set different options; perhaps you prefer to save snapshots to a different directory or to disable the volume on certain games. There are various frontends available.

If you're interested in playing 2600 games on other platforms or other emulators, you have several options:

- StellaX, a Windows port of Stella with a GUI interface (*http://www. emuunlim.com/stellax/*)
- KStella, a KDE frontend for Unix systems (*http://kstella.sourceforge.net/*)
- DCStella, the Dreamcast ("Find a Hackable Dreamcast" **[Hack #50]**) port of Stella (*http://our-arca.de/DCstella/*)
- z26, another fine 2600 emulator for DOS and Windows (*http://www. whimsey.com/z26/z26.html*)
- AtariAge's 2600 Emulation page, with links to other emulators (*http:// www.atariage.com/2600/emulation/?SystemID=2600*)

HACK #4 Use Atari Paddles with Your PC

Use a proper controller for the right games.

If you remember the original Atari 2600 hardware, you likely have fond (or not so fond) memories of the paddle input device. Instead of using a joystick for Breakout-like games, you turned a paddle left or right. Some games play much better this way.

Fortunately, enterprising hackers have sorted out hardware, drivers, and relevant emulator software to make Atari paddle controllers work on the PC, so you can play classic reissues of Atari 2600 games on modern hardware with the original controls. Some emulators even recognize and take advantage of the special analog properties of the paddle controller.

Finding a 2600 Paddle Controller

How do you find original paddle controllers? You might try your local thrift store—classic consoles and computers appear with alacrity. Otherwise, eBay comes to the rescue again; there are several auctions at any given time that offer a pair of paddles for $5 to $10 plus shipping.

De-Jitter Your Paddles

Try to pick an auction that clearly says that the paddles are jitter-free. Atari 2600 paddles suffer from an infamous jitter effect after constant hardware use. Unfortunately, the use of WD-40 or similar lubricants will fix your paddle in the short term, but will also end up making it gunkier (in a scientific sense) in the long term.

Of course, if you don't play often or you think you can beat the odds, constant WD-40 squirtage may do the trick. Some sites are vehemently against it, however, so the *proper* way to fix a jitter-tastic Atari 2600 paddle is to follow the Atari Guide site's guide to taking it apart and soaking all the goop out (*http://www.atariguide.com/help/care.htm*). You need to follow the somewhat complex web site instructions to complete disassembly, but there are some particularly important points to note:

Remove the knob carefully
    Pull the paddle knob straight up; don't pry it up with a screwdriver or lever. If the knob comes off at an angle, it'll break the potentiometer.

Handle the potentiometer with care
    When it comes time to disassemble the potentiometer itself, don't bend the tabs holding it in place too much. If they break off, you're in real trouble.

Swab gently
    Use a lint-free cloth you don't mind ruining to soak up all the liquid you can from inside the potentiometer. Try not to snag the cloth on the sharp bits inside lest you ruin its delicate mechanics.

There are three ways to use an Atari 2600 paddle on a PC: the hard way, the easier way, and the easiest way.

Atari 2600 Paddle to Joystick Port Adapter

If you play 2600 games on your PC, you might use the excellent Atari 2600 emulator Stella ("Play Atari ROMs Without the Atari" [Hack #3]). The Stella user's guide explains how to build your own 2600 paddle to PC adapter

(*http://stella.sourceforge.net/docs/stella.html#Adaptor*) using common electronics components found at Radio Shack. The site says it'll work with the
DOS and Linux versions of Stella automatically. You'll need to be handy
reading schematics and soldering—and beware of the disclaimer that you
may short out your hardware—but several people have reported success in
using classic controllers with emulators.

Before you start, you'll need a 15-pin joystick/MIDI connector on the PC
end. Many sound cards such as the SoundBlaster Live (*http://www.
soundblaster.com/products/sblive/specs.asp*) include them. Other hardware
includes two DB9 male connector ports for the paddles to plug into on one
end and a DB15 male connector to plug into your PC on the other. You'll
also need four 115k resistors and plenty of wire to wire everything up. See
Figure 1-5 for the schematic.

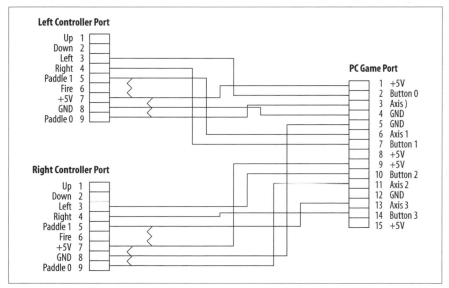

Figure 1-5. The Atari paddle schematic

On the left controller connector, connect port 3 to port 2 on the PC game
connector, port 4 to port 7, port 5 to port 6, port 7 to port 1, port 8 to port
4, and port 9 to port 3.

On the right controller connector, connect port 3 to port 10 on the PC game
connector, port 4 to port 14, port 5 to port 13, port 7 to port 9, port 8 to
port 5, and port 9 to port 11.

You should end up with six wires from each controller connecting to the
game connector. Be very careful that you don't short out the +5V and GND

connections with sloppy soldering, because you're liable to blow your PC game port, the paddle controllers, or if you're very unlucky, your whole PC.

For each controller, solder one 115k resistor between the wires coming from controller ports 5 and 7 and another between the wires coming from controller ports 7 and 9.

You can cut up a joystick extension cable for the PC instead of using a standalone DB15 connector, much like the Xbox extension cable in "Adapt Old Video Game Controllers to the PC" [Hack #37]. This may be even easier, if you can find one cheap on eBay or at an online computer retailer.

Atari 2600 to USB Stelladaptor with z26 Emulator

Here's the bad news. You can be all macho and mess with 15-pin joystick controllers and lots of solder and resistors, but in 2004, the excellent Pixels Past released a Stelladaptor 2600 to USB interface for Mac, Windows, and Linux. This device works perfectly with the paddle controllers using the z26 (*http://www.whimsey.com/z26/z26.html*) Atari 2600 emulator, which has built-in support.

This is the real deal, and for only $30 it's a decent value, too. It also works with Atari 2600 joysticks and driving controllers, though it's worth reading the caveat regarding compatibility:

> Stelladaptor will work with any emulators that support standard USB controllers. Paddle controllers will only work in emulators that allow configuration of analog USB controllers (such as MAME32 and MacMAME), or emulators that have been updated to directly support the Stelladaptor (such as z26).

If you'd like a second opinion, the Back N Time site's Stelladaptor review (*http://www.backntime.net/Hardware/Stelladaptor/FrameSA.html*) is very positive, though they do point out that you need one adapter for each controller you connect to your PC. You'll need two Stelladaptors to play two-player games.

JAKKS Atari Paddle Controller TV Game

If you think the Stelladaptor's wimpy, then the JAKKS TV Game Atari 2600 paddle controllers are for cowards because you don't need to buy original controllers or even own a PC. This software/hardware bundle, designed by retro master developers Digital Eclipse, should come out around the time this book goes to press. It apparently includes a great reproduction of 11 classic Atari 2600 paddle games within the controller and will cost between $20 and $30.

Unfortunately, the ever-gorgeous Kaboom! didn't make it, but plenty of other classics did, including Circus Atari and Super Breakout. The whole thing is available in both one- and two-player variants, so it's an easy way to get 2600 games running without digging out your own console. Rumor has it that this iteration is much better than the Atari 2600 joystick (see "Play Reissued All-in-One Joystick Games" [Hack #9]), which suffered from noticeable software issues.

In the end, whether you do it the hard, easier, or super-easy way, you can soon twiddle knobs to your heart's content and praise the geniuses at Atari for classic early '80s engineering feats.

HACK #5 Run Homebrew Games on the Atari 2600

How do you play a homebrew 2600 game on the actual console hardware?

One of the coolest things about the current emulator and homebrew scene for the Atari 2600 is the amount of new development going on—recently coded, freely distributable games of various kinds. (See the section "The Best 2600 Homebrew Games" in [Hack #6] for a good list.) If you want, you can play those newly developed games on rather cool Atari emulators such as Stella ("Play Atari ROMs Without the Atari" [Hack #3]).

What's not so peachy is that it's tricky to play these new games on the genuine hardware, especially with cartridges involved. There's no straightforward way to put the homebrew title on your 2600, but there are a few ingenious pieces of hardware, often custom-made by others or do-it-yourself that can transfer code to your classic console.

Yes, you can run that Atari 2600 game as God originally intended it—on the 2600 itself.

Oldest of the Old

As discussed earlier, the Atari 2600 itself has a vibrant homebrew scene oriented around sites such as Atari Age (*http://www.atariage.com/*). It's definitely not straightforward to play homebrew games on your 2600, but there are options.

Starpath Atari 2600 Supercharger. Released when the Atari 2600 was still being produced, this rare but ingenious utility allows the player to load third-party-developed games via cassette tape. The cart doesn't save anything, so you need to load the game again every time you power up your 2600, but it's still a great hack. There were specific games produced this way (for example, the Supercharger version of Frogger was much closer to arcade perfect than the regular cartridge version because the Supercharger also allowed more RAM than normal carts), but the only games available at the time came from Starpath and its affiliates.

However, with utilities such as BIN2WAV available on modern computers, it's possible to turn an Atari ROM into a .*WAV* file and load it via Supercharger by plugging in the output of your PC to the input of the Supercharger. Your modern PC thus functions as an early '80s tape player. Bob Colbert has a good explanatory page about using the Supercharger to load 2600 ROMs (*http://members.cox.net/rcolbert/schookup.htm*). However, the Supercharger will play only about half of the 2- and 4-KB games using this method; it takes some complex hardware modification (*http://www.atari2600collector. com/scmod.htm*) to make the others work.

The Atari 2600 Collector site also has a good overview of homebrew development using the Supercharger (*http://www.atari2600collector.com/sdev. htm*). You can find a Supercharger with games on eBay for $50 or less, so it's a fun gadget to play with, even if many games won't work properly with it.

Schell's Electronics Cuttle Cart. Since the Supercharger was such a neat idea, Schell's Electronics licensed the technology and created the Atari 2600 Cuttle Cart (*http://www.schells.com/cuttlecart.shtml*). These wonderful beasts work much like the Supercharger, using WAVs of games loaded via audio cable from an external sound source (see Figure 1-6). Even better, they lack the compatibility problems of the Supercharger!

The Schell's Electronics site maintains a massive list of compatible games (*http://www.schells.com/gamelist.shtml*)—almost everything is there. However, with only 206 Cuttle Carts ever produced, they're incredibly rare. If you ever see one at any reasonable price, snap it up immediately and store it in some kind of bulletproof vault.

The description of why this clever add-on has such an odd name is worth reprinting:

> The Cuttle Cart is named after the marine creature the cuttlefish. Cuttlefish are a type of cephalopod, a relative of the octopus. They are amazing animals capable of incredible shifts in both pattern and color, all in the blink of an eye. If I called this cart the Atari 2600 Chameleon, I think people would understand—chameleon because the cart can take on the appearance of other carts.

Schell's Electronics Cuttle Cart 2 for Atari 7800/2600. Also referred to as Cuttle Cart 2: Electric Boogaloo, this cartridge is a sequel mostly in name. It runs only on the Atari 7800, playing both 7800 and 2600 games, and uses a completely different method of transfer (*http://www.schells.com/cc2.shtml*). It

Figure 1-6. A peek inside the innards of the Cuttle Cart

uses a multimedia card (MMC) with RAM flashable from a PC via an inexpensive USB device. Because the MMC carts range up to 128 MB in size, you should easily be able to fit any homebrew games you want onto it. There are also none of the unwieldy transfer methods of the previous two crazy devices.

The first run of these Cuttle Cart 2 add-ons went to production at this book's press time. It's possible that enough demand will force a second run, so register your interest right now; these may also have very limited numbers. Remember, though, that you'll need an Atari 7800 to run it.

Atari 2600 custom homebrew carts. AtariAge (*http://www.atariage.com/*) has an especially impressive shop (*http://www.atariage.com/store/*) that sells special cartridge versions of many Atari 2600 homebrew games. AtariAge does a wonderful job of publishing many excellent 2600 homebrew games (see "Create Your Own Atari 2600 Homebrew Games" **[Hack #6]**). They also provide several services to homebrew authors who want to see real versions of their games in the marketplace (*http://www.atariage.com/store/services.php*).

Most of these homebrew titles cost between $20 and $40, and they're lavishly repackaged, with manuals, labels, and boxes. Even better, much of the money goes directly to the homebrew authors to help them continue making their excellent titles, always distributed in ROM form for free. So buy, and you'll help encourage further homebrew development. We like this option.

Homemade Atari 2600 multicartridge. This final option, building your own cartridge, is, frankly, a little bit too complicated. You'll need to modify an Activision 4-KB Atari 2600 cartridge with a really complex set of dipswitches, use an EPROM burner, and other craziness. Bob Colbert's site provides good directions (*http://members.cox.net/rcolbert/multi.htm*), but it's really suitable only for experts: you'll have to modify the circuit board in order to refit it inside the cartridge sleeve.

Multicarts

As well as these possibilities, you can sometimes find fixed-content multi-carts advertised on the Internet with a lot of games on them. They don't often feature homebrew titles, and therefore aren't really that helpful, because you can't flash any new games onto them. Googling for `Atari 2600 multicart` will help illuminate some of the possible choices, although there are no major current distributors as of press time.

HACK #6 Create Your Own Atari 2600 Homebrew Games

Join a vibrant scene devoted to creating and distributing new Atari 2600 games.

Even though the Atari 2600 is one of the oldest game consoles around, it has a vibrant homebrew scene. These coders produce a remarkable amount of new material, with everything from RPGs to bizarre puzzle games up to altered updatings of classics. Best of all, the Atari 2600 scene seems to exist in an atmosphere of harmony and mutual understanding, with no beefs, group wars, or other shenanigans.

How can you learn how to create new game levels, or even entire games, for the 2600? Good question.

Creating Homebrew 2600 Games

Suppose you're fed up with merely playing homebrew marvelousness (though shame on you if you are). Maybe you want to create your own levels for games. Maybe you want to go whole hog and code entire homebrew titles from scratch. Either way, you have several available resources.

Using 2600 custom level creation tools. If you just want to mess around with level design, Atari Age runs a series of excellent contests in which you can create new levels for games under development. Often, the finished and produced homebrew cart will include the winning levels. More importantly, entrants often make their tools available for others after the contest closes.

In particular, the Indy 500 XE Track Designer (*http://www.atariage.com/features/contests/Indy500XE/index.html*) is a lot of fun if you're a wannabe race driver. Figure 1-7 shows the "easy-to-use Windows-based track editor that allows the easy creation of new tracks, loading and saving of tracks... and the ability to generate a binary so you can immediately test your creations." The Combat Redux Playfield Design tool (*http://www.atariage.com/features/contests/CombatRedux/index.html*) works similarly. It's a whole lot of fun to block out a level and then test it straightaway in an emulator.

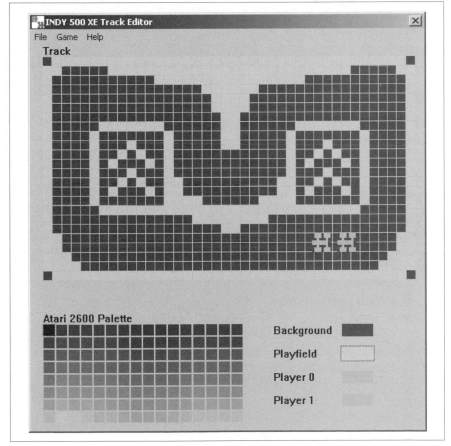

Figure 1-7. Designing a track with Indy 500 XE

These two appear to be the only fully featured level design tools currently available. Other tools require complex, time-consuming binary hacking (*http://www.atariage.com/software_hacks.html?SystemID=2600*) or are more unwieldy and general, such as Hack-O-Matic II (*http://www.dacodez.tk/*). However, it looks like the development community may produce further advanced tools, with an Adventure dungeon editor under serious development as we write—and more tools planned.

Changing graphics in existing games. I mentioned before that binary hacking is a can of complex, time-consuming, and unwholesomely difficult worms, especially if you want to rewrite large chunks of the game. If you'd rather mess around a little with an existing ROM, perhaps changing the sprites in your favorite 2600 game, that's somewhat simpler.

Adam Trionfo's *Changing Atari VCS Graphics—The Easy Way* (*http://www. gooddealgames.com/articles/changing_atari_vcs_graphics_the_easy_way.pdf*) is a perfect beginner document. It modifies a Space Invaders ROM, explaining how to use two programs called ShowGFX and EditGFX (available from *http://www.lizardmaster.com/tlm/dev.cfm*) to create plain-text files listing all vital information in the 4,096-byte ROM. The magic is in the following DOS command:

```
C:\> showgfx spaceinv.bin 0 4096 > spaceinv.txt
```

Because it's a pixel-by-pixel representation of each space invader, you can then load the text file and look for the graphics hidden within the information. The tutorial points out that you can change the player's ship* to a smiley face simply by replacing the appropriate Xs in the text file and then converting the text file back to a binary again with the following command:

```
C:\> editgfx spaceinv.txt testspac.bin
```

You can then run the binary in an emulator or via another method of your choosing.

Coding 2600 titles from scratch. The exhaustive Atari Age even has the last word with regard to coding resources, with an excellent 2600 coding page (*http://www.atariage.com/2600/programming/*) that links to Kirk Israel's superlative "2600 101" (*http://www.atariage.com/2600/programming/2600_ 101/*) basic tutorial. The introduction notes that the Atari 2600 is "a very quirky beast [since] it has very little memory or other resources to work

---

* The ship actually appears upside down, as do many of the other sprites in 2600 game ROMs.

---

with" before explaining the vagaries of the game system. You'll obviously need to program using assembly language all the way—no wimpy C++ here.

If you want specific coding tools, try the DASM Assembler (*http://www. atari2600.org/dasm/*) or the Distella disassembler (*http://www. atari2600collector.com/distella.htm*). They're both excellent tools, providing plenty of functionality considering the age of the console. Adam Trionfo's previously mentioned tutorial actually helps a great deal by describing ways you can disassemble existing Atari 2600 ROMs and then change their content.

Many homebrew developers also provide their source code for free, with highlights including the source to SCSIside (*http://www.pixelspast.com/ games/scsicide/scsi131.s.txt*) and Space Treat Deluxe (*http://www.atariage. com/2600/archives/source/SpaceTreatDeluxe_source/index.html*). Sorting through someone else's successful game code should help you out.

As for already produced homebrew titles, to find Atari Age's list of 2600 homebrew games, go to the search page (*http://www.atariage.com/software_ search.html?SystemID=2600*), pick Homebrew from the Rarity drop-down menu, and hit the Search button. Although Atari Age has the best overall set of homebrew games, links, and information, Erik Eid has the best single Atari homebrew web page (*http://www.wwnet.net/~eeid/station26/homebrew. html*). It lists the available homebrew 2600 games with basic info about each title. Though it's slightly out of date at the time of writing, it provides a good general look at the diversity of the 2600 scene.

The Best 2600 Homebrew Games

There are a few homebrew titles in particular worth singling out; all are available in cartridge form (see "Run Homebrew Games on the Atari 2600" [Hack #5]), but they're also freely downloadable and playable on emulators or on the hardware itself via suitable peripherals.

SCSIcide by Joe Grand. This ingenious, surreal action title from 2001 lets you assume "the role of a hard drive read head and your mission is to read the color-coded bits of data as they scream past you on ten separate data tracks." It's especially fun because of the bright, fast-moving blobs of color. The genuine cartridge version also uses the paddle controller. Learn more at *http:// www.pixelspast.com/games/scsicide/index.php?ID=games&subID=scsicide*.

Marble Craze by Paul Slocum. This advanced split-screen game uses dual paddle controllers to simulate vertical and horizontal tilting of a playfield to move the titular marble around the world. Because it required the use of paddles, it was unplayable in emulators until recently. Fortunately, with the help of the Stelladaptor Atari controller to PC plug-in (*http://www.atariage. com/store/product_info.php?products_id=267*), you can now play it on an emulator, so go ahead and download the ROM release. Oh, and any game with a random Super Mario Kart reference is fine by me: one of the levels is "Rainbow Road." See *http://www.qotile.net/marble.html*.

Oystron by Piero Cavina. A relatively ancient homebrew title from 1997, this fast-paced arcade title may remind you of other classic games while demonstrating a twisted style all its own. The bright sprites with the clever color variations are also neat. The homepage includes *.BIN* files containing many of the early prototypes for the game; it's great to see how it progressed over time. Download it from *http://www.io.com/~nickb/atari/oystron.html*.

Warring Worms by Billy Eno. This is a souped-up version of the classic Snake-style game, with trailing tails, missiles, 256 game types, and both one- and two-player modes. Being able to pass through your opponent's tail by firing is a neat twist, and the basic gameplay is as super-addictive as ever. This 2002 release is definitely a homebrew to try, so head on over to *http://www. baroquegaming.com/projects/WarringWorms/warring_worms.htm*.

Skeleton+ by Eric Ball. This conceptually fun 3D maze game has skeletons galore for you to find and destroy, a corresponding undead locator, and even pseudo-stereo sound—on appropriately modded 2600s—so you can tell where the skeletons are coming from. This is addictive and rather scary, provided that pixelated zombies (as seen in Figure 1-8) fit your idea of terrifying. I dare you to visit *http://www.atariage.com/software_page. html?SoftwareLabelID=2381*.

> The ultimate accolade for homebrew creators came in 2003, when the Game Boy Advance version of the Activision Anthology game (check out *http://www.metacritic.com/ games/platforms/gba/activisionanthology/*) featured several homebrew Atari 2600 games, including Climber 5, Okie Dokie, Oystron, Skeleton+, SpaceThreat Deluxe, Vault Assault, and Video Euchre. Although only the GBA version has these homebrew Atari treats on it—avoid the PlayStation 2 version, they're not on there!—it's well worth seeking out to see some homebrew classics in portable form. It's a wonderful piece of reappropriation by the games industry.

As well as the previous titles, there are a multitude of other neat possibilities from both released games and forthcoming gems. Check out the homebrew

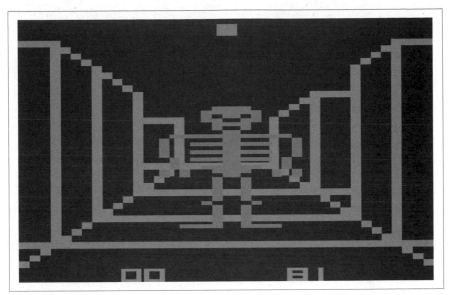

Figure 1-8. A not-so-scary skeleton

games currently in progress, and download early demos from the Atari Age In Development page (*http://www.atariage.com/development_list.html*).

In particular, Paul Slocum's upcoming Homestar Runner RPG (*http://www. qotile.net/rpg.html*) is an excellent example of retro fun with a modern twist. This Atari 2600 homebrew title has official endorsement from the creators of the cult webtoon. It includes turn-based gameplay and the ability to fight bad guys from other Atari 2600 games—a mouthwatering prospect for those addicted to the Homestar Runner (*http://www.homestarrunner.com/*) humor factory.

Whether writing an entire game or not, you may still want to test your works in progress (or other people's in-development or completed titles!) on an actual, honest-to-goodness Atari 2600. That's where "Run Homebrew Games on the Atari 2600" [Hack #5] comes into play.

HACK #7 Play Classic PC Graphic Adventures

One of the most loving, well-crafted interpreters around plays Monkey Islands and Maniac Mansions on current operating systems.

ScummVM is a cross-platform set of multiplatform game interpreters. The authors describe it as "a 'virtual machine' for several classic graphical point-and-click adventure games." It's named after the Script Creation Utility for Maniac Mansion (SCUMM) engine used in classic LucasArts adventure games, including Maniac Mansion, Sam and Max Hit the Road, and Full Throttle, but it's diversified somewhat; it now handles Revolution games such as the Broken Sword series.

Running ScummVM

ScummVM is particularly clever because it *interprets* the original Scumm source files, whatever the platform. In other words, it doesn't try to emulate the original hardware platform, but like the Inform text adventures ("Download, Compile, and Create an Inform Adventure" [Hack #85]), it takes the information in the source files and interprets it independently of the platform. Obviously, each individual hardware platform's version of ScummVM then has the information necessary to turn that information into pictures and sounds.

Let's consider the Windows version of ScummVM. Download it from *http://www.scummvm.org/downloads.php*, install it, and then run ScummVM.exe. You'll see a straightforward windowed menu system to which you can add games by navigating to the directory the datafiles are in (even if they're on a CD). It's really as simple as that, although there are a host of command-line and in-game options.

To play a game, you need the original media. Sources for this vary: perhaps you have floppy disks stashed away in your closet from the DOS versions of some of these games, or perhaps you can hunt around online and pick up the CD versions on eBay or other online auction shops. We'll discuss ways to pick up multiple games a little later.

You won't need every file from the original media to play the game. The ScummVM site has a handy page that summarizes the necessary data for each working game (*http://www.scummvm.org/documentation.php?view=datafiles*). It may be wise to copy the files to your hard drive to prevent wear and tear on the floppies.

 If you can't find originals, you can test ScummVM with demos that various collectors have put online for your downloading pleasure. See *http://www.scummvm.org/demos.php*.

Best of all, the wonderful folks at Revolution Software have made their classic graphic adventure, Beneath A Steel Sky, available from the same downloads page (*http://www.scummvm.org/downloads.php*). Although it's not for the Scumm engine, this is a majestic, adult, brooding adventure title worth your while. Kudos to Revolution for allowing free redistribution.

Alternative Operating Systems and a Scumm LiveCD

You're not running Windows, you say? Well, as ScummVM's web site says, "Currently tested platforms are Win32 (Windows 95/98/ME/NT/2000/XP), Linux i386 and PPC, BeOS, Solaris, Mac OS X, Dreamcast, MorphOS, IRIX, PalmOS and WinCE," so there's plenty of choice. The previously mentioned downloads page has binaries available for all these systems.

What if you just want to run ScummVM despite whatever platform you have installed?

That's the realm of the Scumm LiveCD (*http://www.scummlinux.org/*). As with some of the other Linux self-boot CD distributions (KnoppixMame, for example; see "Autoboot into MAME Heaven" [Hack #15]), it runs independently of the operating system. It's distributed as an ISO that allows you to copy games into the distribution and burn it onto a CD. There's also a special version with USB memory stick support. Copy the games you want across, run the special generator.exe (or its Linux equivalent), change your BIOS to boot from the USB stick, and Bob's your uncle.

Rescumming Mac OS Originals

So far, we've assumed you're trying to use the files from the Windows or DOS version of the original LucasArts games. You can also use files from the Mac OS originals, but there's an additional complication: you need to "rescumm" them to extract the relevant datafiles. In the Mac versions, the entire game is packed into a single file, so the interpreter can't access individual files.

There's an excellent FAQ on how to fix this problem on PS2Cheats (*http://www.ps2cheats.com/randomstuff/scumm/*), but it's really as simple as downloading the ScummVM toolset (*http://scummvm.sourceforge.net/downloads.php*), finding the datafile on your LucasArts game CD, copying it to your hard drive, opening the Terminal window, and then running the rescumm utility on the file. It'll magically extract all the datafiles you need to add that game to your ScummVM install. This is particularly felicitous because there are major compatibility problems with classic LucasArts titles and Mac OS X.

Let's reiterate, since this is a little confusing. You *can* use your Windows datafiles from your Windows CD version of the game to play LucasArts Scumm-totin' games on your Mac. If you're trying to use an original Mac version of one of the games on ScummVM, you'd better rescumm it. Got it?

Recommended ScummVM-Compatible Games

Recommending ScummVM games to play is easy. LucasArts created some of the most delightful adventures using the Scumm engine. Here are some particular favorites you should consider.

Sam & Max Hit The Road. What is there to say about Sam and Max? It's one of the best graphic adventures of all time. Steve Purcell's crime-solving bear and rabbit team have the most absurd, wry, odd, and delightful adventures of any anthropomorphic crimebusters, ever. "You know, Max, I can't help but think that we may have foolishly tampered with the fragile inner mechanisms of this little spaceship we call Earth."

The Secret Of Monkey Island. "Guybrush. Guybrush Threepwood." The original Monkey Island game has classic puzzles, amazing dialog, and a tremendous sense of fun, in addition to its stand-out sense of humor. There's no need for talking skulls to liven up this original piratical jaunt. Apparently, you can always press Ctrl-w to win the game on many versions of it; in that case, there's no need even to play!

Loom. Brian Moriarty's haunting, otherworldly experience was underappreciated at the time, featuring musical notes that created spells. Don't miss the CD-ROM version. If you're really an insane Loom freak, the MixNMojo page (*http://www.mixnmojo.com/php/site/gamedb.php?gameid=14*) points out that the 256-color Japanese FM Towns version is a direct conversion of the 16-color PC version, including all the cool cut-scenes left out of the PC CD-ROM version for space reasons. It's not cheap or easy to find, mind you, though it's very much worth it.

Flight of The Amazon Queen. Okay, this isn't a Scumm game, but it is a stylish and funny classic graphic adventure that richly deserves banding with the LucasArts titles for ScummVM compatibility. It's also freely downloadable, courtesy of John Passfield and Steven Stamatiadis, the original creators. Some reviews describe it as Monkey Island meets Indiana Jones.

When you analyze the titles supported by ScummVM, notice some odd non-LucasArts titles that apparently use the Scumm engine. These children's adventure games, developed by Humongous Entertainment, came about because Ron Gilbert, the Monkey Island cocreator and one of the original programmers of Scumm, founded Humongous and actually went to the trouble of licensing his engine back from LucasArts! Although heavily modified, you can at least load titles such as Putt-Putt Joins the Parade, in ScummVM. That's the kind of thing that can win you a geek bar bet.

If you can find it, the LucasArts Classic Adventure compilation (*http://www. mobygames.com/game/sheet/gameId,2477/*) from way back in 1992 is the best way to find multiple games at once. It includes Zak McKracken and the Alien Mindbenders, Indiana Jones and the Last Crusade, Loom, and The Secret of Monkey Island. That's some seriously good retro mojo.

The new Scumm engine (but not ScummVM!) using LucasArts Entertainment Pack is also good; it includes Sam & Max Hit the Road, Full Throttle, The Dig, and Grim Fandango. Aaron Giles's page (*http://www.aarongiles. com/scumm/*) has more information on this enhanced Windows engine. As of press time, it's available only in the United Kingdom.

Although you can't run it in interpreted form in ScummVM because it's stuck on a cartridge, highly modified, and unreleased, Video Fenky has a web site that exposes the unedited Nintendo Entertainment System version of Maniac Mansion (*http://www.video-fenky.com/features/rg/maniac.shtml*).
Apparently, the Big N wasn't too happy with dialog such as Dr. Fred telling Sandy about "getting your pretty brains sucked out," as well as Nurse Edna's rather suggestive speeches. Fortunately, what was a little much for poor sheltered NES users ended up being fine for those unmoderated PC users.

ScummVM as a Platform

How about creating brand new games for ScummVM? Isn't that possible? Possibly, but the Scumm construction tools have never seen the light of day. It's clear the engine was extensively hacked to construct the games, so construction sets such as AGS ("Adventure Game Studio Editing Tips" **[Hack #79]**) do the job a lot better. As the ScummVM FAQ says:

> While it is theoretically possible to write a new game that uses ScummVM it is not advisable. ScummVM has many hacks to support older games and no tools geared towards creating content usable by ScummVM.

Maybe we're just lucky that some of the all-time classic graphic adventures have already been created using Scumm. It'd almost be a shame to create more and ruin the Scumm reputation.

HACK #8 Play Old Games Through DOSBox

Run glorious old DOS classics on modern operating systems.

Every now and then the urge may strike to play the game that kindled your interest in computer gaming, perhaps X-Com, Master of Orion, or something from the Ultima series. Unfortunately, today's modern operating systems rarely play well with the relatively ancient games of the early to mid '90s. If you're lucky, you can convince some games to run without sound in Windows XP, but they may run far too fast to be playable. That's where DOSBox comes in.

DOSBox (*http://dosbox.sourceforge.net/*) is a four-person open source project that emulates an x86-based PC running DOS. The version used for this hack is 0.61 for Windows. Don't let the version number scare you; it features excellent support for many classic games and can provide Sound Blaster, General MIDI, or Gravis Ultrasound sound support. The DOSBox homepage has a freely downloadable installer as well as the source code and ports to various other platforms.

Getting Started

After you've downloaded DOSBox, run the EXE and pick a location to install to. There's no special setup required to kick off the program at this point. If you run it, you'll end up at a Z:\> prompt. DOSBox, by emulating a DOS PC, hands you a DOS environment just like the one you remember.

If this is your first time in DOS because you're boning up on your game history (commendable!) or if you just need a refresher, there are some commands you need to know. mount mounts a drive under a particular letter so that you can access it from within DOSBox. On startup, by default, DOSBox will put you on drive Z:, a virtual directory it creates to start itself up. You'll need to mount the drive in the computer on which your games reside before you can play them.

If your games are on drive D:, use the mount command as follows:

```
mount C D:\
```

This maps a C: drive within DOSBox to the contents of the current D: drive in your PC. It's important to know how this works, but you can simplify things by editing the *dosbox.conf* file; I'll explain that later.

Depending on the media you need to use for installation (floppy disks or CDs), you'll want to mount those drives as well. DOSBox doesn't automatically know that A: is your floppy drive, so use a similar command to set it up:

```
mount A A:\
mount E E:\
```

This makes A: your floppy drive and E: your CD-ROM. If you now type any of those letters you've mounted followed by a colon, at the Z:\> prompt, you'll switch to the specified drive. You're only an installation away from playing a game now!

Installing Games

To install, you need to know two more important DOS commands. The first is dir, which lists the contents of your current directory. The second is cd, which changes your directory (for example, to the directory containing the file you want to execute). The command dir /W displays directory contents across the screen instead of down, making it easier to find what you're looking for. dir works on any drive and in any folder. Use cd with the knowledge you've gained from the dir listing. For example, to run X-Com, type:

```
cd MPS\UFO
```

This changes directories to X-Com's default installation location. From there, type UFO, and you're off battling aliens! DOSBox executes *.BAT*, *.EXE*, or *.COM* files. It works just like standard DOS, so while these simple instructions will help you to play games, there's a bevy of commands available when you're ready to tinker more.

Once you've mounted everything properly, change to the installation disk and directory and start your game's installation program. This works just like the original, including sound setup.

If you want sound, it's crucial that you now choose either a Sound Blaster or Gravis Ultrasound sound device. Beware that not all games have GUS support. If General MIDI is available, use it because it always provides the best sound quality.

After the installation completes, you'll probably be in the same directory as the game executable. Type the name of the main executable—for example, *UFO.EXE*—and the game will attempt to start.

This Thing Runs Too Slow!

Inevitably, after mounting drives and installing a game to your hard drive, you'll find out that performance isn't quite as you remember. Now's the time to tweak DOSBox for optimal performance. Before you start, though, check the web site for any known problems with your game. The DOSBox web site has an extensive and searchable list of games (*http://dosbox. sourceforge.net/comp_list.php?letter=a*) with a scale ranging from runable to playable to completely supported. This will help you determine if you're better off playing something else.

Provided that you're running a supported game, your next step is to increase the cycles DOSBox uses to run the games. As noted in the *dosbox.conf* file (see Start → All Programs → DOSBox-0.61), cycles refer to the number of instructions DOSBox tries to emulate each millisecond. A very high number can have adverse effects on the program and your PC, so prepare for trouble if you go crazy. On a midrange PC, most games seem comfortable with values between 5,000 and 10,000.

You will have to spend some time tweaking this number to find the ratio of stability to speed. X-Com locked up at 10,000 but played fine at 8,000, for example. The old Amtex pinball table conversion for Eight Ball Deluxe had a nearly transparent ball at 10,000 but played perfectly at around 7,000. Needless to say, you'll probably spend most of your tweaking time on this setting.

Editing dosbox.conf

To make your life easier, once you've done some manual setup and understand how DOSBox works, you can add some lines to the *dosbox.conf* file to avoid having to repeat the process each time you want to play. In the [sdl] section, set the fullscreen value equal to true, because DOSBox performs best in fullscreen mode. Hit Alt-Enter to switch between the fullscreen and windowed modes.

The [cpu] section holds the cycles setting. Here you can put the value you determined earlier. Related settings are cycleup and cycledown. When DOS-Box runs, the keys Ctrl-F8 and Ctrl-F12 can increase or decrease the value of cycles. Set your default at 8,000 or so to start, and change it after you've tried some games.

Finally, you probably want to add your mount statements to the [autoexec] portion of *dosbox.conf*. This allows the program to configure the drives you use for installation and game playing as soon as you come to the initial Z:\> at DOSBox startup.

There are a lot of other flags in the configuration file, but you can leave most of them alone unless you encounter trouble with a game.

It's Easier than It Sounds

If you're new to DOS, you'll need some time to acclimate to its text-only interface. Don't worry, we've all been there. One nice feature of DOSBox is how well it makes the needed amount of memory available to games. Back in the '90s, when these games were new, you often had to perform voodoo, sit a particular way in your chair, and then pray to whatever deity you worship to convince a game to run. DOSBox makes this straightforward. A little DOS knowledge goes a long way, though, so don't hesitate to bone up. See Claymania's DOS Primer (*http://www.claymania.com/dos-primer.html*) for an introduction and The DOS (command) Environment (*http://www.primerpc.com/dos/dos.htm*) for detailed help.

You'll have to track down the original games or pull out your old discs (or disks) to start playing. DOSBox supports most of the big names of the time with varying degrees of success, including Ultima, X-Com, Master of Orion, Master of Magic, and more. It might seem silly once you've installed DOS-Box, but be sure to try old games under Windows XP first just in case. Sometimes you won't need emulation, though it seems like it should be your first choice. The old Simtex classic 1830: Railroads and Robber Barons works just fine in Windows XP without emulation.

Above all, have fun exploring or reliving the golden era of PC gaming. Many of PC gaming's most beloved games come from the DOS era. Besides buying and refurbishing an old 486 DX2/66, this is the best way to enjoy these games. Now excuse me while I stop an alien invasion for the tenth time!

HACK
#9
Play Reissued All-in-One Joystick Games
Can't find your old Atari? An *N*-in-1 TV game collection may be worth your money.

In the last couple of years, the officially licensed *N*-in-1 TV Game genre has grown in popularity. These are small, battery-powered devices that contain conversions and emulations of classic games licensed from the original manufacturers—including Atari, Namco, and Intellivision. Add some batteries—generally four AAs—plug the device into your TV, and hey presto!, you have a complete retro gaming system for around $20. This is a neat hack from the manufacturer's point of view.

This approach seems successful, in that the TV games seem to sell well. What's out there? How faithful are the conversions? Are they hackable to play other games? I'll answer all these questions. Read on …

Atari 10-in-1 TV Game

JAKKS's Atari 10-in-1 game was the first officially licensed, legitimate repackaging that really generated buzz when it hit the market in 2002. It comes in a replica of the original Atari 2600 joystick (officially called the CX-40) that immediately endeared it to retro fans.

The games include Asteroids, Adventure, Missile Command, Centipede, Gravitar, Yars Revenge, Breakout, Real Sports Volleyball, Circus Atari, and Pong. At first glance, this looks like a perfect conversion, but when Atari die-hards get a hold of it, they tear plenty of holes in its armor, as you can see in the BackNTime review (*http://www.backntime.net/Atari%20Interactive/ Teninone/Frame10in1.html*).

Although the basic playability of the classic Atari games translates better than the review intimates, the reviewer does point out actual changes in some of the games. Grindle, the green dragon from Adventure, has mysteriously turned purple. Even worse, the previously well hidden dot (the first ever video-game Easter Egg) is deliberately obvious. Activating it leads to a screen that, instead of crediting Warren Robinett, the original coder, simply says TEXT. Is this a preproduction flub? In any case, these games are not straight emulations. Instead, they're probably recreations done by looking at the original cart, though they might theoretically involve partial emulation.

What's really inside the Atari 10-in-1 joystick? Steve Witham and his handy web site (*http://www.tiac.net/~sw/2003/10/tvgame/*) disassembled a joystick to reveal actual game chips deliberately covered in black epoxy. He also found a 27-MHz clock crystal and muses that the deliberately obscured chips are the video chip, as well as the processor, memory, I/O, and ROM. There doesn't appear to be a way to add other Atari 2600 games into the unit, unfortunately, probably because it's not really a proper emulation. It's interesting to see the insides, anyhow.

One additional reviewer complaint worth mentioning is that several games (especially Circus Atari and Pong) really deserve a paddle controller. JAKKS plans to bring out one- and two-player versions of an Atari Paddle TV Game (see "Use Atari Paddles with Your PC" [Hack #4]) around the time this book goes to press. There's a new developer handling the emulation and recreation, and the initial indications point to significantly better results.

Namco 5-in-1 TV Games

JAKKS also released another desirable TV Game set in the Namco 5-in-1 pack, which includes Pac-Man, Dig Dug, Galaxian, Rally-X, and Bosconian. This version emulates no specific console, though some people speculate that the emulation comes from a particular home conversion set. That's almost certainly not the case.

This set has one peculiar problem, however: it's hard to move diagonally. Bosconian has severe control difficulty, which is unfortunate, because diagonal motion is vital to gameplay. Some of the other games feel a little odd too.

As it turns out, Rob Mitchell at the Atari Age forums has two solutions (*http://www.atariage.com/forums/viewtopic.php?t=44435*), one simple, and the other complex. The simple solution involves changing the four-way diamond travel limit so that it's actually round, meaning you can hit the diagonals properly. The complicated option includes unsoldering the battery wires, really taking the whole thing to bits, and then soldering connectors to attach an Atari joystick into it. A joystick plugged into the innards of a joystick? Wacky.

Unfortunately, there are also some unsolvable problems. In particular, the radar overlaps the playfield for Rally-X and Bosconian. This is both disorienting and disappointing, considering that the original games also used horizontal, not vertical, displays. The sound effects also seem diminished and otherwise blurred from the original arcade versions.

Intellivision 10/25-in-1 TV Games

The oddest release of all is the 10- or 25-in-1 Intellivision game from Techno Source (*http://www.intellivisionlives.com/retrotopia/direct2tv.shtml*). Why odd? As their page itself explains:

> It is based on the Techno Source TV Play Power technology, which means what they are doing is having NES hardware emulate an Intellivision.

What's odd about this? If this is correct—and I guess that it is because it's printed on the official Intellivision page—someone has ported all of these Intellivision games to work on the Nintendo Entertainment System (NES), another notable '80s-launched console. Suspiciously, the NES pseudo-hardware may be used surreptitiously, because there's certainly no Nintendo logo on the unit.

Even though the 25-in-1 has an excellent collection of games, including Astrosmash, Baseball, Basketball, Buzz Bombers, Football, Golf, Hockey, Hover Force, Motocross, Night Stalker, Pinball, Shark! Shark!, Skiing, Snafu, Space Armada, Space Battle, Space Hawk, Star Strike, Sub Hunt,

Thin Ice, Thunder Castle, Tower of Doom, Vectron, Volleyball, and Wrestling, it's received uniformly poor reviews. The original Intellivision controllers differed strongly from the basic Dreamcast-looking controllers used in this remake. Worse yet, the games vary from vaguely correct-looking to almost unplayable, with almost no sensible music or sound effects.

This is an example of caveat emptor. Classic TV game remakes may be hideously disfigured clones of the original, and you may not realize this until it's too late. Before buying, look online for reviews, especially in bastions of classic aficionados such as the Atari Age forums (*http://www.atariage.com/forums/index.php*).

Even Better Than the Real Thing?

This first batch of TV games has just scratched the surface of public consciousness when it comes to playing classic titles. Other intriguing new and upcoming titles include the Activision 10-in-1 (make sure to buy the newer joystick version, not the older version with the aesthetically displeasing and otherwise horrible joypad design!), a second Namco unit featuring Ms. Pac-Man and more, and other sticks with content licensed from Midway, Capcom, and others. There's even a Commodore 64 stick on the way, licensed from Tulip Computers, the current Commodore rights holders, which will include Epyx-licensed C64 games.

You may also see very unauthorized *Famiclones*—third-party, unlicensed NES joysticks, sometimes with an attached light gun and not as many games as the packaging says. Not only do the original creators not receive any money from them, they often have weird sprite-rips and otherwise odd game duplicates. Caveat emptor; despite the novelty value, they're not worth the price.

Unfortunately, these TV games are disappointingly unhackable if you wish to change games because they tend not to include the real hardware in them. The beautiful and increasingly scarce SID chip probably won't actually appear inside the C-64 stick, I'll wager, but at least you can disassemble the hardware, file it down, and make joystick adapters.

HACK #10 Play Arcade Games Without the Arcade
Play classics the perfect way, thanks to a host of online emulation experts.

Unless you've been living in a classic-gaming bereft hobbit hole for the past few years, you've probably heard of MAME, the Multiple Arcade Machine

Emulator. Nicola Salmoria started the project in late 1996 and early 1997. It's since expanded to an immensely popular 100-person hydra. As the official MAME FAQ (*http://www.mame.net/mamefaq.html*) explains:

> When used in conjunction with an arcade game's datafiles (ROMs), MAME will more or less faithfully reproduce that game on a PC. MAME can currently emulate over 2,600 unique (and over 4,600 in total) classic arcade video games from the three decades of video games—'70s, '80s and '90s, and some from the current millennium. The ROM images that MAME utilizes are "dumped" from arcade games' original circuit-board ROM chips. MAME becomes the "hardware" for the games, taking the place of their original CPUs and support chips. Therefore, these games are NOT simulations, but the actual, original games that appeared in arcades.

MAME's advantages over the original hardware are obvious: you don't have to deal with bulky boards that may or may not work with your extremely bulky arcade machine and won't fit into your PC or portable PC-like devices. Even recent home conversions (or TV game versions; see "Play Reissued All-in-One Joystick Games" **[Hack #9]**) of classic titles aren't necessarily perfect versions of the original, due to controller constraints if adapting to consoles or, in the case of TV games, adapted, not emulated, conversions.

MAME Basics

Let's start with the obvious steps. The latest versions of MAME for Windows and DOS live at the official MAME download page (*http://www.mame. net/downmain.html*). MAME runs on a whole host of other platforms, including such interesting options as the Dreamcast, OS/2, Sharp Zaurus, and even the Xbox, so see Mame.net's list of ports (*http://www.mame.net/ downports.html*). Installation is a snap; uncompress the archive into your preferred directory.

To launch a game, fire up a command prompt and type mame *gamename*, where *gamename* is a game you've placed in the ROMS subdirectory of your main install directory. You don't need to unzip the game; MAME extracts the appropriate files automatically.

> Be sure to see the official MAME FAQ section explaining how to use the emulator completely legally ("Legal Emulation" **[Hack #1]**). This is particularly important, because you can play many games without even considering downloading any potentially suspect ROMs.

Alternative Tips for MAME Goodness

It would be pretty tedious to recite the entire MAME FAQ, pointing out various typos that might not apply when this book reaches your hands. Instead, I advise you to peruse the FAQ. Done? Okay—let's explore some MAME facts that can confuse even the experienced emulator entourage.

Hardware specs sometimes matter. Some MAME-emulated games have drastically different hardware requirements from others. This may seem counter-intuitive to anyone who's used to playing, say, a Super Nintendo emulator, where most titles will run at the same speed. Remember, MAME emulates hundreds of different types of hardware in one. In particular, 3D-totin' games need fairly up-to-date system specs to run well.

The official MAME site recommends a 700-MHz PC with 64 to 128 MB of RAM to run about half of the MAME games. For the most sophisticated titles, such as Cruisin' USA, even the latest top of the line multigigahertz machine isn't enough. Also beware that some games need large amounts of RAM to run. This particularly affects consoles.

Some games have dependencies. Having one ROM bundle may not be enough to make the game work if the hardware platform requires additional ROMS. The Neo Geo, PlayChoice-10, and, fortunately, few other systems are examples of this. If MAME complains of missing files, you may not have a dud ROM.

Fortunately, only a few games and systems have this problem. Another reason you may have full ROM sets for one particular title but are missing files is if the game is a *clone*, an often unofficial Asian third-party ripped off from the original title. A Pac-Man clone ROM set probably doesn't include the ROMs that it shares with the original. You'll need to find the original ROM set to fix this.

You can sometimes stop the world. Because so many modern games have save features (except for old arcade ports, grr...), you might think that MAME must have an embedded universal save function. Not so: few arcade games even have pause buttons, for obvious quarter-crunching reasons. These games sometimes don't like stopping partway through only to restart mid-game at some point in the future. It's tricky to implement save states without altering the original ROM code—tricky, but not impossible.

Try pressing Shift-F7 and any key to save a state, and F7 and the same key to reload that particular state. You can have as many save states as you have keys.

Fixing Framerate Woes

Suppose that you have a wimpy, underpowered 200-MHz PC to use with MAME. It can handle simple games such as Pac-Man but choke on newer games for the Sega System 16 or even CPS2. What can you do to run gorgeous new games on your puny machine?

Increase frameskip. Reduce the amount of calculations the emulator has to perform by increasing the number of frames to skip between screen updates. Use the F8 and F9 keys within MAME itself to increase and decrease frameskip, respectively. This may have evil, bad effects such as less controllable main characters and odd animation results, but the effect on overall game speed can sometimes mean the difference between playable and unplayable.

Disable sound. Turn off sound altogether. The MAME FAQ suggests using -soundcard 0 in the DOS version or -nosound for the Windows version as a command-line parameter. Sound isn't always essential to gameplay, so avoiding complex waveform manipulations can free up cycles to render more frames. It's definitely worth trying a vow of silence.

Choose a lower resolution. Run with a lower resolution, selectable before you start up the game on the command line. The only problem with this approach is that many resolutions won't display the entire game area correctly. Some resolutions may not display properly on your monitor, either. Also, many arcade games from early in gaming history already run only at low resolutions anyway. Still, you can wring extra speed out of things this way. The command-line switch for this is -resolution $wxh[xd]$, where w is width, h is height, and d is color depth, which is optional. For example, -resolution 640x480x32 is a valid choice.

This basic stuff is all well and good, but how about looking at some more complex, more intriguing things you can do with MAME and its various add-ons?

Arcade Monitor-Like Output

One of MAME's earliest implemented features was a scanlines effect that emulated the appearance of classic arcade machines with gaps between each vertical scanline on the monitor. Aside from its cool appearance, this also doubles the apparent size of the screen with little effect on performance. You can enable the feature from the command line using the -scanlines option.

You can also use the -effect command along with some intriguing effects that include scan75 (75% scanlines that make it look like an arcade monitor). Many MAME variants go several steps further, especially the Advance-MAME adaptation (*http://advancemame.sourceforge.net/*). Its advanced display modes include:

RGB effects

These combine either vertical or horizontal scanline effects with triad effects. The result averages out pixel coloration to produce impressively cool blend-styled effects from normally nonblended output (*http://advancemame.sourceforge.net/rgb.html*).

Scale2X

Originally invented for AdvanceMAME, many emulators support this feature, including Raine and ScummVM ("Play Classic PC Graphic Adventures" [Hack #7]). As the description explains: "Scale2x is [a] real-time graphics effect able to increase the size of small bitmaps [by] guessing the missing pixels without interpolating pixels and blurring the images."

In other words, this effect can improve the look of old, pixelated, low-resolution graphics by making intelligent choices on how to use extra available resolution. The Scale2X homepage (*http://scale2x.sourceforge.net/*) has screenshots from multiple games, including the seminal Metal Slug series.

Blit effects

Enables a feature that averages colors over missing pixels in stretched images, so as not to erase vital parts of the playfield despite drawing with fewer pixels. Combine this with a blurring effect that emulates aging arcade monitors to coax a great picture out of your emulator. See *http://advancemame.sourceforge.net/blit.html*.

Contributing Back to the MAME Community

Suppose you're playing one of your favorite obscure games, and you see some behavior that definitely didn't happen in the original arcade version, such as glitchy sprites, odd AI, or whatever. Why not make the world a little better place while you're looking for a solution? The MAME Testers site (*http://www.mametesters.com/*) has a giant, continuously updated list of known problems with specific ROM sets. You can add your own descriptions of what you think is wrong and why.

To report a problem, first consult the MAME Testers current bugs page (*http://www.mametesters.com/currentbugs.html*) to see what's amiss.

Program an Arcade Machine Emulator? Why Not!

Although the author of this book can't claim to, some readers know C inside and out. Hey, O'Reilly books tend to attract technically literate types! MAME, being open source software, allows anyone to download its source code, fix any bug, or add any feature their hearts desire, then reupload the fix to include in the next version of MAME. Now that's seriously helpful! Find the source code (which is fun to browse even if you don't have anything to fix) on the main MAME download page (*http://www.mame.net/downmain.html*) just beneath the Windows and DOS download links.

See *http://www.mame.net/contribute.html* for information on how to contribute bug fixes and new emulation sets to the codebase.

Remember that someone probably coded the driver for a particular game in the first place, so that coder might be working on the problem.

One of my very favorite pages on the MAME Testers site is the "Bugs That Aren't Bugs" page (*http://www.mametesters.com/notbugs.html*). In itself, this provides fascinating information on problems with the arcade games releases themselves. Most of the reports are genuine problems, but they were either present in the arcade version of the game or expected features that just didn't exist in the arcade game.

Highlights include complaints about the Pac-Man Plus:

> Sometimes one of the ghosts doesn't turn blue when you eat an energizer. Sometimes the maze disappears when you eat an energizer.

to which an indignant bugworker responded:

> That's the Plus in Pac-Man Plus!

I also like one report of Atari's version of Tetris:

> There's no second button to rotate pieces clockwise.

with the response:

> Many ports of Tetris (notably the Gameboy version) have two rotate buttons, but the Atari versions do not.

MAGE for MAME burnouts

The Multi Arcade Gambling Emulator (MAGE) (*http://magenet.tk/*) emulates gambling titles that MAME no longer supports and simulates (not emulates) other popular gambling machines. Either download the Windows executable from this site, or check out the MAME Plus! emulator (*http://*

mame.emu-zone.org/), a project that originally started to add Unicode support to MAME and has since integrated MAGE code.

To see which slot and fruit machines MAGE supports, see the *history.dat* file currently hosted at Mametesters.com (*http://www.mametesters.com/ elcondor/files/history.dat*) for more information. Only a few games have official support (as vendors worry that clever gamblers will figure out how to game the system through emulation and harass the emulator authors). Fortunately, the number of supported systems and titles will only increase in the future, even though emulating video is trickier.

If you're looking for images; information on what's available; or even fan-made, custom slot machines, start with the PoundRun site (*http://www. poundrun.org*). For more emulation-specific discussion, consult the MAGE board at FruitForums (*http://www.fruitforums.com/forums/forumdisplay. php?s=&forumid=7 3*).

HACK #11 Add and Manipulate a MAME Frontend

When launching MAME from the command line leaves you a little blue, add a nice frontend.

MAME is wonderfully simple ("Play Arcade Games Without the Arcade" [Hack #10]); it's a nice, unified bundle of myriad emulators you'd otherwise have to download and configure individually. While launching it from the command line and typing the name of the ROM you want to run is sufficient, adding in options can make things a little more complex.

There's a dizzying array of frontend programs that bolt onto MAME. These provide sophisticated GUI-based menus with which the player can choose particular games to play and options to use. Some frontends also include handy game paraphernalia such as screenshots, cabinet photos, and even related audio and video, giving you a luxurious overview of your game before you even start the emulator.

With multiple platforms and myriad slightly different choices, where do you even start? My top choice of frontends is AdvanceMenu, though I'll also outline some alternatives.

AdvanceMenu

The AdvanceMenu (*http://advancemame.sourceforge.net/menu-readme.html*) site describes the program as "a frontend for AdvanceMAME, MAME, MESS, RAINE and any other emulator... ." It uses the cross-platform SDL multimedia library (*http://www.libsdl.org/*), so it runs on Linux, Mac OS X,

DOS, Windows, and a few other platforms. Because it's from the same team that developed AdvanceMAME, they play together nicely.

AdvanceMenu lacks the crazed 3D virtual reality arcade-roaming of other frontends, and because it's so portable, it doesn't rely on super-complex window layouts and doohickeys. It's not plain, though. You can easily set neat browsing options, as seen in the example screenshots page (*http://advancemame.sourceforge.net/menu-snapshot.html*, or Figure 1-9).

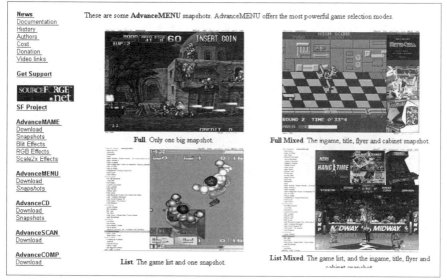

Figure 1-9. The AdvanceMenu page, showing frontend layouts

Here's how to use the program with the normal, vanilla version of MAME:

1. Download the latest version. I use the Windows version from *http://advancemame.sourceforge.net/menu-download.html*. AdvanceMenu automatically detects many emulators, so make sure you have the latest version of MAME. Unzip AdvanceMenu into the same directory as MAME.

2. Load the advanced video driver, if necessary. You will find it useful to fire up a command prompt and run the svgalist /1 command. This loads the *svgawin.sys* driver in Windows NT, 2000, and XP. The AdvanceMAME web site has a page explaining this utility. Basically, it's an advanced video driver that's useful for running AdvanceMenu.

3. Choose your options. Click on *advancecfg.exe*, and you'll see several text menus with options to navigate through. The details here are impressive; they allow you to send your output to a PC monitor, an arcade machine, a TV, or other custom display devices. For this example,

choose PC Monitor. You will see even more complex clock range-related values. I use Generic PC VGA, although I suspect you should look up things in your monitor manual if you can find it. Finally, center your screen appropriately, and save your settings.

4. Create the *mame.ini* file. Make sure there's a *mame.ini* file in your MAME directory, so run `mame -createconfig` from the command line. Let's start simple: have AdvanceMenu find the ROMs directory and load a basic menu that lists each ROM you have in your directory. Edit *advmenu.rc* to add this line:

```
emulator "mame" mame "mame.exe" ""
```

Keep a close eye on *advmenu.rc*, because you'll need to edit it later to customize things further.

In this case, AdvanceMenu figures out the ROM path from the rompath value in *mame.ini*. If you have screenshots or snapshots for games installed on your version of MAME, it'll look at *snap_directory* from the same file to find those. In other words, AdvanceMenu extracts values automatically from MAME's initialization files so that you don't have to. That's the simple approach. Here are a few more advanced options to spiff up your Advance-Menu fun.

Flyers. To allow alternate paraphernalia, such as *flyers* (scans of the original game's promotional sheets), add the following line to *advmenu.rc*:

```
emulator_flyers EMUNAME LIST
```

This line sets the *LIST* directory as the location of the flyers for the games used by the *EMUNAME* emulator. Find these flyers at the ArcadeFlyers site (*http://www.arcadeflyers.com/*).

Video previews. A particularly neat feature is the ability to output MNG (animated PNG image) files from AdvanceMAME, compress them with the AdvanceMNG command-line compressor (*http://advancemame.sourceforge. net/doc-advmng.html*), and then use the animations in the game selection screen. Other frontends provide video ability, of course, but this one makes it easy to record your favorite boss-beating move in the actual game and make it the default video when you load the emulation in the future. This is eye candy and personal bragging rights bundled together!

However, AdvanceMAME supports only MNG, so there may be incompatibilities with other minivideos from other frontends.

To use, place the video in the normal image preview directory. To choose how the video loops, set the `ui_clip` option in *advmenu.rc*.

Flyers as screensavers. AdvanceMenu can segue into a screensaver mode, should you wish it to, displaying the game flyers you've installed. Enable this by adding the following to your *advmenu.rc* file:

```
idle_screensaver 60 30
idle_screensaver_preview flyers
```

This starts a screensaver after 60 seconds of idleness, the first time the screensaver runs, and after 30 seconds of idleness on subsequent occasions. The screensaver cycles through the flyers you have stored, since you've obviously already added them.

Add a completely different emulator altogether. The documentation (*http:// advancemame.sourceforge.net/doc-advmenu.html*) points out that you can attach any emulator you like to AdvanceMenu, as long as you do it correctly. You'll need to specify the emulator name, call it a generic type, and then point to the ROMs, also filtering them by filename if you wish. For example, to run the SNES emulator Snes9X, add something like this to your *advmenu.rc* file:

```
emulator "snes9x" generic "c:\game\snes9x\snes9x.exe" "%f"
emulator_roms "snes9x" "c:\game\snes9x\roms"
emulator_roms_filter "snes9x" "*.smc;*.sfc;*.fig;*.1"
```

Alternatives to AdvanceMenu

If AdvanceMenu doesn't quite fit the bill for you, there are many alternatives and many sites that give advice. The ever-reliable Zophar.net has a very thorough page (*http://www.zophar.net/frontends/mame.html*) that includes brief and very helpful descriptions of your options, along with version numbers and updates. You can also try the massive MAMEWorld site (*http:// www.mameworld.net/*), which has one of the best lists of frontends, appearing at the bottom left of the title page. Unfortunately, the latter is completely unannotated, so you'll have to guess which linked frontends are the best, or just keep reading. Here are some of the best alternatives.

MAME32, a Windows-based all-in-one solution. Although the MAME developers (MAMEDev) sanction their work, the splinter group who produce MAME32 (*http://www.classicgaming.com/mame32qa/*) aren't part of the core MAME group. Nonetheless, they do an amazing job of providing an all-in-one MAME solution for Windows users. The overview explains that MAME32 "has an attractive, elegant, graphical interface which allows the user to forego having to type command line parameters."

After you download MAME32 (*http://www.classicgaming.com/mame32qa/ down.htm*), download the supplemental art packages from the same page.

It's quite convenient to have the sometimes difficult-to-find paraphernalia linked from the same site as the binaries. There's also a very helpful page for installing the artwork packages (*http://www.classicgaming.com/mame32qa/ help/mame32_art.htm*); it explains how to plug these add-ons into the program itself. For example, for the prodigiously large amount of screenshots, just copy them into the *mame32/snaps* folder of your installation. Similarly, for photos of the arcade cabinets themselves, dump them into *mame32/ cabinets* or into one big *cabinets.zip* file that the program can consult when loading.

The MAME32 customization options aren't complex, but as the MAME32 gallery shows (*http://www.classicgaming.com/mame32qa/gallery/gallery. htm*), you can:

- Switch fonts by picking Options/Game List Font from the menu
- Change the game listings to show icons, details, and other information by clicking the icons mounted just below the options menus, or picking the View menu
- Change which GUI items appear when you start up by checking or unchecking any default options from the View menu

The official MAME32 support page (*http://www.classicgaming.com/ mame32qa/help/mame32_support.htm*) isn't quite comprehensive, but it does have a few good tips, especially regarding keyboard shortcuts. For example, if you're in the mood for a little Russian Roulette as your arcade game of choice, choose a random ROM by pressing Ctrl-R in the menu. Just don't blame me if the computer chooses Spy Hunter II, and you end up crying into your expensive arcade joystick. Alternately, if you'd like to skip swiftly to a particular game, use the keyboard to type in its name (or even the first couple of letters). MAME32 selects it automagically, saving you the pain of scrolling up and down maniacally.

3DArcade, the high-end virtual reality approach. 3DArcade (*http://3darcade. mameworld.net/*) shows the insane lengths people will go to in order to select their MAME games: it's home to 3D models of arcade machines. This works best when combined with the sophisticated, Windows-only FEArcade frontend (*http://3darcade.mameworld.net/frontend/frontend.htm*) and allows anyone to set up his own virtual arcade. Stroll up to a machine and press a button to start playing.

Is this 3D GUI over-the-top overkill? Possibly. It's also rather marvellous, not least of which because it's fun to imagine what a collection of classic 1982 arcade machines all looked like together in one place. Anyone can make and export cabinets in the fairly standard *.W3D* format. The

3DArcade models page (*http://3darcade.mameworld.net/models/models.htm*) also includes *.MAX* files for many of the cabinets, if you want to open and adapt them directly in 3D Studio Max.

There are many pictures of the frontend in action (*http://3darcade. mameworld.net/frontend/defaultskin.html*), and you can see some of the really insane arcades created on a special site page (*http://3darcade. mameworld.net/arcades/arcades.htm*). It's particularly worth checking out the Deniros-Domus Arcade, described, trippily enough, as "a futuristic take on Frank Lloyd Wright's Guggenheim Museum set in space." Of course, trying to climb up a crazed 3D world-based spiral staircase into space just to play your favorite arcade game may not be your idea of fun, but it does have style.

MacMAME. MacMAME is a good all-in-one MAME and frontend solution for Mac users, whether they use OS 9 or OS X. It's well worth checking out; for a long time, it was the only real option for Mac users who wanted decent menus with their MAME install. See *http://www.macmame.org/*.

Ultrastyle. This Windows-specific frontend is in early development. It's skinnable and has a neat graphical menu, though it somewhat resembles the Ultracade frontend used for official MAME-style arcade machines running emulated Capcom games. Download it from *http://www.mameworld.net/ ultrastyle/index.html*.

ArcadeOS. ArcadeOS is a DOS-based frontend—particularly useful if you run a PC using MAME exclusively through an arcade stick. Whether you're using TV-out on your television and aren't close to your keyboard or you're using a PC inside an arcade cabinet with a MAME to JAMMA converter, this is the software to beat. You can set your PC to autoboot into this menu without needing a mouse to load a frontend through Windows. Learn more at *http://www.mameworld.net/pc2jamma/frontend.html*.

QMame. This is a Linux/Unix frontend based on Trolltech's QT library. It's a comprehensive, good-looking Linux solution. Although at press time it had not seen an update in a while, it's pretty usable as is. Be sure to install XMame (*http://x.mame.net/*) before installing QMame (*http://www. mameworld.net/mamecat/*).

H A C K

#12

Keep Your ROMs Tidy and Organized
Keep your mass of homebrew emulated games tidy and safe.

One of the joys of collecting ROMs and disc images—even freeware and homebrew ones—is that your collection will soon grow. With that accumulation comes the issue of how to keep them in order. You might even have multiple copies of the same file with different naming conventions from different sources!

With ROM management tools and game databases such as the TOSEC database, you can autorename, checksum, and organize your game image files easily and efficiently.

ROM Management Tools

Your first step is to pick a tool to use. Most of the best ROM managers are available for Windows, but there are decent managers for other systems too. We'll concentrate on the two leading Windows-based managers, CLRMamePro (*http://www.clrmame.com/*) and ROMCenter (*http://www. romcenter.com/*). Both are extremely fully featured.

CLRMamePro, although originally named after MAME, which deals only with arcade games, actually works for multiple DAT files—even those not for MAME.

Unfortunately, these two utilities have different datafiles, which makes metadata compatibility a little tricky. We'll discuss that later. For now the place to start is MrV2K's web-based CLRMame tutorial (*http://www. mameworld.net/easyemu/clrmameguide.htm*).

The *.DAT* files used in these management tools are basically standalone text files. You can download and import new versions and even customize your own copies. Their complexity varies greatly, but at the most basic level, they include the correct filename, the correct size, and the correct CRC checksum for each included game. The tools compare ROMs by checking their file sizes and CRCs. These checksums are alphanumeric values that are guaranteed to be unique for each individual ROM. This allows the system to detect duplicates, even if the filenames have changed.

Because running the tool may cause complex chains of renaming and deletion operations, you may want to back up your entire directory before starting up. Although these utilities generally behave well, most ROM files are small enough that it makes sense to keep your old configuration in case you like things better that way.

After you have the correct DAT file to scan against the ROMs you currently have on your hard drive, run the Scanner option from the main menu of CLRMamePro to cross-check everything against your master DAT. There are several scanning criteria, including whether to check if the ROMs are completely missing, whether there are duplicates, and whether certain files are unnecessary.

At the end of checking, a detailed error report tells you exactly which ROMs failed their CRC check, which have partial missing files, and which need renaming and deleting because of duplicates. Some people suggest that you perform a simple name/case/duplicates check before performing a deeper CRC scan; you're much more likely to have duplicate ROMs than corrupted ones.

If you don't have a suitable DAT file, you can hook existing emulators into CLRMamePro, though this works only with command-line emulators such as MAME. This clever part of the program uses the command-line Information options for the emulator to derive and retrieve information about existing ROMs on your machine. It can then create its own database file from scratch.

Analyzing DAT File Details

Many experts recommend the CLRMamePro format as the master format. Let's explore the DAT file for a real game to see how it works. Here's the metadata for a freely distributable Neo Geo homebrew game, an adaptation of a famous bat-and-ball game you might have heard of:

```
game (
    name neopong10
    description "NeoPong (v1.0, non-MAME)"
    year 2002
    manufacturer "NeoDev"
    cloneof neopong
    romof neopong
    rom ( name pong0_p1.rom size 131072 crc 31b724d7 )
    rom ( name pong_s1.rom merge pong_s1.rom size 131072 crc cd19264f )
    rom ( name sfix.sfx merge sfix.sfx size 131072 crc 354029fc )
    rom ( name sp-s2.sp1 merge sp-s2.sp1 size 131072 crc 9036d879 )
    rom ( name sp-s.sp1 merge sp-s.sp1 size 131072 crc c7f2fa45 )
    rom ( name usa_2slt.bin merge usa_2slt.bin size 131072 crc e72943de )
    rom ( name sp-e.sp1 merge sp-e.sp1 size 131072 crc 2723a5b5 )
    rom ( name asia-s3.rom merge asia-s3.rom size 131072 crc 91b64be3 )
    rom ( name vs-bios.rom merge vs-bios.rom size 131072 crc f0e8f27d )
    rom ( name sp-j2.rom merge sp-j2.rom size 131072 crc acede59c )
    rom ( name sm1.sm1 merge sm1.sm1 size 131072 crc 97cf998b )
    rom ( name pong0_m1.rom size 131072 crc 9c0291ea )
    rom ( name 000-lo.lo merge 000-lo.lo size 65536 crc e09e253c )
```

```
    rom ( name pong0_v1.rom size 524288 crc debeb8fb )
    rom ( name pong0_c1.rom size 1048576 crc d7587282 )
    rom ( name pong0_c2.rom size 1048576 crc fefc9d06 )
)
```

As you might have noticed, many ROMs are variants of other ROMs. This goes for translations and modifications as well as officially released commercial games, which often reuse individual chips on a cartridge or ROM board. The `cloneof` field here allows you to track all the myriad ripoffs of a particular title (in the previous case, a slight variant of NeoPong; a better example is that of the mess of Pac-Man variants). This allows easy organization and grouping within ROM managers, among other things.

Most cleverly of all, the `merge` command within certain of the ROM files allows multiple clones to use the same ROM files if only a few ROMs differ between clones. This can save a lot of space by eliminating useless redundancy.

If you'd like to know a lot more about the various formats, the LogiqX site has an exemplary FAQ section (*http://www.logiqx.com/FAQs/DatFAQs. shtml*) which goes into much greater detail, especially regarding more complex maneuvers such as adding samples and resource files to your database.

Emulator DAT Conversion with DatUtil

Because it stores versions of its databases for both CLRMamePro and ROM-Center versions, LogiqX (*http://www.logiqx.com/*) is one of the best places to look for emulator-compatible DAT files. Since the guys at LogiqX don't merge updates between the databases by hand when things change, they must have some way to convert between the different database formats.

It comes in the form of DatUtil (*http://www.logiqx.com/DatUtil/DatUtil. shtml*), a four-year-old project. This DOS command-line utility converts between multiple formats. It even performs clever comparisons of two different DAT files that may have slightly altered content, spewing out the differences to a logfile.

The DatUtil executable also comes with the C source code, should any ninja coders wish to make custom alterations. You may never need to convert DAT files if you stick with something like CLRMamePro all the way, but if a newer, better ROM naming manager ever supersedes it, it's nice to know that you'll have a way to convert your legacy databases.

Analyzing the Best Master ROM Databases

There are several different ROM databases to explore. The ROMCenter page (*http://www.romcenter.com/*) has a good sampling. However, the most famous two are the previously mentioned LogiqX (*http://www.logiqx.com/*) and the TOSEC team (*www.tosec.info/*).

LogiqX is one of the preferred sources for MAME DATs, especially because of their involvement in CAESAR, the Catalogue of Arcade Emulation Software—the Absolute Reference (*http://caesar.logiqx.com/*). They have fewer files in the more obscure formats outside the most popular emulation platforms, but the DAT files they do have for the latest versions of MAME, Kawaks, Nebula, and others (*http://www.logiqx.com/Dats/Dats.shtml*) are impressively up to date.

On the other end of the spectrum, TOSEC's work in sorting out and compiling massive databases of ROMs is impressive. They're the only people with details on more obscure formats; they keep a list of all Amiga public-domain software or Intellivision ROMs, for example. The TOSEC team is slowly moving from simple, static DAT files to an ambitious web site where you can create DAT files from a master database on the fly—a laudable, if much more complex work. The TOSEC authors explain:

> Eventually [TOSEC 2.0's Database Generator] will fully replace the "solid" data archives we use now and will give you the possibility to generate and download combined and custom dats, making it possible to make dats only containing the files you want them to contain.

It's also worth pointing out that the TOSEC team makes an effort to separate public-domain and redistributable software from ROMs that may have more dubious right issues. This is great news if you want to use ROM database software with legitimate ROMs. For example, the ROMCenter TOSEC page (*http://www.romcenter.com/datafiles/tosec/list.php*) has specific, standalone DAT files for legitimate Atari Jaguar and Atari Lynx PD/demonstration software.

It's likely that TOSEC 2.0 will continue this, making it possible to create custom DATs of every single public domain or freely distributable ROM for any console or computer on the fly. That would be an amazing accomplishment.

HACK #13 Learn Game-Specific MAME Controls

Stop scrabbling around to work out which key does what.

Have you ever loaded a MAME ROM for the first time and found yourself flailing around, trying to figure out which buttons it uses and what they do? Sometimes you'll play for a while before you realize you have a smart bomb button that'll wipe out the mass of enemies onscreen in one fell swoop. Other times you'll completely miss the point of the entire game because you're missing some vital details about keys or objectives scrawled on the cabinet itself, and, obviously, you don't have access to the cabinet.

The *Controls.dat* project (*http://fe.mamehost.com/controls/controls.php*) attempts to catalog the exact controls of every MAME-compatible title ever, along with names and directions. There are even extra fields for information about what to do during the game, in case there are particularly nonobvious game mechanics.

If *Controls.dat* supplies controls information for each title in the MAME library in an abstract dataset (much like the Catlist game listing in "Filter Inappropriate MAME ROMs" **[Hack #14]**), then frontends and emulators can take advantage of it by providing a listing of buttons and their effects. You'll flail no more, at least in figuring out the controls. If you're running a MAME cabinet with light-up buttons, it may eventually even light up the buttons used by that particular game!

A Work in Progress

However, at press time, the *Controls.dat* project is still in progress and is actually in a reasonably heavy state of flux. Right now, and hopefully for the future, the FAQ page for the project (*http://fe.mamehost.com/controls/faq.php*) provides plenty of useful information.

In particular, the site's maintainers argue that "[there] are other sources for similar data, like MAME's listinfo, or KLOV (*http://www.klov.org*), but these sources are either inaccurate or incomplete."

Listinfo

The MAME executable itself actually stores plenty of information about its supported games. You can see this information as DAT files shown at MAMEInfo (*http://www.mameworld.net/mameinfo/*). Any one game's information may contain other recommended games, bugs, instructions for running the game, and even a few key layouts, as well as version histories for updates of the emulation for the game in question.

You can also coax this information out of your existing MAME install by running `mame -listinfo > listinfo.txt` from a command-line prompt. Some ROM management tools ("Keep Your ROMs Tidy and Organized" **[Hack #12]**) also have subsets or supersets of the data contained here.

Obviously, it's not yet easy to add info to the MAME executable wholesale, which is one of the reasons for *Controls.dat*.

Consult the FEDev message board (*http://fe.mamehost.com/yabbse/index. php?board=10*) for information on where to download the latest version of the file, where you can help classify or add items, and to learn about frontends that use the file. It's also possible to browse any individual record for one particular game (for example, *http://fe.mamehost.com/controls/report. php?theGame=19xx*) and see the information in them from the web site. If you register, you can add to the knowledge base by entering game information yourself.

An Example Controls.dat Entry

Here's the example entry from the *Controls.dat* file for the brawler Bad Dudes vs. Dragon Ninja:

```
[baddudes]
gamename=Bad Dudes vs. Dragon Ninja (US)
numPlayers=2
alternating=0
mirrored=1
tilt=0
usesService=0
P1NumButtons=2
P1Controls=8-way Joystick+joy8way
P1_BUTTON2=Jump
P1_BUTTON1=Attack
P1_JOYSTICK_UP=Up
P1_JOYSTICK_DOWN=Down
P1_JOYSTICK_LEFT=Left
P1_JOYSTICK_RIGHT=Right
```

There's extra information in the `miscDetails=` field, too, which can be invaluable for working out how to actually play the game. Here's this game's extra information:

> Holding down attack while standing still will charge up a super punch. Pressing jump and attack at once will do a super kick at the expense of some of your energy.

Other files, such as MAME's *listinfo*, already map out this information, but the notes in the *Control.dat* file tend to be more practical than a straightforward plot/background description.

Frontends That Integrate Controls.dat Correctly

As mentioned before, we're still somewhat in the Wild West when it comes to *Controls.dat* integration into frontends. Here are three ways you can see it in action.

Johnny5 (http://www.oscarcontrols.com/lazarus/archives/000032.html)
> This standalone application shows the layout of controls from *Controls. dat* files. However, it's *not* a fully fledged frontend, just a building block.

Dragon King (http://www.oscarcontrols.com/lazarus/)
> This frontend from the author of Johnny5 uses the latter for *Controls.dat* support. This is a complex but excellent frontend well worth exploring.

MAMEWAH (http://mamewah.mameworld.net/)
> This larger frontend from the United Kingdom also integrates Johnny5 and has many similarities to the classic ArcadeOS frontend.

Controls.dat accounts for about 500 MAME titles right now, with thousands to go. The project continues to make swift progress; you're likely to see it integrated more and more into the existing MAME framework, making for a better, more satisfying emulation experience for all. Hurrah for that!

HACK #14 Filter Inappropriate MAME ROMs
Make sure your kids/young relatives don't see something unfortunate.

When people think of MAME, they probably think of cute, fluffy, kid-friendly old-school titles such as Ms. Pac-Man. The truth is that, among the gigantic amount of MAME ROMs, quite a few titles have lots of nudity, from Arkanoid clones with topless women through Qix clones with topless women and all the way to Puzzle Bobble clones with topless or more extremely unclothed women.

If you have kids (or even parents) who like playing puzzle games, you may not feel comfortable leaving them alone with your unsorted MAME ROM sets. Many of the ROM names don't indicate that they cater to prurient interests. In fact, many have cutesy titles that attract the young. Sure, you could use existing frontends ("Add and Manipulate a MAME Frontend" [Hack #11]), but by fiddling with preferences, it's possible to find masked ROMs again.

Alternately, if you don't have any inappropriate ROMs, but you do want to categorize them better, you can use the same techniques. Better safe than sorry, eh?

MARRT, Your Friendly Neighborhood MAME Adult Filter

Enter MARRT (*http://www.timsarcade.net/news/marrt.html*), a Windows utility that can move or delete all adult-themed ROMs from your MAME directory, using the gamelist in *mature.ini* as the basis for its categorization. You'll need Microsoft's .NET Framework installed to run this.

Thanks to the Catlist project's categorization of MAME ROMs (*http://www.mameworld.net/catlist/*), there's no need for you to identify the adult titles: just fire and forget. Obviously, with the Catlist adult game list, you can probably code a simple Linux or Mac script to do the same thing, but MARRT is nicely packaged already.

Figure 1-10 shows the GUI; here's how to use it:

1. Install MARRT into the */MARRT* subdirectory of your MAME install, using the handy and included Windows installer. Don't run it yet.

2. The distribution includes only a test version of the *mature.ini* file, so download the MAME32 version of Catlist (*http://www.mameworld.net/catlist/files/cat32.zip*), which includes a current *mature.ini* file. Unzip it into the */MARRT* directory.

3. Launch *MARRT.exe* and enter the ROM directory that you're acting on, as well as whether you moved or deleted the files.

4. To delete another game not in the mature category, type in the name of the ZIP file and click Add ZIP to add it to the list.

5. Click the Move ROMs/Delete ROMs button, and MARRT will make it so.

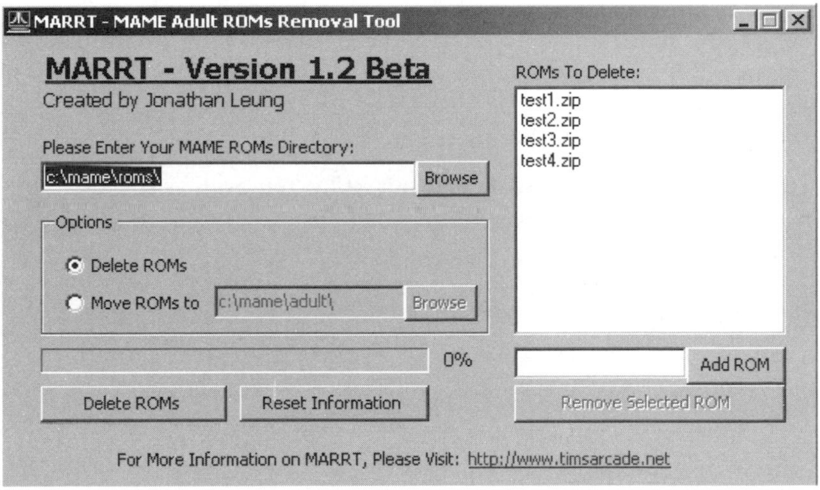

Figure 1-10. The MARRT GUI

If you hate puzzle games, you can slip the puzzle game list in there, instead. Open *genre.ini* in the MAME32 Catlist file, search for the Puzzle genre, and select only those files as *mature.ini*. Heck, you could also move all the adult-themed games *into* your MAME directory, just by moving all your ROMs to a new directory and making your destination directory your conventional MAME ROMs location. Be creative.

ROM Filtering Alternatives

There is an alternative to MARRT in the form of MCM, or MAME Content Manager (*http://www.mameworld.net/mcm/*), an older but still working piece of ROM management software that allows you to rename or remove not only ROMs, but also Snapshots, Flyers, Marquees, Cabinets, and Title Snaps.

This particular utility uses the *CATVER.INI* file, also available from the Catlist site (*http://www.mameworld.net/catlist/files/catver.zip*). Be aware that other versions of *CATVER.INI*, even those that claim to be up to date, don't carry the Mature tag on genres, so you won't be able to tell which games are adult.

In some ways, MCM is more comprehensive than MARRT, although it's less specific with regards to adult games. As it's had no updates in a year or two, it doesn't quite deal perfectly with mature titles. You have to pick the mature version of each of the individual genres from *CATVER.INI*, so it takes more clicks than MAART to perform the same behavior.

However, the added ability to search for particular games by string, as well as the neatness with the removal of other non-ROM-related artifacts that could still cause kid-related consternation, means this is well worth checking out, especially if you're not just interested in banning adult games.

There are still more alternatives for adult ROM removal, as suggested by an official MAME FAQ answer (*http://www.mame.net/cgi-bin/wwwthreads/ showpost.pl?Board=mamefaq&Number=254&page=3*), on *http://www. mame.net/*, which covers the subject in detail. In particular, you can try the tactic of keeping a different MAME directory and user for adults and kids, and making sure you can't access the adult version unless you log on to your Windows or Mac machine as a different user altogether.

On the other hand, software solutions that don't require user-setting complications are good things.

HACK #15 Autoboot into MAME Heaven

Create a self-booting CD to run your arcade games on any PC.

Thanks to enterprising hackers, you can now run MAME on your PC without even touching the contents of the hard drive. How? By using self-booting, Linux-based CDs created exclusively to run the arcade emulator. There are several advantages to this method; for example, you can give copies to less computer-savvy friends without worrying about complex installation and setup problems. The disc is also easily portable; if you want to play at a friend's house, just take along your CD and pop it in her computer.

The Abundance of Self-Boot MAME Choices

There are several MAME-loving Linux CD kits around, so you actually have a choice. Each comes with its own advantages and disadvantages, which often include some practical problems you may run into trying to make them work. The following section details the most popular.

AdvanceCD. AdvanceCD is by far the most compact of the options; it packs a fully working autoboot MAME system into just 20 MB and leaves lots of room on the disc for ROMs. AdvanceCD uses the rather smart Advance-Menu (*http://advancemame.sourceforge.net/menu-readme.html*) frontend ("Add and Manipulate a MAME Frontend" [Hack #11]), as well as the AdvanceMAME and AdvanceMESS emulators, which are particularly known for their custom code to produce the correct screen resolution. As the site explains:

> The Advance versions are able to directly program the video board to always get a video mode with the correct size and frequency.

The AdvanceCD setup comes with three ROMs: Gridlee, Poly Play, and Robby Roto. The SYS2064 legal ROMs page (*http://www.sys2064.com/legalroms.htm*) describes these ROMs as freely distributable. If you're feeling particularly adventurous, you can build AdvanceCD from source in Linux (*http://advancemame.sourceforge.net/doc-buildcd.html*).

Overall, this is one of the most attractive autobooting MAME packages, not least because it has frequent updates to keep in step with the new Advance-MAME and AdvanceMenu releases. Although it's not very customizable or full-featured in terms of the Linux side of things, you can switch to a Linux console by pressing Ctrl-Alt-F2 from within AdvanceCD.

For more information, see *http://advancemame.sourceforge.net/cd-readme.html*.

KnoppiXMAME. KnoppiXMAME is probably a second choice for most, but it's still an excellent self-booting CD/DVD option. It has no games installed by default and uses nearly 150 MB for the installation without ROM files.

On the plus side, KnoppiXMAME is definitely more versatile because it uses the very customizable Knoppix Linux CD distribution (*http://www.knoppix.net/*), a great project in itself. It unfortunately lacks many of the more complex resolution-related features of AdvanceCD. Along with the footprint issues, this is less preferable than AdvanceCD, but is still an excellent effort.

Visit *http://sourceforge.net/projects/knoppixmame/* to learn more.

XMAME on CD. XMAME on CD is mostly a roll-your-own project. It started in Japan and has spawned a separate site in the United Kingdom (*http://www.phased.co.uk/xmame/*) with step-by-step information on how to build your own self-booting XMAME CD from scratch (*http://www.phased.co.uk/xmame/cookbook.html*). Unfortunately, these instructions are old; they refer to Red Hat 6.2, released in March 2000.

Nonetheless, this provides an interesting guide to doing it yourself, particularly with regard to making RAM disc images and creating a read-only filesystem in Linux. Maybe you could look at this page, pretend you understand it, and then download AdvanceCD.

See *http://www15.big.or.jp/~yamamori/sun/tech-linux-2/index_e.html*.

AdvanceCD Tips and Tricks

Since AdvanceCD is probably the best of the available options, let's presume you will use it to make your own self-booting MAME CD. Here are some things you should know to make your games run with maximum efficiency.

Bundling and burning the image. To burn the CD image in Windows after you download it, unzip it to your hard drive, add all the ROMs into the correct directory (*/image/arcade/*), and then run *makecd.bat* to create the ISO (*advcd.iso*). Conventional CD-burning software should burn this correctly.

The procedure is similar for Linux users. Run *./makecd.sh* instead of the batch file after putting the ROMs into */image/arcade/*, then use your favorite Linux—not Windows—CD burning software. Cunning, huh?

Do be careful about the case of the filenames of your ROMs. Only lowercase names will work properly. This may be a problem; it's easy to find ROMs with irregular filenames or all uppercase characters.

Running the CD. Even with intelligent, self-booting CDs, there are some known issues with a few video and audio cards. Onboard audio cards are the main culprits. AdvanceCD's SourceForge page has a massive list of compatible video (*http://advancemame.sourceforge.net/doc-cardcd.html*) and audio (*http://advancemame.sourceforge.net/doc-audiocd.html*) setups. Read that ahead of time to forestall a nervous rush of confusion later.

This may be obvious, but it's worth mentioning; if you have a relatively old machine, MAME may run into speed problems, even with self-boot versions. This is most evident on more complex and recent ROMs. You can't just give the disc to your grandmother with the Pentium 90 and expect games to run at full frame-rate.

Study the manuals and details for AdvanceMAME and AdvanceMENU in detail to understand all the options for screenshots, flyers, background music, and so on. This advice isn't specific to AdvanceCD; you can use these utilities on their own even outside of the self-booting CD. They are covered further in "Add and Manipulate a MAME Frontend" **[Hack #11]**.

HACK #16 Play Emulated Arcade Games Online

Can't find four friends to crowd around your home arcade cabinet? Look online for team play.

One of the few arcade features that consoles, PC ports, and emulation can't always provide is socialization. It's fun to have the high score in a shooter, to take on all comers in a fighter, and to enter battle with three friends in a quarter-eating adventure game. You can recreate the games, but unless you have your own arcade cabinet ("Buy Your Own Arcade Hardware" **[Hack #58]**) or an appropriate emulator ("Play Arcade Games Without the Arcade" **[Hack #10]**) and can convince your friends to play along, you might think you're stuck.

Fortunately, the clever Kaillera bridging software can play emulated titles online.

Introducing the Kaillera Middleware

As the word "middleware" suggests, there's a key difference between Kaillera and the other retro emulators we've discussed. Kaillera software actually interfaces with existing emulators to allow multiplayer arcade games—not originally playable over any network—to play online. However, to make this work, the emulator developers must have incorporated Kaillera into their software.

The main Kaillera-enabled emulator is a MAME variant named MAME32k. It's available with the Kaillera client itself on the site's download page (*http://www.kaillera.com/download.php*). This is sufficient to play games. If you want to host games, you'll need a completely different Kaillera server. The server is a standalone application also available from the download page. In general, the client is embedded in the emulator in some way, but the server always stands alone.

Fortunately, as with many FPS games, you may be able to find a public server without having to run your own. The front page of Kaillera.com lists several such servers (see Figure 1-11). The biggest servers can hold up to 100 people. You may wish to host your own server for ping, ease of use, and privacy issues, however—but it's up to you.

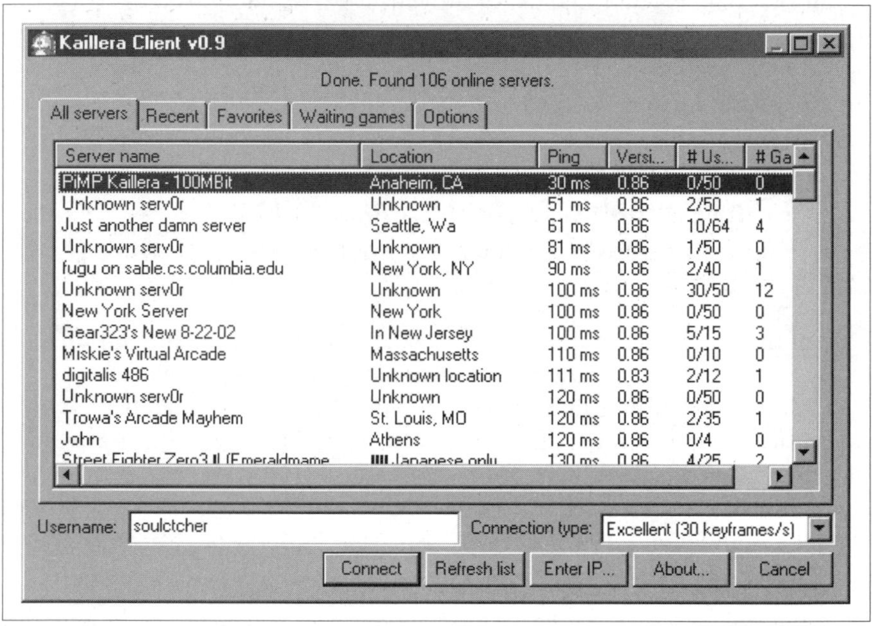

Figure 1-11. Listing the servers in Kaillera

The Kaillera site also has a fairly decent visual explanation of how to start up a game and to find the gaming partner of your dreams; see its screenshots page (*http://www.kaillera.com/shots.php*). The whole process is fairly self-explanatory, presuming you understand the basic network gaming concept that the lower the ping, the more likely you are to have a smooth game.

Troubleshooting Kaillera Play

The designers of these old games never designed in Internet play, and in many cases, the games predated the modern Internet. You'll likely run into several similar problems. Fortunately, the Kaillera page has a quality FAQ (*http://www.kaillera.com/faq.php*) that explains many of the more common problems. Let's highlight a few of the less obvious ones:

Lag is always an issue in online gaming. Some of the largest Kaillera users are in the East, particularly China and Hong Kong, so the FAQ makes a good point about trying to play on a server over very long distances.

However, Kaillera uses UDP, not TCP/IP. Lost packets are gone forever, but the lack of nondelivery acknowledgement in UDP tends to reduce lag. From a practical point of view, try to pick low-ping servers to play on, ideally within the same continent as yourself (see Figure 1-11). Keep your Connection setting on Good to send out enough packets to prevent a choppy connection.

Desynchronization can be a major problem. This slightly more serious problem occurs when network packets are dropped or possibly corrupted. Without in-game error checking, Player 1 may correctly press the A button to pick up a power-up and receive 1,000 points, but the packet that explains this never actually reaches Player 2. Now both players have encountered divergent behavior. One good way to check for desync is by comparing the scores, according to the FAQ. Both players should see the same point values because they're playing the same game.

The Kaillera server comes with optional Unix flavoring. If you're having trouble starting the Kaillera server, bear in mind that there's a version that runs as a Unix/Linux daemon: `./kaillerasrv`. You can treat it as a standard Unix utility. For example, to count the number of visitors, pipe the output to a log, and then type this at the prompt:

```
grep connected kaillerasrv.log -c
```

If you're not quite that elite, there's also a Windows version available from the Kaillera download page (*http://www.kaillera.com/download. php*).

Selected Kaillera-Compatible Emulators

MAME32k is the first and most obvious emulator that uses Kaillera (think anything from great old titles like Rampage, through later '80s games such as Arkanoid, right up to '90s cult titles such as Cadillacs And Dinosaurs, plus many, many more), but there are several other cool alternatives in various stages of development. The following sections describe the highlights.

Kawaks. Though much more contemporary in terms of the material it emulates, and with some MAME overlap, Kawaks is often the most popular emulator over the entire Kaillera server sets. It handles Neo Geo and Capcom CPS2 games, although these games are sometimes commercially available elsewhere; it's often a little shady in copyright terms. Still, it's excellent software, especially for one-on-one fighting titles such as the King Of Fighters series, classic Street Fighter II variants, and newer one-on-one fighters such as Garou. See *http://kawaks.retrogames.com/*.

NESten. This fairly simple, vanilla NES emulator for Windows comes with Kaillera built in, so you can play some of your favorite Nintendo games against others over the Internet. This isn't just neat, it's spectacularly good; who can resist a little Duck Hunt or even a little Tengen Tetris? Download it from *http://tnse.zophar.net/NESten.htm*.

WinUAE Kaillera. This marvelous software allows Commodore Amiga fans to get their game on in a multiplayer fashion, thanks to an adaptation of the popular WinUAE Amiga emulator—think of amazing old titles like Sensible Soccer, IK+, and Speedball. Unfortunately, a second release has seen years of delay, at least at the time of writing. The available version is still an excellent start. Find out more at *http://kaillera.abime.net/*.

Bliss. On the wild side of cool, Bliss allows you to play multiplayer Intellivision games over a network with the help of Kaillera! Who'da thunk that such an old console would ever work online? Maybe you'd better boot up some of the entertaining sports titles such as Intellivision Football, or crazier Tron-style fare such as Snafu, and blast through them multiplayer-style. Learn how at *http://bliss.emuviews.com/*.

Stats, Damned Stats, and Kaillera Stats

One of the coolest things about the Kaillera web site is the statistics page (*http://www.kaillera.com/stats.php*), which shows the top-played titles in several different genres. This is surprisingly useful because it displays the titles that work best online over moderate connections.

As for highlights of this information, Taito's marvelous Bubble Bobble sits atop the most played Platform Games chart, despite being over 15 years old. The tremendously addictive Puyo Puyo installments top the Puzzle Games chart, with the Neo Geo's great Magical Drop 3 shortly behind. It's also notable that the Adventure Games chart includes the classic Capcom brawler Dungeons and Dragons: Shadow of Mystara, an oft-neglected title so popular that the Taiwanese IGS PGM arcade console is producing gameplay clones even now. Finally, there's even a Quiz game chart for general knowledge-style questions, headed by the SNK title Quiz King Of Fighters.

All these games are worth checking out, although the usual caveats about intellectual property and trying to acquire legal ROMs apply. See "Legal Emulation" [Hack #1] for more.

Play Classic Pinball Without the Table

You too can play mean pinball on modern tables with this great emulation suite.

Suppose you want to play some of the classic pintables (pinball tables) from the '80s and '90s, before the market crashed (the only remaining pinball manufacturer seems to be the revitalized Stern). Visual Pinball ("Create and Play Pinball Tables" **[Hack #80]**) is an amazing start—a fully featured, freeware pinball-table-creation suite that's actually pretty easy to use. Thanks to this program and some reasonably complex setup instructions, Windows users can play emulated versions of their favorite old pinball machines in no time.

The Magic of VPinMAME

Although MAME is one of the most well-known, coolest emulators around, another project carrying the MAME name may be both lesser-known and cooler. VPinMAME combines the very cool Visual Pinball with MAME emulation of the dot-matrix display (DMD) on recent games. That's the area that keeps track of the score as well as the logic for controlling the more complex parts of the table, such as when to release multiball and actual minigames you can play with the flippers.

The VPinMAME emulation uses the MAME codebase, but obviously, you can't play the pinball game ROMs in any standalone fashion because you need the table as an interface. By hooking up the amazing physics and layout tools of Visual Pinball to the MAME-style emulation of the DMD display, you can play pinball with relevant dot-matrix score and mini-game feedback at the same time. Smart.

VPinMAME Installation

The (Windows-only) installation is a little strange because VPinMAME must live in its own directory. Your Visual Pinball standalone executable is probably in *C:\Program Files\Visual Pinball*. When you install VPinMAME (from *http://pinmame.retrogames.com/downloads.html*), it should unzip into *C:\VPinMAME*. Run the installation program, and all should be fine and dandy for that part.

However, you will need a bunch of extra software before you can run the games. Unfortunately, since there's no commercial release, the installation process is tricky:

1. Download the VBS Script Files from *http://www.vpforums.com/vptables/tables.php* and extract them to *C:\VPinMAME\Tables*.

2. To make the fonts look right on the tables themselves, you'll also need the latest Font file from *http://www.vpforums.com/vptables/tables.php*. Because they're normal Windows fonts, you can unzip this into your *C:\ Windows\Fonts* directory.

3. Finally, you'll need the default sound samples for every game. Download these in ZIP form from the same site to your *C:\VPinMAME\ Samples* directory, but do not—repeat do *not*—unzip them.

Okay, it's not that tricky. Everything's easy with good directions, if you put your mind to it.

VPinMAME Games of Choice

Before you can play an emulated game, someone has to convert it. AJ's VPinMAME page (*http://www.vpforums.com/vptables/tables.php*) is one of the only really comprehensive conversion lists. It also includes download links if you register. At the time of writing, there are over 400 tables available—an amazing fan-based effort—with many more new titles and improved versions of existing games to come. These games span almost all of the post-electromechanical era, from manufacturers such as Bally, Midway, Stern, Williams, and Sega. There are also some earlier titles in there.

Although each individual dot-matrix screen type had different hardware, which meant there were several chipsets to emulate, the vast majority have support now. The approach is similar to that of MAME: bundling emulators for several individual arcade board types. The collective emulator is extremely powerful.

However, please bear in mind that not all of these tables are completely finished. The makers have spent days playing the original machines and tweaking the physics and layout so that they accurately recreate the original articles as much as possible, but many tables are still works in progress. You may be able to estimate how complete the table is by looking at the version number, but some tables are so easy that V1.0 is all they need, and some still aren't perfect after multiple versions, so your mileage may vary! Check out the *README* file in ROM distributions or poke around the boards for user comments on a specific table.

In any case, it's easy to recommend some of my favorite pinball tables of all time. Not coincidentally, they're often the most polished, so they're well worth checking out.

The Addams Family. Pat Lawlor (designer of many of my favorites) created what may well be the most popular pinball table of all time in his adaptation of Barry Sonnenfeld's big-screen *The Addams Family*. If you haven't had the opportunity to play it in real life, what should you know? The infamous Thing (a disembodied hand) pops out of the playfield and grabs the ball. Also, there's the famous Thing Flips reward in which the pinball machine itself activates the flipper for you to try to make the shot; it automatically corrects for you the next time it misses! Besides these special features, the seminal layout offers the ultimate in smooth play with wonderful game modes. See *http://www.ipdb.org/machine.cgi?id=20*.

White Water. Mixing things up a little, this Williams title riffs on white-water rafting and includes an interactive Bigfoot character on the playfield; try to sneak the ball past him! It also has a gigantic ramp down the right side of the playfield, which will hit the front glass on the way down should you be lucky enough. Although not as well-known as the two titles it's sandwiched between, this Dennis Nordman-designed title is a cult favorite. You can find more information at *http://www.ipdb.org/machine.cgi?id=2768*.

The Twilight Zone. Another Lawlor creation, renowned as one of the most complex but deepest pinball tables of all time, this draws on the lore from the classic TV series to create a super-complex, super-enjoyable table. As with the Addams Family, it's notable because of playfield magnets that change the direction of your pinball unexpectedly. The Twilight Zone messes with things a little further by having a Powerball, a ceramic pinball unaffected by the magnets. This is amazing and obviously tricky to emulate, but the effort is valiant. See *http://www.ipdb.org/machine.cgi?id=2684*.

The Adventures of Rocky and Bullwinkle and Friends. "Hey Rocky, watch me pull a rabbit out of my hat!" The cheerful tones of Bullwinkle J. Moose are a great starting point for this super-addictive Data East title, one of their more notable games. It features several slightly deranged modes, including the famous WABAC Machine that will send you back in (pinball) time. This officially licensed game didn't have a huge mass-market appeal, but you can tell that the designers had high respect for Jay Ward's original 'toons. The ramps are well-positioned for smooth play; plus, there are moose ears atop the actual cabinet. Who can resist that? You can find more information at *http://www.ipdb.org/machine.cgi?23*.

If you're interested in emulators for older, classic pintables without any complicated ROMs to emulate, see IRPinball (*http://irpinball.ztnet.com/*), which has a massive list of recreated tables from the '40s to the early '80s for download. They may not have complex dot-matrix mini-games or cheesy movie licenses, but they're still rather smart. They don't actually require VPinMAME to run, just Visual Pinball.

Loading and Playing VPinMAME Games

It seems that nothing's ever entirely straightforward with VPinMAME, including loading in games. Many games are distributed in two parts, one being the table design itself and the other, the DMD ROM to run in the emulator.

When you find a table in the standard *.VPT* format, unzip it into the *C:\ VPinMAME\Tables* directory. When you find the DMD ROM, probably from somewhere else entirely, put it in *C:\VPinMAME\Roms without* unzipping it. Then, when you load the table and play it normally (by pressing F5), it should recognize and include the VPinMAME features.

> If you're stuck on installation, the VPForums.com site has a FAQ area with basic troubleshooting tips (*http://www. vpforums.com/modules.php?name=FAQ*). There are also plenty of very friendly people on the boards there who will help you with potential issues.

A Short Legal Note

Of course, this brings about a difficult issue. At least with some emulated titles, you can own the original and feel a little more justified in playing the emulated versions. If you wanted to play five of these titles with full legality, you'd need a garage just to store the originals. Hopefully, the original pintable producers will release officially licensed ROM versions of some of these amazing emulations. In the meantime, use your discretion.

H A C K #18   Emulate the SNES on the Dreamcast

Make your Dreamcast act like an SNES, Neo-Geo, or even a home computer.

Although we've dealt with emulators for consoles in several other hacks, Dreamcast emulators really deserve a hack of their own. For one thing, it's easy to burn your own discs full of emulators and ROMs without having to use any legally dubious hardware hacks to boot unofficial discs. For another, the cheap, aging, and fairly easy to buy ("Find a Hackable Dreamcast" **[Hack #50]**) Dreamcast has a relatively swift Hitachi SH-4 RISC 200-MHz processor, so it can run many faster emulators. However, the spartan 16 MB of main memory limits some of the larger ROMs that need more memory. This problem afflicts even the mighty 64-MB Xbox on some MAME ROMs.

Nevertheless, there's plenty of emulation fun available for your DC. Possibly the best example of Dreamcast emulators is DreamSNES, the Super Nintendo emulator.

DreamSNES

Vying for the title of best emulator on the Dreamcast, this Super Nintendo emulator is a conversion of the seminal PC emulator SNES9X. Its features include the ability to save SNES games to your VMU; a handy and functional upfront menu; working four-player support; and mouse, keyboard, and lightgun support.

Making self-booting CDs isn't completely easy, but the DreamSNES creators have a custom application that allows you to add ROMs and burn the CD in one fell swoop. This clever move takes away all the hassle of finding compatible burning software. See the tutorial at *http://www.lysator.liu.se/dreamsnes/tutorial/* for a little more insight. Here are the basic steps:

1. Let Pike install. The ZIP file for Windows includes a copy of the Pike programming language (*http://pike.ida.liu.se/*). It'll take a little while to install unless you already have it.

2. Check for ASPI drivers. If your CD-ROM drive doesn't show when you first load the utility, consult ASPI Drivers Explained (*http://www.ncf.carleton.ca/~aa571/aspi.htm*) to clear up the messy situation.

3. Edit your ROM names. After selecting your burner of choice, switch to the ROM list and add in the ROMs you want to burn. If you'd like a choice of freeware ROMs, try PDRoms (*http://www.pdroms.de/*). From here, you can edit the names under which the games and demos appear in the menu.

4. Burn a CD or image. Switch to the Burn tab, and burn the CD. Alternately, you can write out a Nero disc image if you prefer to use your normal disc-burning software, or if you need the flexibility of an image.

   CD-RWs generally don't work on the DC.

DreamSNES also supports standalone ROM discs. As usual, DCEmulation explains how to create them (*http://www.dcemulation.com/roms-dreamsnes.htm*). Here's the scoop:

1. Organize your ROMs to burn. Take the ROMs you want to burn to CD and put them in a separate *roms* folder. This is *very* important; the next step may arbitrarily rename any other files in the folder.

2. Make a ROM list. Download the *Provlist.exe* Windows executable from *http://www.dcemulation.com/files/needed/Provlist.exe*. Copy it into the new ROMs directory, and run it. This creates the *ROM.LST* file that the emulator needs.

3. Add menu music. If you'd like to listen to music while selecting ROMs, add a *sound* subdirectory with the MP3s of your choice.

4. Burn a multisession CD. Unless you've filled up the CD completely, use your CD-burning software to create a multisession CD. This allows you to add more ROMs later.

Now boot your Dreamcast with the normal DreamSNES disc, then switch to the ROMs disc of your choice.

The Best of the Rest Dreamcast Emulators

The very first place to look for other Dreamcast emulation-related material is DCEmulation.com (*http://www.dcemulation.com/*). Not only do they have a great, comprehensive list of Dreamcast emulators, but they host all the emulator executables locally. As long as the site stays up, you won't have the problems of broken external download links that plague many other sites. In addition, it features an up-to-date news section and often runs tutorials on installing many of the emulators.

Here's a quick run-through of other wonderful and sometimes obscure emulators you can use on your Dreamcast.

Dream-O-Rama. An example of why the Dreamcast is also home to some intriguingly different emulators, Dream-O-Rama reproduces the Japan-only Sega SG-1000/3000 hardware. For those wondering what it is (I also had to look it up), it's Sega's first piece of games hardware, properly released in Japan back in 1983. There are several neat, waaaay out-of-print titles for it, including classic arcade titles such as Galaga and even a James Bond 007 game, so this emulator is well worth checking out.

Download it from *http://www.dcemulation.com/dcemu-dorama.htm*.

DCFrotz. You can find out more about making your own text adventure ("Download, Compile, and Create an Inform Adventure" [Hack #85]), but if you have a keyboard or keyboard adapter for your Dreamcast, you can play text adventures here. There are plenty of freeware Z-Machine interactive fiction pieces available. DCFrotz even supports sound effects if you want to use or program a game that plays spooky WAV files.

Learn more at *http://www.c99.org/dc/frotzdc/index.php*.

MDCNG. This Neo Geo-specific emulator isn't exactly well-tested or stable yet (it runs somewhat short of a 100% frame rate, although turning off sound will improve that a little), but it's impressive nonetheless. It works best for early-'90s Neo Geo titles that haven't blossomed past the Dreamcast's memory limit. You'll need to use the Selfboot.exe Windows utility to create a self-booting Dreamcast CD with both the emulator and then ROMs contained on it (see *http://www.dcemulation.com/selfboot-mdcng.htm*). Even better, DCStuff (*http://www.sesonsite.com/Ten-321/DCStuff/Apps.shtml*) includes a helper application that explains how to make a self-booting DC disc from the plan files of the Neo Geo CD emulator.

See *http://www.dcemulation.com/dcemu-mdcng.htm*.

DreamZZT. Finishing with another ravishing obscurity, DreamZZT is a Dreamcast conversion of Tim Sweeney's famous ZZT PC game-creation tool. (Back in the early '90s, he wasn't yet famous for Epic's Unreal series.) ZZT graphics are entirely made up of ASCII characters. There's a multitude of public-domain games available, both turn-based and real-time. Many are RPG-like. The Chocobo.org site has a decent ZZT game selection (*http://www.chocobo.org/~butz/zzt.htm*) if you'd like to try some third-party titles, all of which seem to run reasonably well.

Find it at *http://www.c99.org/dc/dzzt/index.php*.

As well as these different choices, several emulators mentioned elsewhere have Dreamcast versions, including Frodo for the Commodore 64 (*http://www.dcemulation.com/dcemu-dreamfrodo.htm*) and Stella for the Atari 2600 (*http://www.dcemulation.com/dcemu-stelladc.htm*). Again, see the DCEmulation.com page for more details and thank your lucky stars that the Dreamcast is such a cheap and versatile engine for cool software.

CHAPTER TWO

Playing Portably
Hacks 19–27

Nintendo's Game Boy series has enjoyed a 15-year lead as the portable gaming platform of choice. This has spawned an odd and occasionally bewildering array of add-ons, accessories, and modifications.

The Game Boy isn't the only portable out there, though, nor are you limited to conventional notions of what is and isn't a portable gaming system. For example, did you know that you can play and write simple choose-your-own-adventure-style games that run on the iPod? Have you ever wished your Nintendo were more portable? Why not pick up a battery-powered NES-compatible handheld?

If you're on the go and want a little bit more from your gaming fix, consider these alternate ways to play portably.

HACK #19 Play Games on Your iPod
Make and add simple games to your playlist.

It's commendable of Apple to avoid the whole convergence idea by making the iPod a good music player and not an amazing portable video game system with PDA functions and a built-in phone. However, this move has annoyed those contrary types who want to play games on the iPod. Fortunately, the perverse rule is in full effect; you can now download and even create your own basic, choose-your-own-adventure homebrew games for the iPod.

The iPod Gaming Concept

The trick of playing new iPod games comes from subverting the Notes format, also known as Museum Mode. By design, this mode presents individual pages with hypertext-style links. The original intent may have been to store album information or perhaps reminder notes. Whatever the reason, it's easy enough to offer multiple-choice stories in a hyperlinked tree of pages.

 Caveat hacker! At the time of writing, only the third-generation iPods and the mini-iPods officially support the Notes mode. It appears that you can update older hardware to newer firmware, although Apple will probably never support this. Otherwise, if you have an earlier version of the iPod, you won't have Notes mode, and you can't try out any of this stuff. D'oh.

Playing Existing iPod Games

The iPodSoft site (*http://www.ipodsoft.com/Downloads.aspx*) is the main free area for iPod gaming. They've compiled a list of the only free games available online right now. Particular highlights (yes, yes, I could only find two) include:

Who Wants To Be A Millionaire?
> *http://ipodsoft.com/downloads/istory/istories/Millionaire%20Vol.%201.zip*
>
> Okay, so it's not precisely an official license, and it has a paltry amount of questions, but this recreation of Regis Philbin's greatest suit-and-shirt-matching moment has sound, a clear objective, and works into the quiz format that seems to function best in the very limited Notes structure. In other words, it's kinda fun the first time.

Harry Potter Adventure
> *http://ipodsoft.com/downloads/istory/istories/HarryPotter.zip*
>
> This unofficial adaptation of the Brunching Shuttlecocks' also unofficial Harry Potter choose-your-own-adventure humor site is both amusing and *very* unofficial. If you were a fan of those Steve Jackson and Ian Livingstone *Fighting Fantasy* books in the early '80s (and who wasn't?), it works very well as a piece of fluffy, slight interactive fiction.

If you're *really* considering buying a game, the XOPod site (*http://www. xoplay.com/xoplay.php*) sells several choose-your-own-adventure titles at prices of up to $15 each. Titles include Herbert's Big Adventure (very Leisure Suit Larry–esque) and Bum–Rags To Riches (with a suitably bizarre illustration) to tempt your fancy. Honestly, though, you're paying for the novelty of playing a new game on your iPod. Because you can recreate that experience by downloading the free games, and because the pay titles aren't that much more sophisticated, you may be okay staying with the free content unless you have the need to collect every possible game.

Making Your Own iPod Games

There's only one tool to build your own pseudo-games on iPod right now: iStory Creator (*http://ipodsoft.com/*). This completely unofficial software works only on Windows and, bizarrely enough, requires the Microsoft .NET Framework, a significant irony given the target platform.

It does work, and it definitely makes some of the basic content-creation tasks a little easier, especially organizing things and cranking out stories in a hurry. You can still do everything you want in a text editor, however, so it's not a requirement.

The iPod Notes format. If you want to get down to the nitty-gritty and do some more fun stuff, see the iPod Note Reader documentation on the official Apple site (*http://developer.apple.com/hardware/ipod/ipodnotereader.pdf*). However, there aren't many details because there's so little to the Notes format. You have two tools at your disposal for creating crazy interactive stories:

Text links

> You can have as many text links as you like within each individual Notes *.TXT* screen. More than one of them can point to the same place, too. If you're running a quiz program, you may want to point three of the links to the *false.TXT* text file for that question and the other to the *true.TXT* file. The syntax of a link is:
>
> ```
> <a href="15.txt">Selection 1</a>
> ```
>
> where `15.txt` is the next file to load, and `Selection 1` is the name of the link to appear on the screen.

Music references

> Because the iPod is a music player at heart, you can insert links in Notes to songs on your player. You'll have to import these songs onto the iPod before you start playing the game, but when they're there, you can play little snippets as sound effects, speech, and so on. These will play after the player makes a selection. The particular syntax is:
>
> ```
> <a href="ipod:music?song=songname&NowPlaying=false">Song</a>
> ```
>
> where `songname` is the actual song title on the iPod.

Tricks and limitations. In addition to the actual iPod Notes features, there are a few important caveats to keep in mind:

- You have a maximum of 1,000 notes. If you try to emulate an inventory system by crafting slightly different room descriptions to remember which item is where, you'll soon run out of locations.

- Notes have a maximum size of 4KB each, so *War and Peace*–style descriptions are out.
- Full pathnames must fit into 255 characters, which seems large, but be careful if you're trying to structure your adventure using lots of lengthy subdirectories. If you exceed this length, you'll see no error message. The documentation notes:

  Files whose pathnames are too long are not loaded, and no error is reported.

A short example. What would I be if I failed to show how to write your own game? Here's a template you can use to start. Fill in the parenthesized words to create your own text adventure!

```
You are (verb) in a (location).  You see a (adjective) (noun one) on the
(noun two).  A (portal) leads (direction).
What do you do?

1.  <a href="page2.txt">Pick up the (noun one).</a>
2.  <a href="page3.txt">Go (direction).</a>
```

Fill in the blanks, save this as *page1.txt*, write pages 2 and 3, copy them all to your iPod, and go! Of course, you may want to brush up on your interactive fiction ("Download, Compile, and Create an Inform Adventure" **[Hack #85]**) skills first, though.

Limitations Breed Creativity

Now that you know the simple syntax of iPod Notes, what can you do? You'll have to work around some severe gameplay limitations. You can't save data or select links randomly. Every move happens when the player chooses an option. Maybe you can go crazy and create chess in less than 1,000 notes. An enterprising hacker may be able to use ASCII art to fake the look of actual graphics.

Still, until someone works out how to alter or add to the built-in games without breaking everything, these are the best homebrew games there are for the iPod. Go ahead, improve the art.

HACK #20 Mod Your Game Boy
Hardware hacks for your favorite portable console.

What if you have an older-model Game Boy Advance and want backlighting? Suppose you have a newer Game Boy and miss the chunky bass sound of the older monochrome Game Boys. You're not stuck buying a newer or older machine; there are reasonably straightforward hardware modifications you can do to fix both problems.

Game Boy Advance AfterBurner

First, let's be clear: if you decide to modify your Game Boy Advance (GBA) with a frontlight at this stage in the GBA's life, you're hardcore. When Nintendo saw the immense popularity of the AfterBurner frontlight add-on in 2002, they introduced the Game Boy Advance SP, which features frontlighting of its own.

You're also hardcore because there's a definite failure rate when it comes to the tricky frontlight installation. An acquaintance ruined more than one GBA before getting it right! It's also becoming difficult to find the After-Burner kit because its creators at Triton Labs (*http://www.tritonlabs.com/*) have discontinued it in favor of composing music instead.

If all this doesn't put you off, it's still a challenging and interesting project.

Start by reading the Triton Labs FAQ (*http://www.tritonlabs.com/ ?page=faq#11*) to understand the requirements. You will need:

- An AfterBurner kit. This comes with the light guide and source, electrical wire, and a dimmer switch you can choose to install or not. The dimmer switch can be a little unreliable if installed badly.
- A soldering iron, solder, and wire strippers
- A Dremel drill. You'll need to remove some of the plastic under the screen for the light to fit.
- A can of compressed air. While you have the screen exposed, it may attract specks of dust. They will stay there forever after you reseal your GBA—not good.

Fortunately, the AfterBurner kit itself comes with very good instructions. It's worth running through the steps nonetheless:

1. Open your GBA by removing the special screws from the back of the system. Multiple sources recommend using a 1/16-inch flathead screwdriver. When unscrewed, you can separate the screen from the GBA's cover; be *very* careful here, because the two may be stuck together.

2. Make sure that all dust is out of the way before you mount the antireflective film to the GBA's LCD screen. This is one of the trickiest parts of the entire operation; the film is difficult to apply without trapping air bubbles in the film and extremely tricky to reposition when you've placed it. Be careful!

3. Solder wires from the light guide to two points on the GBA specified in the AfterBurner instruction manual. Carefully reassemble everything, including the new light guide and light source. Use the compressed air

to blow all specks of dust out of the screen area before replacing the front cover.

Presto. You should have a working frontlight for your previously vanilla GBA!

The Triton Labs site says:

> You can expect to spend at least a half hour to an hour to do the job right, possibly more if you've never done anything like this. If you are completely inexperienced in electronics, you should consider going with a professional installer.

The frontlight definitely affects battery life, just as it does with the Game Boy Advance SP. Conservative estimates vary, but expect a reduction of at least 30% in battery life after installing a frontlight. Fortunately, the After-Burner doesn't take power in any underhanded manner; the GBA is under the impression it's powering an external wormlight (an adjustable light that attaches to it). You'll see no power-related glitches if you've installed the device properly.

Frontlighting Versus Backlighting

The whole concept of frontlighting and backlighting is a little confusing, with many people convinced that the Game Boy Advance SP has a backlit screen. This isn't actually correct. Both the AfterBurner kit and the GBA SP add frontlighting, illuminating the LCD screen by projecting light in from the front (specifically, across the front from the sides). If mounted properly, this still provides excellent lighting, although some people claim noticeable issues such as washed-out colors.

Other portable consoles in the past have had proper backlighting, even as far back as the Atari Lynx in 1989.

Bass Sound Modding the Game Boy Color

Although this is a specialized mod, it's pretty neat. The Game Boy is becoming increasingly popular as a machine with homebrew music-creation software ("Compose Music on Your Game Boy" [Hack #22]). One of the limitations of creating sound on a GB is that the original, monochrome Game Boy produces better sound than any other version of the hardware. The Game Boy Color (GBC), an otherwise excellent candidate, has poor bass output and produces extra noise by the time the audio reaches the headphone socket.

The resourceful Timothy "Trash80" Lamb decided to open up the GBC to see what he could do. He produced an ingenious method (*http://www. littlesounddj.com/awkiawki/index.cgi/Prosound/*) of coaxing sound out of the GBC more directly without the garbling that happens through the current headphone socket. Your GBC can now also be a potent sonic weapon.

What do you need?

- A soldering iron, wire strippers, and solder.
- A Dremel or other type of drill. You'll need to cut a small hole in the Game Boy Color's plastic case
- An audio lead with a normal male 3.5mm headphone jack on one end. It doesn't matter what's on the other end; you'll cut it off.

Here's Lamb's procedure, step by step:

1. Open the back of your Game Boy Color by undoing the screws holding it in place. As with opening up the GBA, you'll encounter problems, because the screws are custom-made. Try the same 1/16-inch flathead screwdriver suggested earlier. If that fails, you can buy a Tri-Wing Screwdriver, specifically designed to open this type of screw, from online retailers such as ConsolePlus (*http://www.consoleplus.co.uk/*) in the United Kingdom and Hong Kong's ever reliable Play-Asia (*http:// www.play-asia.com/*).

2. The volume potentiometer is easy to find: it includes five pins and connects to the normal headphone socket. Cut off the other end of your 3.5mm headphone jack cable and strip the wires as necessary. Solder the two audio wires into pin 2 (left) and pin 3 (right). This bypasses whatever junk causes signal degradation on the normal headphone socket.

3. Unscrew the actual circuit board and turn it, looking for the connection labeled "4" under the headphone jack. Solder the last remaining lead, the audio ground, into that connection. Finally, make a small hole at the base of the GBC unit, just large enough for the audio lead, and close the GBC again. Congratulations, your Game Boy Color is now a bass monster.

Please note that this mod will work only for direct sound output, not for headphone output. This is good for recording to your PC when you're done, but not so good for listening on the move. This is a minor issue compared to the extra bass boom it produces, however.

Take and Print Photos with Your Game Boy

HACK #21

Fun things you can do with Nintendo's playful printer and camera peripherals.

Nintendo comes up with some cool geek toys. Many of them are in wide circulation right now, particularly the Game Boy Advance and the GameCube. Some of their older gems are still well worth buying to hack, exploit, and otherwise fiddle with; the Game Boy Camera and Game Boy Printer are foremost among these. Let's check out what you can do with them.

Introducing the Game Boy Camera and Printer

Many people have fallen in love with Nintendo's rudimentary Game Boy Camera, which shoots up to 30 pictures in four shades of grey at 128×112 pixel resolution, and stores everything in 128 KB of battery-saved SRAM. Originally released in 1998 in Japan and then in the West in the days of the black-and-white Game Boy, the camera still works with subsequent Game Boy models, including the Game Boy Advance and Game Boy Advance SP.

Due to its low-resolution, black-and-white look, the GB Camera feels even older than its actual vintage. While snapping, the camera lens itself either swivels to point toward the Game Boy user or faces outward to take pictures of your surroundings. It's surprisingly versatile, though. Not only can you take pictures and create simple stop-motion animations, the camera provides a large variety of stencils and silly add-ons (including fake noses, hats, and other accoutrements) that you can paste onto your picture. It even includes mini-games, as well as a musical DJ mode that allows very simple song composition, although this is nothing like the sophistication of Nanoloop or Little Sound Dj ("Compose Music on Your Game Boy" **[Hack #22]**).

The best thing about the GB Camera is the price. They're spectacularly cheap nowadays, and you can find them in large quantities on eBay for anywhere between $5 and $10 plus shipping.

The fun Game Boy Printer, released concurrently with the Game Boy Camera, is geared toward printing out the pictures you've taken, especially on sticker paper. Although the Game Boy Printer paper is extremely cheap (small rolls of thermal paper cost as little as $1 per roll on eBay), the Printer itself is scarcer than the Camera, fetching $20 or more on auction sites. However, it's strictly optional for most of the fun you can have here.

It's worth steering clear of third-party Game Boy Advance color cameras as an alternative to the Game Boy Camera, because all they offer is a way to take pictures and view them on your GBA screen. You can't perform any of the fun picture manipulations. Although these cameras provide an easy USB connection for transferring pictures to the PC, they're like a poor man's digital camera—not sufficiently lo-fi to be attractive, not nearly hi-fi enough to be worth the money.

Taking the Best Pictures Possible

Although it may seem like normal photographic rules apply, the odd resolution and number of colors mean there are several things to learn in order to take good photos. Here are some compositional and situational tips that'll help you coax the best pictures out of your Game Boy Camera:

- Light levels are very important when taking Game Boy pictures. Any night or dusk-time shots will be almost impossible to make out because the device has no flash. You may be able to take pictures with strong lighting or neon around, but unless you have a backlit screen on the Game Boy itself, you won't see much through the viewfinder. The Game Boy Camera is a sunny-day toy.

- Large, manmade objects such as buildings, vehicles, and statues often photograph better than rolling hills and smooth panoramas, because sharp edges and local contrasts in shade stand out a lot better in just four shades of gray. Forget about anything with subtle details! Figure 2-1 shows some of the best work I've done.

- Use the directional pad to adjust the contrast and brightness controls on the viewfinder screen before you actually take your picture or start your movie running. A couple of notches one way or the other, especially with the brightness control, can make the difference between an unusable and a perfect picture. Don't crank the contrast too high, though, unless you like the novelty of an either entirely black or entirely white pixelscape. This effect can actually look quite good if unleashed at the right time.

- If you're trying to make a movie that'll look good at a later date when looped as an animated GIF, pick start and end points close to each other. For example, do a 360-degree pan in one direction and stop just before completing a full revolution so that the first and the last frames fit together. Alternately, find a piece of machinery or another filmable object that loops—a revolving fairground attraction, for example—to make your GB animation go on forever.

Figure 2-1. Game Boy Camera pictures, taken by author, from San Francisco, Las Vegas, and London

Transferring Pictures to Your PC

There are a variety of methods for moving the images from your Game Boy to your PC for editing. Unfortunately, none of them are easy; Nintendo isn't particularly interested in making non-Nintendo hardware work with your Game Boy. However, if you want to display your Game Boy pictures on your web page, make animated GIFs of your movies, or store your old photos for safekeeping, you need to transfer your photos to your PC in some form. The following sections describe some possibilities.

The Game Boy Xchanger. By far the most efficient method is plugging your cartridge into dedicated hardware that connects to your PC via the parallel port. The most famous of these is the Bung Xchanger, as seen at *http://www. robwebb.clara.co.uk/backup/bung/bungxch.html*. Unfortunately, this device also theoretically allows you to copy Game Boy games if you buy a Flashrom cartridge, so Nintendo has cracked down and banned Bung from selling them.

If you can find an Xchanger, you can transfer the entire SRAM save of the Game Boy Camera cartridge to your PC, and then use either the gb_cam_dump or Gh0st Camera software (available from drx's page at *http://a-blast.org/ ~drx/lo-tech/gameboy/howto/index.en.html*) to save the pictures out into image form.

There's also a very strange device called the MPXchanger from Blaze that has some Game Boy memory card functionality and is available very cheaply, if you can find it. No one knows much about it, and it reportedly works only with Windows 95 and 98 and uses custom save-game formats.

Commercially built printer emulator cables. Although much slower and able to transfer only one picture at a time, a class of ingenious cables and software emulates the Game Boy Camera to Game Boy Printer connection from your Game Boy to your PC. These allow full-quality image transfer. The only one of these peripherals I know about is the MadCatz Camera Link. Unfortunately, it's spectacularly difficult to find; it must have had limited production runs. It comes with its own software to save the photos.

Homebrew printer emulator cables. Hardcore hackers can build their own Game Boy Printer emulator cables, using the instructions in Martin Eyre's software/schematic combo ZIP file (see drx's page again at *http://a-blast.org/~drx/lo-tech/gameboy/howto/index.en.html*). You'll need to adapt a Nintendo Universal Game Link cable and add a PC parallel port adapter onto its end. Documentation is scant, so this is not for the faint of heart.

Take pictures of your Game Boy's screen. This final option is sneaky but workable. There are a variety of methods to get your Game Boy Camera pictures to display on a TV; the easiest and most up to date uses a Game Boy Player for your GameCube. This official device plugs into the bottom of your GameCube and allows you to display Game Boy games through your GC. The Game Boy Camera works perfectly well with it.

You can either take pictures of the screen with a digital camera (a very rough way of doing things) or, even better, use a video capture card on your PC and grab pictures and movies straight from your Game Boy Camera into your computer. You may need to adjust the resolution and deal with the resulting blurriness, but it's definitely better than nothing.

Maximize Snaps with a GB Mega-Memory Card

Now that you're a wizard Game Boy Camera photographer, you may find that 30 pictures just aren't enough, especially for filming animated sequences. Fortunately, the obscure Game Boy peripherals market has provided keen shutterbugs with more space, in the form of the Interact Mega Memory Card for Game Boy Color.

This sometimes clear yellow peripheral, originally made to cash in on Pokémon fever by giving kids five extra save spots in which to save Pikachu from accidental deletion, connects to your Game Boy Camera cartridge. Each extra save spot can hold 30 pictures, increasing your storage space to 150 snaps plus the 30 on your camera. The card comes with its own menu for saving and restoring the SRAM, but it's a little clunky. It just won't fit in an original black-and-white Game Boy, but it works, and there are almost always multiple copies of the peripheral for sale on eBay for less than $5.

By the way, one handy and often overlooked tip related to picture management on the GB Camera cart itself can delete all your photos at once. Instead of laboriously removing each of the 30 pictures individually on the main GB Camera title screen, press the Select button, then choose Edit and

Album, and finally press Up, Select, and Start simultaneously to reach a dialog offering deletion of all.

Adding Color to Your Black-and-White Images

Wouldn't it be cool if there were a Game Boy Camera featuring color with the same cool-looking resolution and picture tone? Unfortunately, such a piece of hardware doesn't exist, but David Friedman's Rule Of Thirds camera page (*http://www.ruleofthirds.com/gameboy/*) showcases an ingenious method for producing color Game Boy Camera pictures:

1. You'll need red-, green-, and blue-hued filters. You can find these at a camera store, which may even give away sample books containing colored filters. Place these filters over the lens of the camera and take a picture from exactly the same angle for each filter. Transfer the pictures to your PC in some fashion and load them into Photoshop.

2. Convert the first picture to the R (red) values, the second picture to G (green) values, and the third picture to B (blue) values. Combine the three into a single RGB picture. If you do all this correctly, you'll see something approximating a color picture. However, the colors will likely to be faint and washed-out, because, as David discovered, the camera still collects infrared light of all types.

3. For ideal results, use a hot mirror filter lens to block out infrared light. Fit the red, green, and blue lenses over the top of this filter. If you want to go all the way for perfect color, these lenses cost between $30 and $40 at photographic stores, so it's probably more expensive than the Game Boy Camera itself, actually. However, the results, as shown on David's page, can be spectacular. See *http://www.ruleofthirds.com/gameboy/pictures.html*. It's great to see the low resolutions with vibrant colors.

HACK #22 Compose Music on Your Game Boy
When you can't take your studio with you, turn your portable into a studio.

Handheld gaming devices aren't just for children or for playing games. They can potentially be productive work devices! Okay, perhaps that's hard to swallow, but you can use your Game Boy to make music. One of the top Game Boy utilities is Little Sound Dj.

Introducing Little Sound Dj

Johan Kotlinski's Little Sound Dj (or LSDj) is very flexible and can enhance your musical ideas. It's also very fast to use once you've learned how.

Feature-wise, it boasts a soft synthesizer with resonant filters, sampled drum kits, and an internal speech synthesizer. All in all, it's more like a portable music studio than anything else.

Little Sound Dj cartridges are hard to find these days, but occasionally show up on eBay. During the last year, used cartridges sold for between $150 and $350. You can also download a free demo version from *http://www. littlesounddj.com/*. There's hope for some kind of reissue sometime in the future, though it's likely it'll still lack Nintendo's imprimatur.

Alternatives to LSDj

The Nintendo Game Boy Camera ("Take and Print Photos with Your Game Boy" **[Hack #21]**) also features a small DJ game with very basic sequencing and sound-programming capabilities. Although it's really a toy, this program aroused a lot of interest in making music on the Game Boy.

Jester Interactive developed the Nintendo-approved Pocket Music program for the Game Boy Color and Game Boy Advance. It is more capable than the Game Boy Camera but less fun, with a dull user interface that does not encourage creativity.

Oliver Wittchow originally created Nanoloop (*http://www.nanoloop.de/*) as a design school project. The program resembles a 16-step drum machine and is easy to use. It's mostly useful for making experimental, loop-based music with spaced-out sounds. It is less useful for making traditional songs, because it lacks support for traditional music concepts such as instruments or notes; program it by moving dots around on a 16-step pattern.

Nanoloop did enjoy some independent production onto actual GB cartridges a few years ago, but now it's hard to find except occasionally on eBay. There, used cartridges typically sell for between $50 and $100. The web site also promises to sell new cartridges for around $80 in the future, but they will run only on the Game Boy Advance.

Aleksi Eeben (*http://www.cncd.fi/aeeben/*) created the freeware Carillon music editor to produce music for games and demos, so the program focuses on making an efficient playback routine. Experienced users can compose good songs on the Game Boy. However, because its focus is technical rather than musical, the editor is not really a musician's dream, even if it is a big step up from Pocket Music.

Running Your Music Editor

Some Game Boy music editors (notably LSDj and Carillon) have download-able ROM image files. You can use these with a Game Boy emulator running on your computer or place them on a flash-ROM cartridge using a backup device connected to your PC.

Emulators can be nice in many ways. Of course, you won't be able to use the program on the real thing, but the sound can be cleaner than on the original hardware, and you can easily perform backups to minimize the risk of data loss. The price is also much nicer (at least if you already have a computer), and the screen is likely to be more legible.

The recommended emulator for Windows is No$GMB (*http://www.work.de/nocash/*). For Mac OS X, KiGB (*http://www.bannister.org/software/kigb.htm*) works well. VisualBoy Advance (*http://vba.ngemu.com/*) runs well on several platforms, including Windows, Mac OS X, Linux, and BeOS. All these programs are free to use for emulating the classic Game Boy.

Finding a backup device to program your own cartridge can be difficult these days, as all production for the classic Game Boy has ceased. If you are lucky, you can find a used device. Look for the brands Transferer, Xchanger, E-Merger, or PC-Linker. An alternative is to use a Game Boy Advance backup device with the Goomba emulator (*http://www.webpersona.com/goomba/*).

If you are handy with electronics, you can also build your own cartridge. Reiner Ziegler put up a page with all the info you need at *http://www.ziegler.desaign.de/readplus.htm*. Be sure to see the Game Boy Dev'rs site (*http://www.devrs.com/gb/*) for all the technical information you could need about the Game Boy.

Getting Started with Little Sound Dj

Enough chat; let's play.

First, download and install your choice of emulator. Then proceed to the Little Sound Dj file archive (*http://www.littlesounddj.com/latest/*) to download the files you need. There's a demo version Game Boy ROM image in the *demo* folder and documentation in the *documentation* folder.

After starting LSDj, you'll see a screen resembling Figure 2-2.

The title at the top left of the window indicates that this is the song screen, the window in which you arrange your songs. The four columns with dashes each represent a Game Boy sound channel. There are two pulse wave channels, one custom wave channel (which uses sampled drum kits or soft-synthesized wave forms), and one noise channel. You can move between the different channels using the cursor key.

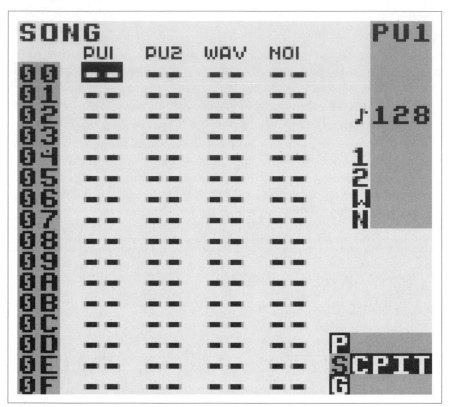

Figure 2-2. The LSDj song screen

Little Sound Dj uses several screens, laid out on a 5×3 map found at the bottom right of the screen. The most useful screens are in the middle row, also called the main row. These are the song, chain, phrase, instrument, and table screens. The screens provide increasing levels of detail from left to right. The leftmost song screen presents an overview of the entire song, and the rightmost table screen shows detailed instrument programming. Navigate between the different screens by holding Select and pressing the cursor key.

The song, chain, and phrase screens control sequencing and work together in a tree-structure fashion. The phrase screen is a 16-step sequencer in which you'll enter actual note data. The chain screen is a 16-step sequencer in which you can enter sequences of phrases to play. The song screen is a 256-step sequencer in which you enter sequences of chains.

Creating some noise. Navigate to the song screen and put the cursor on the PU1 column. Tap the A button twice to insert a new chain. The digit 00 should now appear at the cursor. Edit that chain by pressing Select plus

Right to enter the chain screen. There, go through the same procedure. Tap A twice to insert a new phrase and press Select plus Right to reach the phrase screen.

Here you can enter notes. Move the cursor to the note column and press A to enter a note. The text C-3 will appear, C being the note and 3 the octave. Press Start to play back the phrase. Note how the phrase plays back from the top of the screen to the bottom. You can change the note value by holding A and pressing the cursor button. Pressing A plus Left or Right changes the note, and A plus Up or Down changes the octave.

You can now move the cursor up and down and insert more notes in other positions. To delete a note, press A while holding B. When you have finished listening, press Start again to stop the phrase.

The clean pulse sound might grow a bit dull after a while. Move on to the instrument screen by pressing Select plus Right.

The instrument screen is the place to make the sound a little bit more interesting. Change the envelope and wave fields by moving the cursor there and pressing A plus Left or Right. Modify the envelope setting from A8 to A3. Now press Start again to hear any change in sound. The sound amplitude should decay after the note plays.

The type field sets the instrument type. These instruments are specific to individual channels; pulse instruments play back only in the pulse channels, wave and kit instruments in the wave channel, and noise instruments in the noise channel.

Let's try out the sampled drum kits. First, change to the wave channel. Return to the song screen, move the cursor to the wave channel, and create a new chain and phrase as you did before. Then, move over to the instr column in the phrase screen and tap A twice to insert a new instrument. Press Select plus Right to edit that instrument, change the instrument type to "KIT" by pressing A plus Right once on the type field, then return to the phrase screen. Now you should be able to enter drum sounds in the same way that you entered notes before.

LSDj automatically stores songs in the battery-powered SRAM, so you don't have to save them explicitly. Version 3 also has an option to store several songs on one cartridge. Find this feature in the project screen located above the song screen.

If you want to back up your creations, use either a backup device connected to your computer or the independent Mega Memory Card (typically found for a few U.S. dollars on eBay). The easiest way to record your song to send to friends is to use the headphone output as input to a recording device.

See Also

This short tutorial explained how to make some interesting sounds with your Game Boy. There's much more to learn about Little Sound Dj. For example, the user-maintained Wiki links to several beginner tutorials, and the LSDj mailing list is full of friendly, helpful, and social people:

- Little Sound Dj documentation (*http://www.littlesounddj.com/latest/documentation/*)
- Little Sound Dj Wiki (*http://wiki.littlesounddj.com/*)
- LSDj mailing list (*http://groups.yahoo.com/group/lsdj/*)

HACK #23   Explore the GP32 Handheld Gaming System

This underpublicized, open-access portable is a hidden treasure.

Many people suggest that there's not much room in the gaming handheld market, considering Nintendo's 15-year Game Boy monopoly. Obviously, Sony is challenging this with the PSP, but the Korean company Gamepark has an entirely different approach to proprietary storage and development methods for gaming handhelds. They decided to allow much more open access by including a USB port on their GP32 handheld and compatibility with normal SMC (smart media memory cards). Unfortunately, the GP32 has had limited distribution so far.

GP32 Hardware Details

The dimensions of Gamepark's GP32 resemble those of the first Game Boy Advance, although the GP32 is slightly wider and taller. From there, however, you can see a major difference in screen resolution for its built-in LCD: 320×240 pixels compared to the Game Boy Advance's 240×160 pixels. This leads to significantly sharper-looking games, emulators, and utilities on the GP32. Other than that, the GP32's specifications (a 32-bit ARM9 RISC CPU, 8-MB SDRAM, and up to 128 MB on the aforementioned SMC) make it fairly powerful, at least compared to the GBA. However, please note that you'll need to buy a Smart Media Card separately.

As for availability, that's the tricky part. As we'll lament later, the GP32 has very little commercial software support, so it's not really worth stocking for many brick-and-mortar retail stores within North America. You'll need to order online, and this means going outside the country to Hong Kong retailer Lik-Sang (*http://www.lik-sang.com/*) or searching carefully for an American retailer who actually sells the rare handheld. Expect to pay around $150 for the normal version and $200 or more for the frontlit, modified version.

Software and Hardware Overclocking

One interesting part of the GP32 is that the processor defaults to 40 MHz, but the software can decide how fast it wants the machine to run, up to and over 100 MHz. This is probably one of the first times that you have such a large degree of control in a custom device, but note that overclocking has a direct effect on the battery life of the console. Some emulators allow you to set CPU speed to whatever you wish. The generally agreed sensible maximum is 133 MHz. There are even warnings in the instructions for a PC Engine (Turbografx) emulator that:

> Speed selection over 133mhz is pure overclocking, and not recommended! It might even destroy your GP32 and won't be stable on most machines!

Be careful what you select and especially what you load. Although no one has created a deliberately malicious excessive-CPU-selection program for the portable, it's possible. This would be another inadvisable hack that ranks right up there with the hardware-shredding trick of generating musical tones on the Commodore Amiga's variable-speed floppy-disk drive.

In a related, but extremely hacktastic move, a very daring Netizen has opened up a GP32 and overclocked the hardware by increasing the CPU core voltage (*http://www.cobbleware.com/gp32/gp32oc.html*). This allows reliable overclocking up to 170 MHz. The online instructions go beyond this overclocking with the similarly insane experiment of replacing the 8 MB of RAM with a 32-MB memory chip (*http://www.cobbleware.com/gp32/gp32ram.html*).

While these are very impressive feats (the 32-MB memory chip installation involved soldering pins on the CPU that were 0.5 mm away from each other!), there's not really much software taking advantage of either innovation, although the 32-MB trick could allow the loading of larger ROM files for emulators, providing the applications supported such a thing.

Installing the Alternate Wind-ups Operating System

Interestingly, some homebrew GP32 coders have gone whole hog to create a modified operating system for the handheld. Wind-ups (*http://www.wind-ups.net/*) allows you to navigate via a file browser, easily copy programs from your PC to your GP32, set up neat-looking icons in configurations of your choice, specify custom backdrops, and check out GIFs with a picture viewer. Figure 2-3 shows a sample desktop.

While this isn't tremendously sophisticated—and the built-in OS already does a decent job of providing simple scrollable menus for loading programs with some similar functionality, with new official firmware, better

Figure 2-3. The GP32's Wind-ups OS

graphics, and more options in the works—Wind-ups goes a step further by providing extra utilities. These include:

kReader

> A very straightforward but usable eBook reader that takes *.txt* files and allows you to scroll through pages of text using the shoulder buttons. The most interesting part of this program may be the dictionary functionality. It comes from a Spanish coder, so it uses an English-Spanish dictionary as the default, but if you wanted to learn another foreign language, you can conceivably load an eBook in French and then find a suitable French-English dictionary to plug into it.

kEditor

> Without any touchscreen and stylus combo or mini-keyboard, the GP32 is not suited for writing notes, essays, or even haiku. However, the fairly ingenious Quad-9 tree onscreen typewriter uses the GP32's joypad to divide up the alphabet, allowing two keypresses to select the right character. With this program, you can jot down your latest genius thoughts on your GP32, in between watching movies, listening to MP3s, and playing homebrew games. Having said that, the program's author claims he can input up to 60 characters per minute. Considering that each character takes three separate actions (including the selection keypress) to enter, that target may be optimistic.

Age2K

> This is a surprisingly full-featured address book with well laid-out entries that even allow users to embed pictures of their friends into each entry. However, although you can enter all of the details on the GP32, this would obviously take a long time. Allegedly, the Wind-ups site has

a Windows version of Age2K. Unfortunately, it wasn't available for download at press time.

The Best Original Homebrew GP32 Software

The GP32 has a fairly vibrant homebrew scene, with several original games and utilities. Because it's easy to copy and run them, the barriers to entry are a lot lower than many other proprietary systems. This has led to a lot of creativity, especially for a machine with such a small user base. Here are some of the best homebrew games and utilities available:

GP32 Darts
> Although darts may be a strange, often alcohol-fueled pastime, playing darts on your GP32 (*http://207.44.176.77/~admin28/gbaemu/ homegrown/*) is strangely addictive, thanks to an announcer, realistic physics (the dart bounces out if it hits the metal border areas of the dartboard!), and correct reproduction of the Byzantine darts scoring schemes.

GPMad MP3 player
> This utility (*http://www.robertsworld.org.uk/gpmadmp3.html*) is stylish and much more functional than the original default MP3 player from Gamepark, which had trouble with VBR and other encodings of many MP3 files.

Giana's Return
> A reimagining of the classic, limited-edition late '80s Super Mario–esque platformer, this title (*http://www.gianas-return.de/*) has been released with permission from the original developers. It's one of the slickest 2D platformers available on the GP32, commercial or homebrew.

Gloop
> A recent GP32 homebrew competition winner, this excellent title (*http:// 207.44.176.77/~admin28/cgi-bin/15days.cgi?site=1&filename=GlooP.zip*) plays out a little like the classic puzzler Lemmings, except that it uses water instead of suicidal rodents. It'll make sense if you play it, I promise.

Besides the games named here, there are plenty of other interesting public-domain (PD) titles being coded from scratch, most recently showcased in the 15 Days GP32 Coding Competition (*http://15days.gp32emu.com/*) and the LlamaSoft-style goodies for both GP32 and Game Boy available as part of the PDRoms coding competition (*http://pdroms.de/pdrc2-submissions.php*).

Best of all, try GpKat (*http://www.toxicbreakfast.com/tb/downloads.shtml*), which has a single, genius purpose in mind:

> First find a cat. With cat in place and GpKat loaded up on your GP32, press one of the buttons, move the joystick and one of twenty possible cat noises will sound out. Your cat may be confused and try to find the "other cat".

Of course, no set of homebrew software would be complete without a Linux conversion. SourceForge hosts a project dedicated to putting Linux on the GP32 (*http://sourceforge.net/projects/gp32linux*). However, as of press time, it's currently stalled at the stage of getting a working SMC driver working. Currently, there are only nonfunctional pre-alpha versions available.

The Brightest Emulators and Conversions on the GP32

As far as conversions go, many classic games have conversions to just about every exotic format out there. The same goes for high-quality emulators that can run freeware and PD ROMs from multiple computers and consoles. Why should the GP32 be any different? Here are some of the highlights:

GP2600
> An excellent emulator for the Atari 2600 (*http://207.44.176.77/ ~admin28/gp32emu/gp2600.htm*), which has seen an increasing amount of neat homebrew games recently.

GPDoom
> Where would we be without a conversion of the id Software FPS classic? This version (*http://www.gp32us.com/doom.htm*) includes "high resolution, full sound and music, and full support for the original DOOM, DOOM II, and Final DOOM. There's even external WAD support, so you can load up all your favorite WADs." The GPDoom page also has a really useful CPU speed chart, so you can understand how your CPU speed affects your game speed and battery life.

Frodo GP32
> A rather smart Commodore 64 emulator (*http://dexy.mine.nu/gp32/ frodo/*), it's especially refreshing because there are a lot of PD and homebrew games, demos, and utilities available. Running anything that requires a lot of text entry is probably a major mistake, though.

SpeccyalK
> Another classic '80s computer emulator, this time for the Sinclair ZX Spectrum (*http://www.speccyal.be/*), this comes with a virtual keyboard, savestates, and other neat bells and whistles.

Take Your Console with You

Track down exotic add-ons, find obscure originals, or make your own portable gaming setups.

Suppose you have a favorite console such as the Nintendo NES and its associated game cartridges. Sure, you can play your NES in your living room on your TV, but that isn't good enough for you. You'd really like to scratch your gaming itch wherever you go. You could cheat by putting an NES emulator on an open-to-homebrew machine, such as the GP32 ("Explore the GP32 Handheld Gaming System" [Hack #23]), but not only is that unhackish, it may be legally questionable.

Why can't you play the original NES cartridge in a weird, bootleg, or add-on portable game machine? You can—for many consoles. Here are some options for running official console games in a different, more portable way than originally intended.

Finding Obscure Official Portables and Add-ons

The easiest way to play TV-based console games on the go is to dig out the sometimes forgotten, often unsuccessful official portables. These were often released during the early '90s as limited editions. Now they're hard to find or otherwise neglected, but are still cool; their bulkiness is retro, briefcase-cell-phone chic. Or maybe not. Anyhow, the following sections detail the prime contenders.

Sega Nomad. Released back in 1995, fairly late in the life of the Sega Genesis, the portable Nomad system plays all Genesis and Mega Drive titles. The backlit 2.5-inch LCD screen is pretty good quality. The extra port to plug a normal Sega Genesis controller into is a neat touch.

Having said all that, the Nomad definitely suffers from a short battery life (six AA batteries will last for four to six hours). An AC adapter really helps. Sega Genesis Model 2 adapters are compatible, as well as multi-plug AC adapters; the plug on the Nomad is the same as that on the Sega Game Gear. Oh, and you can't plug in a 32X adapter, but that's no great loss, considering the small amount of good 32X games. Unfortunately, the Nomad is fairly heavy, but perhaps you can accept that for a chance to play Sonic The Hedgehog on original, unemulated hardware.

NEC Turbo Express. Another relatively rare handheld version, NEC's official Turbo Express portable plays games created for the NEC Turbografx 16 (called the PC Engine in Europe and Japan). Originally released in 1991, it had relatively limited success, but its good quality, backlit screen, and a stable of classic Turbografx games mean that it's still a cult hit today.

For starters, the credit card–sized HUCards are perfect for playing in a portable system; a large NES cart can mean trouble for a small handheld system. Battery life is still rather scant, somewhere on a par with the Sega Nomad. Also be aware that there are region compatibility problems, even if you use a cart adaptor. Those problems aside, the stylish design makes this one of the most desirable portables, especially when combined with the relatively scarce TV Adapter.

Finding Arcane Unofficial Portables and Add-ons

Although probably not officially licensed by the original hardware manufacturers, you may be able to find either add-ons or complete standalone pieces of portable hardware that will run your nonportable console games in fully portable form. The following sections describe a selection.

Game Axe: Famicom/NES. The NES-playing Game Axe handheld, originally launched in Asia in 1995, is an excellent example of a very unofficial and rather smart way to play console games portably. Someone has coaxed pictures of the handheld's schematics from the Game Axe creators (*http://members.fortunecity.com/davidlevine/gapics.htm*). There are two models: the FC-812 has a green power LED and a smaller, three-inch LCD screen, whereas the much more common FC-868, built from 1997 until recently, has a four-inch LCD screen and a red LED.

Unfortunately, there are some important caveats. In its normal state, the Game Axe will play only Japanese Famicom titles, not American NES games. You'll need a 60- to 72-pin converter to make that work. This simple add-on, available from companies such as Lik-Sang (*http://www.lik-sang. com/*), allows any Japanese Famicom device to play American and European NES games. If you do this, though, the NES cartridge, already sticking out a long way from the top of the unit, protrudes a whopping nine inches. Another optional add-on is a third-party Famicom controller, tricky to find outside Asia, that plugs into the Game Axe's controller ports.*

As usual, battery life is a major issue. The portable takes six AA batteries and can drain in fewer than two hours. There's an AC adapter that works just fine at the expense of portability. You can also plug AV cables into a television and un-portable-ize the Game Axe, but that's hardly our goal

---

* Apparently, the Japanese Famicom had no actual controller ports. The wires disappeared inside the machine without any way to unplug the controllers.

here. Also, many people complain of screen blurriness and uneven lighting with this highly unofficial toy.

Even with these issues, the Game Axe is still fun. It sells for around $100 on eBay or Asian game sites. However, there may now be better NES-related options.

Game Theory Admiral: Famicom. Until recently, the Game Axe was the only standalone portable NES clone, but now there's the rather cool Game Theory Admiral (*http://www.nesworld.com/gametheo.htm*). It sports a thin-film transistor (TFT) screen—a design that makes it look very suspiciously like Nintendo's own Game Boy Advance, all the way down to similar dimensions and a similar-sized built-in screen. It solely plays Famicom games, which plug into a special slot adapter perpendicular to the console. Oh, and it has one of those marvellous nonsense names that only unofficial pieces of hardware sport (see "Super Wild Card," "Super Magic Griffon," etc.).

Again, there are plenty of positives and negatives for this gray-market product. Positive features include the TFT screen, which is much less blurry and better-looking than the Game Axe, with good brightness and contrast controls. The form factor makes it less bulky than the Game Axe. The battery life also seems to be significantly better than the Game Axe, needing only four AA batteries.

> There's no official AC adapter released as of press time. Some people claim that the Game Axe adapter works, but most experts recommend not using an AC adapter, even one set at the correct voltage; it's apparently very easy to blow a fuse in the Game Theory Admiral. Running American NES cartridges is a trial.

It's also worth noting that the systems are color-coded in terms of the external AV cables. A blue Game Theory Admiral produces a PAL (European) TV signal, and a pink Admiral (aren't those butterflies?) emits an NTSC (American) TV signal. If you want to play the Admiral on your TV as well, buy the right color portable.

Other odd options. There are several other unconventional portable console devices; most involve the much-loved NES and Famicom. The AdFami (*http://www.the-magicbox.com/Mar04/game030404h.shtml*), newly released in Japan, is a unique add-on for the Game Boy Advance SP that plays Famicom games. It's even color-coordinated to match the special-edition NES version of the SP, which should be available in the United States by the time you read this. There's also an official Famicom-to-NES converter for the AdFami that solves a lot of the problems with the other devices. This is very tempting, although there haven't yet been any reviews that describe compatibility and quality.

Rolling Your Own Portable Console

This is where the insanity begins. There's little chance I could actually explain how to redesign an existing console to fit into a portable unit within the space of this hack. It's definitely possible, though, if you consider the misleadingly named Atari 2600 Portable Page (*http://www.classicgaming. com/vcsp/*), which is the center for clever research in making hitherto unportable consoles portable.

Some of the highlights include making a portable Atari 2600, of which there is a step-by-step, if extremely complex, guide (*http://www.classicgaming. com/vcsp/Step%20by%20Step%20Hacking.htm*). The Portable PlayStation is true insanity (*http://www.classicgaming.com/vcsp/PSp/PSp1.htm*), while the Super Nintendo Portable (*http://www.classicgaming.com/vcsp/SNESp1.htm*) is ingenious.

If you consider that the Atari 2600 Portable is probably the easiest hack of the bunch (and even that needs expert tools and detailed electrical know-how), you may do best just loading homebrew Atari 2600 games into your emulator on your up-to-date handheld and pretending that you went to all that trouble, even if it makes you a lazy hacker.

HACK #25 Explore the Bandai WonderSwan
How to recognize, buy, create, and emulate the best handheld you've never heard of.

Other hacks cover notable and obvious handhelds, such as Nintendo's Game Boy and Game Boy Advance ("Mod Your Game Boy" [Hack #20]), as well as the marvelously versatile Korean GP32 handheld ("Explore the GP32 Handheld Gaming System" [Hack #23]). There are other, more obscure fish in the sea worth exploring; primary among these is Bandai's WonderSwan, released only in Japan and Asia. It includes both unofficial and official homebrew game-creation options.

Many Hardware Models, Much Confusion

It's vital to note that several different types of the WonderSwan exist. All are pretty inexpensive. You can find even the most extravagant version, the WonderSwan Crystal, for $40 or less on eBay at the time of writing, though you may have to pay for shipping from Japan or Hong Kong. With the small differential in price, make sure you buy the latest and best variant!

WonderSwan (a.k.a. WonderSwan B&W). The original, monochrome Wonder-
Swan came out in early 1999 and fared pretty well. This thin, Game Boy-
style handheld console has a 2.1-inch diagonal, 224×114 pixel screen and
512 KB of RAM. One unique feature is that you can play games either horizontally or vertically, thanks to two sets of direction pads. The horizontal
mode is very similar to GB or GBA, with a direction pad and two buttons.
You can often find this version for under $20 on eBay (though shipping may
cost you more than that!), but there's no point in buying one when a WonderSwan Color or SwanCrystal costs just a few dollars more.

WonderSwan Color. This variant shows up on auction sites more often than
any other. It launched in December 2000 and sold right through to the Crystal's launch. The main upgrade for this version is a color screen, with up to
241 out of 4,096 colors available onscreen at any time. It has particularly
good battery life, playing for up to 20 hours from one AA battery, and is
backward-compatible with all black-and-white WonderSwan games. At the
time of writing, the average eBay price was $30 plus shipping.

SwanCrystal. The final iteration of the WonderSwan hardware launched in
July 2002 in Japan. It featured a much higher-quality TFT LCD, which fixed
a lot of the ghosting* troubles of the WonderSwan Color and WonderSwan
B&W. The better-quality screen is the only major change, but it significantly improves the games. Settling for the WonderSwan Color is also
acceptable. It's often tricky to find a SwanCrystal, of course. Expect to pay
$30 to $40 on eBay, only slightly more than the previous iteration.

The WonderWitch Homebrew Development System

One of the absolutely coolest things about the WonderSwan is that Bandai
actively supports homebrew development. Their special WonderWitch construction kit (*http://wonderwitch.qute.co.jp/*) included a 4-Mb flashROM cartridge with 2 MB of SRAM, as well as a special cable to connect the PC to
the WonderSwan and a host of C-based PC development tools. You can still
find this kit through Lik Sang or similar companies.

The bad news is that there's no opportunity to use any of this in English.
Not only do you need to be a reasonably serious coder to use the system,
you need good Japanese skills and a J-Windows install to consider using it.
This is a serious shame, but if you have the technical and language-based
skills, by all means go for it.

---

* Seeing trails after moving sprites, for example.

However, we can still live vicariously through some of the successful graduates of the system. In 2004, amateur games have now seen official releases. Highlights include the great-looking shmup Judgement Silversword (Rebirth Edition) (*http://wwgp.qute.co.jp/products/jss_rebirth/*) and the marvellous RPG Dicing Knight (*http://wwgp.qute.co.jp/products/dk_period/*), both of which placed highly in the yearly WWGP programming contests. You can buy cartridges of these and play them in your WonderSwan normally.

You can freely download all other fan-developed WonderWitch games, including competition entries. See the 2002 competition (*http://wwgp.qute. co.jp/2002/*) for some examples. However, you can play these games only if you have a WonderWitch and a WonderSwan, or possibly a WonderWitch emulator. Many console homebrew coders have similar problems. As with the PlayStation Net.Yaroze (a semiofficial homebrew device), there's no easy way to distribute the finished product in a form playable on handhelds.

WonderWitch Alternatives

There's a hackier alternative to the official WonderWitch way, of course. There always is. You can program a game on your PC, checking out things in an emulator as necessary, and then transfer it to your WonderSwan itself via the Wonder Magic flash linker and a special WonderSwan flashrom cart.

Unfortunately, these Wonder Magic flashrom devices are rarer than hen's teeth. If you look carefully enough online, you can find some from Asian sources. Don't forget that you'll need both the linker and the cartridge. The carts top out at 32 Mb (4 MB), which is plenty to play a smartly coded game. You can also use them to play backups of commercial WonderSwan software—perhaps another reason they're difficult to find, as are the Game Boy Advance flash linkers—but if you use them only for good, all is good.

Another alternative is emulation. Zophar's well-informed emulation site has a WonderSwan page that links to multiple emulators (*http://www.zophar. net/ws.html*). WSCAmp is best-known, but all of them work and are worth testing. Additionally, the page lists a WonderWitch emulator called MiracleMage, which claims to be able to emulate the environment under which you can run the official homebrew titles. This utility isn't well-tested, but it does have an English translation patch that could come in handy.

If you'd like to see some WonderSwan source, the PDRoms WonderSwan demos page (at *http://www.pdroms.de/roms.php?system=Wonderswan%20/ %20Color&typ=Demos&first=0*) has ASM source for some graphic demos that can get you started, with the obvious caveat that assembly language is scary and difficult.

As for further examples of homebrew titles, the ever excellent PDRoms site (*http://www.pdroms.de/typ.php?system=Wonderswan+%2F+Color*) has several good homebrew games and demos available. The only significant standalone public-domain game is WonderSnake (Figure 2-4), a good-looking effort in which you must not run over your own tail or into walls.

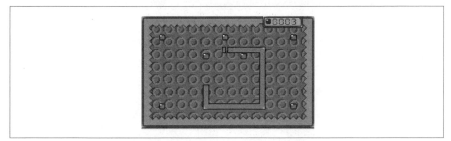

Figure 2-4. WonderSnake for the WonderSwan Color

Bored of Hacking? Try Playing!

I can't leave this subject before highlighting the best WonderSwan games worth buying if you can find them. Bandai negotiated a few rather smart exclusives due to its marketing clout in Japan, but due to the handheld's obscurity in the West, hardly anyone outside Japan has played them.

Rhyme Rider Kerorican
> Nana OnSha, the developer that brought us the amazing PlayStation titles Parappa The Rapper and Vib Ribbon, produced Rhyme Rider, a Vib Ribbon–style game that asks you to press the right buttons in the right rhythmic order to destroy enemies onscreen and make music at the same time. This is fiendishly addictive and fairly forgiving to boot.

Final Fantasy I and II
> For a long time, these rejigged versions of the original FF titles were the sole reason to own a WonderSwan. However, the remakes are, naturally, very heavy on Japanese text, so they're rather incomprehensible to English-only speakers. Fortunately, you can now buy versions for the GBA in English. Though FF IV also had a WonderSwan remake, only I and II were big smashes.

Klonoa: Moonlight Museum
> This wonderful black-and-white 2D action platformer in Namco's Klonoa series, a WonderSwan exclusive, was soundly ignored and buried at the time. It cleverly switches screen resolution at times. It's fairly rare even for WonderSwan games, yet worth staking out.

#26 Play Real Games on Your PDA
High-quality portable gaming without the Game Boy.

Many of the portable gaming hacks we've discussed relate to proprietary consoles ("Take Your Console with You" [Hack #24]). You may need to buy flashcart devices, for which Nintendo will chase you down with legal papers and raised voices. Let's now discuss a portable device that can play classic titles through emulation, is free for anybody to develop on, and is easy to transfer data onto: a palmtop computer.

PocketPC Versus Palm

There are two main branches of portable devices. One is the multimanufacturer PocketPC, running a portable version of Microsoft's Windows operating system. The other is Palm-compatible devices running the Palm OS, mostly manufactured by Palm and its offshoots.

There's one major issue with the form factor of all of these devices: they're primarily portable productivity devices for keeping appointments, surfing the Web, or writing down notes—not for playing games. They lack the easy game-oriented controls of game-specific devices such as the GP32 ("Explore the GP32 Handheld Gaming System" [Hack #23]) or the Game Boy Advance ("Mod Your Game Boy" [Hack #20]).

Also, there are two main new PocketPC processor types, both produced by Intel: XScale and ARM. PocketGame has a good synopsis of the different processors found in PocketPCs (*http://www.pocketgamer.org/links/ppc.php*), including older processors such as MIPS and SH3. Fortunately, almost all new PocketPC titles are ARM-compatible, so they also work with XScale; some also work with MIPS-powered devices. Notable overall brands are the Toshiba series, the Dell Axim, and the HP iPaq, although the ASUS PDAs seem to have the lead among gamers concerned about benchmark performance and controllability. However, to be honest, there's not a lot of difference between the machines. A faster processor may mean faster emulation, of course, which is especially important for insanely high-end emulators like the PlayStation One. Other than that, you pays your money and takes your choice.

The big hit in the Palm arena right now is Tapwave's Zodiac (*http://www. tapwave.com/*), a powerful color PDA designed to look like a Game Boy Advance–style console. It runs an enhanced Palm OS with an ATI Imageon graphics accelerator and retails at $299 for the 32-MB version and $399 for the color version. Although expensive compared to other portable consoles, even the relatively upmarket GP32, you'll also be able to run a lot of Palm software.

The Tapwave stacks up well against official Palm hardware, such as the fairly enticing $299-retailing PalmOne Zire 72 (*http://www.pdabuyersguide. com/palm_Zire_72.htm*), a powerful portable that sports extra features such as a camera, though its ergonomics almost preclude comfortable game playing. In fact, the Tapwave seems have the most buzz of any handheld for gaming right now because it's designed well for Palm software as well as Zodiac-specific enhanced software that takes advantage of the graphics accelerator—even emulators.

To keep up with what's hot with the devices, not necessarily games, start with *Pocket PC Magazine* (*http://www.pocketpcmag.com/*), the granddaddy of Pocket PC–specific web sites. *Wireless Gaming Review* (*http://wgamer. com/*) has better games coverage with commercial software reviews. Another good way to stay up to date is to look in the forums of major gaming sites such as PocketGamer (*http://www.pocketgamer.org/homeindex.php*) to see what kind of hardware the pocket gamers use and what they recommend to others.

PocketPC Emulation Options

The obvious (but delightful) starting choice in PocketPC emulation is MameCE, the MAME emulator for PocketPCs (*http://www.mameworld.net/ mamece3/*). While it is out of date at the time of writing (it requires ROMs for MAME 0.36; Version 0.86 has just been released), it still works with many MAME titles. It performs better than any other handheld MAME emulator, thanks to the speed of the fastest PocketPC hardware.

The PDArcade site keeps a list of PocketPC emulators (*http://www.pdarcade. com/modules.php?name=Sections&op=viewarticle&artid=102*), regardless of quality or age. Start there to find out what's available.

The Click Gamer site also has some neat commercial emulators. In particular, their Commodore 64 emulator, Pocket Commodore 64 (*http://www. clickgamer.com/moreinfo.htm?pid=4*), now has an official license from Tulip Computers, the current Commodore rights holder, making it one of those rare, completely legal hardware emulators. The $25 program, shown in Figure 2-5, has seven kernel ROMs and two disk ROMs built in, so that you can try programs that require variant ROM sets easily without scrabbling around obscure FTP sites for not-necessarily-legit variants.

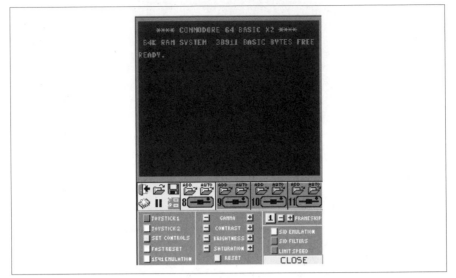

Figure 2-5. PocketC64 emulator for PocketPC

The site also hosts copies of the totally free PocketVCS (*http://www. clickgamer.com/moreinfo.htm?pid=61*), an Atari 2600 emulator that has a neat graphical menu system and excellent compatibility.

PicoDrive (*http://www.finalburn.com/cyclone/pico.html*) is another good Pocket PC emulator from the creator of the Final Burn emulator. This freely downloadable Sega Genesis/Mega Drive emulator has good functionality despite its youth.

Finally, the FPSEce emulator (*http://www.fpsece.net/*) is both smart and likely to run into legal issues. It admirably emulates Sony's PlayStation 1 on Windows CE devices.

You'll need a reasonably fast PocketPC—the emulator's *README* file specifically recommends the ASUS A620 (*http://www.asus.com/products/pda/ event/a620/*)—and at least 16 MB of RAM. You'll also need some way to grab the ISO files that were originally on CD, as well as a PlayStation BIOS file not distributed with the emulator. This is not for the faint-hearted.

Palm and Tapwave Zodiac Emulation Options

Due to the nature of the niche Palm market, many of the available emulators are both good and non-free. Nonetheless, it's worth pointing out some of the pay ones, in addition to others that are, blissfully, completely gratis.

KalemSoft (*http://www.kalemsoft.com/products.html*) is a good source of commercial Palm emulators. They're particularly notable because their NES

Emulator, the cleverly named NESEm, actually plays multiplayer titles over Bluetooth. They also have excellent PC Engine/Turbografx emulators and Sega Master System emulators for Palm OS 5.x, with further enhanced Zodiac versions. All of their emulators cost under $20.

CaSTaway (*http://www.codejedi.com/shadowplan/castaway.html*) is a surprisingly good Atari ST emulator. It's completely free, although the author has a donation box on his site. The same coder has also produced a limited but excellent Palm OS 5.x MAME emulator called XCade (*http://www.codejedi. com/shadowplan/xabout.html*). The registered version ($9.99) has more features and better support.

If you want a good current overview of state-of-the-art Palm emulation, a recent article at *The Gadgeteer* (*http:// www.the-gadgeteer.com/palmos-emulators-review.html*) sums up the situation admirably.

Nokia's Underwhelming N-Gage

You may have noticed that I haven't mentioned the other pocket platform: Nokia's N-Gage, a Symbian 60–compatible device with some other wrinkles. I haven't for two reasons. First, the first N-Gage was universally reviled and saw comparatively little adoption. Second, the N-Gage QD, Nokia's updated device, has just launched to better reviews but still a chilly reception.

Although the N-Gage's commercial games have had mostly bad reviews and its vertical screen isn't perfect—this flaw affects several other PDA devices—there are several half-decent emulators for the machine. If you find the hardware on sale somewhere, it might be worth considering.

The N-Gage News fan site (*http://ngagenews.netfirms.com/*) has a good list of the current emulators on the left side of the page. Emulated platforms include the Commodore 64, Genesis, Game Boy, NES, Spectrum, and some limited, much earlier MAME titles. Some of the vertically oriented games such as Pac-Man make a lot of sense, though!

As for the souped-up Tapwave device, there are multiple emulators claiming to be "enhanced for Tapwave Zodiac." The most notable of these is the completely free Little John Z (*http://yoyofr.fr.st/*), a conversion of the GP32 NES emulator. Actually, it's less a conversion than a rebirth, since it contains NES, SNES, Game Boy, Game Boy Color, Neo Geo Pocket Color, and WonderSwan emulators all in one! At the time of writing, it's available only for Tapwave developers because the author is waiting for Tapwave to make its license GPL-compatible. This should happen in the very near future, so be sure to check out this emulator conglomerate.

The ZodiacGamer fan site (*http://www.zodiacgamer.com/*) has plenty of other information on Zodiac-specific emulators and other homebrew titles. TapLand (*http://www.tapland.com*) also provides great coverage on the whole Zodiac-specific scene, which is likely to continue to burgeon.

Finally, there are also completely official licensed commercial products for the Palm that emulate classic software, including Atari 2600 Retro Packs (*http://www.mobilewizardry.com/multi-platform/atariretro/index.php*).

HACK #27 Install a PlayStation 2 in Your Car
Keep your eyes on the road but your games close at hand.

If you're one of millions of drivers in the world, you know that your car almost defines the concept of portability; you can drive anywhere you like. If you want to take your gaming on the road, why not combine the two and make your console run in your car?

There are two schools of thought on the subject. One worries more about connecting the hardware and electronics appropriately. The other concentrates on good-looking trim and flashing lights. I'm not judgmental, but being a tech geek, not a car geek, I'll cover the former. While you may eventually want to trick out your ride, simply being able to play games in the back of your car while someone else is driving is the important thing.

I'll concentrate on the PS2, though the underlying issues are similar for other consoles.

Cars and Console-Connection Power Issues

As you might have guessed, one of the big stumbling blocks to installing a PlayStation 2 in your automobile is feeding it electricity. There are a couple of options:

Use a DC inverter. A DC inverter that plugs into the cigarette lighter converts the 12-volt output from your car's battery to normal 115-volt wall-socket ratings. You can find this equipment almost anywhere. Watch the wattage, though; both the PlayStation and PS2 drink around 72 watts of power. Depending on how thirsty your monitor or TV is, you may need 300 to 400 watts from the inverter.

It's also worth noting that many inverters will either shut off or warn you when the battery runs low (for example, if you've been running the PS2 while stationary for a long period of time). This saves embarrassing situations where you need to call a tow truck for a jump start because you were trying to beat a boss in Metal Gear Solid.

Convert your PlayStation 2 to run 12V.   A more extreme and hack-like idea is to convert your PS2 to run on 12V DC power natively. Some people suggest that this is overkill, but if you're comfortable opening your PS2, removing the power regulation board altogether, and putting in extra wiring, including capacitors, you can simplify things. Asdffdsa.net has a very detailed explanation of the process (*http://www.asdffdsa.net/projects/ps2.htm*). These directions produce a PS2 with a 12V plug and jack that connects to the car battery just as a car radio does.

This approach won't indicate that you're draining the battery too far, but it's easier to integrate the console into the car. If you want to make your PS2 look like it belongs in the car, this is the way to go. As the page also notes, you draw less power from your car by running directly and skipping the two voltage-conversion steps.

There are advantages and disadvantages to both methods. Using an inverter is better if you take your console on trips only occasionally. Modifying the console works better if you want a permanent setup with the console in the trunk, for example.

Choosing a Monitor

With the console actually working in your car, your next step is to attach some sort of display. There are several choices here too:

Buy a PS2-specific monitor.   Several companies make monitors designed to attach atop the PS2, including Interact's Mobile Monitor (*http://gear.ign.com/articles/361/361296p1.html*) and Intec's PS2 game screen. These products sell for between $100 and $150. The advantages are that these monitors match the PS2 nicely, and they're easily portable outside the car. One major disadvantage is that they don't really match anything but the PS2. If you want to suspend your display from the ceiling, this makes little sense.

Mod the PSOne screen.   There's nothing intrinsically different about the PSOne LCD screen that prevents it from working with the PS2. This device slides onto the small-form, white PSOne console (which also works nicely in a car). Asdffdsa.net has another interesting project of interest (*http://www.asdffdsa.net/projects/screen.htm*). By removing part of the LCD screen's casing, cutting holes in the bottom of the rotating section of the PSOne monitor, and installing 1.5-inch suction cups, you can hang the monitor from the car's ceiling.

However, if the monitor hangs from the ceiling, won't the LCD picture be upside-down? Fortunately, the modders have thought ahead. There are plastic clips on the back of the main housing. Snip these off, and rotate the whole screen 180 degrees before reassembling the casing. Now you have an LCD monitor that can hang from the ceiling *and* provide right-way-up gaming. Will wonders never cease?

 The PSOne screen is remarkably versatile. Not only can you hack it to turn it upside down as a car monitor, but other cunning hackers have removed the LCD part of the screen to use for exotic PC modding (*http://bit-tech.net/article/136/*) by mounting it in the front of a PC case as a second monitor. This isn't particularly game-like, but it's gorgeously hacky, so we'll let this one pass.

Install a car-specific LCD monitor. Yes, there are actually monitors designed to install in cars; check out your local brick-and-mortar electronics store. The cheapest models start at around $60 but aren't very large or good. You can spend thousands on the biggest and coolest-looking LCD screens. They work with both DVD players and video game consoles, so there should be no trouble for gaming. Some models plug into the cigarette lighter; most connect directly to the car's battery.

These monitor ideas aren't just for PS2, either. Fortunately, the mobile-monitor idea, with a nicely designed LCD monitor that clips to the top of your console, has extended to other consoles; similar plug-in LCD monitors exist for the PSOne and even the GameCube. The sky's the limit.

Now how do you play Game Boy in your car?

Playing Well with Others
Hacks 28–34

Even though arcades have diminished in the United States, gaming can still be a social experience. Of course, if you play online often, you might consider it an *antisocial* experience, but there are ways to alleviate that. Part of improving your online experience is finding the right crowd. Another part is avoiding the wrong crowd. This chapter will help you do both.

The crown jewel of social gaming these days seems to be Massively Multiplayer Online Games. If you play for entertainment, not work, the requirements of knowledge and dedication can feel overwhelming. How can you fit in? What's the point? How can you make the most of your limited time online to meet your goals?

Though there's no substitute for experience, this chapter has a few ideas you may not have considered. For all terminology questions, please refer to Table 3-1 in "Understand MMORPG Lingo" [Hack #29].

Practice Proper MMORPG Etiquette

HACK #28

Learn the basics without playing all day every day.

As with any type of game, Massively Multiplayer Online Roleplaying Games (MMORPGs or MMOGs) have a learning curve. Many single-player games offer tutorials to help new players understand the basics before diving in. A few MMOGs have this feature, but they concentrate on movement and use of controls. No Massively Multiplayer Game can actually teach you how to behave and play with dozens or hundreds of other people.

Although starting with the original Multiple User Dungeons (MUDs) and MUD Object-Orienteds (MOOs) in the '80s, the advent of Ultima Online began a modern MMO gold rush. Titles such as EverQuest, the Lineage series, Final Fantasy XI, and City Of Heroes now provide a monetized, massively multiplayer experience that millions of people have signed on to worldwide.

This, then, is a guide for the new player and a refresher for the seasoned hand. Here we'll discuss what a MMOG is, some guidelines for dealing with your fellow players in a social game, and an analysis of what exactly you'll receive from playing a Massively Multiplayer Game.

MMOGs are somewhat unique in that they can help fulfill fantasies of heroism, mercantile success, or international fame. It's rare for a game accomplishment to have such an impact on the real world. The first group of players to slay a powerful creature can become famous to thousands of people in the space of a few days, such as the large group of players who defeated the legendary hundred-billion-hitpoint monster Kerafyrm, a.k.a. The Sleeper, in EverQuest late in 2003. The social environment within the game world distinguishes a MMOG from any other type of game.

Social Interaction

The undertone to the gameplay in a MMOG is a backdrop of social interaction. Understanding the motivations of other players is important no matter which game you choose to play. Some players want to prove their skills. Others enjoy the ability to explore worlds and involve themselves with a worldwide plot inhabited by real people. Many players simply enjoy talking to other people.

Regrettably, a visible few players enter a MMOG because they enjoy the ability to control, frustrate, or hurt the other players of the game through their characters. The Player Killing of the early days (1997–98) of Ultima Online has gone down in MMOG history as one extreme. Fortunately, the game now features a very free implementation of Player vs. Player combat and stronger NPC city guards to stop excessive player carnage.

Of course, even Non-Player Characters (NPCs) have a social context. These computer-driven constructs always provide a service to other real players. Some games allow players to destroy vendor and guard NPCs, affecting the experience of other players.

For example, high-level characters often attack the guards of Qeynos in EverQuest to take out frustrations. They are also a respectable challenge, because the average Qeynos guard is probably around level 55. Slaying these guards can expose new characters to danger, however, as they provide protection for adventurers in the newbie zones.

The Darker Side of Social Interaction

Despite the fact that most people you'll meet in-game are pleasant, friendly, and helpful, there are occasional bad eggs. Some people have trouble separating their behavior in a single-player game from their behavior in a MMOG. The lack of context in free-form chat makes translating behavior from a single-player environment more difficult. "Ha ha, you suck" could be either a friendly jibe or a bold insult.

Beyond that, no major commercial MMOGs have a minimum age requirement, so immaturity can sometimes be a factor in awkwardly social situations. Teenagers and children let loose in a virtual environment may be tasting true freedom for the first time. Some quickly leave the bounds of polite society just because they can. Of course, this isn't always a function of physical age. Some people are old enough to know perfectly well that their actions affect other people. Online anonymity can be a powerful draw for individuals who can't express their darker emotions in real life. These people are commonly referred to as *griefers*.

Kill stealing, or KSing, is a common grief tactic. Some games have trouble doling out credit for killing a monster appropriately, and KSers use that to their advantage. By attacking the monster after you've already weakened it, they can take equipment and experience that should have rightly gone to you.

EverQuest has experienced serious problems with this since launch time. The Zone of Blackburrow, as a very popular low-level zone, has often had multiple parties jump on named monsters. The system now rewards the character or group that did 75% or more of the damage.

Final Fantasy XI takes another approach. A character who attacks a monster has a claim on it. No other player can even target a claimed monster unless the original combatant cries for help with a specific command.

Some people honestly don't know that KSing is a bad habit, so keep your temper. Just state that you'd appreciate if they didn't do that, and go about your business. Chances are that it won't happen again. If it happens on a persistent basis, you're likely being griefed. Report such harassment to a customer service representative.

Some people take issue with swearing and crude language in their games. Many players are casual with crass language, so be prepared for that eventuality. Some games have profanity filters to help you ameliorate uncomfortable chatter. A few players will take it to an inappropriate level and begin harassing specific individuals. Almost every MMOG allows players the ability to ignore other people, usually through the /ignore command. If another player begins to treat you poorly and does not respond to repeated requests to desist, use your ignore list to make your chat channels blissfully quiet.

If you ever feel threatened or harassed, remain calm. After all, there's nothing people can do to you physically outside the reach of the game. Ask the offending person to leave politely and try to get on with what you're doing. Ignoring the person will help. Nine times out of ten, if you stop giving him the attention he craves, the bully will move on.

If the harassment persists, don't hesitate to call in a *Game Master*, an in-game customer service representative. These people are paid to assist players in tense social situations and with technical problems. The support staff in Mythic's Dark Age of Camelot are well-known for their short turnaround times and quality of attention. SOE's Star Wars Galaxies, on the other hand, has had issues since launch with customer service representatives answering petitions in a timely fashion. Regardless of their speed, GMs take harassment very seriously.

Explain the situation calmly and try to remain unemotional about the experience. If a player is harassing you, chances are he's done it before or will do it again. Asking a GM for help will reduce your stress and the stress of those around you. Don't let one bad experience ruin your opinion of your fellow players.

Being a Courteous Player

Courtesy is the watchword of multiplayer gaming. Simple common courtesy is the easiest way to ensure that you'll have fun playing a MMOG. Most players understand this. Curiously, I have met few people in real life as courteous as players I've met in-game.

Many new players are afraid of appearing ignorant in front of other people, especially in a culture that labels players with less experience as "newbies," or, less pleasantly, "newb," "noob," or "n00b." You may find this attitude disrespectful, but don't feel ashamed of your lack of experience. All of your fellow players went through a similar period of learning. Similarly, treat even newer players with respect, as they'll go through the same experiences you did.

You may also run into people who overcompensate by being too nice. Overly conciliatory or ingratiating language often sounds phony.

Simply treat others respectfully. Even though the social environment is different from real life, the rules are based on everyday interactions. This congenial attitude should extend to both questions and combat. If you need help, ask one of your fellow players, though try to avoid asking questions out loud in public channels.

Many games support a mentoring or guide system that allows players to flag themselves as willing to answer questions. Final Fantasy XI's mentoring system is very mature. New characters begin the game with a red question mark by their name. This indicator remains in place until the player has played approximately 15 hours or has reached level 5. During this time period, everyone else in the game knows that the character may need help adjusting to the game or the genre, or may just need some advice. In addition to this system, players can join a mentoring on-call system. This system supports new players during their earliest time in the game (statistically the most likely time a player will quit) and gives experienced players the opportunity to give back to the community and show off a little.

Look out for these people if you have a simple question that needs answering. If someone helps you out of a tight spot or heals you, be sure to thank her. Similarly, if you think you can help someone out in combat without getting both of you killed, give it a shot. It's a good idea to ask if the other player would like assistance, though; some players hate the thought of needing help.

Someone fighting several monsters at once or a monster of much greater strength may need assistance. If you can, examine the player's hit points and statistics, and make your decision.

The most common way for players to interact is through *grouping* ("Build an Effective Group" [Hack #33]). Grouping with other players is usually the most efficient method of gaining experience, and it's almost always more fun, too. Don't be put off, though, if some people turn you down. Playing by yourself sometimes is a nice break.

Be aware that some players don't make a goal of socializing. They tend to view the gameworld as an extension of the single-player games they've played alone. They may not feel at all weird about randomly and unexpectedly inviting other players with no explanation, so be prepared for these phantom invites. Accept or deny the request based on the limited information you have about the other player.

When dealing with other people and their goals, find out what they want to accomplish. It's less awkward just to turn down a request than to leave it suddenly later. If you accept, there will likely be a looting mechanism available for "pick up" groups of this sort, so you shouldn't have too much to worry about. Be friendly; hopefully, other players will begin to view you as more than just another bunch of pixels on a screen.

Loot

Beyond simple social graces, you'll also have to consider the material concerns of game equipment, money, and loot. The biggest thing to remember is that it's just loot in a game. Losing a piece of equipment is not the end of the world.

Of course, if you're playing with others, make sure to agree on a fair division of loot before setting out. Groups move through monsters much more quickly than an individual. The increased rewards make it even more important that everyone receives a proportional amount of treasure.

Some groups roll dice for highly valued equipment. Others cast lots, and some use old-fashioned sweet talking. If you come across a piece of equipment that is appropriate for your class, make an argument without whining. The odds are good that your companions also want class-appropriate items, so use this opportunity to find something you can use. If all else fails, you can always offer to buy a piece of equipment from the other player. This may net you a significant discount from buying it at auction or through a more formal sale.

Player trading is the mainstay of most MMOG economies. If you're selling small, common, and inexpensive items, you're better off trading with NPC vendors. Larger, more powerful, and rare items usually earn more profit when sold to other players. The means by which you sell items varies between games. Some offer large marketplaces or in-game auction systems. Others allow you to hire NPC vendors.

Whatever your method of selling, be courteous when going about your sale. Many players dislike having sales shoved into their faces, so avoid spamming a common chat channel. Also, be aware of the accepted costs of your goods before you set a price. A high price won't net you any sales, while a low one will give you a poor return on your investment of time and energy. Well-established games often have several web sites that offer common costs for even the rarest objects. Otherwise, ask around for several opinions on how much an item is worth. Chances are you'll find someone who has bought or sold the item before and can give you a fair estimate of its value.

This guide has attempted to be a bridge between the new player tutorial and your first steps as a new player in a wider world. I've tried to lay out some basic information on becoming an active and participatory new player. The skills you learn and the friends you meet through actual play, though, are what will keep you playing for years to come.

HACK
#29 **Understand MMORPG Lingo**
Learn the language of your chosen MMORPG.

While there are plenty of interesting lands to explore in MMO games, you'll stick out like an ugly American tourist unless you speak the highly specialized language. Some of the lingo may be obvious even to newbies, but if holding down a day job for several years has reduced your street credibility to Vanilla Ice–fan levels, you'll find it hard to succeed until you know how to communicate.

Fortunately, I can help you sell items for a profit, adventure in a group, or seem like an old hand at monster-whacking. Table 3-1 shows a glossary of training, twinking, ganking, and more.

Table 3-1. The A–Zs of MMORPG speak

Term	Definition
AC	Asheron's Call, by Turbine Entertainment.
AC2	Asheron's Call 2, by Turbine Entertainment.
Achiever	One of the four Bartle Player Types. Achiever players play MMOGs for the purpose of advancing their characters as far as they can go in an attempt to beat the game.
Add	A monster that attacks an individual or group already engaged in a fight. Often used as a warning.
AFK	Away From Keyboard. Said when a player leaves the computer but stays logged into the game. Can also be a mode entered on purpose to alert other players that there is no one at the keyboard.
Aggro	Also known as Hate, Aggro is when a creature begins to attack a character. The act of initiating this is called Getting Aggro. The area around a monster where players can activate it is the Aggro Radius.
AI	Artificial Intelligence. The behavior or programming of an NPC.
Alpha	Shortening of Alpha testing. Alpha testing is the initial internal test of a Massively Multiplayer Game.
Alt	Alternative Character. A character other than the one most often used by a player.
AO	Anarchy Online, by Funcom.
AOE	Area of Effect, also sometimes abbreviated AE. Used to discuss the area something will strike or to state that a spell or ability will target multiple creatures.
Armor Class	The defensive capabilities of a character, usually due to equipment. Abbreviated AC.
ATITD	A Tale in the Desert, by eGenesis.
Aug	Augmentation.
Avatar	A representation of a real person inside a virtual space.

Table 3-1. The A–Zs of MMORPG speak (continued)

Term	Definition
Bartle, Richard	One of the original programmers of MUD1, one of the first Massively Multi-player spaces. Mr. Bartle is perhaps best known for his article "Players who suit MUDs" (*http://www.mud.co.uk/richard/hcds.htm*), which categorizes MMOG players into distinct types.
Beta	Shortening of Beta Test. This is usually the first portion of a MMORPG testing phase that includes individuals outside the company. Some games feature a phase where anyone with the ability to download the client can test the game. This is an Open Beta.
Bind	The location within the game world where a character respawns after being defeated. The specific location is the Bind Point. Some games use a Bind Stone or Statue to represent the Bind Point.
Buff	A beneficial spell cast on an individual, such as a spell that increases a character's hit points. The act of casting such a spell is buffing. An individual who casts such spells on a regular basis is a buffer.
Camping	An activity where an individual or group stays in a particular location for an extended period of time for the express purpose of killing a particular monster or type of monster. Usually considered antisocial.
Carebear	Derogatory term for individuals who prefer PvE combat or Roleplaying to PvP combat.
Caster	Shortening of Spellcaster. Refers to any character with the ability to use magical abilities or cast spells.
Character	The in-game representation of the Player as represented in game elements such as a name, hit points, mana (see Mana Points), equipment, abilities, skills, and spells.
Client	The program installed on the Player's computer that allows him to connect to the gameworld.
COH	City of Heroes, by NCSoft.
Con	Abbreviation for Consider. Considering a monster reveals the difficulty of the creature in relation to the level and ability of the character.
Crit	Shortening of Critical Hit. Many games allow for the possibility of striking a blow of higher damage during combat. This is a Critical Hit.
DAoC	Dark Age of Camelot, by Mythic Entertainment.
DD	Acronym for Direct Damage. Refers to a combat ability or spell that inflicts damage directly to its target as opposed to Damage Over Time.
Debuff	A negative spell cast on an individual. The act of casting such a spell is debuffing. An individual who casts such spells on a regular basis is a debuffer.
DoT	Acronym for Damage Over Time. Refers to an effect that inflicts damage over a preset period of time. Poisons and spells are common DoTs.
DPS	Acronym for Damage Per Second. Refers to the damage done per second by a spell or weapon. Also a term used to describe a character or character class that is adept at causing a lot of damage quickly. For example, "The rogue will do DPS for the group."

Table 3-1. The A–Zs of MMORPG speak (continued)

Term	Definition
Emote	A repeatable physical action that shows emotion. Usually accessed via slash commands. Some games allow direct slash command emotes (such as /hug). Most games allow freeform physical actions via the /emote command. If your character's name were Paul, typing /emote does a little dance displays Paul does a little dance.
Experience	A common game metric used to determine character progression. Experience usually comes from defeating monsters or completing quests. Gaining a certain amount of experience usually allows the player to go up a level.
Explorer	One of the four Bartle Player Types. Explorer type players typically play MMOGs for the purpose of adventuring and exploring the in-game world.
EQ	EverQuest, by Sony Online Entertainment.
EQ2	EverQuest 2, by Sony Online Entertainment.
Faction	A metric used in some games to determine a character's standing with a specific group within the game world. If your character does quests or completes actions that adversely affects a group, your character has bad faction with that group.
Farming	Repeatedly adventuring in an area and defeating monsters for an extended period of time for the purpose of obtaining equipment or currency.
FFXI	Final Fantasy XI Online, by Square/Enix.
Gank	The defeating of a much lower-level character by a higher-level character in PvP combat.
Gil	The unit of currency of Final Fantasy XI.
GM	Acronym for Game Master, a customer service representative in a MMOG. GMs are typically representatives of the company who assist players in-game with technical and social issues.
Griefer	A player who takes pleasure in the abuse and control of other players' characters. A griefer typically does not play the game in the same sense as other players. His goal is to manipulate and control other players. This activity is griefing.
Grinding	Repeatedly adventuring in an area and defeating monsters for an extended period of time for the purpose of gaining experience and levels.
Guild	A group of players with formal recognition within the game world. Guilds are influential social organizations that usually form the backbone of player society.
Healer	Anyone who can provide HP treatment during a fight. Many healers also have the ability to resurrect characters if necessary. Traditionally, this is a Cleric or Doctor.
Hit Points	A game mechanic used to represent a character's health resources, usually measured in points. Also Health Points, often abbreviated HP.
Inc	An abbreviation of Incoming. Used to warn others that a monster has joined an ongoing battle.

Table 3-1. The A–Zs of MMORPG speak (continued)

Term	Definition
Instance	A term used to describe a private portion of a gameworld created just for an individual or group of players. The technology as a whole is Instancing. Normally used to ensure that dungeons or specific adventuring areas are always available for those who wish to access them.
KK	Chat slang for ok. Used instead of ok because hitting the k key twice is quicker. Chatters are lazy.
Killer	One of the four Bartle Player Types. Essentially a synonym for Griefer.
Kiting	A combat technique in which a character attacks a monster and then runs out of range of the creature's melee attacks while continuing to attack the creature. In some cases, this may allow a character to defeat a monster she couldn't otherwise take on in a stand-up fight.
KOS	An Acronym for Kill On Sight. Used to describe the reaction of an NPC (not a monster) who attempts to kill characters of opposing factions.
Koster, Raph	One of the original developers of Ultima Online, Raph Koster is a well-known developer who has influenced numerous Massively Multiplayer projects, including Star Wars Galaxies. Currently creative director at Sony Online Entertainment.
KS	Acronym for Kill Stealing. An antisocial behavior in which a character attacks a monster already under attack by another character with the intent of gaining the resulting experience and equipment.
Lag	A condition caused by network traffic or server slowdowns that results in a slowdown in responsiveness within the game. May result in a long pause between a player's command and the character's response.
Level	Exactly like the system used in Pen and Paper roleplaying, levels determine a character's power within the gameworld. Characters usually gain levels by obtaining a set amount of experience. Often abbreviated Lvl.
LD	Acronym for the phrase Link Dead. Indicates that the player's client has lost its connection with the game server.
LFG	Acronym for the phrase Looking For Group. Usually used to make a generic request on a chat channel, almost always accompanied by a statement indicating the character's level and class. "Lvl 8 War LFG" indicates that the character is a Level 8 Warrior looking for a group.
Log	Shorthand for the phrase Log Out. For example, "Excuse me, I have to log."
Loot	A generic term used to refer to items taken from defeated foes. The act of taking items from defeated foes is looting.
Lum the Mad	Scott Jennings, a MMORPG commentator who ran the site entitled Lum the Mad in 1999. The site and Lum's opinions became very popular, and the Lum site became one of the most respected sources of MMOG news on the Internet. Mythic Entertainment hired Mr. Jennings in 2001 to work on Dark Age of Camelot.
Mana Points	A game mechanic used to represent a character's magical resources, usually measured in points. Often MP or mana.
Main	The particular character a player considers primary or plays the most.

Table 3-1. The A–Zs of MMORPG speak (continued)

Term	Definition
Med	Abbreviation for Meditation. A generic term used for a period of downtime used to regain consumable character resources such as mana or hit points.
Melee	A hand-to-hand fight in contrast to ranged combat or spellcasting. A melee fighter specializes in hand-to-hand weapons or brawling combat.
Mez	Abbreviation of Mesmerize, a generic term for any effect that incapacitates a monster.
MMORPG	Traditionally used acronym for Massively Multiplayer Online Roleplaying Game. MMORPGs are virtual persistent worlds located on the Internet in which players interact with each other through avatars.
Mob	Abbreviation of the word Mobile. The term originates from text-based game-worlds, in which programmers referred to every NPC as a mobile.
Moogle	A personal assistant creature in Final Fantasy XI.
MUD	Acronym for Multi-User Dungeon. The name of the original text-based massively multiplayer game created by Richard Bartle and the generic name for the genre of text-based gameworlds.
Mulligan, Jessica	A well-known games programmer and author. Ms. Mulligan is currently Executive Producer at Turbine Entertainment.
Mule	A character created not to play but to hold equipment.
Newbie	Term used to refer to someone who is new to the game or to Massively Multiplayer games in general. Can be negative depending on context. Abbreviations include noob, newb, and n00b.
No Drop	A descriptive element for an item in a game. No Drop on an item means that players cannot trade the item to another character by dropping it on the ground. You may be able to sell it to a vendor.
NPC	Acronym for Non-Player Character. A character controlled by the computer or gameworld, not directly by a human.
Nuke	Either a high-damage spell or a character capable of casting high-damage spells. Thus, a Fireball spell and a Mage character could both be Nukes.
OOM	Acronym for the statement Out of Mana. Stated by a spellcaster to alert others that he cannot cast any spells for the moment.
PC	Acronym for Player Character. The representation of the Player inside the game world.
Permadeath	An uncommon design decision in MMOGs where a slain character is deleted, effectively killing the character. Also referred to by the acronym PD.
Plat	Abbreviation of Platinum, a form of currency used in several Massively Multiplayer games. For example, "I'll trade you my sword for 5 Plat."
Player	The actual human playing a game.
Pet	An NPC creature that a player's character can control or influence. While often a monster or demon, Pet can refer to any nonplayer character entity that a player's character commands.

Table 3-1. The A–Zs of MMORPG speak (continued)

Term	Definition
PK	Acronym for Player Killing. Player Killing is a PvP act in which a character kills another character. While not functionally different than normal PvP, Pking is seen as a negative PvP act done at random. A player who Player Kills is often a Pker. Often considered griefing.
PnP	Acronym of Pen and Paper. Used to refer to tabletop Roleplaying.
Pop	Synonym for Spawn. For example, "The orc boss just popped! Let's get him!"
Powerleveling	An activity in which high-level characters assist a lower-level character to combat creatures in a high-level area. The goal is to provide the lower-level character with a rapid increase in experience and levels without minimal effort.
Proc	Abbreviation of the word Process. A proc is an effect attached to an item. The effect (usually a spell) has a random chance of activating, or procing. For example, "This sword has a 15% chance to proc Fireball."
PS	Planetside, by Sony Online Entertainment.
PST	Acronym for Please Send Tell. A request for someone to send a private message directly to the individual. Normally used after another request. For example, "Looking for good hunting spots! PST."
Pull	To attract a monster's attention. Functionally the same as going Aggro, though in a controlled fashion. Normally used by an individual to lead a monster or monsters to other members of a group. A person who pulls is a puller. For example, "Do you want to Pull for this next group of orcs?"
PvE	Player vs. Environment. Also sometimes referred to as PvM or Player vs. Monster. Combat in which a player-controlled character engages in combat with a computer-controlled character. The typical form of combat in modern games.
PvP	Player vs. Player. Combat in which two player-controlled characters engage in combat. Frequently a restricted form of conflict in modern games.
Raid	A large social gathering in which many characters band together to assault a difficult dungeon or creature.
Regen	Abbreviation for Regeneration. Regeneration typically refers to the refilling of a consumable character resource, such as mana or hit points.
Rez	Also Res. The act of Resurrecting a character after the character has died. For example, "Can you rez me please?"
RP	Acronym for Roleplaying.
Rubberbanding	A phenomenon wherein characters and monsters can seem to teleport backwards along their path of movement. Caused by server slowdowns or network bandwidth that result in the game client believing that an actor is further along its path than the game server expects. When the client and server reconnect, the server resolves the discrepancy in its favor, causing the characters to fall back a short distance.

Table 3-1. The A–Zs of MMORPG speak (continued)

Term	Definition
Server	A copy of the gameworld. Every MMORPG consists of several servers that spread the player population as evenly as possible among available resources. Each server is made up of dozens or hundreds of individual computers to keep the server up and functional. Characters are often identified by which server they reside on. For example, "My character is on the Rallos Zek server."
Slash command	A command that can be issued via a word or words following a forward slash. /attack might initiate an attack, for example.
Socializer	One of the four Bartle Player Types. Socializers play MMOGs for the purpose of interacting with other people in interesting and stimulating ways.
SOE	Game publisher Sony Online Entertainment.
Spawn	The location where a monster appears within the game world. Also the act of the creature appearing in the game world. Used synonymously with Spawning or Respawn. For example, "The boss spawned! Let's get him!"
SWG	Star Wars Galaxies, by Sony Online Entertainment.
Tank	Term used to describe a character whose role within a party is to take damage. Traditionally held by a melee class. Tanking is the action of being a Tank for a group.
Taunt	An ability designed to increase Aggro against the character using it. Usually used by a Tank to ensure that the Tank is the center of the monster's attention.
Tell	A personal message sent via in-game chat to another player. Sometimes referred to as Whispering.
Tick	A duration of time, often a second. Normally used to refer to an effect of some sort. A Damage Over Time spell could do five points of damage per tick. That is, the spell does five points of damage per time interval.
Train	A line of monsters. Usually results from unexpected monsters attacking a character already in combat. The character's player panics and runs, taking the monsters he was fighting with him. As he flees through the area, more monsters attack him. This line of monsters is the train. Trains are dangerous because when the original character is killed or flees, the monsters begin to make their way back to their appropriate places and continue to attack characters they encounter on the way. Can also be created on purpose by higher-level characters to inflict frustration on lower-level characters. The term is usually used as a warning, often with a notice of where the train is headed. "Train to Zone!" means that a character is fleeing for the edge of the area map with a train following behind him, and other players should beware.
Twink	A character outfitted with equipment, spells, or assistance beyond her normal level. A 5th-level character possessing a sword appropriate for 25th-level characters is Twinked. Twinking is the act of outfitting a character in this manner.
Uber	Used to refer to something or someone that is very powerful. For example, "That sword is uber!"
UO	Ultima Online, by Origin Systems. Often considered the original modern MMOG.

Table 3-1. The A–Zs of MMORPG speak (continued)

Term	Definition
Vendor	A nonplayer character that buys and sells items.
WoW	World of Warcraft, by Blizzard Entertainment.
WTB	Acronym for the phrase Want to Buy. Placed before an item the player wants to buy, normally used in auction chat channels. For example, "WTB the One Ring."
WTS	Acronym for the phrase Want to Sell. Placed before an item the player wants to sell, normally used in auction chat channels. For example, "WTS Sword of Power + 1."
Zone	A self-contained area in the original generation of Massively Multiplayer Games. Moving from one area to another is Zoning. Zone can also refer to the act of zoning. For example, "There are a bunch of orcs following you! Quick, Zone!"

HACK #30   Grind Without Going Crazy

Gain levels, find loot, and reach the end game while minimizing your boredom.

The standard form of advancement in massively multiplayer games is through experience gain and level acquisition. *Grinding*, or repeating an action over and over to gain experience and levels, is often the quickest way to move through online games.

In this hack, we'll discuss moderately grind-heavy games more familiar to Westerners, such as EverQuest and Final Fantasy XI. However, it's worth noting that many titles popular in MMO-crazy Korea, particularly the Lineage series, are even more grind-heavy than Western titles. If repetitive actions really appeal to you, by all means seek them out.

> This guide assumes that for the most part you are grinding alone. Grinding with others is easier and more fun, but if your only goal is to gain experience, partying up will only slow you down. See "Build an Effective Group" **[Hack #33]** for tips on party adventuring.

If you're serious about gaining levels quickly, be prepared for tedium and frustration. Fighting monsters as you stumble upon them is not grinding. Spending several hours at a time in an area that you know will give you good XP for doing nothing but fighting monsters, though you wish you were doing something else, is grinding. The key is to grind without boring yourself to tears.

Preparing for the Grind

When you begin a grinding session, prepare as much as possible before-hand. Your goal is to extend your time in the field, so make healing a priority. EQ (see "Understand MMORPG Lingo" [Hack #29]) players should stock up on bandages and healing potions. FFXI players who already have a well-established character class can craft potions for leveling another class. SWG players can purchase stimpacks to restore their Health bar.

Buffs and debuffs. In addition to supplies, take care of any poisons or afflictions before leaving civilization. You'll likely catch something nasty in the wilds, so why make things harder on yourself than they have to be? SWG players should make a point to visit a cantina to remove any battle fatigue.

Also consider buffing your character before beginning the hunt. Be as strong and fast as you can, with as many hit points as possible.

> EQ characters can find buffs from other spellcasting characters. The best buffs location to obtain a Spirit of the Wolf (speed increase) or Temperence (HP increase) is the Plane of Knowledge (PoK). Many people there advertise their buffing services over the PoK out-of-character channel. Luckily, these are usually high-level characters whose buffs last a long time.

Galaxies and Final Fantasy XI players should obtain as much food as they can get their hands on. Even simple food and drink can provide stat increases to characters in these games. Keep an ample supply of buffing foods on hand to help you take on more difficult creatures than normal. Galaxies players should also look to their fellow players for assistance. Like most things in SWG, the player community is the best way to get ahead. Doctors can craft and apply medicines that can buff all aspects of the Health and Action pools, while Dancers and Musicians have the ability to buff your Mind pool.

Tools. Supplies and buffs make the character, but you need the right tools for the job. Most modern MMOGs place a great deal of importance on armor and weapons. Sell off any and all loot you've been meaning to get rid of. This will give you spending money and make room to pick up new loot.

If you're playing straight without twinking, the best armor and weapons for your level should be obvious. Choose the best equipment that suits your playstyle. Several web sites offer helpful advice on outfitting. Two of the best are the Warcry network (*http://www.warcry.com/*) and Allakhazam's

Magical Realm (*http://www.allakhazam.com/*). The latter in particular has excellent item resources.*

Location, Location, Location

At this point you are cocked and loaded for bear (or bunny). The proper hunting ground depends on your level. Do a little research online to find the best place to invest your time.

EverQuest. Your initial choice of grind location is out of your hands. Most newbie zones are fairly similar, so start grinding your way to level 10 in whichever racial zone you start in. Table 3-2 shows some recommendations.

Table 3-2. EQ grinding locations

Level	Alignment	Zone	Notes
Levels 1 through 5	Good	The halfling zone of Misty Thicket	A wall separates the lower-level area of the zone from the 5+ area, allowing new characters to hunt relatively unmolested.
Levels 1 through 10	Evil	The Nektulos Forest	This location offers plenty of variety in monsters to hunt. If you don't mind staying put, you can grind into your early teens.
Early to mid teens	Either	Blackburrow, outside of Qeynos; the Crushbone orc camp.	Traditional haunts.
Levels 15 to 20	Either	The undead haunt of Befallen; the Lake of Ill Omen.	If you hit the Lake of Ill Omen, make sure not to target the Sarnaks, no matter how tempting the XP. They play a major role as NPCs throughout the continent of Kunark. If you lose faction with them, it is very hard to restore.
Level 20 and up	Either	Everywhere except the continent of Velious	Norrath opens up to your character here. Your path to the level cap should take you across the length and breadth of Norrath and beyond, to the planes.
Further along	Either	Paludal Caverns; the Lost Dungeons of Norrath.	The instanced zones of the lost dungeons provide excellent experience and fantastic money.

* Use the navigation bar on the upper right side of the page to choose games besides EQ.

Final Fantasy XI. The world of Vana'diel offers three choices of starting location: the nation-states of San D'Oria, Bastok, and Windhurst. Each nation state is home to one or two of the various races and has a very similar starting zone. If you begin at your character's racial home, you'll receive a nice ring that offers increases in your health and mana. At level 1, even a few points of health can mean the difference between life and death, so it's worth your while to follow the crowd at the start.

Though in other games there are advantages to grouping even at low levels, FFXI almost punishes you for grouping at the lowest levels. From levels 1 to 10 it is very much in your best interest to solo. Even if you're alone, you're likely to have a lot of allies. Friendly red and white mages often cast healing spells on beleaguered adventurers as they wander by. Once you pass level 10, soloing quickly becomes an effort in futility. Luckily, there are almost always players on the lookout for hunting partners.

Table 3-3 gives further advice on locations.

Table 3-3. FFXI grinding locations

Level	Solo/group	Location	Notes
Levels 1 through 10	Solo	The Bastok proving grounds; the Gustaberg areas	Stay in the initial starting zones and their adjacent dungeons. FFXI zones are a genuine pleasure to play in, so you won't be too bored.
Early teens	Solo/group	The Konschtat Highlands; La Theine Plateau; Tahrongi Canyon	Many other groups of similar-level adventurers will be glad of your assistance.
Mid to late teens	Group	Valkurm Dunes	The creatures that drop the all-important items for your subjob are somewhat common here (mostly the ghouls). Great monsters and experience are icing on the dune cake.
Level 18	Group	Selbina or Mhaura	Do your sublevel quest! The Selbina quest is much easier than the alternative. Find Isacio on the ocean front to begin the quest.
Level 19 and up	Group	Jeuno	Hook up with other adventurers of your level and begin thinking about your all-important Chocobo license.

Star Wars Galaxies. SWG offers two choices for a starting city, Theed on Naboo and Mos Eisley on Tatooine, but the choice is not critical. Both Naboo and Tatooine are very well-populated planets with many options. If you want to learn about the game without being overwhelmed with other players, I suggest Naboo. Otherwise, Mos Eisley offers a real dose of *Star Wars*–ness. Either way, the grind begins right away.

 Unlike other games, Galaxies uses a straight experience system that allows you to gain components of a profession as you choose. Grinding has as many different facets as there are ways to play. All of these differing ways of playing the game can be combined within one character, and that makes grinding in Galaxies an especially laborious process. Table 3-4 shows some strategies for various professions.

Table 3-4. SWG profession grinding strategies

Profession	Levels	Location	Notes
Brawler and Marksman	Low levels	Areas outside each major city on Naboo, Coruscant, and Tatooine	Grinding combat skills is much like grinding levels in any other game. The low-level monsters here are extremely squishy.
Elite combat professions	Intermediate	Talus; Dantooine; Rori	These planets all present harsher and more forbidding landscapes and adversaries.
Elite combat professions	Advanced	Dathomir; Lok; Endor	The creatures on these planets are anything but small and squishy. Big or small, they also provide materials and XP for the Scout profession.
Artisan	Any	Any	A foremost artisan talent is surveying for resources. Grinding through the profession requires a lot of metals, chemicals, and power.
Entertainer	Any	Any	Entertainers gain experience by performing for other players.

Grinding guidelines. For all the preparations and planning you can do, the only way through the grind is to do it. Keep in mind the following guidelines as you play:

Have goals. If you grind away for hours on end with no purpose, you'll burn out very quickly. Aim for something, perhaps a timespan to grind in or a specific amount of experience to gain. Even a goal as simple as "gain a level before I log off tonight" will help you to know when it's time to stop.

Pace yourself. While you may intend to take on the most difficult creatures you can in order to make the grind go more quickly, that tactic will likely lead to serious wounds. Taking on less challenging creatures will give you less experience per creature but will allow you to fight longer between healing breaks.

Take risks. While fighting small fries is a consistent way to meet your goals, there's little glory in it. Girding for a major battle, taking on wave after wave of tough enemies, and cheating death the entire time is a great way to earn experience and is a refreshing change of pace.

Make friends. While you'll probably do most of your grinding alone so as not to annoy others, having people to assist you will make your grinding far and away more pleasant. Fellow adventurers can buff or supply you, heal you after a long series of battles, and even just hang out while you whittle your way through the bunny population. Friends are the best tools for the grind.

Have fun. While you should concentrate on whatever task you have set yourself, stop and smell the roses occasionally. The fun parts of massively multiplayer games vastly outweigh the boring parts. If you don't remind yourself of that, you'll cancel your account faster than you would have thought possible.

Avoid burnout. This is the bottom-line guideline to keep in mind. You're gaining levels to have more fun, not to turn a game into a job. Many powergamers treat the leveling aspect of massively multiplayer gaming as the core of the game. Instead, look at grinding as a temporary annoyance that will allow you to enjoy the game more after you have completed your short-term goals.

Designers realize that some people prefer to grind their way through certain aspects of gameplay, but the grind of the game can involve more than just repetitive combat. Repeated use of commands and endless clicking can wear down a player. That's why the designers of many new games, such as Final Fantasy XI, World of Warcraft, and especially Star Wars Galaxies, include a macroing system ("Write MMORPG Macros" [Hack #32]) to save and refine automated functionality.

Make a Profit in Vana'diel

How to make good money in Final Fantasy XI through auctions and smart sales.

Final Fantasy XI Online (FFXI) is the most heavily subscribed Massively Multiplayer Online Roleplaying Game as of early 2004. It is a great game, carrying on the traditions of the single-player Final Fantasy franchise and fantasy online games such as EverQuest.

There's an old adage that money makes the world go 'round. It applies just as much in the world of Vana'diel as it does in real life. The unit of currency in FFXI is the gil, and to succeed as an adventurer you'll need a lot of it. At

higher levels, monsters drop gil on a regular basis, but to begin with you'll
make most of your money through questing, selling to NPC vendors, and
one of the best features of FFXI: the Auction Houses.

Questing for Profits

Questing in Final Fantasy XI is a lucrative and entertaining way to add
meaning to the everyday grind. Each starting city has a variety of simple
quests that can net you a decent amount of gil for a minimum of fuss. To
start you on your way, Table 3-5 shows a few quests for each of the three
starting cities.

Table 3-5. FFXI city quests

City	Zone	Grid/location	Quest description
San d'Oria	North San d'Oria	F-6, looking out over the deck	Speak with Secodiand. He is looking for bat wings. Every 2 bat wings you bring him nets you 200 gil. Repeatable.
San d'Oria	San d'Oria Port	G-7, in the pub	Speak with Nogelle. She wants Lake Lufet Salt, which drops from River crabs. Every 3 units of salt nets you 600 gil. Repeatable.
San d'Oria	San d'Oria South	K-6, in the pub	Speak with Legata. He seeks flint, which drops from worms. Every 4 flints nets you 100 gil. Repeatable.
Bastok	Bastok Markets	L-8, in the Trader's Home	Salimah is looking for ingredients for a dish she's working on. She takes Treat Bulbs, Wild Onions, and Sleepshrooms. You'll earn a 100-gil reward, unless you time it right. Repeatable.
			From 6:00 to 11:59, Treant Bulbs are worth 200 gil. From 18:00 to 5:59, Sleepshrooms are worth 200 gil. From 12:00 to 17:59, Wild Onions are worth 350 gil.
Bastok	Bastok Mines	F-8	Gerbaum is looking to have Zeruhn Mines creatures slain. Bring him 3 Zeruhn Soots and he'll reward you with 150 gil. Repeatable.
Bastok	Bastok Markets	K-9	Aquilina is looking for flint to light her oven. They drop from worms. 4 flints will net you 100 gil. Repeatable.
Windhurst	Windhurst Port	G-5, behind the warehouses	One of the best early-level quest stories around. Speak to Kohlo-Lakolo to start the Star Onion Brigade quests. You'll need to turn in a rarab tail, dropped by a bumblebee.

Table 3-5. FFXI city quests (continued)

City	Zone	Grid/location	Quest description
Windhurst	Windhurst Woods	H-6	Illu wants someone to clear crawlers out of the area. Bring her 3 silk thread or 3 crawler calculi to net 600 gil. Repeatable.
Windhurst	Windhurst Waters	L-6, in the Aurastery	Moreno-Toeno is looking for a Two-Leaf Mandragora Bud and a Bird's Feather. The turn-in nets you 250 gil. Repeatable.

Dealing with Vendors

The first and easiest means of selling goods you'll discover is using NPC vendors. Every NPC vendor in FFXI will purchase any item you have in your inventory, and all vendors purchase items for the same prices. A weapons vendor will purchase weapons at the same rate that an armor vendor will purchase weapons.

At low levels, you'll likely find better prices from randomly dropped loot than you'll see at the Auction House. Don't ever sell equipment to a vendor, however. Almost every piece of equipment will sell for much more on auction than it will to a vendor. Vendors are useful only for serious moneymaking when you can set up a sweet deal between vendor prices and Auction House prices.

Merchants at the various crafting guilds sell materials for their crafts. Sometimes you can purchase these items, such as lumber or cotton, via the guild halls for relatively little and resell them at the Auction House for a high profit. Otherwise, avoid selling to NPC vendors. The Auction Houses are almost always the way to maximize the profits of your labors.

Player trading is the mainstay of most MMOG economies. If you're selling small, common, and inexpensive items, you're best off trading with NCP vendors. Larger, more powerful, and rare items usually earn more profit when sold to other players.

Auction Houses

Every major city has a few Auction Houses where players can buy and sell goods. The AHs within a city tie into one another, so a sword up for sale in Windhurst Waters will also appear in Windhurst Walls.

There are different categories of items available for you to peruse. When putting an item up for sale, look under the category of the item you want to sell. If you're selling a Bronze sword, bring up the Weapons screen. On the screen you can choose the type of item you wish to sell. Select Bronze Sword to place a bid if there are any up for sale, sell an item, or review the item's sales history.

Before selling an item, always check the price history. The AH is a powerful tool for valuing equipment and goods. A sale occurs when a player places a bid on an item at or exceeding the amount of money the selling player asks for the item. If there are many items with the same price that meet those criteria, the buyer buys the oldest item up for sale. If Bronze Swords are selling for 150 gil, you might place it up for auction for 170 gil, hoping to make a better deal. If your item is the only Bronze Sword up for auction, the first bid at or more than 170 gil will win your item. Your house Moogle will hold onto the gil you gain from an auction until you retrieve it from him.

That's how to buy and sell. How do you profit? Two of the best ways to work the Auction House are farming and timing.

Farming items. Farming items from locations and monsters, if done in the right places, can lead to a lot of money. The most lucrative item to farm is probably ore from the Bastokian mines. Iron ore from the mines sells for around 700 gil, and the much rarer Darksteel ore can net over 6,000 gil per piece. Fire crystals, dropped from monsters, are also valuable on almost every server. A stack of 12 could fetch as much as 3,000 gil. Both methods work for low-level characters to raise a stake in Vana'diel.

Timing the system. Timing is much trickier. Japanese players are much more advanced in the game and generally have more gil than their American counterparts. While prices for a particular item during American gameplay times can be too low to consider selling, placing items in the Auction House for sale during Japanese play times can rake in higher profits.

Muling. If you want to combine all these methods to maximum effect, consider using mule characters. Final Fantasy XI accounts allow one character by default. Buying additional character slots will cost an extra dollar per month. If you're willing to deal with the additional cost, three additional slots will make for a very wealthy primary character. Remember to create these additional slots on the same server as your primary character. Use a Worldpass or trial and error to ensure this.

Create three characters and station one at each of the cities. Every Auction House has slightly different rates for equipment and loot. Pass gil and equipment back and forth between characters via Moogle mail. Send the appropriate piece of loot to the mule character who can sell it for the maximum amount of gil, then pass the gil to the primary character.

If you don't mind a little more work, you can also use these mules to complete lucrative one-off quests. Equipment from low-level quests often sells for a good deal at the Auction House, such as the Justice Badge in Windhurst.

With only a few guidelines in mind, you should have no trouble keeping your primary character properly armed and armored. The art of making gil requires knowing how to use what you have to greatest effect. Once you have some experience in the art of the Auction House, making gil hand over fist becomes almost second nature. Keep your eyes out for bargains and good luck!

HACK #32 Write MMORPG Macros
Turn tedious sequences of commands into click-and-forget aliases.

Like real life, MMORPG play has its moments of repetitive tedium (especially while you're grinding—"Grind Without Going Crazy" **[Hack #30]**). Fortunately, computers are very good at doing repetitive tasks; they rarely slip up and never complain. Many modern MMORPGs offer macro features to help you record and play back long sequences of events; Star Wars Galaxies and Final Fantasy XI are two examples of this phenomenon. In particular, Galaxies includes good macro features to automate your gaming experience.

Star Wars Galaxies Macros

In order to access the macros menu, hit Ctrl-A or the small firework symbol on your menu bar. This will open the actions menu, on which the macros tab hangs. To start a new macro, hit the New Macro button. Give the macro a name, choose an icon that represents it, and type the macro into the text box.

Capitalization counts in commands. If your macro doesn't behave properly, double-check your spelling, capitalization, and semicolons.

To refer to other macros or to loop self-referentially, a macro must call a slot in the User Interface toolbar. Grab your toolbar and drag it to encompass two rows so that you have as many slots as possible for actions and macros. To refer to a toolbar slot, use the call /ui action toolbarSlot*xx*, where *xx* is the number of the slot. Keep in mind that the first slot in the upper right corner is slot 00, not 01. The last slot in the lower left is slot 23.

Now that you know how to define macros, let's explore some useful ones.

Bleed pull. This macro can begin combat with an accurate shot that will cause your opponent to bleed health over time:

```
/prone;
/pause 2;
/mindshot2;      Replace this with any bleeding shot
/pause 2;
/stand;
```

AFK combat. You can grind on combat and scouting without being at the keyboard. Your first task is to find a place to run the macro. Choose a low-risk location far from other players. This macro won't differentiate between unclaimed creatures and those already under attack by others, so this is a highly antisocial macro.

The macro targets the nearest creature and moves you toward it. In order to stay in the same location, move the camera directly above your character, and use your options menu to increase your field of view to its maximum:

```
/ui action targetSelf;
/pause 1;
/ui action cycleTargetOutward;
/follow
/pause 5
/attack;
/pause 1;
/loot;
/ui action toolbarSlotxx;
```

The final command is self referential, so place the macro in slot *xx*.

This macro has several tweaks. Train your scouting skills by adding the following line just after the /loot command:

```
/harvest hide        Or meat or bone
/pause 1;
```

If you have a pet, train your creature handling by adding this just before or in place of the attack command:

```
/tellpet attack;
```

Then add a command to the end of the macro, before the self-referential command, to command your pet to heel.

Healing. Healing in SWG is just another action that queues up with other commands. To heal yourself promptly, use this macro:

```
/ui action clearCombatQueue
/healdamage self
```

Crafting. Grinding artisan skills can be the most tedious clickfest of your game experience. Thankfully, the following macro makes it much easier:

```
/ui action toolbarSlotxx;   Reference to crafting tool
/sel 57;                    Schematic number; see note below
/pause 8;
/nextC;
/nextC;
/nextC;
/createPrototype Practice No Item;
/createPrototype Practice No Item;
/pause 2;
/ui action toolbarSlotxx;   Reference to next macro in line
```

To use this macro for an extended session, place a series of crafting tools on the toolbar. Refer to these tools in turn at the start of the macro. The macro will choose the schematic you want to create. See the datapad for the number of the appropriate schematic. The macro then pauses for eight seconds, during which you must click furiously to fill the schematic slots with resources. The macro then moves through the next screens and finishes the product as a practice item. This will give you the XP for the item (with a slight bonus) without actually creating the item.

For an extended crafting session, duplicate this macro and refer to the next example of the macro on the UI toolbar in the last line.

AFK entertainer. Combine the following macro with another macro referencing several dancing or music flourishes (labeled flourishrun here) to gain Entertainer XP without attending to your character. Remember to start this macro in a cantina. Replace startdance with startmusic as necessary.

```
/stand;
/pause 5;
/startdance rhythmic2;   Use your highest level
/macro flourishrun;
/pause 72;
/macro flourishrun;
/pause 72;
/macro flourishrun;
/pause 72;
/macro flourishrun;
/pause 72;
/macro flourishrun;
/pause 72;
/stopdance;
/pause 5;
/sit;
/pause 60;
/ui action toolbarSlotxx;   Recall this macro
```

Final Fantasy XI Macros

FFXI macros are much more basic than their SWG counterparts. These macros are simple ways to improve the combat experience of soloing and grouping. Each character has 20 available macro slots. To access the macros on a PC, hit Alt or Ctrl to bring up the two sets of 10 slots. On the PS2, hit R2 or L2. To edit them, select a macro slot and choose Edit. To access a macro in combat, hit Ctrl or Alt and the number of the macro you wish to use.

Here are some sample macros to start your adventures.

Stat ping. This simple macro alerts your teammates to your health, technique points (tp), and mana status:

```
/p HP: <hp> TP: <tp> MP: <mp>
```

Aggro warning. Alert party members to the possibility of an aggroing monster:

```
/p Warning! Possible Aggro! <call0>
```

Pull announcement. Alerts party members to the name of the creature you are pulling:

```
/p Targeting a <t>. Get ready! <call1>
```

Spell macros. Use the /ma command followed by the name of a spell and a target indicator to cast a spell quickly:

```
/ma "Cure" <t>       Casts cure 2 on current target
/ma "Protect" <me>   Casts protect on yourself
```

Group spell announcement. Use this to announce your plan to cast a group spell:

```
/p I'm going to cast a group cure! <call0>
/wait 5
/ma "Curera# " <me>
```

These examples, while specific to Final Fantasy XI and Star Wars Galaxies, are just a small selection of your options. EverQuest, Dark Age of Camelot, and World of Warcraft also have macro systems of limited degrees with their own specific syntaxes and quirks.

Of course, you can also produce macros using third-party programs. UOCurse, a third-party, text-based Ultima Online hack, is one such tool. A host of other programs bring results both legitimate and, much more often, illegitimate. Not only do most MMOG players consider them immoral, they often violate Terms of Service agreements. If the publisher catches you, they can ban you and may even seek legal relief against you. For most simple tasks, internal macroing should be more than enough to assist you.

Build an Effective Group
Fight the monsters, not each other.

It's fairly easy to find a group of adventurers, but not everyone in your new group may be as on the ball as you are. Once in a group, infighting, confusion, and misunderstandings can lead to a distinct lack of adventuring.

You can avoid this fate with a bit of planning and a bit of common courtesy. The following section shows you how.

Finding a Group

If you've ever spent time in a mid-level area, you've undoubtedly heard "LFG" over the general channels at least one too many times. Leave the public desperation at home.

Most games feature a toggle to set to announce quietly that you're looking for a short-term group. Some also allow you to search through nearby players to see who has that flag and which class or race they are. Star Wars Galaxies has the most advanced player-matching setup of any modern game, allowing you to search based on personal interests as well as in-game abilities. When you find some likely results, start /telling or /whispering people to see if they're interested in your goals. Be specific, friendly, and understandable. "Hi. I'm looking to take on the ogres across the lake. Care to join me?" is a good opening line.

If you find someone willing to give it a try, start the group with yourself as the leader. Once you have one or two people together, you can start advertising. A group looking for players is often much less annoying than a player looking for a group. Similarly, if you see a group looking for a player, make sure to speak up. Someone else has gone to the trouble of putting together a group, and the best thing you can do is to support them. If they have their own goals, hear them out. Their goals may be similar to or physically near yours. Groups can handle challenges more quickly than a solo player can, so having multiple goals when you start the group might work nicely.

If you don't have a grand goal and you notice a few other people hunting in the same area, consider starting a small group—even with only two people. Look for the obvious signs that you and others have the same goals. If you and another player are about the same level and are obviously hunting only a particular type of creature, chances are that you could aid each other in the short term. Don't be shy; send a /tell with your proposal.

Setting Out

If you are leading, check with the other group members to understand what everyone wants out of the experience. If the quest has any requirements, such as having a quest logged, being at a certain level, or having a certain item, make sure that everyone has that taken care of before you start. If you are a participant, make sure that you prepare for the task at hand before you enter the group. Nothing frustrates players more than supposedly quick preparatory side trips before a mission.

Take a few moments to figure out appropriate group roles. Who's the Tank? Who's the Healer? Who's pulling, and who's doing DPS? (See Table 3-1.) These roles don't have to be formal, but do plan ahead and set your expectations appropriately.

EverQuest players should have a good stock of bandages, food, and drink. If you are participating in an instanced adventure for the first time, be sure to obtain an adventure stone from a member of the Wayfarer's Brotherhood. Galaxies players should be sure they have access to a steady supply of high-buff food tailored to their prey. If you're hunting creatures that target minds heavily, have mind-buffing food at the ready.

With your group members ready and your roles assigned, strike out on the trail. Many games have a /follow option that allows one character to follow another as you move through the world. This is a convenient way to travel long distances, because only one person really needs to drive. Before you start, discuss hunting on the way to your destination (if you have one). Some people will want to head right there, and some folks will want to stop and kill every bunny along the way. Discuss that up front.

Combat Techniques

Once you have reached your destination, consider your combat techniques. The technique you use to enter combat will determine the most effective use of your party members. The most common method, and the only one I'll discuss here, is *pulling*. This is where one party member, usually the Tank, attracts the attention of a monster or small group of monsters and leads them to the group, waiting in an area free of monsters. Once the Tank has led the monster to the group, he leads the attack against the creatures. Nukes and DPS characters attempt to bring the beast down as quickly as possible while the Tank and Mez characters ensure the safety of their damage-dealing compatriots. Healers and Buffers use the time between pulls to practice their arts.

While this may seem tedious, pulling ensures that only a limited number of creatures enter combat with the group at a single time. A large group is much more likely to awaken every monster in the cave, but a single individual can attract the attention of a smaller group and draw them to the rest of his party.

Pulling is common in large dungeons where dangerous creatures tend to gang up on parties, such as the train-heavy gnoll dungeon of Blackburrow. Outside of a dungeon, the odds of a large number of creatures ganging up on the party is much smaller. Additionally, there is more room to maneuver outside, so pulling may be unnecessary.

Pulling is less common in Star Wars Galaxies, which has alleviated the need for these tactics. Most hunting parties become targets of an entire enemy group by attacking only one creature of that group. Crowd control is the key to a successful hunt.

Have the group leader designate a primary target. Use the most powerful hunters to take out this target as quickly as possible. In the meantime, have the rest of the group perform disorientation effects, knockdowns, and fear-attacks against other enemies. Most Galaxies hunting groups have a Doctor or Medic with them. To keep the others players alive, have the doctor monitor their HAM bars. Droids with the proper Stimpack Dispensation Module can hold stimpacks, which can ease the load of your medics.

On the Hunt

Now that you're in the field and in the thick of things, stay flexible but on task. If you're not the leader, your primary objective is to keep up with the group. If you fall behind, you jeopardize the group by your absence—and by the fact that the group might have to come save you from a respawn.

Congratulate the other folks in your group for finding good loot and for gaining levels. Don't complain if someone found a better item than you did just by the luck of the draw. If you really are interested, offer to trade them something for it. Stay on the lookout for monsters that might wander in during combat. Players traditionally announce additional monsters by saying "Add!" or "Inc!" for "incoming."

Distributing Loot Equitably

You'll soon start earning loot, which is one of the points of a group in the first place. Most games have specific styles of group looting mechanisms in place. Before you kill a single monster, it's crucial to decide which style to use. Looting is the single most stressful group activity.

If you don't have the option to limit the ways in which people can loot corpses, a round-robin approach is probably the fairest way. If you have a frequent group of players, designating one player as the official looter might work best. At the end of your hunting session, the looter can hand out items to players who are interested in them. Split looted coin evenly among the party members; most games do this automatically or at least give you the option.

Working with Other Groups

Once you've reached your destination, you may have to deal with camping. When a creature spawns infrequently, and players have a high interest in killing it, groups often camp out at the monster's spawn location. Camping is a fact of life in Massively Multiplayer games. Be polite. The group that's waited the longest has the first rights to the monster. Make sure that you and your group members respect the wait the other group has endured.

If possible, offer to help the other group. Many boss-type monsters spawn with attendants, making a difficult fight even harder. If the boss monster is the only creature the groups at the spawn are interested in, offer to take on the attendant spawns while the other group tackles the boss monster. This gives you more experience and less boredom, and the other group may offer to reciprocate.

Your group might complete the initial goal more quickly than you imagined and float another goal as a reason to stay together. Now that you've gone to the trouble of playing together with these people, be open to the possibility of doing something else with them. There are likely to be several options open to you, so state your preference. If you're voted down, decide whether you'd like to assist with the new goal or whether you'd like to move on. Helping out other folks can have a turnabout, though. If the goal has already changed once, it's possible that it may change again to something more to your liking.

Your assistance and friendly behavior may have future payoffs. All modern games have some capacity to designate people as friends. Many people use the friend list as a way to keep track of reliable individuals for grouping. The friend designation is most formal in Final Fantasy XI and requires an okay from both parties to enact. At the same time, FFXI players are very ready to recognize worthwhile group members as friends. It's too useful a technique to pass up.

Taking Your Leave

With your adventure successfully completed, the only thing that remains is to leave the group. If you and your group have decided to divvy up treasure at the end of the session, make sure you get your cut before you take off. You may have picked up an item or two along the journey that another group member might want. Offer to trade, if you like, or just give it away if you're feeling generous. As courteous as you may have been, nothing makes a better impression than philanthropy. Thank your group members for helping you out and then take your leave. Ungroup yourself from the group before you leave the area so that it's clear that you are gone. Some games allow you to gain experience from fights you had no part in, so ungrouping is a courtesy to the other players.

The most important part of grouping is courtesy. Helping out other folks in the interesting and dangerous world you inhabit will ensure that there are people around in the future to watch your back. What else is a group for?

Catch Half-Life FPS Cheaters Redhanded
Identify, catch, and call out people who cheat in certain online FPS games.

The developers of FPS titles such as Half-Life are making it easier and easier for users to create modifications. This increases the longevity and enjoyment of the games, but it also puts power in the hands of the clients. Giving up some control means that users can surprise you, but it also makes it much easier for people to create cheats. Cheaters are almost inevitable and commonly difficult to identify.

How can you recognize a cheater in, say, Counter-Strike, and what can you do about it?

Identifying Cheats

To understand the problem, you first need to understand what kind of things cheaters can do. One of the best places to find out about anticheating software is at the Counter Hack site (*http://www.counter-hack.net/content.php?page=typesofhacks*), which lists hacks common to games. They even go one step further and specifically describe Half-Life-specific hacks (*http://www.counter-hack.net/content.php?page=halflife*), as seen in Figure 3-1.

Here are some of the most common hacks:

Aimbot
> This type of cheat locks the cheater's crosshair onto other characters. It is commonly configurable so that players can aim automatically at

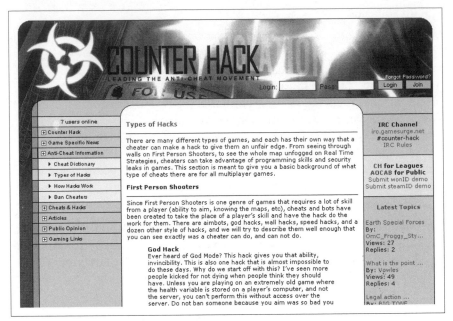

Figure 3-1. The magisterial Counter Hack site

different parts of their targets. In some instances, players may also use auto-shoot in conjunction with auto-aim to fire without having to click the mouse button.

Early Half-Life aimbot hacks worked by making the computer fire at certain onscreen colors, requiring cheaters to change their character model colors to very bright hues. This method saw swift defeat, both by anticheat programs and by enterprising anticheaters running around the level daubing the walls with colored stencils. If you saw another player firing uncontrollably at your bright red wall stencil instead of at your character, you knew he was cheating.

Wallhack

This cheat allows the cheater to view other players through walls, usually by making the walls partially translucent, not transparent, often by messing with the graphics drivers. (With transparent walls, you'd continually run into invisible barriers.) Wallhacks can be quite confusing to play, but having the equivalent of X-ray vision can give cheaters quite an advantage.

Radar and Map ESP

When you play Counter-Strike, your radar normally shows dots for your teammates and various other gameplay objects you're allowed to monitor. Some hacks add your enemies to the radar readout, making it trivial to track down your opponents. In a similar vein, people have managed to put a friend-and-foe mini-map in the corner of the screen in some later versions of Counter-Strike.

Modified player skins

Most players consider bright skins (either retextured or full-brightness character models) a cheat. Basically, this technique colors the character textures of other players so that they stand out from the background more. It's much easier to find a high-contrast clown hiding in the shadows.

Stopping Cheaters with Anticheat Software

There are a variety of installable anticheating software mods for Half-Life, all of which have good and bad facets. Let's check them out.

Cheating-Death. There's an excellent explanation of "why Cheating-Death is different" on its official web page (*http://www.unitedadmins.com/cdeath. php*). In short:

> The main difference between Cheating-Death (C-D) and the other anti-cheating packages available is that it does not have cheat specific detection methods. Instead, it tries to make cheats less effective, and to prevent cheats from getting information. In most cases this leads to cheats simply not working.

Cheating-Death is particularly good because it works from both the client and server side. Servers have the option of requiring clients to run the C-D client software or allowing clients to run without it while marking them as less trustworthy. This flexibility, combined with regular and excellent updates, make Cheating-Death the third-party anticheat utility of choice at the time of writing.

HLGuard. HLGuard (*http://www.unitedadmins.com/hlguard.php*) was once the best anticheat utility around. It's still one of the few Half-Life tools with current updates. The downloadable server-only version (*http://www. unitedadmins.com/hlguard-dl.php*) can't do some of the clever stuff Cheating-Death can, such as preventing cheating or incompatible players from ever joining the server in the first place, but it does stop some of the most obvious wallhacks, aimbots, and other hacks.

There's also an excellent FAQ (*http://docs.unitedadmins.com/hlguard/en/*) for the title, which explains some of the neater features, including a Filescan feature to detect modified game files and some good aimbot detection. The latter is especially tricky; like many other systems, it calculates the accuracy of any given player and flags warnings and triggers actions (such as bans) if that player's aiming skills obviously exceed human capabilities.

Valve Anticheating System (VAC). Because Half-Life, Counter-Strike, and other Valve products are gradually transitioning over to a more secure framework on their Steam content delivery system, it's natural that Half-Life creators Valve would eventually make their own in-house anticheat system. This has the distinct advantages of having input from the creators of the game and more concrete punishments for the bad guys, as you can see by the message if you join a VAC-enabled server over Steam:

> You are joining a server that implements Valve's anti-cheat system (VAC). Please note that the use of Cheats is a violation of your End User License Agreement for the software and/or your Steam Subscriber Agreement.
>
> If Valve or the game host detects your use of Cheats on an VAC-enabled server, your Steam Subscription and/or your product key for the software will be banned from playing on VAC-enabled servers for one (1) year.

On the other hand, it's hard to learn about the actual anticheat mechanisms and which cheats VAC detects, because the update information usually reads "New detections and detection strategies." That's very nonspecific when compared to the other, more transparent anticheat systems. On the other hand, while Cheating-Death is more watertight than VAC, it looks like VAC is catching up.

There's no separate download location for updates to VAC. Steam automatically pushes down the latest fixes and patches automatically. Valve also promises VAC functionality for the forthcoming (at press time) Counter-Strike: Steam, hopefully meaning many more months and years of no cheating.

Identifying Cheaters by Behavior Alone

Suppose you can't rely on technology because you're playing on a server without anticheat devices installed, or you're just obtuse and don't want to use any of the anticheating tools mentioned earlier. Identifying a cheater can be difficult or even impossible. Competitive players are often so good at FPS games that they play better than people who cheat!

Fortunately, there are behaviors that may lead you to suspect that someone isn't relying on skill alone.

Spotting a wallhack cheater. For example, a good player will know exactly where you are based on the sounds you make throughout the level. Based on those sounds, he can accurately predict your next move. However, this is also characteristic of someone using a wallhack, so what can you do?

For one, someone using a wallhack will spend a lot of time looking at otherwise uninteresting walls. Seeing someone strafing with his face up against a building, for example, should raise your warning flag. In a similar vein, if you see someone make good strategic judgments without ever looking into open space to get his bearings, he may already see open spaces—through the walls!

Spotting an aimbot cheater. It's difficult, but not impossible to identify someone using an auto-aim cheat. Such a player will usually make a series of extremely quick, unfluid movements, too precise or odd to come from a human hand on a mouse or trackball. You may also see him lock onto other characters without first looking in the appropriate direction.

These cheats are never completely accurate, can be ineffective in laggy situations, and may not function well with projectile weapons, so pay attention to a suspect's choice of weapon. The best weapons for auto-aim use superswift bullets that reach the target immediately.

> Auto-aiming is less effective with weapons that use projectiles because it takes too long for the projectile to reach the target, which often moves in the meantime.

Identifying Other Cheats

Unfortunately, from sight and play experience alone, it's almost impossible to identify someone using bright skins, radar, map ESP, or similar hacks. (You can, at least, identify the very simple speed hacks; if someone's running much faster than normal, he's probably cheating.)

In these situations, because cheating can be very subtle, you can definitely identify only flagrantly obvious cheaters. The player will display similar characteristics to the very best conventional players. Fortunately, software anticheating measures can stop this little blighter from ever entering your Half-Life server in the first place.

Playing with Hardware
Hacks 35–46

The world of gaming doesn't end when you stop looking at pixels.

Like many other hobbies (such as miniature gaming, car modding, and model trains), half of the fun is building new things or adapting old things in new ways. Perhaps you have a beloved controller that doesn't quite connect to your new system or you want to have the coolest, quietest PC at the LAN party. You can have game-related fun while getting your hands dirty with hardware, wires, and even a soldering iron or two.

Maybe you'd rather make your gaming experience more immersive by improving your video or audio setup. There are plenty of ways to combine your home-theater setup with your game playing. Here are a few ideas to keep you involved while you're waiting for the next killer game to come out.

HACK #35   Build a Quiet, Killer Gaming Rig
Make your game worlds more immersive by quieting the real world.

The highest-end monster PC is likely a noisy tower with fans and hard drives spinning away. That may be fine when you're blasting hordes of alien zombies to a heavy metal soundtrack, but a 10,000-rpm drive spinning up at the wrong time can ruin the suspense of sneaking around in the dark. Even with 1,000 watts of power driving your speakers, sometimes nothing beats the sound of silence.

A quiet, distraction-free environment can make your game experience more immersive. Fortunately, you can modify your current rig to run more quietly. The same tips apply if you're building a new PC. Here's how to assess where you stand now and plan to make your computer quieter.

Understanding Noise

Understanding how to attack your computer's noise problem is closely related to how audio compression algorithms (such as the one in MP3s) work. Your brain will hear only the loudest noise at any given time; you won't hear any quieter noises. In order to compress sound, audio engineers drop the quieter information because listeners won't hear it. When you attempt to quiet your computers, this phenomenon applies in reverse. Removing one loud noise often unmasks another noise beneath the sound threshold of the first one.

Quieting your computer as much as possible is often a matter of trial and error. It might take several attempts to reach an acceptable noise level. To identify your biggest problem areas, start by purchasing an inexpensive Radio Shack SPL (sound pressure level) meter.

Using an SPL meter. Set the meter to C weighting and the response time to "slow." Set the SPL meter on your work area a couple of feet away from the computer, and point the business end right at your rig. Now fire up your computer and take readings. You can unplug your various components to see which are the biggest offenders and diagnose what to change first. It's also satisfying to take before and after volume readings.

In fact, there are people who actually make a hobby out of getting the quietest PC possible. Check out the SilentPC Review forums (*http://forums. silentpcreview.com/*).

Choosing Soundproof and Quiet Components

If you're building a computer from scratch, start with an aluminum case. This material will act as its own heat sink, naturally reducing the internal temperature. A well-designed steel case can also be cool, and the denser material will dampen sounds from spinning components. Make sure to buy a solid case, because thin walls vibrate more easily.

Next, do your homework: pick your components based on reseller dB ratings, if possible. Be aware that there is no set standard for how to measure component noise. Manufacturers often reengineer their specs in order to make the product look better on paper and generate more sales, so use your common sense, and buy from trusted manufacturers.

Second, your case should contain some noise-absorbing material to soak up internal fan noise. The goal here is to limit noises of high frequencies. To do that, use a porous, noninsulating foam material. Any soft, pliable packing foam will do the trick, but you probably need more than what came packed around your motherboard. Muffled Computing (check out *http://www. muffledcomputing.com/*) sells a hybrid porous/semiporous foam material with a sticky backing on one side (*http://www.muffledcomputing.com/foam. html*). This Whispermat is the best white-noise-deadening foam on the market today. It comes in half- and 1-inch thicknesses on 12-inch square sheets. You'll probably need two or three sheets to do your entire case.

> Some people claim some success using standard car-audio sound-deadening material (like Dynamat) inside their computer case. Dynamat is a heavy, nonporous material used for soaking up low-frequency noise—ideal for use in automobiles. It also does a fantastic job of insulating your car from outside heat due to its high density.
>
> However, these aren't desirable properties for computer-case soundproofing.

Sound will leak out of any available space in the computer case, including unused drive bays, card slots, and venting—anywhere. Try to cover every space inside the case without a vent or fan, especially around the GPU and CPU. This will absorb most of the sound that bounces around the case before it can escape out the fan or vent holes. Most cases have vents intended to pull air across your hard drives. Be careful not to cover those vents unless you use auxiliary hard-drive cooling fans.

If you are building a new rig or upgrading your motherboard, consider a board with a fanless chipset. If your board has a fan, you can add an after-market heatsink with little risk of malfunction as long as you have adequate airflow.

Finally, before you start replacing noisy components, think about your wire management. Even floppy-disk drives come with rounded cables these days, but you can go one step further; use plastic wire wraps to group and tuck away your cables as much as possible, making an unobstructed path for air to stream through the computer.

Reducing Component Noise

Now that you have reduced case noise, it's time to concentrate on lowering component noise. Here are the most common noisy components, in order of loudest first.

Power supply unit. The power-hungry components of an elite gamer require more juice than a normal computer user needs. Heavy power supply units (PSUs) can be extremely noisy, however. The biggest mistake you can make is to buy an overpowered PSU. Monster 500+watt power supplies are notoriously noisy, and unnecessary for most of us.

If you're building your own rig, determine your maximum power needs before springing for an oversized power supply. There is quite a lot of "spec engineering" when it comes to PSUs, so stick to a good brand like Antec or Enermax. One tried-and-true (if unscientific) method is to buy the heaviest PSU available in the wattage category. This usually guarantees quality components and good heatsinks in your new PSU.

If you have a bigger budget when building a computer or are ready to upgrade your PSU, several manufacturers offer quiet PSUs, including the excellent Zalman (*http://www.zalman.co.kr/english/product/cnpsma.htm*) and Nexus (*http://www.nexustek.nl/index_headquarters.html*) lines. These power supplies have temperature-regulated fan speeds and often have aluminum housings that draw away heat.

Completely solid-state and dead silent, fanless PSUs have started to enter the market. These types of power supplies will work well with carefully conceived cooling strategies; unlike most PSUs, they contain no fans themselves to provide heat exhaustion from the computer case. They're also reliable only in a low-power computing environment, making them unsuitable for a high-power gaming computer. Stay away from them for now.

Finally, if a brand new PSU isn't in the budget, consider an inexpensive Fan Muffler (*http://www.muffledcomputing.com/mufflers.html*), also from Muffled Computing. Their universal ATX PSU fan muffler attaches to the back of your case and routes the exhaust through a noise-absorbing channel. For under $30, you can even make a mammoth 550W PSU livable. Download the PDF template to see if your case will accept a muffler. They also make mufflers for your auxiliary and front fans. They are extremely well-made, are surprisingly effective, and come in three different colors.

CPU fan. It's often a toss-up between your CPU fan and your PSU cooler in regards to which one is the loudest. After replacing just one, you may often find that the other is nearly as loud. If you are serious about quieting your computer, consider replacing the PSU and the CPU fan at the same time to improve your overall noise level dramatically.

Keep in mind that a modern computer will regulate the rpm of your CPU fan automatically, besides letting you control your own parameters through software, so a larger heatsink combined with a quieter fan is extremely effective at limiting noise. I really like the Zalman CNPS7000 Cu "flower" CPU cooler (*http://www.zalman.co.kr/english/product/cnps7000cu.htm*). It's quite large and won't fit on every motherboard, so check your case dimensions first.

GPU fan. Some of the more recent high-end video cards are infamously loud, so much so that they might even make the top of your noise list. This will also happen after you've quieted your CPU fan and PSU. Several manufacturers make quieter graphics-processing-unit (GPU) fans and even giant heatsinks that eliminate the need for a fan on your GPU altogether. You can also often buy third-party video cards that incorporate these solutions out of the box, if you want to avoid a complicated installation.

A GPU cooler is easily the most intricate of any of the recommended mods on this list, so a prebuilt solution is a great idea. Keep in mind that these heatsinks often take up an additional PCI slot next to your AGP input; budget some room.

Case fans. Extreme gaming rigs can't survive on only one exhaust fan; your machine needs a clear airflow path for best performance. Matching the cubic-feet-per-minute rating of your intake to your exhaust fans is also a good idea, because it will make your overall cooling strategy as efficient as possible. Start with fans that spin at or below 2,500 rpm and look for the lowest dB rating you can find. Newer fans have a three-wire connector that will allow modern motherboards to self-regulate all the case fans according to internal temperature. Even without this type of motherboard, you might still want to purchase the three-wire units; you can always throw an add-on fan controller into an unused drive bay. These controllers can be fully automatic, with programmable modes that spin your fans at a certain speed when the interior of your case reaches a preset temperature. Some also have manual dial controls to set the fan speed, which is also quite effective.

Hard drives. If your loudest component is your hard-disk drive, this can be good or bad news. If you have 10,000-rpm RAID arrays, invest in an auxiliary hard-drive cooling fan that incorporates a noise-dampening mounting solution as well and surround the drives with noise-absorbing foam. There are also fanless heat pipe coolers on the market that will silently help your HDD keep a stable temperature. If you have an especially noisy HDD array, consider a separate enclosure and tossing the whole thing in the closet—just the drive enclosure, not your high-end gaming PC.

If you're on the market for a new hard drive, you may have a tough time finding a dB rating on the spec sheet, but there are a couple of guidelines you can go by. As common sense dictates, a faster-spinning hard drive will make more noise than a slower one, and larger hard drives (3.5 inches) are noisier than smaller (2.5 inches) ones.

Start with a 5,400-rpm hard drive if you're building a second computer for a quiet environment, such as a bedroom. These drives are also great for infrequently accessed deep storage archives on your main rig. If you have a noisy drive that you use only for storage, schedule it to shut down after a period of inactivity. See the Power Options menu on your Control Panel if you run Windows, for example.

Some of the newest drives on the market come with very quiet fluid dynamic bearings. These drives typically have high-performance platters that spin at 10,000 and 15,000 rpm, but we'll probably see this technology move to slower drives. If you have a drive with fluid bearings, expect a volume decrease of 4 dB over conventional bearing drives of similar speed. Drives with fluid bearings that run at 15,000 rpm are often quieter than some drives with standard bearings spinning at 7,200 rpm.

See Also

- Choosing the Right Power Supply (*http://www.firingsquad.com/guides/power_supply/default.asp*)
- Muffled Computing (*http://www.muffledcomputing.com/*)
- Zalman Quiet Computing Products (*http://www.zalman.co.kr/english/product/cnpsma.htm*)

Find and Configure the Best FPS Peripherals
Stop blaming your poor first-person shooter performance on the wrong tools!

While it's important to have actual first-person-shooter (FPS) skills to do well in them, when it comes to how you control your onscreen avatar, your weapon of choice also makes a big difference. Not only do professional FPS gamers have certain choices for their mice and keyboards, careful configuration can make a massive difference to how well you do in the heat of a frantic online fragfest.

Mousin' Around

The mouse is the single most important device for a committed FPS gamer. There's one obvious selection criterion to start with: does your mouse have a ball in it, as did all mice of old? If you still use a standard ball mouse, invest in an optical mouse of any kind. These are leaps ahead in accuracy from ball-based mice, which tend to skip, need frequent cleanings, and are not as sensitive as optical mice. Even a basic optical mouse is a major improvement.

Microsoft's Intellimouse and Logitech's Optical Mouse are generally considered among the leaders in the market and are relatively inexpensive to boot. However, there are many types of optical mice from a variety of different manufacturers. They often boast fancy features such as dual optical sensors or a variety of extra buttons.

Microsoft's multidirectional mouse wheel (which moves from side to side as well as up and down) may be excellent for some desktop use but can be annoyingly imprecise with FPS titles. It's easy to trigger inadvertently the sideways motion while moving up and down on the wheel. Even if you don't have mappings for the side-to-side motions, they can still put off the smoothness of your up-down mouse wheel spinnin'.

On the top end, the Razer Boomslang, a semimythical, fairly expensive mouse that many hardcore gamers swear by, is a famous example of a gaming-specific mouse. However, some feel these fancy-featured mice make relatively little difference when playing FPS games because the difference in quality of input from different optical sensors is negligible, and the extra buttons can be awkward. Your mileage, of course, may vary.

Better players almost always use mice with connected wires. For one thing, older wireless mice may have a slight amount of lag or may lose signal strength irregularly. This can be fatal.

Any additional buttons besides the basic right and left normally aren't useful, but they may be convenient to activate extra features, such as voice communication. In general, a mouse with extra buttons is no better than one without. The only extra button you really need is a wheel, commonly used for switching weapons.

A trackball mouse is another option, but I don't advocate it. It's too difficult to control your crosshair effectively. Similarly, professional gamers almost universally testify that joysticks or other controllers are ineffective with shooters. That said, if you do choose to use a trackball, much of the mousing information available here still applies.

Mouse configuration. Mouse configuration may be even more important than your choice of mouse. When configuring your mouse, pay the closest attention to its sensitivity. You want a level of sensitivity that's quick enough to allow you to turn around quickly yet slow enough to aid in precise aiming. If you can't turn a full 180 degrees easily in one motion, increase your sensitivity. If you find it difficult to aim, lower your sensitivity. Play around until it feels right.

Inverting the mouse movements is also an option. If inverted movements feel natural to you, do it.

Mouse pads can also be important, though you can certainly choose to use none at all. Everglide, Ratpadz, Ice Mat, and Func Industries all sell mouse pads designed specifically for FPS games. Some would argue that these aren't any better or any worse than a basic cloth mouse pad or even a piece of cardboard. As long as your mouse pad isn't too small, it will work fine.

Keyboardin' Around

There are two aspects to consider when it comes to keyboards and FPS titles: type and configuration.

When it comes to the type of keyboard, your current keyboard is probably perfectly adequate for just about every FPS game imaginable. The most basic keyboard will work just as well as the most extravagant. Any buttons other than the basics are unnecessary, and you likely won't use them for playing games. However, you should concern yourself with comfort. A hand rest is usually a good idea. Better yet, use an ergonomic split keyboard. The last thing you want is a sore wrist after playing games for a hour.

Configuration is much more complicated. If you're anything like me, you've found assigning the 30+ different keys very intimidating. My best approach is to assign keys based on a common configuration across every FPS I play, making exceptions only for unique functions. This ensures that you won't need to remember a different arrangement for each game.

The most common layout is the WASD arrangement. W moves your character forward, and S moves backwards. A strafes left, and D strafes your character right. The spacebar most commonly jumps, and the Shift or Ctrl keys crouch. The number keys work well for selecting weapons, but advanced players often use the mouse for this task. The keys surrounding WASD control each game's unique functions. For example, the R key commonly reloads weapons in games that require it.

With this configuration, you'll need to remember very few keys from game to game, and you'll have the optimal settings by default. When you first start a new game, make sure it uses the standard WASD setup, and go from there.

The only problem arises for gamers who mouse with their left hands. As a left-hander, you need a configuration based on the opposite side of the keyboard, unless you have a desk that's big enough to allow you to shift your keyboard further to the right. Otherwise, you'll need to set up your keys for every game based on the right side of the keyboard. The arrow keys often work well.

Monitorin' Around

Gamers ignore their monitor configurations all too often. This includes the brightness, refresh rate, and resolution settings. A higher-than-normal brightness setting can aid in games that have dark scenes and dark characters—making it easier to see the characters. However, a normal mid-level brightness setting is often best.

Many web sites can help you find the optimal settings. Use your preferred search engine to search for something like `correct monitor brightness` to find a web site with meters to test with. Also make sure that your refresh rate is the highest supported by your monitor and video card. By going to Display Properties → Settings → Advanced → Monitor → Screen refresh rate, you can adjust the setting.

Resolution is often a controversial issue among gamers. Some people believe a lower resolution makes the characters larger, but this simply isn't true. You will want a resolution that is high (1024×768 or higher) but doesn't cause your frame rate to dip too far (below 60).

HACK #37 Adapt Old Video Game Controllers to the PC

Want to play your favorite PC game with your favorite console joypad? No problem.

If you enjoy playing arcade-style games on your PC, you may have found that they benefit immensely from a joypad. (Trust me, they do.) However, although you can buy PC joypads that will do the trick, you probably already have a perfectly good Xbox or PlayStation controller. Thanks to the wonders of hacking, you can adapt that console controller to work on your home computer. This is great for console ports, MAME, other emulated titles, and your wallet.

The Easy Way: Buying Adapters

Before hacking any hardware, consider that you can buy several third-party USB adapters, particularly for PlayStation joypads, but also for the Xbox and more exotic consoles. However, you may not be able to use your choice of homebrew drivers for this equipment. Sometimes, the hardware adapter is a little bit proprietary, so you'll have to use the manufacturer's drivers or write your own. On the plus side, the hardware is already built.

Be aware that several available PlayStation adapters have a few compatibility problems. They do complicated things, and most adapters have only Windows drivers. As well, some commercial USB adapters will not work properly with Dance Dance Revolution pads, if you want to play DDR or

DDR clones such as Stepmania on your PC. The parallel port adapter we'll build *does* work in concert with the DirectPad drivers—another reason to hack it yourself. Junta's DDR modding site (*http://junta.cromas.net/adapters. html*) has a good list of DDR adapter problems.

In general, you should be perfectly safe buying an Xbox-to-USB converter, because the Xbox controller is already a USB device. All the converter does is change the gender of the adapter. Of course, this makes it much easier to make your own.

Beyond these two popular classes, you can buy several more exotic prebuilt adapters, converting everything from the NES through the Neo Geo controllers to your PC. Start by looking at Smartjoy.com (*http://www.smartjoy.com/*), now a division of Hong Kong retailer Lik Sang. The site has some commercial impetus that could skew things, but it still seems good at comparing a large range of adapters.

 If you're feeling really lazy, look for Sega's new PC USB version of the classic Sega Saturn. There's no need to do any hacking at all; just buy it and plug it in.

The Hard Way: Building an Xbox-to-PC Adapter

You'll need several items for this hack:

- A soldering iron to reconnect the wires
- Electrical tape to make sure you don't short out anything along the way
- A USB-to-USB cable, available pretty much everywhere
- An Xbox breakaway cable, easily found online from eBay or many third-party retailers

With the breakaway cable, you can cut and snip without affecting your actual joypad. Naturally, if you're feeling confident and don't want to play your Xbox controller on the Xbox anymore, you can skip this piece.

Cut the breakaway cable (the half of the Xbox controller cable closest to the console itself) either just before or just after the nodule that appears halfway down its length. Then strip the sheathing so you can see the five colored wires. Strip all of the wires (red, white, green, and black) *except* the yellow wire.

Now do the same with the USB cable, cutting it near one end and stripping the sheathing to expose the colored wires (red, white, green, and black). Now solder together the wires of the same color on the two cables. When you finish each individual solder, wrap a small amount of electrical tape around each connection to prevent it from touching other soldered wires and shorting out.

Finally, when you're done, tape everything shut with electrical tape, plug the USB cable into your PC, and turn on your PC. If you're using Windows, use the XBCD drivers (*http://redcl0ud.hostrocket.com/xbcd.html*) to make analog joysticks, the directional pad, and all 12 buttons work in PC games. The Mac (*http://homepage.mac.com/walisser/xboxhiddriver/*) and Linux drivers, at least, as part of the Xbox Linux project (*http://cvs.sourceforge.net/viewcvs. py/xbox-linux/kernel/drivers/usb/*), are at various stages of construction, but all of them basically work.

The Hardest Way: Building a PlayStation-to-PC Adapter

The PlayStation adapter is significantly more complicated but still fairly workable. The easiest approach involves using the parallel port to plug your adapted PSX controller into the PC. It requires more advanced use of a multimeter and diodes, as Figure 4-1 shows.

You'll need:

- A soldering iron
- A multimeter
- A male DB-25 connector
- A PlayStation extension cable, easily found online or at your local store
- Five (5) diodes of type 1N914 or 1N4148
- A small piece of extra bare wire, an inch or so long

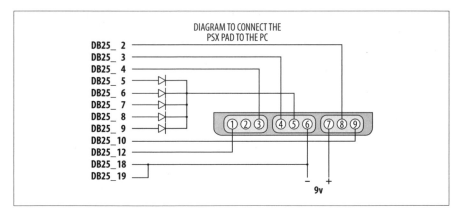

Figure 4-1. Pin map for the PS2 controller

First, cut one end of the PlayStation extension cable, and strip the sheathing, exposing the wires in a similar way to the Xbox adapter. This time, you'll see one wire without any insulation on it at all. Ignore it. If the controller is Dual Shock–compatible, you'll see eight other wires. Otherwise, you'll see seven.

Unfortunately, there's no easy way to know which wire connects to which connection on the other end of the extension cable, so grab the multimeter. Put one contact in the first hole of the PSX connector and keep testing the wires until you have a positive result. Write down the hole and the color. Repeat for each of the PSX connector holes.

Now take the diodes and cut short (half an inch or less) the end furthest away from the marked ring on the diode. Solder these diodes to holes 5, 6, 7, 8, and 9 (the top center holes) of the DB-25 parallel connector, with the short end closest to the connector itself.

Finally, solder the PSX connector's wires onto the DB-25 connector in the order shown in Figure 4-2. Connect hole 5 on the female PSX connector to all five diodes, using the extra piece of wire.

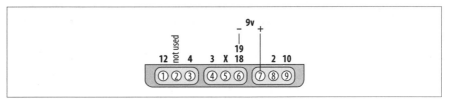

Figure 4-2. DB-25-to-PSX controller schematic

Finally, close the DB-25 connector and plug it into your PC's parallel port. Several software drivers will work with your adapted PlayStation joypad, but DirectPad Pro (http://www.aldostools.com/dpad.html) is one of the best, because it also supports SNES, Sega Genesis, and other console joypads. PSXPad (http://www.psxpad.com/index_e.php) also comes highly recommended and supports a multitude of consoles.

HACK #38 Choose the Right Audio/Video Receiver

Treat your ears to some candy too.

There is more than meets the eye when it comes to coaxing the best possible performance out of your gaming console and your audio/video system. All three of the current crop of consoles can produce incredibly sharp and detailed video and excellent surround sound, but they all do it in different ways.

The recent revolution in home theater affordability has made it possible to put together a great setup on even the most modest of budgets. Having a home theater provides a great venue for viewing DVDs and digital television at home as well as an awesome gaming experience.

Unlike the PC-gaming world, console games use the same audio formats as the movie industry. Therefore, once you've put together a killer audio setup for your consoles, you will have simultaneously assembled an awesome home theater. How do you choose the right equipment? First, you have to know what the equipment can and cannot do.

Understanding Audio Processing

All of the home surround-sound formats in use today have direct roots in the motion picture industry. This genealogy traces back to the '70s when theaters equipped themselves with Dolby Labs's emerging audio technology to play *Star Wars*. Due to its revelatory effect on moviegoers, George Lucas's 1977 hit became the progenitor of a common era of movies offered in Dolby Surround Sound.

At the time of *Star Wars*, surround processing was in its infancy. Thanks to the digital era, surround sound has become exponentially more powerful and infinitely more immersive than the surround systems that captivated those audiences years ago. Almost more incredibly, these powerful and complex systems are available for our homes; it's quite feasible to equal or exceed the experience of the cinema without breaking the bank.

Today's systems take advantage of discrete audio technology. Each speaker has a specific input channel. In a typical six-channel system, movie and game producers can place sound exactly where they wish.

The brain is an amazing machine. By merely listening, you can determine distance, direction, speed, and location of an audible object, in addition to sensing the overall environment. For example, it's possible to tell whether you are in a cathedral or inside a coffin from audio cues alone. When you combine what you hear around you with what you see onscreen, the synergistic effect is extremely powerful. Game and movie producers have become experts at providing audiences with this potent combination, but you can only achieve this with a properly set up system.

Choosing a Home A/V Receiver

The most important part of your gaming A/V system is the home theater receiver. As your rig becomes more and more elaborate, you might jockey between three or more consoles, a DVD player, and satellite or cable input, as well as any other components that you add later. A good receiver will allow you to switch between sources—provided it has the proper audio and video inputs. The receiver also decodes incoming digital surround information and powers all your speakers.

Choosing the right receiver can be tricky. Surround formats are constantly changing, to say nothing of the ever growing complexity of high-end video connections ("Tune Console Video Output" [Hack #41]). That said, it is very tempting to buy a receiver based on video-switching capabilities alone, while ignoring audio properties. This can be a very expensive game to play; the biggest mistake you can make is purchasing a receiver with an underpowered amplifier.

Unlike years ago, all the channels in modern Dolby Digital home theater systems can now handle a full-range signal. This means that if your speakers are up to it, the receiver will send them a full bass signal, two or three octaves below what they might receive from an older Dolby Pro-Logic system.

Modern movies and games often tell your receiver to play full-range signals on all speakers at once. This places an unbelievable load on your amplifier. If your amp is not up to the task, it will give up, sending out a truncated signal. This type of waveform is extremely dangerous and will quickly deteriorate your speakers by forcing them to play a sharp-cornered signal that a weak amp produces. This is also called *clipping*. Under heavy loads, some receivers may shut down from excess heat. To help prevent this, never block the top of your receiver and be sure to give it adequate ventilation. Even if your amp never grows hot enough to shut down, you will increase its life greatly by giving it room to breathe.

Signs of quality components. The size and type of power supply is also vitally important. The power supply links your amplifier to the AC from the wall plug, so it is a limiting factor of how much power your amp can deliver to your speakers. The weight of the receiver says a lot about the quality of the power supply because it is by far the heaviest component; quality components tend to weigh more than their cheaper counterparts.

If you can afford it, buy a toroidal power supply. This type of construction provides higher efficiency, greater power delivery, and cooler operation. It also provides much more juice than a standard rectangular "EI core" supply. You can recognize a toroidal power supply by its doughnut-shaped core. EI core supplies are square.

Check that your prospective purchase has a glass-epoxy main circuit board. You can tell a glass-epoxy board by its green color. Brown boards are made of pressed paper and are very susceptible to solder joint failure due to expansion and contraction as the board heats and cools. Glass-epoxy boards are much more durable and withstand extreme heat without deforming. A receiver with a glass-epoxy board will last longer; this is generally a hall-mark of quality construction found on higher-end receivers.

Another indication of a quality rig is a five-way binding post for connecting speaker wires. This is a large knurled knob that allows you to connect spade lugs, banana connectors, and even bare wires. This is the best kind of terminal to have because it is very versatile; it's often present on high-quality speakers. Spring tab terminals are the worst because they offer a tiny connection surface area and no alternative to the very small pin-connectors only they support. Worse still, it takes very little movement to knock pin connectors out of the terminal because the small springs that hold them in place weaken over time. Avoid receivers with spring tab terminals; they often have poorly conceived overall designs.

Audio power consideration. One of the lesser-known evils in home theater amplifiers is dynamic compression, i.e., when your equipment electronically limits the maximum output of the amplifier. You'll often find this in the convenient and inexpensive home-theater-in-a-box (HTIB) systems. Since the manufacturer sells you a receiver and speakers in a single package, they know precisely the limitations of the system, which allows them to cap the volume at a set point. While this prevents your speakers from clipping, preserving their health and longevity, this seriously limits the capability of a system to play at a realistic volume for many rooms. This is the biggest drawback of the HTIB system. Always test a prospective purchase and listen for punchiness in the bass and clarity in the dialogue during a loud scene. Weak amps will show their true colors here, and you will find it hard to understand what is going on in busy, loud sequences.

A powerful amplifier will grab your speakers and tell them what to do. It is always better to have too much power than too little. Speakers often have power ratings and general recommendations for amplifier strength, though they usually focus more on the minimum end of the scale. If your amplifier is much more powerful than the recommended rating on your speaker, don't worry; it will provide your speakers with a nice clean signal at all times. Obviously, there are limits, but you will wreck 100 speakers with too little power before you break one with too much.

Audio/video switching. Finally, you may not have to use an A/V receiver for audio and video switching. Modern televisions, especially HDTV models, have abundant audio and video inputs that allow you to switch between multiple sources using the television itself.

You can still send the audio signal to a home A/V receiver via the audio output jacks. Many TVs have two sets of audio out jacks: one fixed-volume and one variable. The fixed-volume jacks work for using an amplifier or receiver and using the volume control on those instead. This is a great way to use an older receiver whose only limitation is a lack of video inputs. The receiver controls the volume of the sources. Look for a menu function that disables the TV's speakers.

The variable outputs work best when you have an amplifier with no volume control; the TV's volume control will control the overall volume of the system. You can also use the variable output with an A/V receiver, but having two volume controls is confusing and will likely degrade your signal. Your A/V receiver most likely has a better-quality volume control anyway, so it's better to use it with the variable output on the TV.

Please bear in mind that using the TV as a switching device can quickly lead to a confusing and difficult-to-operate system. Most televisions don't have digital audio inputs, so if you want the benefits of digital audio, you have to send video signals to the TV and audio signals to the A/V receiver. Once the two signals go their separate ways, make two input changes when you change sources: one video input selection on the TV and another on the receiver. Using an A/V receiver that switches both at once will be more convenient for you, but, more importantly, for your family and friends.

Switching Devices

If you have the impression that I'm steering you toward the highest-grade video connection that you and your gear can muster, you're reading this section correctly. Unfortunately, as your system grows, you will soon run afoul of the correct type and amount of inputs. One of the best switching devices that I've come across is the Audio Authority 1154 Component Video switcher (*http://www.audioauthority.com/*). It has four component video inputs and automatically switches to the active source, meaning you can add devices to your system and switch to them transparently with this handy doodad.

Another great device is the Pelican System Selector Pro (*http://www. pelicanperformance.com/*). While not as high-end as the AA 1154 (it doesn't handle 720p/1080i signals), it has eight component video inputs as well as several digital-audio and Ethernet jacks. It's not automatically driven, but it does have a standard component footprint and won't look out of place next to your other gear. If you still own wood-grain-finished consoles, consider the Pelican System Selector Pro.

One hallmark of a great system is when someone besides the owner can operate the system easily. A properly set up A/V receiver will help you achieve that goal.

HACK #39 Place Your Speakers Properly

Make the most of your room by optimizing your speaker locations.

With the right home theater equipment chosen ("Choose the Right Audio/ Video Receiver" [Hack #38]) and in hand, your next step to great console gaming sound and video is connecting everything. This can be quite complex, but following the following guidelines will lead you to success. Here's how to connect your audio equipment for the best possible experience.

Check Your Wiring

When first setting up or reviewing a system, start by checking the wiring. Don't be afraid to disconnect everything. While you're verifying your connections, you have the chance to straighten and untangle your wires. Do it! This is a great time to label all of your system wires. Do it! You can buy small plastic labels, but masking tape works fine. You'll feel better about your system if everything is neat, labeled, and connected correctly.

To avoid confusion and tangles, run your components one at a time. To confirm that you've connected the inputs and outputs in the right direction, consider where the signal flows.

> If you're connecting a Dolby Digital–compatible component to a DD 5.1 receiver, the receiver's display will often indicate the presence of a 5.1 signal. This helps to determine a good connection.

If you're connecting your console or DVD player to a surround receiver with a Toslink or coaxial digital cable, set the device to Dolby Digital mode in its audio menu. (They're usually set to two-channel analog by default.) Some devices also have a PCM mode. Although this is a digital mode, it supports any two channels, so switch to Dolby Digital to send a 5.1 surround signal to your receiver.

Speaker wires are always marked somehow from one side to the next (positive versus negative). Usually, there is a bit of writing or imprinting on one of the two wires. I follow the writing-equals-negative convention, but you can go either way, as long as you're consistent. You must connect the positive lead to the positive side of the speaker and amplifier. Reversing one of these sets produces out-of-phase sounds that will kill your speakers' imaging properties; one speaker's cone will travel outward while the other travels inward.

Test and setup DVDs, such as the Avia Guide to Home Theater (*http://www.ovationmultimedia.com/*), allow you to determine correct wiring through sound checks, but it's easier to do things right the first time.

Speaker Placement

Unlike subwoofers, which play sound frequencies so low that the human ear can't determine the speaker's location, normal full-range audio speakers readily reveal their position. It's important to place your speakers in the right spots and position them correctly.

The main two left and right speakers should form an equilateral triangle with the prime listening position, directly front and center of the screen. In other words, the viewing distance from the speakers to the front row of seats should equal the distance between the speakers. Point your front three speakers directly at this position, as precisely as possible.

Some people use masking tape or even fancy laser devices to make a perfect triangle and correct their aim. You can do well without that work, as long as you understand that you won't have much imaging if your speakers fire directly ahead into your couch.

You can improve the sound of your system quite a lot by reaiming your speakers. This is the best free tweak I can tell you about: do this right away. Align the main speaker's tweeters at the height of your ears in your seated listening position. If your speakers sit on the ground and fire into the furniture, raise them to the correct level. You don't need expensive stands; just be creative and set your speakers at a better height.

This advice also applies to the center-channel speaker. Wherever you have this speaker mounted, point the tweeter directly at your head when you're watching a movie or killing zombies. Use an empty CD case or two AA batteries taped together to tweak the center channel up or down correctly.

Surround sound speaker placement. Surround speakers are more complicated. Many new formats benefit from specialized setups. Some receivers even have provisions for multiple types of speakers that deploy under certain conditions. I'll concentrate on the bread-and-butter Pro Logic and Dolby Digital 5.1 formats used by consoles today. In a perfect world, you'd own dipolar surround speakers, which help create a null area of no sound from the cabinet sides. By design, they fire equally to the front and rear to mimic a movie theater's surround array, creating an enveloping sound field at the rear of the room.

Many people simply use a spare pair of small speakers for surround channel sound. This is fine until you can upgrade to a set designed for home-theater use. These speakers produce unidirectional sound. You can spread this out by reflecting it into a corner first, instead of directly at your head, like the front three. You may like it this way a lot more, especially for movies. This method will create multiple reflections that will approximate a dipolar speaker, but you'll need to experiment a bit with positioning.

If you listen to a lot of multichannel music, you may appreciate a configuration in which you can switch back and forth between reflected and direct-fire modes. If you have the space, place the speakers themselves above and behind the prime listening position by about three feet in each direction. If your couch is right up against the back wall, at least put them to the sides, not in front of the couch. The corner trick applies here as well.

You can reinforce the bass output of your main speakers greatly by putting them very close to the walls or corners of the room, but this placement will affect only one or two frequencies, according to the dimensions of your room. This kind of bass reinforcement sounds muddy if the speakers are too close together and isn't very pleasing to the ear in the long run. Pull each of your front speakers at least a couple of feet out and away from the side and front walls if possible.

Rearrange your room. One of the biggest factors in your sound setup is your room and its orientation. If you can't position your speakers as I've described, consider a room makeover. Some people insist on placing the TV in the corner of the room, which is a nightmare for sound. Aligning the sound along a diagonal axis makes reflection problematic, volume inconsistent (especially bass), and imaging poor overall. Set up the screen and speakers on the square axis of the room—along a main wall instead of the corner—to maximize the potential of the room to reinforce the speakers' loudness and bass.

Reducing Noise

You will find that 60-Hz noise is inherent in and around AC power line cables, so people commonly want to reduce it. Start by routing the AC lines away from the interconnect cables as much as possible. Especially avoid running them parallel to each other! I've found that bunching the AC lines together does cancel out noise somewhat.

Hands down, an incorrectly wired subwoofer is the biggest hum and noise generator. This often comes from a ground potential difference. In short, the subwoofer connects, via a grounded plug, to a different outlet than the main system, and the differences in the ground wire lengths cause a hum. One easy fix is to defeat the subwoofer's ground altogether with a ground cheater plug, though it may leave you open to damage.

If you are experiencing ground hum from another source, such as cable or a satellite connection, try running a separate ground wire to reground coaxial cable lines. The best place to do this is from the splitter, because there are often ground wire connection screws. If this doesn't do it, you will need an isolation transformer (available at Radio Shack). See the Curing Ground Loops site (*http://www.siber-sonic.com/broadcast/GLoopFix.html*) for more information.

Do-It-Yourself Grounding

Attach your ground wire to a cold-water pipe, not a gas pipe. I know it seems elementary, but please, please check thoroughly. Attaching to the house's main ground rod is your best option, because it will eliminate ground potential differences. The outside surface of the fuse box or circuit breaker is also an acceptable bonding point.

If this kind of home wiring sounds complicated and dangerous, that's because it is. If you are not comfortable with this kind of work, you should call in the cavalry: a licensed professional electrician.

Hardware Settings

Now that you have everything wired, placed, and grounded correctly, let's talk about hardware settings. Even though I fly solo on Christmas morning when I put together my little nephew's Lego set, when it comes to my gear, I read the instruction manual to save myself time and frustration. Do the same for your surround processor and TV.

People often overlook the bass management setting in their surround processors. Dolby Digital systems have different speaker settings, including Large and Normal (or Small). This affects the bass output of the receiver and the bass load it places on the speaker. Bass management is smart enough to reroute any bass you take out of the center channel to the main speakers, subwoofer, or both. Remember to set the speaker profile to match your system.

Large center channels are still rare, though growing in popularity, so check your speaker's specs to see if it can handle loads below 80 Hz. If not, set it to Small. The same rule applies to your surround speakers and subwoofer. The sub setting has three modes: off, on, and both. Use "both" when you have large mains that can also handle deep bass and a subwoofer. The low-frequency effects (LFE) channel is the .1 in 5.1; it's automatically routed to wherever you have sent these bass signals. If you don't have a sub, set your subwoofer to "off/no" to route the LFE signals to your mains instead.

Subwoofer settings. The subwoofer has settings on its back panel to help determine its location. First, wire your sub with the line-level or single interconnect (RCA) wire to take advantage of the receiver's digital bass processing. Your sub might also have speaker-level connections—actual connectors for speaker wire inputs and outputs—but this is a very inefficient and costly way to connect your sub.

The sub may also have a "crossover" setting on the back to determine where it starts to reproduce the bass signal. Ideally, you'd like it to pick up where your main speakers leave off. To set this correctly, you'll have to find where the speakers stop producing a strong bass signal. Usually, you can find this in the documentation, but magazine reviews from reputable publishers are also great sources of independent and unbiased information.

If your mains roll off at 40 Hz, set the sub for about 40 Hz. If they're small, play with settings from 80 to 120 Hz. It may sound complicated, but it is really that easy. A little time spent experimenting will pay off in the long run.

Let's talk about placement again. Consider where you set the sub to start making bass. The lower the frequency, the less directional the signal is. Not all subs can go this low; if you have smaller main speakers, you'll need to make more mid-bass at higher frequencies. The higher the frequency, the better your ears can locate it.

If you have your sub set up to complement smaller speakers by producing higher-frequency (mid-bass) sounds, you're better off placing it in the front of the room near the mains to reinforce them. This way, the entire audio spectrum will sound as though it all comes from the main speakers. If your mains don't need reinforcement, and the sub reproduces only the low-frequency channels from about 20 to 80 Hz, feel free to experiment by placing it anywhere in the room. For maximum effect, I recommend first trying a spot closer to your listening position, perhaps just to the side.

Finally, let's discuss level settings. Again, in a perfect world, you'd have five speakers with identical sound properties and matching timbre. When you don't, it's impossible to control the volume precisely because the sound character changes so much from speaker to speaker. One of the best investments you can make is an analog Radio Shack sound pressure level (SPL) meter. This tried-and-true device will help you dial in the perfect volume level for each speaker. Using the test tones from the receiver, you can equalize the speaker volumes with accuracy not possible using your own ears. This makes for smooth transitions around your room and maximizes your immersion as sounds fly from speaker to speaker.

HACK #40 Connect Your Console to Your Home Theater

Put your shiny new stereo system through its paces with a few rounds of zombie-blastin'.

With your AV receiver selected ("Choose the Right Audio/Video Receiver" [Hack #38]) and your speakers connected ("Place Your Speakers Properly" [Hack #39]), it's time to connect your console to your home theater. All three of the current generation of consoles have slightly different approaches, so we'll tackle them one at a time.

Sony PlayStation 2

Sony's PlayStation 2 is not only the most popular console, but also the longest in the tooth of the three major consoles. It offers you the most modern connections, with Firewire, USB, and even component video with the right cables. Unlike the Xbox and GameCube, there is also a Toslink digital output jack conveniently located right on the back of the chassis.

As for the Playstation 2, from the outside, it looks like a sexy and capable temptress. At the end of the day, looks are all it has. In game, the PS2 produces Dolby Digital 5.1 output only in *some* cut-scenes. Unless you have money and digital inputs to spare, it just doesn't make sense to connect your PS2 using the digital output.

If you use your PS2 to play DVD movies, you might have a good argument to hook up that digital output. This is one mode in which you can take advantage of Dolby 5.1 surround because it is on full-time. Sadly, the PS2 is a lackluster video machine and does very little with DVD movies. We'll talk about some alternatives in "Tune Console Video Output" [Hack #41]. Until then, stick with the standard analog RCA audio hookup for 95% of the PS2's full capability.

Microsoft Xbox

The Xbox a versatile piece of kit, all Dolby Digital, all of the time. If you have the goods to support it, a digital connection is essential. You will need to buy some extra equipment, but there's a big payoff.

Of the two available options, I recommend the Microsoft Xbox High Definition AV Pack (*http://www.xbox.com/en-us/hardware/highdefinitionavpack. htm*), which allows you to connect Component Video to your HDTV along with a Toslink hookup for digital audio. The kit doesn't include the digital Toslink cable, so be sure to pick one up. The Monster Cable Products (*http:/ /www.monstercable.com/monstergame/*) Gamelink 400 X video kit and their Lightwave 100 X Toslink audio kit is the high-end approach. If you don't have a high-definition television, Monster also sells an S-Video kit (Gamelink 300 X) that incorporates a connection for the audio kit as well.

After connecting your Xbox to your A/V receiver's digital input, don't forget to activate the Dolby Digital 5.1 output on the settings menu. Once you've done that, you'll have surround sound all night long.

Nintendo GameCube

Nintendo has, as usual, gone its own way. The GameCube uses a new type of surround processing called Dolby Pro Logic II, an update to a venerable older format. Pro Logic II produces a surround experience that is very close to Dolby Digital, but it requires only two-channel analog source material. You don't need to connect your GameCube with a digital (optical Toslink) cable; you're free to use a normal set of RCA audio cables. All of the GameCube audio/video cables on the market today incorporate these, so you need no extra cables to coax the best possible sound from your GameCube.

There is a catch, however. Pro Logic II is a fairly new development in the surround-format world, and only fairly recent A/V surround receivers contain appropriate decoding circuitry. Here's the good news: this decoding circuit is newer but not exclusive to the most expensive models of receivers today. Nearly every new receiver, including inexpensive entry-level models, have Pro Logic II decoding chips. The other good news is that any two-channel stereo-encoded material will benefit from having an A/V receiver with a Pro Logic II decoder. You'll hear all of your CDs, stereo VHS movies, and games from any stereo gaming system in surround sound with this kind of receiver.

Conclusion

When you consider all of the ways in which you'll use a great surround system, its advantages are many. A properly set up sound system will provide you audio cues that will help your gameplay and enhance cinematic moments in games by producing an epic soundstage. Not only is surround sound an improvement for gaming, it provides an immersive environment that can take you and your friends away to a different world for a while—that's what great games and movies are all about.

HACK #41 Tune Console Video Output

Understand the video options that your system does and does not support.

If you read "Choose the Right Audio/Video Receiver" [Hack #38], you already know that I'm a bit of a home theater nut. One of the coolest things about setting up a great-sounding home theater is that it makes an excellent gaming rig at the same time. The same is true for improving your video system. Buying the right monitor and adjusting it for the best performance for movies will also give you the greatest gaming experience possible. In this hack, I will discuss how to adjust your monitor for the highest performance and the best way to hook up the consoles that you own.

Audio Versus Video Upgrades

If you're on a budget and have to choose between investing in either your audio or video system, choose audio. Quality audio components depreciate slower than any type of video display. Good speakers won't be much cheaper next year, but higher-end televisions will be. Video technology advances rapidly, so next year's high end will replace this year's top performer, driving down prices.

Audio technology moves more slowly, making it a a solid investment that will pay good dividends for years to come. For example, a solid receiver and quality speakers will often last for 10 good years. That just isn't true for televisions today.

If you're ready to run out and buy a brand new display, don't let me stop you. There are a ton of really great monitors now with improved HDTV adoption.

Whether you are ready to hook up a brand new set or are taking a courageous wait-and-see approach, here's how to prep your current display for an optimum gaming experience. I'll first talk about each of the big three consoles, then show you how to optimize your television settings.

Video Connection Types

Because video technology moves so quickly, there are quite a few new things to learn about in the context of today's technology. Here are a few definitions to keep in mind:

Composite video
> This is the most basic video connection and comes standard on all consoles today. Composite video is a combination all of the video signals produced by the video source. A single cable, usually terminated by a yellow RCA connector carries this signal to your TV. Filters inside your television separate the different parts of the signal, but even high-end TV comb filters can't match the video quality of the other superior connection types. Composite cable connections are very basic. Avoid them, especially for detail-intensive games.

S-Video
> The name S-Video (or *Split Video*) comes about because there are two parts to an S-Video signal: *luminance* (or brightness, designated as Y) and *chrominance* (Color, designated as C). Because there are two parts, there are two small cables inside a single S-Video cable. An S-Video connection bypasses your television's comb filter that would otherwise separate these signals, in turn degrading the picture. The biggest visual payoff is in improved edge-definition, an especially big benefit for detailed games.

Component video
> A video signal is actually made up of three parts, the luminance (brightness) and two subcomponents of chrominance (color), red and blue. The luminance channel carries the third color, green. Separating the video signal into its three component parts enhances detail and increases color saturation to realistic levels that S-Video alone cannot achieve. Component video has become the de facto standard for DVD and high-definition video. Also, component video allows the transfer of a progressive-scan signal. To be clear, you must have a component video cable connection to display 480P (progressive scan) and higher resolution signals.

Progressive scan and interlaced video
> An interlaced video signal draws one half of the frame in 1/60th of a second (the odd lines of a frame), then goes back to draw the in-between even lines in the next 1/60th of a second, completing a full

frame in 1/30th of a second. This produces one full frame 60 times per second, or 30 frames per second using interlaced video, but separates each frame into two different parts. Drawing a picture in this half-and-half way produces a noticeable flicker and is generally inferior to a progressively scanned picture.

Progressive-scan video draws a full frame from top to bottom in one pass, every 1/30th of a second. This one-pass drawing tends to look smoother and contains fewer artifacts, especially at lower resolutions. This is the way your computer produces its picture and the reason why it looks so smooth and solid in comparison to a standard analog television.

16:9 and 4:3

Some high-definition screens now have a widescreen shape, or aspect ratio, of 16:9. Aspect ratio is the relationship of the monitor's width to its height. Older, square-shaped TVs have a 4:3 aspect ratio. This ratio can also be expressed as a whole number, as in 1.33 to 1 (4:3) or 1.78 to 1 (16:9).

HDTV, SDTV, EDTV

There is more to HDTV than I can cover here, but high-definition games begin and end with the 720p and 1080i (interlaced scan) formats. The generally accepted definition of a high-definition-quality picture is that it generates over one million pixels per frame. Conversely, 480i is essentially the theoretical upper limit of older televisions' (NTSC) capabilities; today this is standard-definition TV.

The 480p format falls somewhere in between these two categories. You'll sometimes hear it referred to as enhanced definition or EDTV. Note that some 480p signals are meant for display on a 4:3 TV, and some are optimized for a 16:9 aspect ratio widescreen television.

Widescreen 480i and 480p signals are called *anamorphic* video. You can tell if a DVD or game has been optimized for a widescreen television if it says "enhanced for widescreen TVs" or "anamorphic video" on the rear of the software package. Sometimes games are marked "high definition/480p." While this may not be true in the strictest technical sense, it generally means that the game plays at an EDTV resolution and is also anamorphically enhanced for 16:9 widescreen TVs.

High Definition Games Database

One of the best resources on the Web is the High Definition Games Database (*http://hdgames.net/*) enthusiasts site. Game review sites frequently regurgitate misinformation fed to them by the game developers concerning the HD capabilities of new titles. Often they report that games support progressive scan, high-definition capabilities, and 16:9 modes, but those features often fall under the twin knives of budget and time pressures. Hdgames.net is an open forum for gamers to post whether these features are actually present in shipped products.

Hooking Up Your Consoles

Enough theory. Remember how television and output standards move fast? This is apparent when you consider how every console handles things a little bit differently.

Sony Playstation 2. The PS2 is a little dated and out of fashion, but I still dig Sony's mullet approach to connectivity, with business in front and party in the back. There are a ton of connections right on the unit: Toslink audio, USB, IEEE 1394 FireWire, and the hard-drive bay. Sony's hairdressers have been busy though, chopping off overgrown locks and shaping new sideburns as it has matured through several version changes. There are three versions of the PS2, each with significantly different video capabilities. The easiest way to determine the version that you own is to check the model number on the back:

SCPH-10001, SCPH-15001, and SCPH-18001
> The earliest versions of the PS2 don't play DVDs in 480p progressive-scan mode, nor do they play 480p games. The highest-grade supported video signal is 480i interlaced mode.

SCPH-30001 and SCPH-30001 R
> The second version of the PS2 produces progressive video (480p) output on supported games. It doesn't support DVD movies, however. The R version is the Limited Edition of the PS2 in white, blue, silver, yellow, and red. As a mnemonic device, remember that if your PS2 doesn't match a Model T, you can game with 480p.

SCPH-50001
> The latest and greatest version of the PS2 includes several design changes. It adds 480p support for movies and drops FireWire support. In addition to being 30% quieter, it has increased DVD capability and allows gamers to play DVD-R, DVD-RW, R+, and RW+ discs on their systems for the very first time.

Sadly, Sony has chosen the path of the other consoles when it comes to video; you can upgrade your video connection only by purchasing a different proprietary cable. The standard video connection is composite video (the yellow RCA connector). Now you need to find which aftermarket video connection to purchase. The three most important considerations are what kind of video connections you have on your TV, which model of PS2 you have, and whether you'll use your PS2 as a DVD player.

Knowing these three things, you can make a shrewd decision. First, all three versions support aftermarket S-Video and component video connectors. Before you run out and buy that expensive component video cable, remember that most users run a first-generation PS2 where component video is overkill. In 480i mode, there really isn't much of a case for components, but S-Video over the standard composite cable will make a visible difference. If you have a spare S-Video slot on the TV, you'll be glad that you made the investment.

The same is true for the second-gen PS2 as well. So few 480p PS2 games exist (and 720p/1080i ones really don't exist) that such a high-end purchase has no payoff. If you are considering the expensive Monster Cable GameLink 400, use the money to purchase a decent progressive-scan DVD player instead.

If you end up with the upcoming third-generation PS2, its integrated IR receiver and 480p DVD capabilities might just convince you to use it as an all-in-one game/DVD player. At this point, buy the component video cable to take advantage of these features. However, note that the previous generations' DVD video playback quality was extremely poor, even compared to the most modest standalone DVD players. Without seeing the quality for yourself first, I'd caution you against buying a third-generation PS2 expressly for DVD movie viewing.

There are only a handful of 480p games on the PS2. Because the graphics engine is a bit older, the quality is a toss-up between 480p and 480i. In fact, several sources state that 480p actually looks worse than 480i on some games. Support is so limited thus far that you usually must hold a certain combination of buttons on the controller to unlock the 480p mode upon booting. Check your game's manual to find out how to turn on these modes —and off if you don't think they make an improvement.

Microsoft Xbox. You can take your thinking caps off now. The Xbox is a no-brainer. If your TV supports component video, pull the trigger right now and buy the Microsoft HD expansion pack or an aftermarket component video cable such as the Monster Cable GameLink 400. You'll need either one to hook up the digital-audio signal anyway, so it's well worth the investment.

The Xbox doesn't support 480p for DVD movies, but games have the star treatment; most are available in 480p these days. More importantly, some are even available in high-definition 720p and 1080i formats. These formats produce extremely rich resolutions on a high-definition set that make for completely immersive gaming. If you have an older analog TV, I suggest using the Monster Cable GameLink 300 S-Video cable. You can still attach their digital-audio kit to this video cable system. Strangely enough, Microsoft's own HD expansion kit includes only component video, not S-Video output, so you'll need the Monster kit to add digital audio to an analog display.

Here's the sticky part about some high-definition Xbox titles: some fully support 16:9 aspect ratios and some don't. That is, some games play in HD mode in an anamorphic widescreen and will fill your screen, but some will place a 4:3 frame inside a 16:9 picture, nullifying the widescreen effect completely. If you prefer a full-framed widescreen game, switch off the 720p and 1080i modes in your Xbox menu. Your game will play in 480p 16:9 mode instead.

Nintendo GameCube. The GameCube supports 480p for progressive-scan-capable standard-definition and high-definition televisions. To achieve this, you must purchase and install the Official Component Video Cable from Nintendo. If you don't have a progressive-scan TV, I also recommend the Official Nintendo S-Video cable, because it is affordable and a solid performer.

By the way, if you have the component cables hooked up, turn on progressive mode by holding down the B button while your system starts. Then select the progressive mode in the menu.

H A C K **Tune Your TV for Console Video**
#42   Calibrate your video display device to see more of the game.

Today's games have resolution and details that will tax your display to its limit. A properly adjusted sharpness setting will reward you by showing off the spectacular details in Halo, and a correctly set black level will allow you to see Sam Fisher lurking in the shadows of Splinter Cell. Hooking up your console with the best connection possible ("Tune Console Video Output" **[Hack #41]**) is only half the battle. You must calibrate the monitor settings: the brightness (black level), contrast, sharpness, and color balance controls.

Setting Up Your Television the Right Way

There are many misconceptions about what looks good. Default television settings that make them stand out from one another on the showroom floor are disastrously horrible (and potentially damaging) if you keep these settings once the set is in your home. The best and most efficient way to tune your TV yourself is with a testing-and-calibration DVD such as Digital

Video Essentials or Avia Guide to Home Theater. These test discs will guide you through all the adjustments necessary in order to calibrate your display for its highest possible performance. They cover a wide gamut of settings, including audio setup help. Although they're expensive, they are a great investment. Currently, outfits such as Netflix.com don't offer these discs for rental, but a local video shop might have them available.

> You might already have a calibration disc at home without even knowing it! Many THX-certified DVDs (*http://www.thx.com/*), including *Star Wars Episode I* and *Episode II*, *Monsters Inc.*, and *Finding Nemo*, include the THX Optimizer calibration program. Dedicated calibration discs include a blue plastic lens to help you fine-tune your color and tint. You can order this lens from THX online.

To give you a great example of what tweaking your video settings can do to improve your television's picture right now, go into your TV's menu settings and turn the sharpness control all the way off. Setting the sharpness control at a high level turns on an artificial edge-enhancement that produces ringing or noise around objects in your picture. This added noise actually obscures the picture and makes small details impossible to see.

On some televisions, turning the sharpness all the way off also deactivates Scan Velocity Modulation, a dubious enhancement. Be aware, however, that some televisions actually induce an artificial blur at a low sharpness setting that can obscure the picture as much as a noise-inducing high setting can. This is where a test disc comes in handy to guide you to the optimal setting.

ISF Calibration

Another approach is to contact the nearest Imaging Science Foundation (*http://www.imagingscience.com/*) technician to calibrate your monitor. This servicing will take your display to the next level. The technician will set the grayscale, calibrate the brightness, and dial in the convergence to a degree that you or I probably can't. He will enter the television's service menu to set some very high-level adjustments. Almost all monitors will benefit from this level of calibration.

I'm sure that you can dig around the Net and find the service menu codes yourself, but this is one hack that I don't recommend. You can really, really screw up your set by doing the wrong thing in there. Leave that stuff to the professional hackers—the ISF guys.

Make Your Monitor Remember

Many monitors today have the ability to set up different modes, meaning that you can calibrate and save different settings underneath, say, theater and normal modes. If you have direct sunlight on your monitor during part of the day, consider separate settings for day and night. You might even consider rearranging your setup to minimize ambient light hitting the screen.

A good way to make a day/night mode work for you is to go through your settings in the evening with a calibration DVD and set your monitor "by the book" for optimal lighting conditions. Then, save these settings to the movie or theater mode that almost every modern TV has. After you've set everything up according to Hoyle, feel free to experiment with boosting the contrast and brightness to overcome daytime lighting conditions. For the daytime settings, use the normal or game modes. You might use your calibration disc again, or simply set it up for what looks best to you with your favorite game. Now you have two different modes optimized for daytime and evening lighting conditions.

Be aware that extremely high amounts of contrast (sadly, often the factory setting) will allow your monitor to bloom or overdrive the white signals on your set. This kind of overvoltage will overpower other colors on the screen and distort the geometry of the picture. Worse still, a high contrast setting will shorten the life of the picture tube, especially on rear-projection and plasma displays, increasing the likelihood of burn-in.

Try to find the setting that allows you to see the greatest degree of difference between black and white, without blooming on the monitor or washing out the blacks. Even the best-performing monitors are no match for direct sunlight. Consider spending $100 on quality blinds or a weekend to rearranging your living room; you could coax another year or two of useful life from your television.

You can also sometimes save a mode to a certain input or turn off unused inputs, depending on the TV. I'm as big of a Han Solo as everyone else, but this is where reading the manual comes in handy.

HACK
#43   PC Audio Hacking

Trade flimsy computer speakers for an atmospheric surround sound stereo experience.

One of the best weapons in the elite gamer's arsenal is a killer audio system. With the advanced audio performance in today's games, you will often hear your enemies well before you can see them. Our amazing ears and brains can sense distance, location, direction, and environment from audio information cues. Unless you have eyes in the back of your head or another monitor behind you, gaming with a surround sound system is the best way to check straight behind you. If you want this kind of advantage, you must invest in a high-end sound card and surround speakers.

For PC gamers, surround sound is a bit different from standard console audio fare. Most modern games use DirectX's Direct3D audio standard. Direct3D simulates 3D environments better than Dolby Digital (*http://www.dolby.com/*) can. This format supports everything from two speakers all the way up to 7.1 and 8.1 systems, as long as the software renders audio to that many speakers.

Connecting a computer surround speaker package is straightforward because the speaker set usually includes connection cables. Be sure to follow the guidelines for speaker set up and positioning in "Place Your Speakers Properly" **[Hack #39]**.

Some high-end speaker packages from Logitech (*http://www.logitech.com/*), Creative Labs (*http://www.creativelabs.com/*), and Klipsch (*http://www.klipsch.com/*) have started to include onboard Dolby Digital decoders as well, allowing them to function as limited-use A/V receivers. In addition to the analog inputs, they have up to three separate digital inputs. If you connect your PC to the analog input, you can save the digital inputs for a DVD player or game consoles.

The Meaninglessness of Computer Speaker Power Ratings

If you need even more versatility, an alternate setup is to attach your computer to a home theater A/V receiver and use conventional, nonpowered speakers. This approach provides a great advance over most low-fidelity computer speaker systems. Computer speakers are not subject to the same regulations regarding how they specify amplification power.

In a standard A/V receiver, the manufacturer must specify wattage using the RMS method; the given rating represents the power that the amplifier produces when it drives all channels simultaneously. In contrast, computer speaker ratings show the peak capacity of a single channel. The reason that manufacturers can get away with this is because the amplifier is mounted outboard (usually inside the subwoofer), and is therefore not subject to the same Federal Communications Commission regulations. Obviously, the RMS method is a much fairer representation of an amplifier's actual power and renders self-powered computer speaker ratings virtually meaningless by comparison.

Because using a personal computer as the center of a home entertainment system is fairly new, PC speakers have remained quite pedestrian and substandard. With the growing popularity of the home theater PC, a few notable exceptions have started to raise the bar. This bar is still low, though; the high end tops out at about $500 for an all-in-one package consisting of five speakers, a subwoofer, an amplifier, and a surround decoder in a single set. This is just a starting point in the realm of a serious set of home theater speakers capable of producing realistic volume levels in a large room. Therein lies the major difference. Computer speakers assume that the listener is right there, so they perform with a near-field environment in mind. Whether you have gone beyond the confines of a small office into a larger room or simply want a high-end experience, it may be time to graduate to an actual home-theater-grade setup for your computer system.

Your ideal setup will probably fall into one of two scenarios: connecting to an existing system or building a dedicated multimedia PC ("Build a Dedicated Multimedia PC" [Hack #45]).

Connecting to an Existing Home Theater

You will need a long cable (or set of cables) to connect your gaming rig to your home theater. Depending on your sound card, you will need a specific cable that connects the two systems. Most SoundBlaster cards require a set of 1/8-inch headphone-jack-to-RCA cables for every two channels you would like to bring over. If you have a 5.1 Dolby Digital receiver, you will need three cables for your six-channel system. If you have a Pro Logic system, you will need just one set of these cables. Your Pro Logic receiver provides surround sound using its own processor.

Most modern A/V receivers today have a six-channel input specifically for SACD and DVD-Audio players. For the most part, these go unused. I recommend connecting the six RCA connectors from the computer here. You can also still play DVD-Audio discs with the Audigy 2 and newer cards from your computer's DVD tray.

Be careful to connect the channels correctly. There are usually very small printed indicators on the back of the card itself, but it may be easier to read the card's instructions instead. Use the card's audio software to produce a test tone to confirm the connections and balance your speaker levels. Once you've connected everything, you can control your volume with the receiver in the same room, making things a bit easier to manage.

Advanced SoundBlaster cards with outboard connection units (the Platinum and Platinum eX models) contain both Toslink and coaxial digital connections on the front panel. The M-Audio Revolution card (*http://*

www.m-audio.com/) has a coaxial digital output directly on the back of the card. Using a digital connection to connect to your receiver saves you having to buy two or three analog cables. Instead, you'll connect with just a single line. However, digital cables tend to be more expensive, so weigh the cost carefully. If your run is short, it is a good idea to go digital. Otherwise, do the math to see which method makes more sense. The biggest benefit of a digital connection is that you can keep your analog connection to the computer's speaker system for gaming and switch your receiver to the digital connection for normal audio without removing and replacing wires every time.

Any of these methods will give you a taste of multiroom audio with access to your entire music collection from the comfort of your couch. Provided you have made the video connection ("Optimize PC Video Performance" **[Hack #44]**), you can enjoy your archived movies there as well.

Hacking an Older Pro Logic Receiver

If you have an older Pro Logic receiver, you may not have six-channel input. Instead, you may have a set of pre-inputs on at least two channels that will allow you to bypass the processor on the receiver, giving you full Dolby Digital performance if you send it the right signals. If you have a Dolby Digital sound card in your computer and three sets of analog RCA cables, plug them into your receiver as pre-inputs. You will have to control the volume from the computer side, however, because this method totally bypasses the receiver's preamplification. There are a lot of great older receivers out there configured this way. They're often inexpensive because they lack the most current Dolby Digital circuitry.

When shopping around for this sort of amp, look on the back of the unit for *jumpers*, those little metal shunts that connect two sets of RCA jacks on the back panel. A Pre-Input section was a high-end feature years ago, but with newer formats, these older but powerful receivers have lost most of their value. Additionally, these receivers also had great features such as learning remotes and heavy-duty amplifier sections. Combining the brains of your computer with the brawn of these receivers is a great way to give these fine components a new lease on life and treat yourself to an inexpensive but powerful audio system.

Optimize PC Video Performance

HACK
#44   Run the best PC video you possibly can.

In 2003, there was a vacuum in the PC power versus gaming software performance race due to delays in the release dates of games such as Half-Life 2 and DOOM III. You could sit back and relax with PCs that ran everything that the software developers threw at you with ease; current PC graphics cards were much more capable than anything the emerging crop of games could challenge them with.

Games in 2004 push the limits again (Far Cry!). With the current lineup of consoles already showing their age, developers who want to use radical physics engines, advanced AI, and revolutionary graphic effects must target the PC market. Graphic resolution in games isn't merely upscaled from standard resolutions like VGA (800×600) as in years past. Instead, developers are taking advantage of today's powerful hardware to support resolutions all the way up to UXGA (1600×1200). This amount of screen resolution represents a six-fold increase over an Xbox running at 480p. Consoles are inexpensive for a reason: they are yesterday's technology.

True, you can purchase all three consoles and a game or two for the price of a single top-end graphics card, but the experience is different for the first person shooter, real-time strategy, or flight simulator fan. Combining the right game and a powerful gaming PC makes any console look like a foofy pocket calculator. As your graphics card and display capabilities become more advanced, your experience will scale to match.

Buying the Right Video Card

With quarterly model changes, the computer industry moves faster than any other in the world. For the high-end gamer, this is good, when new innovations and technology hit the market regularly, and bad, as top-flight equipment rapidly becomes mediocre. A little research will tell you quickly whether or not a high-end or budget mid-end card is the hot ticket for today's games. I won't try to explain which cards are a good deal right now, because the technology changes so fast it wouldn't even be relevant tomorrow. Instead, read independent third-party review sites that conduct in-depth testing of graphics cards. Sometimes they test the card on games that you own or want to play with the new card. Good review sites include HardOCP (*http://www.hardocp.com/*), AnandTech (*http://www.anandtech.com/*), and Tom's Hardware (*http://www.tomshardware.com/*).

As you wait for Half-Life 2, the bargain bins host a ton of classic games that don't require spectacular graphics chips. If you haven't played titles like the original Half-Life, Deus Ex, Thief, or Homeworld, rescue them today and enjoy. I won't tell anyone that you haven't finished them.

LCD Monitors

When it comes time to upgrade your monitor, consider an LCD system. A big, bright display that doesn't take up a bunch of desktop real estate seems like a dream come true. It is, but with a couple of caveats.

LCD monitors respond more slowly to motion than do traditional CRTs (glass tube monitors). This technology is rapidly advancing, however, so motion looks better now than it did a few years ago. The single biggest performance criteria when considering an LCD is the *response time*, the time in milliseconds that it takes for a pixel to toggle from fully off to fully on and then off again. LCD displays that have a pixel response time rating of under 20 ms—approaching the performance of a traditional CRT—are leading-edge technology today.

The other two important factors to consider are overall brightness and contrast ratio. Brightness is measured by cd/m² (candelas per square meter); the higher the better. More important is the contrast ratio of the monitor. *Contrast* is the degree of difference that a monitor can display between white and black. Brightness and contrast ratio on an LCD are closely interrelated. As brightness increases, contrast generally decreases. Sadly, manufacturer specifications are unreliable due to loose rules for monitor ratings. Trust your own eyes instead.

When hooking up your LCD, use a digital video interface (DVI) connection if possible. Many modern graphics cards and displays support this DVI connector. Because LCD displays are natively digital, attaching them with an analog connection means that they must then convert your signal to digital before the information passes to your screen. Worse still, the graphics card must convert its information to analog to pass it through the VGA cable! Each conversion takes its toll on the quality of the signal. Connecting your card and monitor with a DVI cable allows them to converse without any translation and can improve display quality remarkably.

Calibrating Your Display

For the same reasons that you should calibrate your television ("Tune Your TV for Console Video" [Hack #42]), you should also tune your computer's

Hacking a Mac Display

You've done your research and have your heart set on a great big LCD monitor. You've also noticed that Apple offers widescreen LCDs at a very attractive price. The only problem is that they use an Apple Display Connector (ADC) connection.

ADC is a DVI-compatible video format that combines USB and DC power for the monitor in a single cable. While innovative and clutter-reducing, you might think that this type of connector makes these monitors incompatible with your PC. However, Apple makes a DVI-to-ADC converter that works with a DVI-enabled graphics card. Even when you add the cost of the converter to that of the monitor, you will still pay several hundred dollars less for a Macintosh 23-inch Cinema HD than for a standard PC LCD display of similar size from any other manufacturer. The best part is that this monitor requires no other prep work; hook up the ADC converter, and it is plug-and-play from there with Windows XP.

Be careful to use only the first-party Apple ADC-to-DVI converter, however. Third-party products such as the Dr. Bott DVIator can produce unwanted artifacts if you use a Mac monitor with a PC.

display for optimum performance. Brightness and contrast performance are extremely important on your computer monitor. If you use an LCD/DLP based setup, the optimum settings will be very elusive. There are a few calibration programs available out there for graphics professionals, but you can start with DisplayCalibration.com (*http://www.displaycalibration.com/*) a very good free calibration web site.

Setting Up the Optimum Playing Environment

We have already discussed controlling light in order to limit direct sunlight on your monitor's surface, but playing games or watching movies in total darkness can be a buzz-kill as well. If you view something in complete darkness, the only light your pupil reacts to is onscreen. As scenes change from dark to light, your pupil will change from fully dilated to fully closed, fatiguing your eyes in the process. This is why even in a movie theater, there is usually at least some light in the seating area. To prevent this, add a small light source to your gaming area to prevent full dilation of your pupils and eye fatigue. The best place for this is right behind the monitor so that it doesn't reflect directly onto the screen,

Other small sources of light can come from your peripherals. Auravision manufactures a line of backlit keyboards and mice that use Indiglo technology called Eluminx (*http://www.eluminx.com/*). These keyboards are a godsend for the WASD crowd that wants an optimized darkened environment.

HACK #45 Build a Dedicated Multimedia PC

Make your own dedicated PC system for multimedia and gaming, all at once.

Building a dedicated multimedia computer system is one of the most rewarding projects I've undertaken. A big part of that was building a powerful audio system. I'm not talking about adding a mid-performance PC to complement your living room's existing audio system. I've gone off the deep end with my gaming rigs by upgrading at every turn, never missing an opportunity to buy the latest video card or processor. If your system is out of control like this, your next upgrade should be a serious audio system to compliment everything you do on your rig.

For you dorm dwellers, this kind of audio setup can also be the cornerstone of your home theater system after you graduate.

Sound Equipment

Start with a top-of-the-line sound card such as the SoundBlaster Audigy or M-Audio Revolution. Because this is a dedicated system, you'll use the processor in the sound card itself, so use the analog connections from the back of the sound card with a set of three 1/8-inch minijack-to-RCA cables. If you wish to use a higher-grade cable, I recommend the Monster Cable iPod cable because it uses a very compact 1/8-inch minijack connector head. This is important because the jacks there are very close together on most cards, especially those that support 6.1 and 7.1 multichannel formats.

When you've connected your card to the receiver, you will be able to control volume with the receiver's master volume selector. This is a nice feature while you're playing a game. You can also use whatever conventional audio speakers you wish. You will need at least four monitor speakers and an additional center speaker to build a true 5.1 system. Remember to choose magnetically shielded speakers if you use a CRT. If you use an LCD monitor, it won't matter, but most home theater speakers have shielding anyway.

Many home-theater-in-a-box systems on the market today are convenient and value-oriented, but most of these systems suffer from the same problems as computer speakers. Remember why the ratings of PC speakers don't stack up? The same problem exists with HTIB systems that have the amplifier mounted outboard in the subwoofer. Choose at least a system that includes a real separate audio A/V receiver, and make sure that it has a six-channel multichannel audio input on the back. Finally, don't forget a subwoofer. In a smaller room, you can use a modest eight-inch driver-equipped sub so as not to break the bank.

For extreme hackers, the path to audio nirvana is paved with audio separates. Separate amplifiers cost more than receivers for several reasons, mostly due to build quality. Separates also hold their value very well, making the overall cost of ownership quite attractive compared to a top-of-the-mark receiver that depreciates with every new surround format introduced. In a computer environment that contains all the decoding and preamplification (volume control) on the sound card, all you really need is amplification. You can connect a multichannel amp in the same way you normally connect an A/V receiver with analog interconnects. See "Optimize PC Video Performance" [Hack #44] for more.

Connecting Your Consoles

After you have handled the audio setup, you can even connect your other game consoles to make an ultimate all-in-one gaming system. Several devices can convert the higher-resolution video signals of the Xbox and GameCube to VGA that will display natively on your monitor. From here you can also connect an inexpensive KVM switch to toggle between consoles and your computer without rewiring between sessions once the video is in VGA format. Connect the audio output of the consoles directly to the A/V receiver, and you are good to go.

Needless to say, this kind of system is all you really need to enjoy games, movies, or music. Building a multimedia computer alongside a serious home audio system will reward you with scalability, upgradeability, and resale value.

Audio Alternatives

Last but not least, if you don't have the budget for great speakers and expensive high-end audio separates, you still have your options. A general rule of thumb is that headphones sound equivalent to speakers that cost 10 times their price. You can easily hang with the elite by investing in some quality headphones for a fraction of the price of a killer audio setup. Additionally, many current receivers support Dolby Headphone technology, which approximates a 5.1 system by using only your headphones. This technology is extremely convincing and realistic, and will close the gap between you and a truly excellent audio system. See *http://www.headphone.com/* for everything you've ever wanted to know about headphones and headphone amplifiers.

Use a Multimedia Projector for Gaming

HACK
#46   Are your games too big for a TV? Try a projector.

I don't know about you, but whenever I have to sit through a boring Power-Point presentation, I always think, "All right, who's ready for a couple of rounds of Counter-Strike?" Multimedia projectors are a great way to converge your computing, gaming, and movie-watching experiences. Lately, prices for quality projectors have taken a nose dive, and the attraction of PC gaming on a giant display is unassailable. Small projectors today are brighter and display higher resolution than ever. Because they use LCD and DLP technology, they are immune to the burn-in problems associated with rear-projection big-screen TVs.

Projector-Purchasing Criteria

When considering what kind of projector to purchase (or borrow from the IT department), first consider your room's ambient light level. The more you can do to reduce this, the less you need to consider the projector's peak light output. It might be significantly less expensive to invest in better blinds or shades instead of purchasing a very bright projector. That said, remember that contrast and brightness on a projector are closely interrelated; contrast often decreases as brightness increases. Buying the projector with the highest brightness rating will certainly not guarantee you the best overall picture. So again, having a room in which you can control light is of paramount importance.

The next most important factors are the projector's core technology and native resolution. Portable multimedia projectors today generally use single-chip DLP and LCD engines to drive their displays. There are top-quality and value-oriented projectors made with both technologies. The highest-end projectors have one chip for each color group (red, green, and blue). These units are much more expensive and aimed at the home theater market. My hat is off to you if you can afford one of these, but I'll concentrate on the much more affordable portable-projector market.

There seems to be a sweet spot in the resolution range at 1024×768, with projectors only a bit more expensive than the 800×600 units. Since the manufacturers typically intend these projectors for use in business presentations, they have a 4:3 aspect ratio. When you play DVDs on a 4:3 projector, the 16:9 format occupies only a portion of the panel. An XGA (1024×768) resolution panel fully resolves 16:9 DVD information, even though you use only the middle part of the chip.

Hacking a Business Projector for Home Use

Business multimedia projectors generally drop a few home-theater-type features to make them more competitive in the business market. Generally speaking, you won't find component video inputs on the back of a very affordable projector. In fact, the amount of video inputs most likely will scale up or down with the actual size of the unit. The most portable projectors don't have the real estate to accommodate all the various connector types your typical home theater might use. However, if you plan to connect this projector to your PC, you can work with only the computer input—the VGA connector or DVI input. For the reasons that a desktop LCD monitor looks better with a DVI connection, the same holds true for a projector.

Many presentation projectors lack ceiling-mount support. This feature reverses the projected image so that you can mount the unit out of the way on the ceiling. To work around this lack, use your video card's software to send an upside-down image to the projector. The projector's reversed orientation will make the image right-side up again. Your image will have done a 360-degree spin, ending up the right way. You will have to practice your handstands to set up the projector, but once this is done, you are all finished.

ATi users: right-click the ATi icon in your systray, mouse over to Rotations, and select "Rotate 180 degrees." You can also enter your Control Panel, hit the Display Settings tab, and select Advanced to bring up the ATi software settings group. If you still don't see the Rotation tab, enter the registry, navigate to HKEY_LOCAL_MACHINE/Software/ATI Technologies/Desktop/*xxxx*, where *xxxx* is the display device number, and set the value to 01 00 00 00 from the current value of 00 00 00 00. Then select the Rotation registry and change the value to activate the tab. After you change the registry value, you'll see the tab where you can flip your image.

NVidia users: click on the NVidia icon in your systray, select the NVRotate function, and set it to 180 degrees. You can also navigate to the Display icon in the Control Panel and change your settings from there.

Setting Up a Budget Projection Screen

A very important factor in using a projector is what you project onto. The surface must be smooth, even, and perfectly white if possible. You can cover part of your wall with special reflective paint, but drywall typically isn't very uniform and will distort your image. Also, the surface must have a fair amount of reflectivity in order to provide a bright image. Bare walls will often eat up a big portion of the projector's output because they do not meet the above criteria.

Unfortunately, professional-grade projector screens from companies such as Stewart, Da-Lite, and Draper can easily approach or exceed the price of the projector itself. Thankfully, there are a couple of great solutions at a low cost. You can typically buy white melamine-coated MDF (medium density fiberboard) at a big hardware store. Though this type of board has a hard plastic coating that resembles Formica and is often used to make cabinets, I've found that it is a very suitable projection surface. It is extremely flat, and you can screw or nail into it if you want to build a frame around it.

Another material with quite a bit of buzz is the Parkland Plastics PLAS-TEX panel (*http://www.waterproofpanels.com/plas-tex.shtml*). Originally used as a heavy-duty industrial wall covering, this shares many properties of a good projector screen. Home theater enthusiasts have begun using it for this purpose. It has become so popular that Parkland now manufactures these panels in 16:9 aspect ratio sheets. You can find this material at Lowe's and Home Depot stores.

Playing with Console and Arcade Hardware

Hacks 47–62

It's hard to talk about games without occasionally considering the hardware that runs the games.

What do consoles and arcade machines have to do with each other besides taking up too much space under your television?

They're amazingly cool to hack, whether you're doing crazy things Sega never intended the Dreamcast to do or swapping out JAMMA boards in a full-fledged official arcade cabinet. Consider what happens when you insert a disc and turn on the machine or connect your console to the Internet. What if you had some way of intercepting or modifying that process? What cool things could you do?

Maybe you're just interested in the games themselves, but modding the hardware is the only way to play exotic games from other territories. If you ever wanted to run that obscure Japanese NES game on your American machine—or something even more obscure—here's a good place to start.

Play LAN-Only Console Games Online

HACK #47

Official console services don't support your preferred game? You can play online anyway.

Suppose you want to play a console game online, but the box claims the pesky so-and-so supports only LAN play. That game could be anything from Mario Kart: Double Dash!! on the GameCube to the classic Halo on the Xbox. Are you stuck without any way to play with anyone further away than a few yards?

Fortunately, a variety of clever PC-based utilities allow you to route your console traffic through your computer and over the Internet.

Why Do You Need Console Tunneling?

Before explaining these programs, let's discuss why console tunneling is even necessary. Simply put, these games use too much bandwidth or send too many packets to work reliably over most Internet connections. Console manufacturers have fairly stringent rules about acceptable performance lag for playability, and Internet-based console gaming has only recently taken off. Some older, unoptimized, or just plain stubborn titles are only officially available for local area network (LAN) play.

Clever coders decided to *tunnel*, pretending that the local console is talking to a LAN-connected friend while actually shipping the packets back and forth over the Internet. This, of course, requires a computer to mediate. The tunneling utilities have grown increasingly sophisticated; they support chat channels, private or public servers, voice support, homebrew support, and plenty more options. Best of all, most of these tunnelers are freely down-loadable—created by charitable and innovative coders. Some even support multiple operating systems.

Tunneling Bandwidth Requirements

Besides the console, game, a console LAN adapter, an Internet connection, a PC, tunnelling software, and a friend with the same equipment, you'll also need a reasonably fast uplink for smooth play. Unfortunately, many DSL connection plans limit the upstream to 128-Kbps, or 16 KB per second. Depending on the efficiency of the game's networking code, this can be bad news for tunneling applications.

The GameSpy Arcade tunneling FAQ for Xbox (*http://www.gamespyarcade. com/support/tunnel_xbox.shtml*) indicates you'll need 256-Kbps upstream bandwidth per player for Halo. Although this seems a little over the top, there are definitely some issues there, because the game was tuned for LAN com-muncations. Similarly, the Warp Pipe project recommends a 256-Kbps connection for playing Kirby Air Ride online. Of course, a 128-Kbps connection seems fine for other games such as Mario Kart: Double Dash!!. This may be due to the relative inefficiency of Air Ride or relative efficiency of the other GC LAN titles.

Bear this in mind when considering the various console tunneling options.

GameCube Options

The best-known contender in the GameCube tunneling scene by far is Warp Pipe (*http://www.warppipe.com/*), a neat tunneling solution that works for all the LAN-released GameCube titles so far. At presstime, this list was Mario Kart: Double Dash!!, Kirby Air Ride, and 1080 Degrees Avalanche. It's a short list, but all three games are fun, and Mario Kart is a classic, which helps make up for the paucity of titles. Warp Pipe is also an excellent choice because there are versions available for Windows, Mac OS X, Linux, and BSD.

It's worth noting that a broadband adapter is required for your GameCube to make Warp Pipe work because it doesn't come with the console. The add-on costs $50 at the official Nintendo web site or at most retail stores and fits snugly into the back of your Cube. To be honest, it isn't useful right now in any official capacity; only the Phantasy Star Online series supports online play. These games cost an additional subscription fee, so although they're rather addictive, there's no massive demand for the GC broadband adapter.

What if you do have the equipment necessary to take your GameCube online? The excellent Warp Pipe setup page (*http://www.warppipe.com/gettingstarted/network_setup.html*) explains the basic steps:

1. Connect your GameCube to the Net with an Ethernet cable. You can plug into a hub or a router, depending on your Internet setup. A hub may be simplest, and the Warp Pipe FAQ points out it's "based on Nintendo's recommended LAN setup for playing LAN-enabled GameCube games," but you can use a router as long as you understand port routing. You can also put another Ethernet card in your PC and use a crossover cable to connect to your GameCube, but this is less common.

2. Unblock port 4000 for both UDP and TCP. Remove or disable all firewall rules that may block this port. The GameCube uses both UDP and TCP to communicate for LAN games. If you're unlucky, your ISP may block these ports outside your control.

   If you're using a router, use its port forwarding to send the traffic through your PC and out onto the wilds of the Internet. Again, check the excellent Warp Pipe FAQ information (*http://www.warppipe.com/support/router_firewall_support.html*) for lots more details.

3. Install and run the tunnelling software. Warp Pipe works on Windows, Mac OS X, Linux, and the BSDs. Run the software to see a window pop up with pictures of GameCubes and somewhere to enter an IP address.

4. Find someone to play against. At the time of writing, you still need to find a potential opponent's IP address and type it into the software manually (see Figure 5-1). The imminent WarpPipe 0.4 release promises to include an instant-messaging interface, much like the one in the

XLink Kai Xbox tunneling software. It may well be out by the time you read this.

However the version you use, *http://www.warppipe.com/gettingstarted/playing_games.html* will likely explain how to find opponents online. You also have the choice to "listen for connections" instead, allowing an opponent to contact you. One of you needs to host the game. Bear in mind that you need UDP and TCP on port 4000 unblocked to host but only TCP unblocked to connect to another opponent.

5. Play the game. If the connection succeeds, you'll see a ping value (hopefully way below 100!) appear. Now move over to your GameCube and boot the game into LAN mode to play against your new friend and opponent. Have fun and don't drive over too many bananas in Mario Kart!

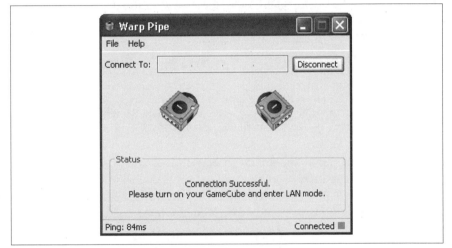

Figure 5-1. Warp Pipe, connecting you to other GameCube users online

A new contender in the GameCube field is XLink Kai (*http://www.teamxlink.co.uk/*), originally created just for Xbox. There are already Mario Kart: Double Dash!! tournaments happening on XLink Kai, and users claiming it's comparable or faster than WarpPipe; this bodes well for the future.

Xbox Options: XLink Versus XBConnect

When it comes to the Xbox, one of the leading services is the Windows-only XLink Kai (*http://www.teamxlink.co.uk/*) from the creators of XLink Messenger. At the time of writing, they've just expanded their tunneling efforts to the GameCube and PlayStation 2. It supports almost 50 games on Xbox alone.

Technically speaking, XLink works similarly to the GameCube's WarpPipe. The only major difference is that it uses UDP ports 34518 and 34519 for the basic setup and UDP port 6073 for voice chat. Refer to the XLink help page (*http://www.xboxlink.co.uk/help.php*) for further help.

XLink's impressive features include the ability to use XLink Messenger to monitor the status of tens or hundreds of avatars currently online in an almost Xbox Live–style fashion. You can tell their nicknames, locations, and current actions; whether they're idling; hosting a game of Tony Hawk; advertising the desire to play a certain title; or just hanging out and chatting. You can add friends as in conventional IM clients and talk to each other via your PC in lobbies. It's all rather impressive.

As for game availability, the former XLink homepage lists the favorite game for any given moment. More often than not, it is original Halo, but other titles such as the UbiSoft stealth action games are known to sneak in there from time to time.

> It's particularly worth playing games via XLink that you can't play on Xbox Live. Microsoft's service is good and fully featured; you should probably patronize it if you're really into online Xbox gaming. Also, multiplayer Xbox Live matchups in games such as Project Gotham Racing 2 tend to be less lag-prone than tunneling software.

In a rather smart move, the ability to play LAN-enabled software over the network means that, if you know how to run homebrew software on your Xbox,[*] you can even play LAN-enabled homebrews such as Quake-X (*http://www.lantus-x.com/ClassicX/*) online via XLink. Clever stuff.

There are other Xbox tunneling programs. XBConnect (*http://www.xbconnect.com/*) is excellent and well-known, if available only for Windows. It supports nearly the same amount of games (45 in total, though it officially lists no homebrew games) and may actually have a larger Halo fanbase. XBConnect seems to lack XLink Kai's ambition to expand to other consoles, but it's well worth checking out.

Another possibility is the GameSpy Tunnel (*http://www.gamespyarcade.com/support/tunnel_xbox.shtml*), which is also free and Windows-only. It reportedly used to have a larger number of overall users than the other two services. This seems to fluctuate, but being tied to a major gaming news web site must help its popularity a little.

---

[*] See Andrew Huang's *Hacking the Xbox* (No Starch), for example.

Finally, Aqueduct (*http://www.postpose.com/aquaduct/*) for Mac OS X works similarly to the Windows-only utilities. You'll probably have to pre-arrange games with specific people, because there are far fewer people using the service.

PlayStation 2 Tunneling

PlayStation 2 tunneling is a little complex. Originally, Sony designed LAN play to work only with a special iLink cable—basically FireWire to connect multiple consoles. You can even use a FireWire hub to connect multiple PS2s to play Gran Turismo 3. However, with the advent of the PSX PlayStation 2 + DVR (digital video recorder) device, the iLink port will eventually disappear on newer PlayStation 2 models. LAN games will still work through the Ethernet port.

Obviously, you need an Ethernet adapter, standard only on recent PS2s, before you can think about tunnelling. XLink Kai has just started offering LAN compatibility for PS2 games through your Windows PC, and it should work by the time you read this. Check out their site (*http://www.teamxlink. co.uk/*) for more details.

Particularly interesting LAN-enabled titles include Gran Turismo 4, Tony Hawk's Pro Skater 3 and 4, and the new Star Wars Battlefront. Obviously, most recent LAN-enabled games also have online support, so there's no startling advantage for one style, as is the case for Halo for Xbox, which just isn't playable online unless you tunnel.

To reiterate, XLink Kai compatibility will work for those games that use the Ethernet port for LAN play; those that use iLink only for LAN play won't work for now, sadly. It's possible there are some iLink-compatible tunneling software packages out there. If these software packages exist, they seem badly documented and will likely be sparsely populated.

The Future of Tunneling

The usefulness of tunneling may wane as more consoles and games support online play out of the box. Halo 2 has online capabilities, for example. For consoles that discourage going online (the GameCube) or certain titles that will never support online play (the original Halo for Xbox), it's worth the hack in order to play in ways the designers never intended. Tunneling can work beautifully after you apply some homebrew creativity.

Hack the Nuon DVD Player/Gaming System

#48   Do unlikely and intriguing things with the cult DVD player and game chip combo.

Failed game systems often attract a certain amount of cult attention and new content as, abandoned in their full-price glory, they're resurrected as cut-price toys for hackers, exploiters, and hardcore fans. This is definitely the case for the bizarre Nuon, the VM Labs–developed game console on a chip. VM Labs made a stealth bid for glory by bundling their game system in as many third-party DVD players as possible. While this attempt failed, the Nuon nonetheless made it to market.

With the ability to burn and play homebrew titles and accomplish other clever hacks with existing content, the Nuon is a fascinating, inexpensive games machine to hack around on. Some models feature the amazingly impressive Virtual Light Machine, which can generate effects you have to see to believe.

Nuon's Short Life and Resurrectory Jaunt

Back in 1994, some of the creators of the Atari Jaguar founded VM Labs (which should partially explain the appearance of a certain shaggy Welsh psychedelic programmer later in this story!). They set up partnerships with major third-party DVD/consumer electronics manufacturers to license what the official FAQ for the now defunct Nuon web page explains is:

> ...powerful and versatile embedded technology that enhances the passive elements of digital video products such as DVD players, digital set tops and digital satellite receivers, while adding high performance interactive graphics and audio. This combination allows consumers to enjoy next generation 3-D video games, interactive family software and other flexible applications all on the same digital platform.

VM Labs originally, quite seriously, billed the Nuon as a Mario killer. Early adverts showed Mario's cap in a puddle of blood next to an X, because the original name of the chip was *Project X*. So, although a few enhanced DVDs took advantage of the extra processor power of the Nuon, and DVD players including Nuon had advanced features such as super-high-quality zoom, the Nuon really turned out to be a single-chip media processor that could play 3D games on a DVD player.

After an extended delay, Samsung finally released a Nuon-compatible DVD player in July 2000. Ultimately, some 10 commercial games saw the light of day. Unfortunately, even though Samsung, Toshiba, and RCA all released Nuon DVD players, and Motorola experimented with Nuon tech in some of its set-top boxes, the technology was not a success. It fizzled out in 2001 and

2002, although a couple of RCA players without easily accessible Nuon features or gameports did debut later in 2003.

VM Labs unfortunately lapsed into bankruptcy in 2002. A company called Genesis, completely unrelated to Sega's classic 16-bit system, purchased the company. They were actually interested in Nuon for its MPEG decoding capabilities.

Picking the Choicest Nuon Hardware

Before hacking a Nuon, you need the hardware, so you'll need to decide which model you actually want. If you're in the United States, there are really only three DVD players with Nuon functionality worth considering:

Samsung N-501
> Samsung's DVD player, released in early 2001, is my first choice by far, because this player comes with built-in controller ports and can play homebrew CDR games without any trouble. In addition, although it's low-resolution, the Virtual Light Machine (VLM) included in the BIOS has a massive range of controllable effects. Unfortunately, it doesn't come with a controller packed-in, though it does include the addictive little puzzle game Ballistic.

> You should be able to find this player in online shopping stores or on eBay for between $75 and $125, although it is getting a little trickier nowadays.

Samsung Extiva N-2000
> The very first Nuon-compatible player, from the middle of 2000, came with Ballistic, a game controller, and a fully featured demo disc with multiple commercial games on it. However, being an early model, it does not have the correct firmware to load the *NUON.CD* files used in homebrew Nuon titles. Besides that, it has serious trouble recognizing CD-R discs.

> This model has 100 VLM effects, but you can't apply them in real time, unlike the N-501 version. At the time of writing, only one store offered the N-2000 on Froogle, for $129.

Toshiba SD-2300
> The Toshiba has a few minor pluses, such as controller ports, and the fact that this player was the only place to get Hasbro's The Next Tetris via a mail-in demo disc offer. (This deal has likely expired by now.) However, it has only a pathetic eight VLM effects, allegedly due to epilepsy concerns. It also won't play homebrew games, which is a major issue. If you can find it online, it'll probably run you $80 to $150.

For European readers, the insanely rare Samsung N-504 is the machine to buy, because it's very similar to the American N-501, complete with controller ports. If you can't find that (and it's very likely you can't), you will have to settle for an N-505, which, tragically, has no controller ports.

Believe it or not, an enterprising European has hacked the N-505 to add controller ports, which are simply missing external linkage; the circuit board inside has the controller port connector. There's more info about this hack on the Nuon Dome site (*http://www.nuon-dome.com/n505hack/n505hack.html*), but, unfortunately, this version needs an extra set of Nuon controller ports to work. You'll need to scavenge them from a broken American N-501 or similar model.

For the very hardware-savvy, Vid Kid has gone one step further, hacking in mini-DIN connectors to the open game port on the N-505. See his web page for more (*http://www.debaser.force9.co.uk/n505hack/*). It requires significant soldering skill; you'll need to open up a Nuon controller and wire mini-DINs onto that as well. For gamepad connector–starved Europeans, it's definitely an option.

Commercial and Homebrew Nuon Software

After you've picked up your Nuon and have a working controller, which commercial games should you consider?

Here's a short list of the games worth looking at: Tempest 3000. See, I told you it was a short list. Jeff Minter's crazed update of the classic arcade game is the only essential title on the Nuon, degenerating into psychedelic mayhem in about three seconds flat. If you enjoy burning your eyes out by gazing intently at the bright, bright screen and flailing spasmodically at the joypad, then you've picked the right console and the right title.

Fortunately, there's also the homebrew scene. VM Labs released the Nuon SDK just before going into liquidation. You can find the SDK in multiple places, including Nuon Dome. This fact, as well as the help of some ex-VM Labs engineers, meant people were soon able to run self-made titles, even overcoming the 4.5-MB limit for the open SDK. The games are incredibly easy to burn: just take the files included in the ZIPs and burn them to the root of a CD-R, using one CD-R per title.

Again, Nuon Dome is the web site with the best file collection and review of what's out there (*http://www.nuon-dome.com/download.html*), so I'll describe what you might want to check out there.

Ambient Monsters (http://www.nuon-dome.com/ambientmonsters.html)
This odd but beguiling relaxation disc isn't very interactive but shows neat attention to detail.

Decaying Orbit (http://www.nuon-dome.com/decaying_orbit.html)
Although very much a work in progress, this is by far the most ambitious original Nuon title around; it's a port of an original PlayStation Yaroze game. It involves flying around the screen while avoiding the pull of various planets. While it's a traditional 2D title, it has a lot of style and pizazz (see Figure 5-2).

DOOM (http://www.nuon-dome.com/doom.html)
One of the original demos from the early days of the Nuon, this runs at a slow frame rate, but it's DOOM running homebrew on your Nuon! This uses the open-sourced code and the official shareware WAD file. It has a custom library to read data from the CD, and there's even a recompiled version for the RCA NUON DVD, running on a faster processor.

Breakout (http://www.nuon-dome.com/breakout.html)
A worthwhile addition to the Nuon homebrew canon, this is a basic but fun interpretation of the classic Breakout. It's still under development and features a delightfully badly Photoshopped Mr. T title screen. I pity the fool who doesn't burn this baby!

The Nuon Boot Loader

In early 2004, one of the most important breakthroughs in the Nuon scene occurred: the Nuon Boot Loader, created by Scott "Skah_T" Cartier, who once worked for VM Labs. According to the Boot Loader site (*http://www. dragonshadow.com/-/bootload/*):

> The Boot Loader allows you to place several NUON applications (called "apps" from here on) on a CD-R and presents you with a menu from which to select the one to run. These can be homebrew games like Breakout or Chomp, applications like the jpeg viewer, or demos such as the ones found in the NUON SDK.

Much like similar utilities for the Dreamcast, this makes it infinitely easier to try out multiple small utilities or games without having to burn a new CD-R for each. You can even customize a menu for each individual utility or game, with colored text and JPG pictures of your choice.

Here are some tips for using the Boot Loader:

- Make subdirectories for each program you wish to support and enter the names of these directories in the *applist.txt* file in the root directory. Anything over eight characters is verboten.

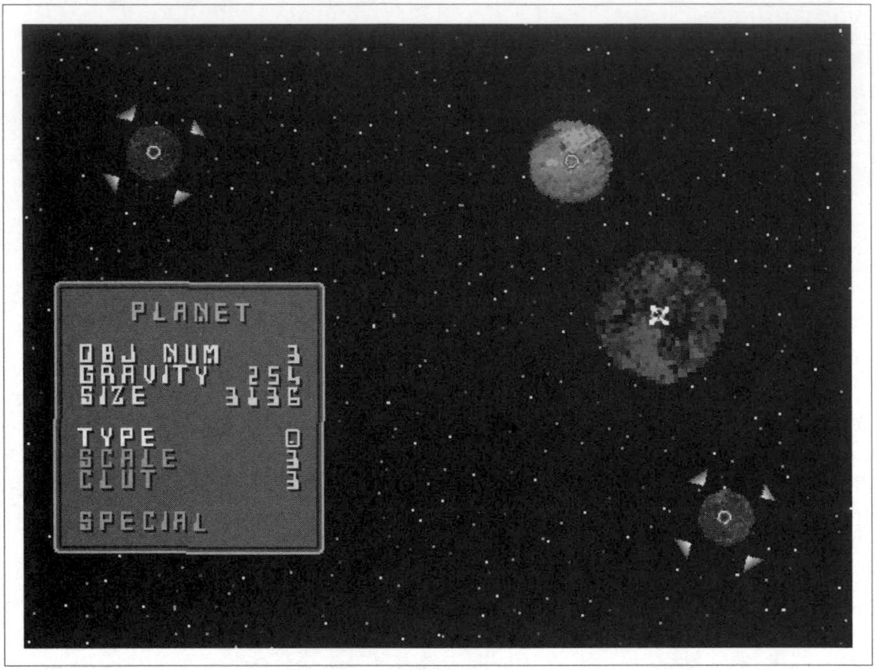

Figure 5-2. Nuon homebrew title, Decaying Orbit

- You can't use multiple *NUON.CD* files on your disc, because they will seriously confuse the boot loader. Instead, you need a *cd_app.cof* executable for each standalone game or utility you want to load.

- If you boot a disc and one of your entries appears in red, it's because there's a problem with the program. Most likely, you're missing the *cd_app.cof* file.

HACK #49   Play Import Games on American Consoles

Defeat regional lockouts with extreme prejudice.

I can see it in your eyes. You're hardcore. Not only will you wait no longer than necessary for your games, you want the best versions available, without censorship or missing features. You also want to play the games that you could only dream about as a child—Japan-exclusive titles that never made it to the NES or Genesis. Well, you're in luck: we'll now explore how to bypass the regional lockouts that prevent you from running Japanese games on your American video game hardware.

The easiest (if hardly cost- or space-effective) solution is to buy the Japanese hardware. Japanese and American televisions use the same NTSC standard resolution, so there are no problems there. Although U.S. power outlets provide 120 volts versus Japan's 100, an extra 20 volts won't damage a PlayStation; I've had my Japanese PS2 plugged in here for years and nothing's happened. (If you're concerned, however, buy a step-down adapter. Good luck finding one at Radio Shack, though.)

What about games from across that other ocean? In general, Europe sees its games much later than the United States and Japan. They're usually not optimized for the continent's PAL television format, so it's rare that anybody wants to hunt down European titles. It does happen, though. For example, Sega's adventure epic Shenmue II was an Xbox exclusive in the United States, but saw a Europe-only, English language Dreamcast release.

Playing PAL games on American hardware can be much more difficult than playing Japanese ones because the video display format is different. In general, this hack deals with regional lockouts, not regional differences. For example, although there are no regional lockouts whatsoever on the Atari 2600 VCS system, some PAL-format games will not display correctly if you try to run them. Because the 2600 has such primitive hardware, though, you can usually solve the problem by adjusting your television's vertical hold.

As for other hardware, even if PAL games work on U.S. systems with no modification necessary, the games might not load at all. There's no easy solution to this besides buying a European system or cracking your hardware open and modifying its guts with a soldering iron and steel courage. If you're up to it, web sites such as GamesX (*http://www.gamesx.com/*) will show you how to do all kinds of things with your old systems, including changing the display frequencies so that PAL games run properly in any country.

Of course, practically everything described here, even the use of external hardware or boot discs, will void whatever manufacturer's warranty is still applicable to your game hardware.

Nintendo Hardware

Though notoriously tough on piracy, the century-old, Kyoto-based Nintendo has generally not taken overly drastic measures to lock out the playing of import games. Their cartridge-based systems have either used a physical lockout or none at all, and even the disc-based Gamecube is the easiest of the current generation of hardware systems to modify.

Nintendo Entertainment System. Nintendo's breakthrough system was the NES in the United States and the Famicom, or Family Computer, in Japan. This was the first system to use a regional lockout; the NES uses a two-stage lockout system, with different cartridge shapes and fewer pins on the ends of the Famicom cartridges than on the NES ones. You'll need a *passthrough converter*, a small device that accepts a Famicom cartridge in one end and plugs into the NES on the other. A company called Honey Bee made these converters (*http://www.atarihq.com/tsr/odd/scans/honeybee.html*) decades ago, but they're hard to find now. Try searching eBay for honeybee NES.

Also, in the early days of the NES, when the Japanese and American software was identical, Nintendo would plug Japanese circuit boards into Famicom converters, wrapping the whole setup in a NES cartridge shell. You can find more-or-less official NES-Famicom converters inside a select few copies of games such as Gyromite, Hogan's Alley, Excitebike, and others. Again, check eBay or the bargain bin of your local game store if you want to make off with one of these beauties. AtariHQ also has an amusing pictorial (*http:// www.atarihq.com/tsr/odd/scans/adapter.html*) that shows exactly how to extract the converter.

Most Famicom carts will slide into an early-model NES, but some are too large. Either shave down the edges of the cart or buy an expensive late-model toploading NES. For the prices they fetch, however, you're probably better off simply hunting down a Famicom clone such as Gametech's Neo-Fami. Now that Nintendo has discontinued their hardware, clone makers produce their wares in mass quantities.

Super Nintendo Entertainment System. Nintendo's next effort, the SNES, was the Super Famicom in Japan. You need to make only a small physical modification to run Japanese cartridges on an American SNES. If you open the cartridge slot on your SNES, you'll see two small plastic tabs behind the metal connectors. These prevent you from inserting a Japanese cartridge; try to put one in, and you'll feel the tabs. Use pliers to yank them out, melt them down with a soldering iron, or heat up and use an X-Acto knife to slice right through them. GamesX has a good page with pictures (*http://www. gamesx.com/importmod/snescon.htm*).

If you don't want to alter your system, you can hunt down a similar passthrough converter or an inexpensive SNES-model Game Genie adapter and modify its tabs. Be aware that some convertors, including the Game Genie, don't have the extra pins that allow you to run Super FX games such as Star Fox.

Another expensive but impressive solution is the rare Tristar 64 (or Super8) adapter, which allows you to play NES and Famicom games as well. If you're lucky, you can find this on eBay.

Nintendo 64. Much like the SNES, the N64 uses only a physical lockout. You can take the system apart and remove the offending plastic pieces altogether, but if you're not careful, you might lose the spring-loaded flaps that protect the cartridge slot from dust. Instead, take a hot soldering iron to the tabs and melt them down, or cut off the pieces with an X-Acto knife, as before. I personally use a passthrough convertor for my N64 because they are very inexpensive and easy to find. There are a plethora of brands, including the N64 Passport Plus III, that also have Action Replay–like functions.

Nintendo GameCube. Japanese GameCube discs won't boot on an American system; a software lockout prevents the game from booting on a non-homeland system. Luckily, the Japanese and American GameCube hardware is identical except for one small connection on the circuit board. It's possible, if tricky, to wire a switch to that connection so you can shift the system between U.S. and Japanese modes. Most online vendors (such as Lik-Sang or Play-Asia) that sell Japanese GameCube games also sell premodified hardware, or they will modify your existing system if you send it to them. With this mod, you need to maintain separate memory cards for Japanese and American games, because the regions use different formats. Otherwise, the system will believe your cards are corrupt and try to format them.

For the hardware-phobic, there is also a software-based solution. An inexpensive, widely available boot disc called the FreeLoader (*http://www.ntsc-uk.com/tech.php?tech=FreeloaderGuide*) can trick the system into thinking that the game you've inserted is American. This has two added advantages: it also works with PAL games, and allows you to use one memory card for all your saves.

The disadvantage of the FreeLoader disc is that newer games may not work with the disc. In that case, wait for a new revision or buy the more expensive Action Replay disc from Datel (*http://www.datel.co.uk/*), which features the same functions as the FreeLoader but also lets you input codes that can fix the errors. See "Cheat on Other Consoles" [Hack #75] for more.

Game Boy series. None of Nintendo's portable systems (Game Boy, Game Boy Color, Game Boy Advance, Game Boy Advance SP, and Virtual Boy) feature any regional lockouts, so you can enjoy all Game Boy games on all compatible Game Boy systems. Nintendo does this because travelers frequently take their Game Boys on the plane to foreign countries and will want to buy games there for the return trip. There is one caveat. The E-Reader attachment for the Game Boy is not region-encoded, but the E-Cards that it reads are, so you'll need Japanese cards for your Japanese E-Reader even if you use it on an American Game Boy Advance.

Nintendo announced its innovative dual-screened, stylus-based portable, code-named Nintendo DS, at the 2004 E3 Expo, but didn't mention whether the machine would feature regional lockouts.

Finally, PAL Nintendo consoles are radically different, and far more difficult to mod for import fun. They may need BIOS and other tricky changes.

Sega Hardware

Woe betide any Sega fan who decides he wants a complete collection of the hardware produced by his favorite company! Before leaving the console hardware business in 2001, Sega produced more hardware variations and regional variations than you can shake a stick at (although the unfortunate early adopters of the Sega 32X probably did more than *shake* a stick at it).

Sega Master System. Sega's Master System, the SMS in the United States, is the Sega Mark III. There may be an extremely rare adapter that lets you play games for the SG-1000 and SG-3000 on the U.S. SMS hardware, but they're almost impossible to find. A rare system called the Dina 2-in-1, or the Telegames Personal Arcade features a slot that plays SG-1000 (but not Mk III) cartridges, but that slot is disabled in some of those machines. In many cases, only the Colecovision-compatible slot works. One solution is to hunt down a Power Base Convertor for the Japanese Mega Drive (Genesis) system, then modify your Genesis to accept Japanese cartridges.

Sega Genesis. The Sega Genesis in the United States is equivalent to the Mega Drive in Europe and Japan.

Much like the SNES, the first two Genesis models used a physical lockout, with small plastic tabs inside the cartridge slot that prevented Japanese games from sliding in. Compare a Japanese cartridge to the Genesis cartridge slot, and you'll see the offending hardware. Remove these tabs by whatever means you prefer. The Genesis 3, released in limited quantities by Majesco Sales, features no physical lockouts.

The problem is that late in the life of the Genesis, Sega decided it would be a good idea to put software lockouts into selected titles. This means that some of the best latter-day Genesis titles, such as Bare Knuckle 3 (Streets of Rage 3) won't work. You'll either need to modify the system internally—see web sites like *http://www.gamesx.com/*—or use a passthrough adapter. You don't want a passthrough adapter that merely changes the shape of the cart; you want ones like the Mega Key that feature external switches on them that change the territory of the system. Some, like the Super Key or Mega Key 2, let you switch PAL frequencies as well.

A cheap, easy, and somewhat kludgey solution is to use the Galoob's Game Genie (available in fairly large amounts on eBay) as a passthrough convertor. Web sites such as *http://gamefaqs.com/* have codes to override any territory lockouts in the game code itself.

Sega CD. Sega sold the console known as the Sega CD in the United States, and the Mega CD in Japan and Europe. It has a hardware chip that locks out foreign games. Adaptors exist that plug into the Genesis cartridge slot, but they don't work with all games or all revisions of the system. As with the Genesis and Saturn, you can fiddle with the system's innards to make it universal, but this requires a complex BIOS image swap. If you do convince it to run, take heart that regional lockouts don't affect RAM cartridges that let you save your games.

Sega Saturn. You can *switch-mod* your Saturn (modify your console to add a switch for choosing a region), but given the availability of cartridge adapters that let you run Japanese games, why bother? The best model is the Four-In-One cart that combines the 4-MB RAM upgrade necessary for hot imports such as X-Men vs. Street Fighter along with an Action Replay code device, a territory lockout–breaker, and lots of space for your saved games. Good luck finding it, though; you may have to scour eBay.

Dreamcast. The Dreamcast, like other modern systems, has more complex region protection. You can't modify it simply by adding a hardware switch. Instead, you'll need a *mod chip*, a hardware device designed to circumvent hardware-protection schemes, or a software solution.

The mod chip only requires soldering four wires to various points on the circuit board. After that, it's pain-free. If you are an expert at hardware tinkering and a quick draw on the soldering gun, you'll probably feel comfortable doing this yourself. Otherwise, hire a professional or stick to software-based solutions. For example, you can purchase a FreeLoader disc or download and burn your own; it's easy to find the files and instructions online. The mod chip is a far more elegant solution, however, because it lets you run any DC disc—including PAL ones—perfectly. If you're still jonesing to do it that way, Wrongcrowd.com has a great, detailed FAQ on how to use NCSX's five-wire mod (*http://wrongcrowd.com/dreamcast/*).

Game Gear and Sega Nomad. The Game Gear is fully region-free, and a simple passthrough converter called the Master Gear (easily found on eBay) will let you play all your SMS games on the portable system. Unfortunately, the portable Sega Nomad is subject to the same caveats as the Genesis.

Sony Hardware

Sony's piracy-prevention methods seem to be more reactionary than precautionary. The first models of their systems on store shelves tend to contain some easily exploited security flaw, which Sony usually fixes. Then the mod-chip makers find some way around *that*, and Sony has to upgrade the system again. Expect a similar cat-and-mouse game shortly after Sony's PlayStation Portable (PSP) releases in 2005; Sony has announced that the system will support region coding.

PlayStation or PSone. Early PlayStation models were easy to trick with the well-known swap trick: hold the disc door open as you hot-swap an American game with a Japanese one at the right time in the booting process. Sony quickly revised the hardware to make this impossible. Finding a working early-model PS is basically impossible now anyway, since they break down with alarming regularity, generally with CD lens–related problems.

You can't deter dedicated importers who design mod chips, but Sony found a way around that too. A small device called a GoldFinger provided an elegant no-modification-necessary solution. It plugged into the system's I/O port, so Sony eliminated that port entirely in the next hardware revision.

PlayStation 2. Mod chips for the PlayStation 2 are widely available, but installation is far from idiot-proof. If you can bear to part with your PS2 for a week or two, some online vendors such as ModChipMan (*http://www.modchipman.com*) will modify your system for you or sell you a brand new, premodded unit for a premium price.

If you don't want to alter the guts of your PS2, consider a system called Magic Slide. This variant of the swap trick method uses two boot discs—one for CD-based PS2 games and another for DVD-based titles—in conjunction with a small plastic card. To use the Magic Slide, remove the front cover of your PS2 disc tray (the long bar of plastic that has the PS logo on it). Be careful lest you permanently destroy the little clips that hold on the cover. Be aware that exerting stress on the drive tray mechanism isn't healthy for the unit in the long run. A gentler modification replaces the top shell of your PlayStation 2 with a little hatch that opens up so you can change discs.

Once the cover is off, boot up the PS2 with the appropriate boot disc. When the screen says "Insert Disc," slide the Magic Slide card underneath the disc tray. Slide it to the right to disengage the lock under the tray; pull on the card, and the tray will come out. You can now swap the boot disc for an import game without the PS2 knowing that you've opened the tray.

The Magic Slide is available at many online vendors, including Japan Video Games (*http://www.japanvideogames.com/*). There is not, as of this writing, any way to play import games on an unaltered PS2. Of course, as the price of the system goes down, purchasing a Japanese unit might be the best way to go.

Other Hardware

Of course, Nintendo, Sega, and Sony aren't the only companies who have manufactured video game hardware across two countries. The following sections describe the other major cross-continent gaming devices.

TurboGrafx-16 or Turbo Duo. This machine went by various names, including the PC Engine, CoreGrafx, and PC Engine Duo in Japan.

First the good news: CD-ROM games for the Japanese PC Engine and American TurboGrafx are entirely compatible. The bad news is that the cartridge games will give you problems. You'll need an expensive passthrough convertor. Tele-Games (*http://www.telegames.com/*) sells them new for about $100.

3DO. All but a handful of Japanese 3DO games will run fine on a U.S. system (whether the Panasonic REAL, or the Magnavox or Goldstar 3DO) with no modification necessary. (Of course, if the game you want to play is in that tiny handful, you're out of luck.)

SNK Neo Geo. All Neo Geo (AES in Japan) home systems play all Neo Geo games regardless of region. That's the good news. The bad news is that the Neo Geo software auto-detects which type of system it's running on and will automatically convert the game language into SNKglish, a strange English dialect characterized by pure nonsense. Worse, the game might auto-censor the blood, turning it white to protect any small children who might somehow have purchased a $500 system and a $300 cartridge.

There are adapters available that let you play the cartridges used in Neo Geo arcade machines on your home system, but they cost between $150 and $200. Of course, that probably sounds reasonable to a Neo Geo collector.

Microsoft Xbox. Upon its entry into the console hardware business, Microsoft initially pleased importers by saying that the Xbox hardware would not feature any regional lockout. This turned out to be technically true, but the discs themselves did. The catch was that region coding on Xbox games is optional, left to the publisher's discretion.

As you might imagine, almost every publisher—including Microsoft—exercised their discretion to put regional lockouts in their software. There are plenty of Xbox mod chips that will let the system play import games, back up games to the hard drive, play media off your computer, do the laundry, and shave your cat. There are also software mods, so search online for more details.

Conclusion

It's difficult to say whether things have improved or worsened for importers. The Internet has helped by allowing dozens of import-game businesses to sprout up, which has leveled the playing field and brought prices down from the insanity of the early '90s, when import Super NES cartridges from sketchy mail-order houses fetched around $150 apiece. The widespread dissemination of information about region encoding and system modification has also taken much of the mystery and risk out of importing.

That said, the actual process of playing import games on new systems has grown more and more complicated. It's not enough anymore just to cut a bit of plastic from the drive tray. You can bet that the next generation of hardware will have even more inscrutable and complex regional lockouts.

HACK #50   Find a Hackable Dreamcast
On finding and hacking the versatile Sega Dreamcast.

When considering consoles to hack, it turns out that the often neglected Sega Dreamcast is by far the best bet for intelligent software hackers. You have no need to modify your console to use it for homebrew gaming or utility purposes; there's a significant development community making interesting games, utilities, and varied hacks; the DC has Internet connectivity; it's reasonably powerful; and most of all, it's inexpensive.

With that in mind, here's some background on the console, as well as where to buy it and what you need to hack with it.

Dreamcast History

The Sega Dreamcast saw a Japanese release on November 25, 1998, and launched in the United States on September 9, 1999, as Sega's hardware follow-up to the Sega Saturn console. It sported an Hitachi SH-4 RISC processor (200 MHz, 360 MIPS), 16 MB of main RAM, with 8 MB of video and 2 MB of sound RAM, special 1.2-GB GD-ROM discs for the games, and a 56-Kbps modem in the United States (although only 33.3 Kbps in Europe and earlier Japanese models). In some ways, it's an intergenerational piece of hardware—more powerful than the PlayStation or Sega Saturn, but with weaker hardware than the PlayStation 2, GameCube, or Xbox.

Although the Japanese version of the console has a Designed-for-Windows CE logo on the front, in reality, a very small amount of games actually use the Windows CE working environment, preferring instead Sega's custom libraries. While reasonably successful in terms of software diversity, the Dreamcast didn't really build up enough of an installed base to break through. Sega finally discontinued it in early 2001, with software support sputtering out shortly afterwards in all territories except Japan, which still sees the release of occasional niche titles.

One major advantage of Dreamcast hacking is the price. You're likely to see it for $30 at most brick-and-mortar retailers or online stores. It's still fairly plentiful in the States, so you should have no trouble finding one. eBay also often has good bundle deals available; try to find a machine with at least one visual memory unit (VMU) memory card included if you want to try VMU hacking ("Hack the Dreamcast Visual Memory Unit" [Hack #52]).

If you're researching that all-important Pop N' Music controller or a Seaman plush toy, you can goggle at them online; the excellent Dreamcast History page (*http://www.dreamcasthistory.com/*) has a multitude of galleries, information pieces, and rare information on obscure titles, bonuses, and peripherals for the DC.

Getting the Right Dreamcast Version and Accessories

When buying or hacking a Dreamcast, common wisdom says that you need a unit manufactured before November 2000. Toward the end of the Dreamcast's life, Sega altered the machine's BIOS so it no longer booted its specialized MIL-CD format; as a result, you may not be able to run any homebrew CD-R discs you've created yourself. It's difficult to be sure, though. DCEmulation has done a survey (*http://www.dcemulation.com/article-supported. htm*) and has yet to find any Dreamcasts that won't boot MIL-CDs, but, naturally, your mileage may vary.

The date of manufacture should appear on the base of the unit; it should even show through a hole in the packaging, should you happen to find an unopened Dreamcast retail bundle anywhere. However, probably only 10 to 20% of all Dreamcasts were manufactured after this cut-off date, so you are fairly unlikely to run into an incompatible second-edition model.

Also, don't be concerned if the prompt to set the Dreamcast's clock pops up when you load the machine; the Dreamcast has a rechargable battery that occasionally fails completely after the console has spent a very long period of time disconnected. If this happens to you, you'll need to set the time each time you boot the machine, but it won't affect more vital settings such as your Internet ISP settings. Those live elsewhere in the Dreamcast's innards and won't be wiped out by this glitch.

Finally, if you happen to find one of the early Japanese Dreamcasts, then you have a very special console on your hands: the first ever water-cooled games machine. Although there are no outward signs, these early launch versions of the DC have a fan at the side, near the front of the machine, attached to the chips that are cooled right in the middle of the motherboard by a metal rod that has liquid (or at least water vapor) running through it—very unorthodox! Some people claim this version of the console is quieter, though that's debatable, considering that it still has a fan. After a while, the screechy GD-ROM drive access is the noisiest thing in the Dreamcast, anyhow. Still, it's an entertaining diversion.

Hopefully, your Dreamcast will come with a controller. If not, pick up one of the standard, first-party white Sega controllers. You'll need it. Otherwise, if you want to save anything in terms of save games, preferences, and such (apart from ISP settings and such for Internet access), you'll need a memory card. Find one of the official Sega VMU memory cards that have 200 blocks of memory. This is enough for multiple saves, though some games take up to 150 blocks. These cards also have LCD screens, making them suitable for further hacking ("Hack the Dreamcast Visual Memory Unit" [Hack #52]).

Play Movies and Music on Your Dreamcast
HACK #51
Turn your favorite bargain console into a multimedia workstation.

Since the Dreamcast is a relatively powerful beast, it's easy to play MP3-encoded music and watch reasonably good quality movies on it using self-burned discs. However, there's a multitude of players available, and some of the rules for encoding or playing content aren't exactly straightforward. Let's sort the wheat from the chaff when it comes to ways to turn your $30 console toy into a jazzed-up multimedia player.

Watching Movies

It's both easy and difficult to play movies of your choice on your Dreamcast, whether it be home videos you've created or freeware movies you've downloaded from the Net. Both easy and difficult? How can that be? Well, it's easy to find good-quality, multiple-format-reading freeware movie programs for the Dreamcast, because there are two of them:

- DC Movie Player (*http://homebrew.dcemulation.com/dcmovieplayer. shtml*), from the Japanese coder Bero, copes with a multitude of complex movie formats, including MPEG-1, MPEG-2, MPEG4 (DIVX4/5 and XviD), and Microsoft MPEG v1, v2, and v3 (Div-X 3), but lacks good English-language documentation.

- DCDivX (*http://www.dcdivx.com/*), despite its misleading name, actually supports a host of different movie formats (OGM, VP3, DivX 3.xx, DivX 4.xx, DivX 5.xx + Pro, OpenDivX, XviD, AVI) and has much better documentation, but lacks the common MPEG formats that DC Movie Player supports.

Both players allow disc switching, and both are reasonable at keeping audio and video in sync, often a significant problem with homebrew console video players.

However, it's difficult to use movie players on the DC, since it has so little RAM for buffering, which also limits the maximum available resolution. This means that almost any reasonably sized movie you download from the Internet may well have too much throughput or too high a resolution to play properly. You'll need to reencode your existing video files for them to play well.

If you want to know exactly how to encode video properly for playback in DCDivX, there's an excellent tutorial available at *http://homebrew. dcemulation.com/zacmcd/DcDivX4dummies/*. Here are the salient points:

- Start with the excellent Sourceforge project VirtualDub for Windows (*http://virtualdub.sourceforge.net/*) as your preferred cross-encoding software.

- Use a bit rate of 500-Kbps and a resolution of 352×288 or less. Use the MPEG layer-3 audio codec with a sound quality of around 40-Kbps 22,050-Hz stereo.

- Build a self-boot CD by downloading a special self-boot kit for Windows, available from *http://homebrew.dcemulation.com/zacmcd/ DcDivX4dummies/DcDivX4Dummies.zip*.

Playing Music

If you want to listen to music on your Dreamcast, the multipurpose freeware DCPlaya (*http://sashipa.ben.free.fr/dcplaya/*) fits the bill. You can also download this popular, French-authored program from the DCEmulation Homebrew site (*http://homebrew.dcemulation.com/dcplaya.shtml*). It sports a full GUI, great graphics, and gorgeous functionality for a free title, as Figure 5-3 shows.

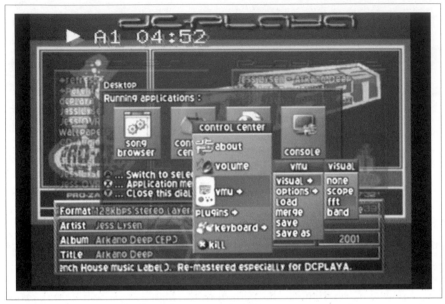

Figure 5-3. A menu screen from the gorgeous DCPlaya

The versatile player works with MP3s as well as the free alternate OGG format, the archaic but cool-sounding MOD and S3M formats, the Atari ST-associated SC68 format, and the even more archaic and funky Commodore 64 SID sound format. It even plays cool-looking VMU effects in time to the music, if there's one plugged in.

You don't need to burn the MP3s or OGGs that you want to play on the actual disc; the DCPlaya executable will stay resident in memory after you boot the CD-R. You can swap in a disc of your choice, and the player will still memory-resident and play anything you throw at it. Unfortunately, the current version of DCPlaya doesn't support variable-bit-rate MP3s, so be careful when burning or using existing MP3s.

Although you can't create M3U files on your Dreamcast, you can burn playlist files onto discs and use them to play MP3s in any order you choose.

DCPlaya uses the Lua (*http://www.lua.org/*) API, a powerful lightweight programming language designed for extending applications. You can find the DCPlaya source code from the project's Sourceforge page (*http://sourceforge.net/projects/dcplaya*). However, nobody has yet built on the DCPlaya base to add visualizations, alternate formats, or anything else; it would be amazing if someone would start. One often requested feature is the use of the broadband adapter to allow Shoutcast or Icecast streaming audio over the Net.

Playing DC Music Without a TV

Suppose you want to put your Dreamcast somewhere in the house where you don't have a TV—for example, next to your amplifier or your hi-fi in your bedroom. The Dreamcast is a versatile console, but it's hard to make up for the lack of visual output. Maybe you can muddle through the menus on something like DCPlaya by memorizing button presses, but that's no real answer.

Well, actually, I lied a little. The Dreamcast can make up for no TV-based visual output by using the Spinal Tap-influenced To 11 MP3 player (*http:// homebrew.dcemulation.com/to11.shtml*). This clever player shows all of its interface on the Dreamcast's VMU, so you won't even need a television to play music.

Apart from the two previous choices, there are alternate players with TV-based visual interfaces; some are definitely worth checking out. Examples include DreamMP3 (*http://homebrew.dcemulation.com/dreammp3.shtml*) and DreamAmp (*http://homebrew.dcemulation.com/dreamamp.shtml*), but they can't really hold a candle to the majesty of DCPlaya.

Finally, if you're interested in trying earlier media players along with home-brew games and other interesting utilities, check out the DCEvolution Dream Selection Vol.1 pack (*http://www.dcevolution.netfirms.com/ds_vol1. shtml*). This 36-MB download has 25 programs on it, including To 11, DreamMP3, and more. It includes a cool-looking GUI to boot.

HACK
#52 Hack the Dreamcast Visual Memory Unit
Play homebrew games on Dreamcast's LCD-toting memory card.

One of the more unique aspects of the Sega Dreamcast is the visual memory unit, a 128-KB memory card with a 48×32 resolution LCD monochrome screen. The VMU has clever uses for memory card management (you can manipulate and delete saves without plugging it into a Dreamcast and even connect two memory cards to trade saves), but we're really interested in it for its ability to store games. It comes with a battery and built-in controls (a D-pad minicontroller and two buttons), so you can play standalone games using it, even though it normally plugs into your Dreamcast controller.

Basically, the device resembles a teeny tiny Nintendo Game Boy. As such, it's eminently hackable.

VMU History

The VMU, also known as the Visual Memory System (VMS) in the United States, never reached its full potential during the height of the Dreamcast's popularity. If connected to your Dreamcast controller, it would sometimes show the game, logo, vital statistics, or other information while playing games. Some multiplayer games provided personal data, hidden from your opponents.

You can also use standalone VMU games with a few commercial titles. Games such as Power Stone use standalone VMU games intriguingly. Sega's Sonic Adventure is particularly interesting because it allows you to grow a cute-looking Chao creature on your VMU and then import this data into the Dreamcast game. There were also several official VMU games download-able from the Internet via the Dreamcast's web browser, for titles such as Namco's excellent fighting game Soul Calibur. However, with the Dream-cast's cancellation and the homebrew scene's interest, the VMU has seen significant and interesting independent development efforts.

Acquiring Your VMU

As discussed previously, you should be able to find a Dreamcast VMU for anywhere between $5 and $10 at your local specialty game store or on eBay. They come in a variety of fetching colors, with even limited-edition VMUs sporting Godzilla and Sonic Team themes. White and transparent are the most common colors, so don't spend too much time collecting. Just pick one up.

When you track down a VMU, whether bought in the store or unearthed in the closet, you may find that its batteries have died. The unit takes two CR2032 lithium batteries, also found in watches and cameras, so it's easy to track down replacements for around $5 for the pair. Just remove the small screw holding on the back compartment and replace the batteries to return your VMU to fighting shape.

Arming Your VMU

Transferring files from your PC to your Dreamcast may not be exactly straightforward. You have several possible choices:

Hop online

> If you can browse the Web from your Dreamcast ("Use Your Dream-cast Online" [Hack #54]), simply type—the Dreamcast keyboard is an optional and handy extra here!—a relevant URL, such as *http://www.*

rockin-b.de/vm/VM-downloads.htm, and then click on the DC links to download VMU games directly to your memory card.

The advantage of this method is that you don't need to burn CDs to manipulate VMU games. A major disadvantage is that you'll need to take your Dreamcast online somehow, which probably means you need a dial-up ISP or an ultra-expensive Dreamcast broadband adaptor.

XDP for fun and VMU profit

A simple if dubious method for acquiring VMU saves is to burn a disc of the XDP Standalone utilities and web browser package from the Psilocy-bin Dreams site (*http://www.psilocybindreams.com*).

Click one of the browser options to reach the main menu, then use the digital controller to choose the Menu option. Finally, choose the VMU Mini Games option to see a web page (as if you were actually online) that includes over 30 freeware, freely distributable VMU games. This includes the vast majority of the games we'll talk about in the next section. However, the disc also contains highly customized versions of Dreamcast browser software that, while possibly being abandonware in some abstract sense, the developers may not have permission to distribute. Bear this in mind before downloading.

This solution works because the developers burned an offline web page and a web browser onto the same disc, so it's a little like you're online.

VMU copy

The final, incomplete solution unfortunately works only for vanilla VMU data saves right now, not VMU games. This comes in the form of a downloadable utility called VMUCopy, available at *http://ljsdcdev. sunsite.dk/dl.php*. VMUCopy allows you to burn up to 19 VMU saves into a \VMUFILES directory on a disc image alongside the VMUCopy executable (called 1st_read.bin). If you then use a boot disc such as DCHakker and swap in your VMUCopy disc, you can run 1st_read.bin and then use the up/down directions on the joypad and the A button to upload them to your VMU (see "Burn Dreamcast Homebrew Discs" [Hack #57]).

While this option is excellent if you have normal Dreamcast save games that you'd like to transfer to your Dreamcast without going online and grabbing them, there's currently no functionality to detect if a save is actually a VMU game, so VMU game support is broken. Perhaps this will change in the future, though.

VMU Development Resources

Do you think you're a hardcore programmer capable of creating your own VMU games from scratch? It's definitely possible, but it won't be easy. Start with the VMU Development page at *http://www.maushammer.com/vmu.html*.

This site provides info on a VMU assembler, available in Windows, Linux, and even Amiga (!) flavors. However, VMU development has poor documentation and requires assembly code, so it's hardly straightforward. Also bear in mind that some of the interest in the Dreamcast VMU scene started to die out when the DC began to fade, so many of these pages have fallen into disarray in recent years.

To aid you in your programming task, and heck, even to run the previously mentioned VMU games on your PC as a test, download a PC emulator that claims to emulate the VMU. This should be handy if you want to check ongoing development. However, both the Windows-based VMU emulators, DirectVMS (*http://www.dcemulation.com/emu-directvms.htm*) and SoftVMS (*http://www.dcemulation.com/emu-softvms.htm*), seem to crash with some regularity on the most recent versions of Windows. You may have better luck with a Mac OS port of SoftVMS (*http://www.bannister.org/software/softvms.htm*).

Finally, if you want to know anything else about the VMU, the VMU FAQ at *http://rvmu.maushammer.com/faq.html* is an extremely useful document that explains many common problems, from how to reset your VMU to animation constraints. However, please bear in mind that its writing preceded the discovery of self-booting methods for burning Dreamcast-compatible CDs, so it doesn't cover any of the self-boot options for running VMUs.

Choosing the Best VMU Games

After you've successfully downloaded a VMU game onto your memory card, you can access it by removing your memory card from its berth in the Dreamcast controller. Press the Mode button on the controller until the playing-card icon flashes, then press the A button to enter the VMU game.

Please note that you can have only one VMU game on your memory card at a time, although you can also store multiple Dreamcast non-minigame saves. The VMU has no multiboot concept; you can't select between multiple games. VMU games may use up to 128 blocks (the official maximum), so you also need to ensure you have enough space, even if the new VMU game writes over the old one.

However, separating the quality games from the mere demos can be tricky when it comes to playable VMU titles. Frankly, it's fun to download everything because the entire VMU pantheon is limited to tens of titles. You can make your own decisions then. If you'd like to do that, you might want to check out the following:

Rockin B's VMU page
> This excellent page has quality ratings for each title, with careful picks and even screenshots of the better VMU titles. Because there's no concept of copy protection for VMU titles, it's very clear which are commercial and which are noncommercial VMU games. This page has no commercial VMU titles. See *http://www.rockin-b.de/vm/VM-downloads.htm*.

PlanetWeb's VMU site
> The people behind the PlanetWeb browser for the Dreamcast still have their page up. It includes a few VMU minigames and massive amounts of VMU animations and normal Dreamcast save games, in conjunction with the fan site Booyaka. Visit *http://dreamcast.planetweb.com/vmu/*.

DCEmulation's VMU Games
> Although it lumps everything together, this resource has some interesting VMU games of various kinds, from the sublime to the ridiculous. Learn more at *http://www.dcemulation.com/covers/index.cgi?browse&Vmu%20Games*.

If I had to pick some homebrew VMU games you should check out because they're wacky, weird, cool, or any of the above, they'd be the following:

Alien Fighter by Soren Gust
> This is an excellent vertically scrolling shooter with sound, a saved high score, addictive old-school gameplay, and all the bells and whistles that come with low-resolution black-and-white VMU fun!

Glucky Labyrinth by Omar Cornut
> This game is a fine attempt at a DOOM-style 3D maze game, with chests to open, levels to ascend, and smooth-scrolling 3D dungeons to traverse—impressive on such a limited piece of hardware.

Snaky by Anonymous
> This classic game featuring the snake with the ever extending tail that the player mustn't bump into, is fairly straightforward but still plenty of fun. It also features a high-score table for your greatest slithers.

Minesweeper by Soren Gust
> You all probably know and have suffered inadvisable addictions to the Minesweeper-style game. This is an excellent version, complete with both sound and save games.

You can download these and others (shown in Figure 5-4) from the Rockin B site.

Figure 5-4. Title screens

HACK #53   Unblur Your Dreamcast Video
Make everything all sharp for boomstick raids.

If you're playing your DC a lot, you may notice that playing through a normal TV is a little blurry. Fortunately, if you want to sharpen the images, you can duplicate a PC setup for playing Quake (keyboard, mouse, VGA monitor) with the relatively unknown Dreamcast VGA Adapter. There are official Sega adapters and a multitude of third-party clones, which tend to do the job just as well. Pick yours up on eBay or other auction sites for about $10.

This peripheral was fairly revolutionary at the time, because it allows you to connect your Dreamcast to a VGA computer monitor for a clearer, sharper picture, something no other console could officially do. Dreamcast games tend to run in a resolution of 640×480, so it makes perfect sense.

The VGA Adaptor is nothing like the VGA converters for other consoles that require much more complex electronics, because the DC naturally outputs VGA. However, bear in mind that a small number of games don't work with the VGA adapter, and some naturally low-resolution games (such as Capcom's fighting titles) may look a little blocky in ultra-sharp resolution.

Here are some notable titles to put through the VGA adapter:

Quake III by Activision/id
> It's special to have a $10 piece of hardware running VGA-quality output on your computer monitor. More to the point, in a game where seeing pixels in the distance makes a major difference in gameplay, it'll improve your playing. This works well both online and offline.

Soul Calibur by Namco
> This all-time classic 3D fighter shines even without the VGA adapter, so if you add crystal-clear VGA output to the weapon-based 3D combat, this can only be a good thing. This game runs only offline.

Phantasy Star Online V1 and 2 by Sega
> One of the best Dreamcast titles, PSO is still a basic hack-and-slash dungeon crawler with excessive item hacking from nefarious noobs online. It's still super-addictive, though, and the gorgeous visuals look even better on VGA. As a testament to the Dreamcast's power, the

GameCube and Xbox versions don't look that much better. This works both online and offline.

Guilty Gear X by Sammy

If you can find a Japanese import copy of the superior 2D fighter Guilty Gear X, you'll be amazed at the difference a VGA adapter makes. Because of the hand-drawn sprites and humble arcade origins, most 2D fighting games support only lower resolutions. Guilty Gear X runs in 640×480 and looks so much better for its VGA upgrade. This is an offline-only game.

Forcing VGA

When is a non-VGA Dreamcast game actually a VGA game? When you can use a boot disc to force it to display VGA, it seems. The DC-X Import Game Player (available from eBay and Lik-Sang), a handy tool in itself for playing Dreamcast games from different regions, actually has a boot option to enable VGA on games that don't have it enabled within the code.

The VGA option seems to be a simple toggle switch that some companies elected to disable because they didn't have time to test it properly or didn't want to support it for some other reason. Most of the titles that lack official VGA support play just fine this way, but you can't force it for some titles that don't actually run in 640×480 in the first place. Examples include earlier Dreamcast versions of SNK's King Of Fighters games and odd conversions such as Capcom's Plasma Sword.

Use Your Dreamcast Online

#54 Take Sega's remarkably versatile console onto the Net.

Though it may seem as if going online with a relatively simple console such as the Dreamcast will be dull and boring, there are actually plenty of cool things you can do. Even now, after the Dreamcast's heyday, you can browse the Web, chat on IRC, and play Quake III with PC-hosted servers. The following sections show you how.

Finding the Right Hardware

Although perhaps an idea ahead of its time, Sega bundled a web browser disc with many versions of the Sega Dreamcast. These programs supported SegaNet, the official Sega ISP, as well as an ISP of your choice, meaning the service still works even today. Additionally, several Dreamcast games allow online play or interactivity of various kinds, whether by downloading add-ons, checking out web pages from within the game, or actually playing against other human beings in real time.

However, the Dreamcast has only a built-in 56-KB modem. (European versions have a 33.6-KB modem, presumably some subtle commentary on the static-filled nature of Continental phone lines.) So, in unexpanded form, the Dreamcast has no way to attach a normal DSL or cable modem to it. Broadband is a major issue.

There is an expensive savior in the form of the official Dreamcast Broadband Adapter. Sega produced this device in very limited quantities during the Dreamcast's lifetime because broadband was much less popular back in 2000 or 2001. Now that the Dreamcast is no more, the connector is a collectible. You're likely to find the Broadband Adapter only on eBay or similar auction sites for $100 to $150. This is not a cost-effective means to hack, by any means, but it is extremely cool if you're willing to shell out the money for it.

> An earlier LAN Adapter, released only in Japan in 1999, does not work with many of the U.S. web browsers and games. Unless you have homebrew plans, steer clear. The Lan Adapter's serial number is HIT0300 or HIT0301, whereas the BBA (Broadband Adapter) has the serial number HIT0400 or HIT0401. Some unscrupulous retailers will deliberately blur the descriptions of the two, so beware.

Suppose you're stuck with dial-up to maneuver your Dreamcast around the wilds of the Net. This is no problem as long as you have a dial-up ISP. However, for many hack-centric readers, you're likely to have DSL or a cable modem, and not actually own dial-up anymore. If you're lucky, your DSL provider may provide free dial-up. Supposedly, Earthlink DSL offers this, as do some other providers. Otherwise, the late-'90s free dial-up ISP boom is over, and there don't seem to be any completely free dial-up ISPs anymore. Ad-supported ISPs such as Juno.com may give you up to 10 hours a month for free, but it's pretty impractical and may not work properly with your DC. This is a palpable problem. Your best bet is to find a broadband ISP with free dial-up, or curse like a sailor and fork out 10 bucks per month for dial-up.

Choosing a DC Web Browser

Although it seems slightly crazy, there are at least three different web browsers available for the Dreamcast. Including different versions, there are at least 10 overall. Which ones will you find in the wild? Which versions are worth using?

The PlanetWeb browser, which a third-party company made for Sega, is the most prevalent Dreamcast browser. Most U.S. versions of the console bundled it, and it appeared on several cover discs of the *Official Dreamcast Magazine*. Version 1.0 is very basic indeed, but the more common v2.0 and especially v2.6 are the easiest browsers to find. Versions 2.0 and later are fairly versatile, and they have MP3 support. Version 2.6 even runs Java 2.0. Finally, the rare v3.0 (available for a $20 upgrade fee direct from PlanetWeb during 2001 and 2002) adds the latest version of Flash that was available at the time (v4.0) and pJava, which enables Java chat not possible in other versions.

If you're in the United States and want to use your Dreamcast with the broadband adapter, you will need a browser that understands the concept of broadband, such as PlanetWeb 3.0 or XDP.

The DreamPassport browser is available almost exclusively in the Japanese language. It's a good, fully featured browser that includes many of the best features of PlanetWeb. It also allows broadband adapter use. However, you're relatively unlikely to see an English-language version anywhere outside of unofficial homebrew-hacked versions.

The DreamKey browser, more readily available in Europe, is a dumbed-down browser that often supported only the SegaNet ISP. It isn't versatile in the slightest, so avoid it if possible. Some Dreamcast games, such as Skies Of Arcadia or Sonic Adventure 2, actually have this browser built-in, even in the U.S. versions. You may have to live with this if it's the only browser you can find.

However, there is a fourth way. An important, but slightly suspect homebrew-adapted innovation trumps all of these browsers. Download the XDP browser from the Psilocybin Dreams page (*http://www.psilocybindreams.com*) and burn it onto a self-booting CD. The disc includes a translated version of DreamPassport as well as a heavily modified version of PlanetWeb 2.6. The site explains the complex changes that have been made to the various browsers, even going so far as to create multiple user agents:

> There are 3 user agents available: Original, Expanded, and MSIE 6.0. "Original" is necessary for changing or setting up Ch@b settings or downloading game saves from certain sites like Booyaka. "Expanded" is the best overall surfing browser. It gives access to Hotmail and most banking sites. "MSIE 6.0" is available for those rare sites that only accept an MSIE 6.0 browser.

However, although the developers have given away these browsers in the past, the team behind XDP do not seem to have permission to enhance them in such a way. Even if viewed as abandonware, this excellent compilation may have suspect permissions.

The Dreamcast for Network Infiltration

To think way outside the box with regard to uses for your Dreamcast online, the hackers of DC Phone Home (*http://dcphonehome.com/*) have turned the console into a network infiltration tool. Drop the Dreamcast in a quiet part of an office building and plug it into a network socket using an included LAN adapter. At that point, as their FAQ explains (spelling and punctuation reflect the original document):

> First it checks for common TCP ports let out of firewalls. If it finds one, it starts vtun. If no TCP port are found, it checks for UDP ports (like 53). If it finds a UDP port, it starts cipe over UDP. It then checks for ICMP, if ICMP is available, it starts icmptunnel. If TCP, UDP, and ICMP fail, it attempts to discover a proxy server. If a proxy server is found, it starts PPP over SSH, via the proxy server, using proxytunnel. Once the device starts the tunnel, it sends its network information over the tunnel to the phonehome system so the attacker can setup routes to the internal network.

Provided you have physical access to a facility, your Dreamcast can be a cheap, effective infiltration tool that works from the inside out—much easier than from the outside in! It's ingenious, though DC Phone Home has never released the software for download, and the scarcity of the broadband adapter raises the expense of a throwaway tool. Still, this is clearly a proof of concept for security researchers rather than an actual black-hat piece of evilness. It's an interesting concept showing off what you can do if you start thinking creatively about cheap and hackable hardware.

HACK #55 Host Dreamcast Games Online

DC online gaming still has a little life left in it, even after Sega has bailed out.

Because each Sega Dreamcast came with an included modem ("Find a Hackable Dreamcast" [Hack #50]), it was one of the first consoles to support mass online gaming ("Use Your Dreamcast Online" [Hack #54]). For a while, Dreamcast online gaming was seriously hot. Unfortunately, Sega shut down the servers for most of their Dreamcast games in June 2003. Many excellent titles such as Bomberman Online, Chu Chu Rocket, Alien Front Online, and the Sega Sports titles are no longer playable on the Net because Sega has not released their server code to third parties.

This is a definite shame, but it doesn't mean that those games are useless. There are a couple of bright spots in the Dreamcast online canon that you can still log on to and play even today.

Quake III

id's (*http://www.idsoftware.com*) Quake III benefitted from synergy with the PC version. PC servers can actually host Dreamcast players, so you'll never have trouble with anyone shutting down the official servers; you can always create your own!

To set up your own server, you'll need a copy of Quake III for the PC as well as various extra free downloads. Then you do a bunch of tinkering. The excellent Dreamcast OnlineConsoles site has the best tutorial on how this works (*http://dreamcast.onlineconsoles.com/phpBB2/content_q3_serversetup.php*).

Briefly, you need to run Quake 3 v1.16n on your PC. Download the special Dreamcast-only *segapak.pk3* map file (*http://dreamcast.onlineconsoles.com/ q3ss/segapak.pk3*) and the Dreamcast map pack (*http://www.fileplanet.com/ files/60000/61677.shtml*). When this is done, you can grab a relevant configuration file, also hosted at the Dreamcast OnlineConsoles site. Create a shortcut with the following Windows syntax (or equivalent on other platforms):

```
"C:\Program Files\Quake III Arena\quake3.exe" +set dedicated 2 +exec ffa.cfg
```

Presto! Your Dreamcast friends can play Quake III. PC gamers who have the Dreamcast map pack installed can even join in, though if your Dreamcast buddies are playing with the joypad, you'd better give them a big head start!

Phantasy Star Online

Phantasy Star Online is still available in more than one theoretical flavor. As of this writing, the European versions of PSO, v1 and v2, still have their servers, although the U.S. servers are gone. If you'd like to play on the European servers from the United States, it's possible to purchase a PAL version of Phantasy Star Online and use the Utopia boot disc (*http://homebrew. dcemulation.com/Utopia.htm*) to boot the PAL version. You will not need an PAL television, in this case, as the Dreamcast will output NTSC. You can then play the game normally. However, there's no guarantee how long these servers will stay online; they may be gone by the time this book is released.

Sega seems to have ignored the obvious alternative: reverse-engineering a PSO v2 Server. Some intrepid folks are doing just that. Their plans and site are very much in flux right now, so you'll need a CodeBreaker tool (an Action Replay–style device) to make things work. Search Google for PSO

Dreamcast homebrew server to find the latest information on this valiant effort to keep a closed-down game working.

Burn Dreamcast-Compatible Discs on Your PC

Burn your own special, personal Dreamcast CD-Rs.

In order to burn standalone self-booting Dreamcast discs on your PC, you need the ability to burn relatively complex CD images. The BIN, CUE, and ISO formats generally lack sufficient disc information. Therefore, most Dreamcast-disc images come in NRG or the more popular CDI format.

As for the media itself, normal CD-Rs will work. There's no possible way to burn GD-ROMs, the Dreamcast's proprietary format, unless you have a special Dreamcast-specific burner and a Dreamcast developer's kit. Unless you've done some very pricey eBay shopping, it's doubtful that you do.

The CDI format originated with Padus Discjuggler (*http://www.padus.com/ products/discjuggler.php*). It's now also available in the $50 utility Alcohol 120% (*http://www.alcohol-soft.com/*). Fortunately, there's a 30-day full-featured demo version. This is one of the best products with which to try Dreamcast CD burning.

NRG, the less common alternative, is a custom format created by the Windows program Nero Burning ROM, more often just called Nero. There's a demo version of Nero available on the official site (*http://www.nero.com/*) that is limited to single-speed burning. The full version costs around $80.

Here's the step-by-step version of burning a CDI image using the trial version of Alcohol 120%:

1. Download the trial Windows version of Alcohol 120% (*http://trial. alcohol-soft.com/en/download_120.php*) and install it to a sensible location on your machine. Launch it. It will configure its virtual drives and should autodetect your CD burner.

2. Prepare your disc image. Use the self-booting CDI image of Great Giana Sisters (*http://www.gianas-return.de/downloads.html*), a sideways-scrolling platformer originally released in the '80s that draws absolutely no inspiration from a certain pair of plumbers. Unzip the file to somewhere obvious. From the File/Open menu in Alcohol 120%, load the image. You'll see support for plenty of other formats mentioned in the file window, including the sometimes-alternative Nero image (.NRG) format.

3. Hit the Image Burning Wizard link on the main screen of Alcohol 120% (or from the File menu), as shown in Figure 5-5. Review your file selec-

tion and ensure that it has two sessions, each with a track. This is the special data structure necessary to make self-booting CDs work reliably. Hit Next, and make sure your CD recorder data is set up properly; then hit Burn. Follow the usual caveats for burning CDs. If your machine is a little sluggish, for example, you might want to reduce the burning speed.

4. Pop the finished CD into your Dreamcast, boot it, and prepare for a little Giana sibling fun and shenanigans.

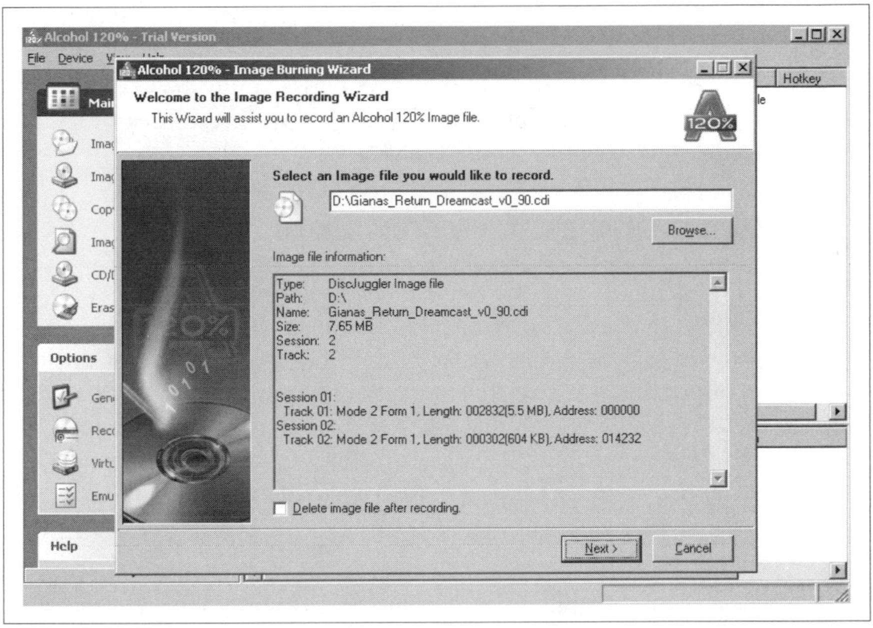

Figure 5-5. Using the Image Burning Wizard in Alcohol 120%

Various other lesser-known programs use both the NRG and CDI formats, but bear in mind that some may try to convert the original formats to the ISO or BIN standards before burning. This can interfere with the complex CD formatting required for self-booting CDs. Burning coasters may be useful at first, but it's a tad annoying when the number of coasters outpaces the amount of people who drink beverages in your house.

Unfortunately, Mac or Linux burning software doesn't often work well with these exotic formats, so you'll have an easier time using a Windows machine to burn these particular hacks. Fortunately, Curmudgeon Gamer has been experimenting with methods of burning on Linux that seem promising (check out *http://curmudgeongamer.com/article.php?story=20040105232756356*).

As well as the simpler, standalone CDI files, you can also burn multiple small homebrew Dreamcast programs onto one disc and then use a self-booting menu to switch between them. Obviously, this doesn't always use a CDI format, because you can select the executables you want to add, which adds some multisession weirdness. This deserves a separate hack of its own ("Burn Dreamcast Homebrew Discs" [Hack #57]).

HACK #57 Burn Dreamcast Homebrew Discs

How to discover and boot the best DC homebrew stuff.

Why does the author have a Dreamcast fixation in this book? For starters, there's a forward-looking, constructive homebrew coding scene for the console. Most importantly, it's relatively easy to burn your own self-booting CDs for the console, saving you having to buy and install complicated, possibly less-than-legal modchips. This, in turn, has led to a real burgeoning of creative homebrew software for people to download and run on the DC.

To start exploring the marvellous world of Dreamcast homebrew software, make DCHomebrew (*http://www.dchomebrew.org/*) your first port of call. Formerly part of the DCEmulation.com site covered in other hacks, it's seen a major revamp and is particularly useful due to their hosted and well-updated lists. The site also stores all the files it covers locally, so, in theory, there are no broken links.

Self-Booting DC Menu Systems for Homebrew Games

If you want to make the most of your Dreamcast, you need some way to burn your own self-booting CDs. I've dealt with the packaged CDI archives in a separate hack ("Burn Dreamcast-Compatible Discs on Your PC" [Hack #56]), but that won't help much if you have lots of tiny programs you want to select, one by one, from a menu.

The basic approach is to burn a standalone CD with a menu system such as DemoMenu or (my favorite) DCHakker, then burn a separate CD with all your homebrew titles on it. The homebrew CD needs a specific directory structure, so use DiscJuggler or a similar specialized CD-burning utility.

The Dreamcast Help site (*http://www.consolevision.com/members/fackue/tut_demomenu.shtml*) has a tutorial on this very subject that's well worth your time. Here are its salient points:

Grab and burn your boot CD . Although there are other, older options, the best boot discs are DCHakker (*http://www.dchomebrew.org/dchakker.shtml*) and DemoMenu (*http://www.dchomebrew.org/Demomnu.shtml*). These allow you to load almost any Dreamcast homebrew executable except those created using WindowsCE. Fortunately, that's a very small percentage of titles.

Burn a multisession disc. Open your favored CD burner (the tutorial uses Nero Burning ROM), select the Start Multisession Disc option after bypassing the Image Wizard, and choose ISO Level 2, Mode 1, ISO 9660, and Joliet. Then add your files. You can drag any homebrew title from Windows to the root of the disc, but remember to rename the *.BIN* file if you have multiple programs to burn, lest multiple files overwrite each other. When you've finished, write the disc.

Boot with the menu disc. You should be able to boot your Dreamcast using DCHakker or DemoMenu. Switch to your homebrew CD. You should then be able to access and run any of the executables on it.

One of the coolest things about this method is that these self-boot menus support multisession burning, so you can keep adding new homebrew DC titles. Since you'll likely want to try new programs or new versions, this can save you from burning dozens of CDs with only about 100 KB of data apiece.

Simply take the CD-R back to your CD burner, and burn extra data to it. In the Nero CD-burning tool, select the Burn ISO option, Continue Multisession Disc, and then add new files before selecting the Write CD dialog as before.

Self-Booting DC Menu Systems

An alternative to booting from one CD and switching to another is to burn CDs that include a self booter as well as multiple homebrew programs. The application in question is the Windows program SelfBoot Inducer[*] (*http://consolevision.com/members/sbiffy/files/*). In some ways, this is the easiest approach, especially because it produces a convenient self-booting CD

---

[*] If the file you want to burn is an *.SBI*, this is your only option.

containing the excellent-looking Dream Inducer menu system. Of course, you can burn this disc only once; there's no multisession fun.

The DCHomebrew site has an excellent SBI tutorial (*http://www. dchomebrew.org/burnsbi.shtml*), but it's really a little simpler than the boot CD method, especially if you have Windows. Grab the SelfBoot Inducer application, copy the *.SBI* files into the *C:\Sbinducr* directory, run the program, and decide whether you want to output the disc image file in DiscJuggler, Nero, or another format. This produces a ready-to-burn CD image that boots with a menu showing your choice of SBI files. It's really as easy as that.

The Best DC Homebrew Titles

I've talked up the homebrew scene pretty heavily. What's worth exploring? The following are just a few of the all-time classic and particularly cool pieces of homebrew software, excluding, of course, any of the emulators ("Emulate the SNES on the Dreamcast" **[Hack #18]**) or music and movie players ("Play Movies and Music on Your Dreamcast" **[Hack #51]**).

Beats Of Rage. Although completely homebrew in construction and coding, be aware that Beats Of Rage uses some sprites and backgrounds unofficially from SNK's King Of Fighters series as well as backgrounds from Sega's Streets of Rage series. However, if you can get past this reuse (and it's a completely different genre of game from KOF), you'll find one of the most delightful, fully formed titles on the DC. Neill Corlett has successfully produced a classic Sega Streets Of Rage–style scrolling beat-em-up, originally created by Senile Team. Though there's also the original PC version and a modchip-only PlayStation 2 version, somehow the DC feels like the right place to play this game. See *http://senileteam.segaforums.com/bor.php*.

Ghetto Pong. Inspired (an odd word to use) by the classic Atari game, this early, unofficial effort from Cryptic Allusion is a two-player funfest. Though it features new backgrounds and music, the main draw is the same great Pong gameplay that has kept people playing for over 30 years. Download it from *http://www.dchomebrew.org/ghetto.shtml*.

Alice. This is an amazing-looking, fully featured platform game. It's a side-scrolling platformer featuring gorgeous pastel illustration-like graphics and fun playability. Though it's still in early development at press time, the DCEmu site has some very attractive screenshots (*http://www.dcemu.co.uk/ alice.shtml*). Alice really looks professional; all the better to give away for free. Learn more from *http://www.dchomebrew.org/alice.shtml*.

Feet Of Fury. This homebrew title from Cryptic Allusion has a nicely featured demo version available for download, but the full version actually comes on a CD and costs money, despite being an unofficial, self-boot-style title without Sega's approval. While you may scrunch up your face at this, the game is a rather full-featured, Dance Dance Revolution–inspired title. It features 22 songs to step along to and works with the Dreamcast DDR controller. It even has a Typing Of Fury section that uses the Dreamcast keyboard and the DDR interface to pastiche The Typing Of The Dead, a cult Sega game in which you have to type words as quickly as possible to defeat zombies. Even if you don't go whole-hog and buy the title, there's a good preview version available from *http://www.feetoffury.com/fof_download.php.*

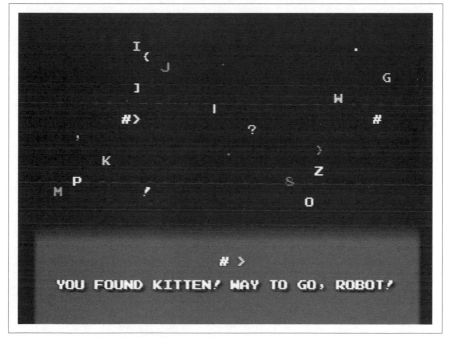

Figure 5-6. Will robot ever, ever find kitten? We hope so.

RobotFindsKitten. This title is one of the most genuinely marvellous pieces of software ever invented. The ASCII-based game bills itself as "yet another zen simulation." The instructions speak for themselves:

> In this game, you are robot (#). Your job is to find kitten. This task is complicated by the existence of various things which are not kitten. Robot must touch items to determine if they are kitten or not. The game ends when robotfindskitten.

As you'll see from the homepage (*http://robotfindskitten.org/download/Dreamcast/*), RobotFindsKitten has ports to almost every system imaginable There's even a version for the GP32 and one for the Sinclair ZX Spectrum (I guess that means you can emulate the Spectrum version on your GP32 and then emulate that on ... Okay, crazy talk).

RobotFindsKitten is less a game and more of a way of life (see Figure 5-6). It's fun to wander around until you find kitten, at which point you feel happy and can start again.

HACK #58   Buy Your Own Arcade Hardware

Know the hardware to buy when it comes to playing arcade games.

Having your own, personal arcade machine is a very cool thing, and there are several ways you can make this a reality. Of course, there are plenty of intricacies to deal with; for example, what's the JAMMA standard? Should you buy a large American cabinet at auction or hold out for a sweet sit-down Japanese minicabinet? Even if you're not interested in the titanic task of building an arcade cabinet from scratch, there's still plenty to learn about buying, understanding, and customizing your own arcade hardware.

Arcade Cabinet Hardware Basics

If you're starting from scratch and know absolutely nothing about arcade machine hardware, think of an arcade machine as a big games console and the games as cartridges. Simply open your cabinet, plug in the cartridge (the circuit board containing the game), and turn on the cabinet to play that game. You don't need any detailed electrical knowledge at all.

However, the console/cartridge analogy doesn't quite hold water because there's no built-in CPU in the arcade machine itself; the arcade game circuit board is a self-contained computer that has all the gaming hardware needed to play that game. Obviously, this makes arcade games potentially expensive propositions. Imagine buying a whole new PlayStation 2 every time you want to play a new game! Fortunately, because arcade operators very quickly switch games, there's a flood of older titles that nobody except collectors want, so secondhand prices for arcade boards are relatively reasonable.

Although there was a mess of conflicting standards early in the life of the arcade machine, the Japanese Amusement Machine Manufacturer Association, or JAMMA, introduced a standard in the mid '80s that most games have since followed. If you have a JAMMA cabinet, you can easily swap Final Fight for Bad Dudes Vs. Dragon Ninja, because they both connect to your cabinet using the same pin-based connector.

However, there are custom variants of the JAMMA standard. Some recent games, usually with custom controllers or cabinets, don't adhere to JAMMA at all. You can still go a long way by buying a JAMMA cabinet, though. Browse the Killer List Of Videogames (*http://www.klov.com/index.php*) to see the percentage that support JAMMA and you'll see what I mean.

If you're really a classic-game fan, you have to accept that Pac-Man won't easily play in the same cabinet as Q-Bert, because they both use nonstandard, non-JAMMA connectors. If your classic games have fairly standard controls, you may be able to find JAMMA adaptors for each in places such as the Multigame.com web site (*http://www.multigame.com/KITS.HTM*), but it's really not straightforward. Worse yet, Pac-Man cartridges rarely exist outside of Pac-Man cabinets, and it's the artwork of classic cabinets that makes them particularly good-looking. You may do best buying specific old arcade titles as separate machines, then buying a generic JAMMA cabinet for everything else.

The other alternative for running those classic arcade titles is to run the MAME emulator through JAMMA. See the PC2JAMMA project (*http://www.mameworld.net/pc2jamma/*) for more information. Heck, you could skip the JAMMA step altogether and make a fake arcade machine. It's not the real thing, of course, though it's workable. It's also ethically and legally dubious unless you own the original boards or run legal ROMs from places such as StarROMs.

Finding a JAMMA Arcade Cabinet

You've made the momentous decision to buy a JAMMA cabinet somehow. What are your options, and how much will they cost you? The following sections describe what's available.

Buying used U.S. JAMMA cabinets. If you're looking for a JAMMA cabinet originally constructed in the States—the larger, stand-up, heavy arcade cabinets, generally made of wood, that you'll see in your local game room or bar—then you have a few choices. Go on eBay, find a live auction, or talk to your local arcade operator.

Because eBay has a Location/International option in its advanced search that will find items local to you, you can search for arcade cabinets in your area. Be aware that shipping cabinets can be as or more expensive than the cabinet itself—even brief freight trips to you, the lucky buyer, can cost over $300. If you can manage it, try to buy a cabinet you can pick up yourself.

You may need to do some detective work to see if the cabinet in that perfect eBay auction supports JAMMA. Search for information on the game currently working in the cabinet with KLOV (*http://www.klov.com/index.php*). Many cabinets that include games won't have the phrase "JAMMA compatible" in their listings, even though they actually are.

Make a note of the button configuration, too. The basic JAMMA setup supports two players with three buttons per player as well as a Start button. If the cabinet you're bidding on has fewer buttons, you may have trouble playing standard JAMMA games without modifying your control panel.

As for auctions, Super Auctions (*http://www.superauctions.com/*, shown in Figure 5-7) is probably the most famous regular arcade game auctioneer in the United States. It holds multiple yearly auctions across the country. Prices range from a hundred to over a thousand dollars, depending on the size and quality of the cabinet and the ferocity of the bidding.

Figure 5-7. Super Auctions, the only major U.S. arcade auctioneers

Finally, it might be worth going into your local (perhaps slightly run-down) arcade to see if there are any old cabinets the owner might sell cheaply. Unfortunately, given the upkeep of a lot of these establishments, you may not find a perfectly preserved artifact, but it's better than nothing.

Buying used Japanese JAMMA cabinets. Although the mid- and late-'90s Japanese arcade cabinets that made their way to the States have the same basic design and no region lockouts, they have quite a different style and form factor than American cabinets. To start with, they're generally made of metal and are much shorter, so players sit, not stand, at them. They also have

Cabinet Auction Fever

If you're at an auction, remember that buying a generic JAMMA cabinet with a poor-quality game already installed in it can be much cheaper than shelling out more cash for a similar cabinet with a particularly well-known game in it.

For example, I was at a Bay Area auction in which a JAMMA cabinet with the X-Men fighting game in it sold for over $600, whereas basic old JAMMA cabinets with early-'90s titles in them went for $100 or so. You can buy the X-Men cartridge for under $100 on eBay, so what are you really paying for?

However, in this case, the cheaper cabinet wouldn't have the Capcom fighting game harness with the extra buttons needed to play six-button Capcom games.

larger monitors—at least 25 inches diagonally—and have generic, good-looking decals on the sides that should suit almost any game you put in them. If you can deal with sitting down to play and sometimes being uncomfortably close to your fellow player when dueling in two-player combat due to the smaller size, then Japanese cabinets are the stylish, cool-looking choice for the JAMMA acolyte in a hurry. Remember, you can play American games in Japanese cabinets and vice versa.

Finding Japanese cabinets is a little trickier than old American cabinets, though. The vast majority of these cabinets enter the United States via container ships steaming into Los Angeles. You'll always find at least one seller on eBay selling generic Japanese JAMMA cabinets. Prices start at around $250 for 25-inch monitor models and can reach $700 or more for deluxe 29-inch versions. These cabinets are actually branded around specific arcade game manufacturers, but will work for all JAMMA titles nonetheless.

Some common Japanese cabinet brands turning up in the States include the Sega Aero City and Astro City, the quirky but excellent-looking Taito Egret, and a variety of SNK Candy cabinets that come ready with the extra JAMMA connections to play Neo Geo games. Most of these cabinets sell without any included games, incidentally. Unlike the majority of U.S. arcade cabinets, which started life with a specific game inside, Japanese cabinets are completely generic by design.

The biggest problem with buying Japanese cabinets is probably location, location, location. Unless you live close to Los Angeles, you'll probably spend $300 to $500 just to ship the cabinet to your house. The problem is similar to that of buying nonlocal American cabinets, which means that the relatively competitive pricing on these Japanese-imported cabinets becomes uncompetitive pretty quickly. Many collectors think the extra shipping is still worth it to pick up good-looking, versatile Japanese cabinets, though.

Building your own JAMMA cabinet. Cabinet building is an extremely complex topic all on its own, admirably covered in another O'Reilly Hacks title, *Hardware Hacking Projects For Geeks*, which you should check out at your leisure. Suffice to say that many cabinet-building projects don't include JAMMA connections; they are set up for the player to simply put a PC and a normal computer monitor into the cabinet and pretend like it's a real arcade machine. I call that cheating, but your mileage, naturally, may vary.

Anyhow, if you want to build a cabinet and then build JAMMA connections into it, the ArcadeRestorations.com site has a good explanation of how to go from an empty cabinet to a JAMMA cabinet (*http://www. arcaderestoration.com/index.asp?OPT=3&DATA=63&CBT=24*). This page explains the full, if complex, wiring setup you'll need.

Safety is really important, even if you're just buying an already constructed video game cabinet, so bear in mind that you shouldn't interfere with the innards of the machine while it's turned on. Make sure the machine is properly electrically grounded (many Japanese machines are not, as they use two-pronged plugs only), and especially avoid the back of the monitor, even when the machine is off. In most arcade machines, if you have the keys to open the cabinet and are dumb enough to wiggle your hands into the dangerous parts around the back of the monitor, there's enough voltage to kill you.

Be careful, and by all means touch the adjustment knobs often situated around the back of the arcade monitor, but try not to expire in the name of playing arcade-perfect Street Fighter II.

HACK #59 Configure Your Arcade Controls, Connectors, and Cartridges

All you need to know about hardware and software arcade controls.

Now that you know about the basic hardware setup and system choice for arcade cabinets ("Buy Your Own Arcade Hardware" **[Hack #58]**), and you have an arcade machine within your sweaty grasp, you probably want to configure it for games. Configuration options include monitor orientation, control panel and connector setup, and even the actual games themselves. The following sections describe how to do it.

Arcade Control Panel Variations

Unfortunately, arcade life isn't as easy as buying a JAMMA cabinet, finding any JAMMA game, and just playing it. To play some of the best JAMMA games, including more recent Capcom fighting titles and several of SNK's great Neo Geo carts, you need to deal with specific hardware variations, sometimes referred to as JAMMA+.

As usual, you plug your JAMMA board into your cabinet. Control-specific signals travel through the connector and up into the control panel. There are also other standard signals such as video, sound, and coin insertion. Unfortunately, each of these major JAMMA types has different control needs for dealing with extra buttons.

Basic, default three-button JAMMA. The standard JAMMA connector configuration provides the obvious audio and video throughputs, a joystick and three buttons for each of the two players, and a Start button. All JAMMA boards, even those with JAMMA+ functionality, should work with this configuration; you'll just be missing extra button controls.

Here's a diagram of those standard JAMMA pins:

```
        PARTS SIDE      SOLDER SIDE
       ---------------|---------------
             GRD   1|A GRD
             GRD   2|B GRD
             +5V   3|C +5V
             +5V   4|D +5V
              5V   5|E -5V
            +12V   6|F +12V
             KEY   7|H KEY
       COUNTER 1   8|J COUNTER
   C LOCKOUT 1   9|K C LOCKOUT 2
     SPEAKER +  10|L SPEAKER -
             N/C  11|M N/C
             RED  12|N GREEN
            BLUE  13|P SYNC
             GRD  14|R SERVICE SW
         TEST SW  15|S SLAM SW
          COIN 1  16|T COIN 2
        1P START  17|U 2P START
           1P UP  18|V 2P UP
         1P DOWN  19|W 2P DOWN
         1P LEFT  20|X 2P LEFT
        1P RIGHT  21|Y 2P RIGHT
       1P FIRE 1  22|Z 2P FIRE 1
       1P FIRE 2  23|z 2P FIRE 2
       1P FIRE 3  24|b 2P FIRE 3
```

```
N/C  25|c  N/C
N/C  26|d  N/C
GRD  27|e  GRD
GRD  28|f  GRD
```

SNK's Neo Geo extended button configuration. The setup for SNK's wonderful Neo Geo cartridge system is almost identical to the JAMMA setup, except that the unused Pins 25/c handles 1P FIRE 4 and 2P FIRE 4, respectively. This is the fourth D button for each player. Few of the basic and classic Neo Geo games, such as Metal Slug, use it, but all of the system's fighting titles, including the King Of Fighters and Samurai Shodown series, do.

> The D button is important even in fighting games in which it doesn't seem useful. For example, the taunt button mapped to D in Art Of Fighting 3 actually charges your power bar—and you thought it was completely useless.

If you have a two-, four-, or even six-slot Neo Geo MVS system in which you can plug in multiple cartridges at once, there's also a Select button to wire in. This button switches control between the different cartridges.

Keep in mind that Neo Geo games expect a specific control setup—some have the A and B buttons on top and the C and D buttons directly below them. Many of the fighting games make attacks and combos out of pressing A+B together or C+D together. If you're rewiring a six-button Capcom-style cabinet to play Neo Geo games, make sure to use this button configuration and leave the two end buttons alone. Otherwise, you'll end up playing finger-Twister to pull off your attacks. Unfortunately, other Neo Geo button layouts put buttons A through D in a row, left to right, which is even less compatible with the Capcom layout.

Capcom extra buttons. The famous Capcom CPS2 cartridge system, which has all the decent Capcom fighting games (Street Fighter Alpha, Vampire Savior, X-Men, Marvel Super Heroes) from the early and mid '90s on it, uses the Street Fighter II button-layout scheme, with a grand total of six buttons per player. There's no way to squeeze the extra buttons for these games onto the existing JAMMA harness, so there's a custom Capcom wiring harness for those extra buttons.

The games will still boot without those buttons connected,* but you'll need all the buttons connected to play properly. Unfortunately, the original versions of Street Fighter II used a different wiring scheme from the CPS2

---

* Some CPS2 games, such as Super Puzzle Fighter, don't use them at all.

harness, so bear this in mind if you happen to pick up a reasonably common Street Fighter II cabinet from somewhere. You can buy CPS2 wiring harnesses on eBay and rewire them fairly easily, however.

Of course, if you want to play Neo Geo games on a CPS2 system, remember that 1P FIRE 4 is now wired into your custom harness, not the JAMMA connector. D'oh.

Four-player extended JAMMA. This system is an extra custom button connector with all the connections for the third and fourth player; it doesn't touch the JAMMA connector at all. This is relatively rare, but games such as Konami's excellent Teenage Mutant Ninja Turtles, the X-Men side-scrolling beat-em-ups, and Midway's classic NBA Jam all have this ability. Fortunately, they all still play through the normal JAMMA connector as two-player games.

In reality, you'll probably never build two extra controllers onto your machine if you don't have them. Four-player games are sometimes no fun to play with one player; the first controller is so far to the left of the control panel, it's difficult to see the screen. If you already have a JAMMA-compatible NBA Jam cabinet, however, this information may be useful.

Choosing the right variation. What's the solution for all of this kerfuffle? If you have a six-button CPS2-style cabinet, the extra button connector also includes the wiring for the fourth button, which some Neo Geo MVS and Sega ST-V games need. This is a major issue, because you theoretically need to rewire every time you switch between the games.

One idea is to use an easily detachable bridging connector with the offending common wires connected. Again, the excellent Solvalou site has something along these lines with its Egret setup (*http://www.solvalou.com/arcade_egret.php*), using an Atari-type joystick connector as a mediator.

Of course, you can always just stick to the one game type you like.

For further reading on this subject, especially for the more exotic controllers such as trackballs and steering wheels, check out the excellent Arcade Controls page (*http://www.arcadecontrols.com/arcade_controls.shtml*). Bear in mind that many older games with exotic controllers don't support JAMMA natively, however. Those recent JAMMA titles that do use exotic controls often have such specific controls that they support only a few compatible games after installing them. I still recommend joysticks if you want to play many high-quality, low-cost JAMMA titles.

Reorient and Align Your Arcade Monitor

HACK
#60
Make the most of your arcade monitor.

Though JAMMA ("Buy Your Own Arcade Hardware" [Hack #58]) has taken much of the guesswork and incompatibility out of arcade games, it's not perfect. The first time you switch out Frogger for Xevious, you might discover that no matter how common the controls, the monitor orientation is too different. Sure, you could play with your head turned sideways, but that's not exactly healthy. Fortunately, there are options.

If you never play games of different orientation, maybe you play games of different resolution. There are solutions for that, too.

Monitor Orientation

First, look carefully at the orientation of your monitor, because arcade games have either horizontally or vertically inclined monitors. The vast majority of arcade titles use a horizontal monitor orientation. If you're buying a cabinet and you can't inspect the insides in great detail, choose one that's already set to a horizontal inclination, especially if you don't know how easily you can change it.

Software rotation. If you launch MAME from the command line, use the -ror or -rol options to rotate the screen clockwise (to the right) or counterclockwise (to the left), respectively.

If you prefer a frontend (see "Add and Manipulate a MAME Frontend" [Hack #11]), you may have options to control monitor rotation. For example, in Mame32, use the Options → Default Options menu. In the lower-left corner, you'll see monitor rotation and flipping options. Choose your orientation, apply the changes, and play!

Physical rotation. Several of the Japanese generic minicabinets, such as the Taito Egret, can rotate their monitors fairly easily via large mounted wheels without any disassembly. Unfortunately, this is much less often the case with the larger American arcade machines that often come from a specific manufacturer for one specific game.

There's a small slideshow of this momentous Taito Egret rotation occasion on the Solvalou page (*http://www.solvalou.com/arcade_egret.php*), in which the author claims that "Rotating a 29-inch monitor might not sound very easy, or safe, thing to do, but with Egret it's actually quite simple." He also makes the important point that you should definitely degauss your monitor (in this case, by pressing a red button inside the coin door) after the rotation.

Why degauss? Rotating the monitor changes its magnetic profile. Because a monitor is basically a gun that shoots electrons at the screen, you'll see distorted colors if the electrons suddenly change their paths.

If you don't have an Egret, you can modify your cabinet to allow for rotation. Your two biggest difficulties will be heat dissipation and the physical modification. Mark Jenison's Mark 13 cabinet (*http://users.rcn.com/jenison/mars/*) is a good example of an existing cabinet that has been modified. He and Rich Schieve mounted the monitor on a wheel-of-fortune device that allows the monitor to swivel. Build Your Own Arcade Controls has a fuller write-up (*http://www.arcadecontrols.com/arcade_jenison.shtml*).

Screen Resolution

Most earlier JAMMA games use normal, standard-resolution monitors, roughly equivalent to a normal television. However, some Atari games from the '80s such as Toobin' and Paperboy, as well as several more recent games, use medium resolution. Make sure your monitor supports this; many do not. Finally, some very recent games such as Sega's Naomi boards (basically cartridge versions of Sega Dreamcast games) use the high-resolution 640×480 monitor. This probably affects only 1% of all JAMMA games, mind you, but it's worth bearing in mind.

Finally, there should be standard television-style adjustment knobs somewhere around the back of the monitor. Use these to stretch or move the screen, but be very careful when making adjustments. Some JAMMA arcade boards actually have a different screen offset from others, annoyingly enough. If you can find a fairly neutral monitor position with some spare space at the edge of the screen, this should deal a little better with errant JAMMA boards.

HACK #61 Buy Cart-Based JAMMA Boards

When it comes to interchangeable arcade games, carts are cooler. Here's where and what to buy.

If you're just starting in on the arcade collector scene, the wealth of great standalone arcade circuit boards can be daunting. Fortunately, it's not as bad as it seems. Because these boards originally cost buyers well over four figures each, manufacturers in the '80s had no problem replicating everything needed (CPU, graphics chipset, I/O chips, and so on) for each individual board, especially for games that used custom hardware. Thus, games such as Pac-Man were standalone computers that plugged into an arcade monitor and controls.

As the '90s dawned, and arcade game companies discovered they used similar hardware models for their games, the idea of lower-cost, interchangeable cartridges started to gain some dominance. These carts plug into JAMMA-compatible motherboards mounted within the arcade cabinet, although the motherboards themselves are swappable like normal JAMMA boards ("Buy Your Own Arcade Hardware" [Hack #58]).

You can play any one of several JAMMA cart-based systems on your JAMMA cabinet. In some cases (such as the Neo Geo MVS), these systems are identical to home systems of the era. Other systems, including the Sega ST-V, adapted solid-state versions of CD-based games. Still more, in the case of Taito's F3 and Capcom's CPS2, use systems completely different from any home console.

By far the best thing about these systems is that the secondhand market for them is relatively slack because you need an arcade machine and interest in more recent titles to pick up the motherboards and cartridges. Games can cost less—sometimes, far less—than a current PlayStation 2 or Xbox game.

Major JAMMA Cartridge-Based Systems

One of the best ways to build a major collection of arcade game software is to buy one of these cart-based systems and then lots of individual carts. The following sections detail several notable systems.

Neo Geo MVS. As created by the divine SNK, the Multi Video System (MVS) version of their Neo Geo hardware is functionally identical to the Advanced Entertainment System (AES) home version. The Neo Geo sports a 50+ game catalog of releases from 1990–2004, after which Sammy's Atomiswave JAMMA system and standalone JAMMA boards have finally taken the 2D crown.

Neo Geo MVS motherboards themselves come in several different flavors, including different revisions with slight compatibility differences. The vast majority of the boards out there are standard one-slots, with room for one cartridge. You may also see two-, four-, and occasionally six-slots; these are the equivalent of a CD autochanger for Neo Geo games. You'll need a Select button wired into your control panel through the JAMMA harness if you want to switch between games yourself, as mentioned in "Configure Your Arcade Controls, Connectors, and Cartridges" [Hack #59]. There are regional differences, generally basic and language-based, with differing BIOS affecting the language you see the game in, but there are no region lockouts.

As for the games, there is a wealth of titles from SNK as well as external developers. Look for the Metal Slug series of side-scrolling 2D shooters; the seminal cult King Of Fighters series of Street Fighter–style beat-em-ups; and a gigantic range of sports games, puzzle titles, one-on-one beat-em-ups, action games, and other 2D sprite-based titles. The excellent Neo Geo For Life site (*http://www.neogeoforlife.com/*) reviews almost every single Neo Geo title in some detail, so that's a great starting point to track down the best titles for the system.

In terms of pricing, the older fighting titles go for as low as $10 plus shipping on eBay. Many of the best titles cost less than $50. This is amazing for large solid-state carts that originally cost hundreds of dollars each. Even the most expensive recent titles rarely cost more than $150.

Sega ST-V. Sega's own mid-'90s proprietary cart system, the ST-V (also known as the Titan in America), is essentially a cartridge version of the Saturn. Many developers either ported their titles to ST-V or made sure they developed games with small enough footprints (that is, no FMV) to make translation to the ST-V easier.

The ST-V/Titan definitely has regional lockout problems. Confusingly, they're completely different for different carts. You won't go far wrong if you buy a Japanese ST-V motherboard, though. Very few games have lockouts on it, and you'll enjoy the full game experience on the much more common Japanese carts. For example, Cotton 2's story mode disappears when the game runs atop the U.S. BIOS.

Game recommendations include the Olympic-sized 3D-totin' duo of Decathlete (a.k.a. Athlete Kings) and Winter Heat, both excellent multi-event 3D sports titles, spectacularly good puzzle games such as Baku Baku Animal, several Columns variants, and Puyo Puyo Sun (which, bizarrely but genuinely, appears with an "Action Against AIDS" charity logo on boot-up). Other games worth considering are Treasure's pricey vertically scrolling shooter Radiant Silvergun and multiple titles in the two-player Puzzle and Action minigame series.

There's one place to learn about the range of games for the ST-V: the amazing System16 site (*http://www.system16.com/sega/hrdw_stv.html*). It has pictures and names for every ST-V title ever released. Sadly, the ST-V lacks its own fan-run review site, presumably because of its overlap with the Saturn. Fortunately, if you want to know something before you buy, search for Sega Saturn reviews of the offending game. Even if it had a Saturn release only in Japan, you'll probably find an English-language review somewhere.

Again, eBay is an excellent source for games, although they appear with less frequency than carts for the MVS. Common carts can cost as little as $10, with only a few costing over $50. Radiant Silvergun is by far the most expensive, given its cult-like status and difficult availability; it can cost over $100, although that's often cheaper than the equally rare Sega Saturn version.

Capcom CPS2. Following the massive success (and, unfortunately, massive bootlegging) of Street Fighter II, Capcom developed a common platform for their subsequent arcade games. This is the CPS2, a completely custom piece of arcade hardware with no connection to any home consoles.

The CPS2 doesn't quite support cartridges as you might expect. Instead, it uses equal-sized A and B boards. The A board is the motherboard, available in blue, green, or gray, depending on its source region. The B board is the game itself. To switch games, pry out both boards and swap out the B board. They're still classifiable as carts, but they're very large—about the length and width of a letter-sized piece of paper and much thicker and heavier.

With regard to regional compatibility, twinning blue (American) and green (Japanese) A and B boards isn't a problem; they'll work without any issues. Should you see any gray (Asian) boards, be careful. Because of an intentionally inverted connector, they'll work only with other gray boards. There's more information on this in the excellent CPS2 text FAQ (*http://members. aol.com/CMull11217/private/cps2faq.txt*), which has pin-outs and everything else you'll ever need to know about CPS2.*

Do beware of the CPS2's strange B board suicide problem. Because Capcom wanted to avoid the bootlegging problems of Street Fighter II, they sealed off everything under plastic and stored a special encrypted key in SRAM on the board. Five to ten years after the board's manufacture, an onboard battery will die, losing the encrypted key from SRAM. The game will then refuse to play, even if you replace the battery. Razoola has a good FAQ about the fairly technical method of dealing with this problem on his site (*http:// cps2shock.retrogames.com/suicide.html*). He's even managed to resurrect dead boards, but it's extremely complicated and involves decrypting game ROMs. It's probably better to swap out the battery before it dies in the first place.

There are around 30 games available. Obviously, six-button fighters dominate, including plenty of Street Fighter games (all the way up to the new-ish

---

* The page had infrequent updates as of the time of writing, which is unfortunate.

Street Fighter Alpha/Zero 3), the gorgeous Darkstalkers/Vampire Savior series, as well as Marvel Super Heroes, X-Men, and Marvel Vs. Capcom. There are also some marvellous cult titles of a different flavor lurking in the library, especially the Dungeons And Dragons side-scrolling action RPG games and the genius Super Puzzle Fighter puzzle game.

Pricing for CPS2 games depends on whether the battery has been replaced. It general, it's a little higher than for MVS or ST-V games. Prices start at $30 for the most obvious and common fighters such as the original Darkstalkers or Street Fighter Zero/Alpha. Expect to pay three figures for rarer and more desirable carts such as Super Puzzle Fighter.

Other systems. There are a few other, less popular interchangeable systems. Taito's F3 (*http://www.system16.com/taito/hrdw_f3_page1.html*) is a very interesting cart-based custom system and is especially good for classic Taito puzzlers. Nintendo's PlayChoice was a pioneer, basically putting NES carts in the arcade. Sega's recent Naomi requires a very expensive JAMMA adaptor to behave properly on most machines.

Buying JAMMA Systems and Carts

If your curiosity is piqued, there are a couple of different places you may be able to pick up JAMMA cartridge-based systems and carts.

eBay. It may be obvious and tedious, but the trading behemoth is one of the best places to find cheap deals on carts, especially Neo Geo MVS and Sega ST-V carts. Be very thorough with searching, though. Some Neo Geo MVS carts lack the string MVS in their descriptions. Worse yet, some people advertise their Sega ST-V carts as STV and others as ST-V. Search carefully.

Hong Kong or Japanese arcade dealers. Several Asian-based retailers, such as the Hong Kong specialists at Cosmicco (*http://home.netvigator.com/ ~cosmicco/*), sell JAMMA cart motherboards and carts themselves. The high shipping prices from the East don't make it worth it unless you're buying a large amount of items or particularly obscure titles. At the time of writing, Cosmicco had carts for the super-obscure Taiwanese IGS PGM cart-based JAMMA system. These rarely surface on eBay at all.

Specialist message boards. Although many of the more obscure systems lack fan pages, the excellent site at Neo-Geo.com (*http://www.neo-geo. com/*) is a major trading hub for MVS games. It also sometimes has other JAMMA-related material for sale by users. Although it has no formal feedback system as eBay does, traders are friendly and will call out scammers and other ne'er-do-wells.

There are other possible places to find these JAMMA boards and carts; however, U.S. arcade vendors are sometimes very expensive compared to the previous options. Trying to buy directly from Japanese auction sites such as Yahoo! Japan is very tricky because many buyers will not ship internationally, and you may have a language barrier.

However you find your JAMMA boards and carts though, I hope you have fun.

When swapping JAMMA boards, be careful how you connect them. If you don't pay attention, it's possible to connect JAMMA boards upside-down so that the first pin on the board connects to the last pin on the connector. This can be horribly bad, because you can fry the board. Some JAMMA connectors physically stop you from doing this by blocking off some of the pins, but most won't. Pay attention to any markings on the JAMMA board, or check the pattern of wires on the connector compared to the available connections on the board itself. You should see a gap in roughly the same place.

HACK #62 Programming Music for the Nintendo Entertainment System

Turn the classic console into a musical instrument.

The Nintendo Entertainment System (NES) was released in North America in 1985, two years after its release in Japan where it was known as the Family Computer (Famicom). It enjoyed a particularly long life, remaining in production for nearly 10 years. Over these years, hundreds of games were released for the console, and it could certainly be argued that it earned the title of king of the 8-bit generation. One of the most memorable aspects of the NES was its distinctive sound—the cute chip melodies many of us can still easily recall today.

However, maybe it's time to stop humming the theme from Super Mario Bros. and start composing your own music for this legendary console. This is where MCK/MML comes in, a toolset that provides you with everything needed in order to program original tunes for the NES. So let's get to it!

MCK/MML Workspace Setup

The first step is to download the necessary files. The first four files are available from *http://www.geocities.co.jp/Playtown-Denei/9628/*:

mck_0228.zip
mckc025.zip
dmcconv005.zip
mckc-e.txt

This file is available from *http://www.magicengine.com/mkit/download.html*:

mkit251_dos.zip

Organize MCK/MML workspace. Create a folder called *workspace,* and unzip all files contained in *mck_0228.zip* and *mckc025.zip* into this folder. Now extract only *nesasm.exe* from *mkit251_dos.zip* into this same folder. Next, create a new folder inside *workspace* called *DMCconv,* and extract the files from *dmcconv005.zip* into this folder.

Create and modify files. Create a new text file, call it *songdata.mml,* and place it in your *workspace* folder. This is the text file from which you will use the Music Macro Language (MML) to program your tune. First, open *make_nsf. txt,* and scroll to the end of the file where you will find several *.include* statements. After the last one, add this line to the file: `.include "songdata.h"`.

Also look for these lines in *make_nsf.txt*:

```
.org    $800E
    db    "Song Name"
    db    $00
.org    $802E
    db    "Artist"
    db    $00
.org    $804E
    db    "Maker"
    db    $00
```

This is the part of the NSF header that identifies the tune. Modify these header fields appropriately, as shown next (be aware that there is a 31-character limit for each):

```
.org    $800E
    db    "My First NES Chip"
    db    $00
.org    $802E
    db    "Nullsleep"
    db    $00
.org    $804E
    db    "2003 Jeremiah Johnson"
    db    $00
```

Generating the NSF File

Create a new text file, open it up, and type the following:

```
mckc_e songdata.mml
del nesmusic.nsf
nesasm -raw make_nsf.txt
ren make_nsf.nes nesmusic.nsf
```

Save the file, close it, and rename it *build.bat*; this is a simple batch file that will run all the commands to generate an NSF file from the MML data. By this point, everything should be set up properly, and you can get started programming MML.

Basic Song Setup

Just like a normal song with a key, a time signature, and musical staves, a MML song needs several pieces of information.

Header credits. After opening up *songdata.mml* in your preferred text editor, you should add header lines to the top of the file; these identify yourself as the composer and note the title of the song. For example:

```
#TITLE My First NES Chip
#COMPOSER Nullsleep
#PROGRAMER 2003 Jeremiah Johnson
```

Note that the incorrect spelling of #PROGRAMER is a typo within MCK itself.

Channel layout. The NES has five channels that are defined in MML as:

A   First pulse channel

B   Second pulse channel

C   Triangle channel

D   Noise channel

E   DPCM channel

This hack covers the programming conventions for each channel; because their operation is identical, A and B are covered together.

Tempo settings. Tempo can be set individually for each channel; however, it's likely that you will usually want all channels to play at the same speed to keep everything in sync. The tempo for all channels can be set simultaneously by typing **ABCDE t150**.

In MML notation, this says: for channels A, B, C, D, and E, set the tempo to 150 beats per minute. The valid range of values for the tempo is 1 to 255.

Volume settings. The pulse wave channels (A and B) and the noise channel (D) of the NES have volume control, while the triangle wave channel (C) and the DPCM channel (E) can only be turned on or off. For the pulse and noise channels, there are two options for setting volume. The first is to just set a constant volume level: **A v15**.

This sets the volume level for channel A to 15. However, in most cases, using a volume envelope is a better choice. Here's a volume envelope example:

```
@v0 = { 10 9 8 7 6 5 4 3 2 }
```

The volume envelope takes values between 0 and 15. The highest volume is 15; 0 is silence. The last value is held until another note is played. Note that if neither a constant volume nor a volume envelope is defined for the pulse channels (A and B) or the noise channel (D), you won't hear any sound output on these channels.

Pulse Wave Channels (A and B)

The next step is to set up each channel individually with the properties it requires. Here is a standard setup for a pulse wave channel:

```
A 18 o4 @01 @v0
```

For channel A, this translates to:

- Set the default note length to eighth notes.
- Set the octave to the fourth octave.
- Set the duty cycle to 01 (25% duty cycle).
- Use volume envelope 0 (defined earlier).

Duty cycle. Think of a pulse wave as a square wave with a variable width. In a square wave, the width is fixed at 50% (half up and half down), but pulse waves have more flexibility. This flexibility is referred to as the *duty cycle* (or sometimes the *timbre*) of the pulse wave. Here are the four possible duty cycle settings for the pulse wave channels on the NES:

```
        _
00   | |              | 12.5% thin raspy sound
     | |_ _ _ _ _ _ _|

      ___
01   |   |            | 25% thick fat sound
     |   |_ _ _ _ _ _|

      _ _ _ _
02   |       |        | 50% smooth clear sound
     |       |_ _ _ _|

      _ _ _ _ _ _
03   |           |    | 75% same as 25% but phase-inverted
     |           |_ _ _|
```

Programming. Now that the pulse channel (A) is set up, here's an example of a note sequence that can be programmed on it:

```
A c d e f g4 a16 b16 >c c d e f g4 a16 b16 >c<<
```

If you know standard music notation, most of this should look familiar. Basically, it's just note values followed by note lengths. Create sharps or flats by adding either a + or -, respectively, after the note value. The notes in an octave, as seen on a piano keyboard are:

```
  c+ d+    f+ g+ a+
| #  # |  #  #  # |   additionally:
| #  # |  #  #  # |   r = rest
| #  # |  #  #  # |   w = wait (rest without silencing
|__|__|__|__|__|__|             the previous note)
  c  d  e  f  g  a  b
```

Because the default note length for channel A is set to eighth notes, this melody plays c d e f notes for an eighth length each, then the g note for a quarter length, followed by the a and b notes for a sixteenth length each. Next is the > symbol, which switches an octave up (to the fifth octave), and then the c eighth note plays. Now the scale repeats again before finally switching back down two octaves (to the original fourth octave set for the channel). Additionally, in reference to note duration, it's possible to use dotted notes. Dotting a note increases the duration of that note by half its value. These examples should help illustrate this:

c8.

C note played for an eighth plus a sixteenth

d4.

D note played for a quarter plus an eighth

e4..

E note played for a quarter plus an eighth plus a sixteenth

f2..

F note played for a half plus a quarter plus an eighth

Now, getting back to the previous example programmed on the first pulse wave channel (A), notice that this sequence plays only once. The full sequence or small portions of it can be looped using brackets followed by a loop count, as shown here:

```
A [c d e f g4 a16 b16 >c c d e f g4 a16 b16 >c<<]2
```

This loops the entire sequence twice, which can be handy for keeping your MML code clean and saving unnecessary typing. To give this sequence a little more of a dynamic feel, set up another volume envelope, and switch between the two. You'll end up with something like this:

```
#TITLE My First NES Chip
#COMPOSER Nullsleep
#PROGRAMER 2003 Jeremiah Johnson
@v0 = { 10 9 8 7 6 5 4 3 2 }
@v1 = { 15 15 14 14 13 13 12 12 11 11 10 10 9 9 8 8 7 7 6 6 }
ABCDE t150
A 18 o4 @01 @v0
A [c d e f @v1 g4 @v0 a16 b16 >c c d e f @v1 g4 @v0 a16 b16 >c<<]2
```

This volume envelope switching puts a slight emphasis on the quarter notes because of the higher initial volume setting of the new volume envelope and its slower decay rate. All of this can be applied identically to the second pulse channel (B) as well.

Triangle Wave Channel (C)

The operation of the triangle wave channel (C) is similar to the pulse wave channels with the exception of volume envelope and duty cycle parameters. The triangle channel has no volume control or duty cycle settings. Taking these things into consideration, the initial setup of the triangle channel is fairly straightforward:

```
C 14 o3 q6
```

These settings should be recognizable aside from the q parameter. The q stands for "quantize," and it can take values from 1 to 8. Notes are divided into eight equal parts, and this value determines how many divisions of the note to play before cutting it. For example, the q6 setting we used will cut the note after 6/8 of it has played.

Here's an example of a bass-line sequence on the triangle channel:

```
C c e g8 g8 a16 b16 >c8 c e g8 g8 a16 b16 >c8<<
```

Noise Channel (D)

The noise channel (D) can be a fairly versatile instrument with a bit of work. A few possible applications include waves crashing on a beach, rocket engines roaring, dark fiery dungeon sounds, and supplemental percussion to enhance your drum samples. Like the pulse wave channels, volume envelopes are used by the noise channel and are an important part of getting good sounds out of it. Additionally, it has two modes of operation: normal and looped noise. The looped noise setting can generate interesting, somewhat metallic sounds. The pitch range of the noise channel is limited and loops every octave, making octave changing unnecessary. The c note seems to be the high pitch, with the pitch moving slightly downwards over e, f, g, a, and finally to the b note, which seems to be the lowest pitch.

Initializing and programming. Here are a couple of simple volume envelopes that can be used for some basic percussion on the noise channel:

```
@v2 = { 15 12 10 8 6 3 2 1 0 }
@v3 = { 15 14 13 12 11 10 9 8 7 6 5 4 3 2 1 0 }
```

After setting up the volume envelopes, initialize the channel:

```
D l4 o1 @0 @v2
```

For channel D, this translates to:

- Set the default note length to quarter notes.
- Set the octave to the first octave.
- Set the noise mode to normal (@1 turns on looped noise).
- Use volume envelope 2.

Here is a little sequence of simple noise drums:

```
D @v2 b @v3 e @v2 b @v3 e @v2 b @v3 e @v2 b @v3 e8 @v2 b8
```

DPCM Channel (E)

The DPCM channel, or delta modulation channel (DMC), plays back samples on the NES. This can be useful for programming drums, sampled bass lines, or even vocal samples. Its operation is simple and fairly straightforward, with few parameters. Like the triangle wave channel, there's no volume control; the DPCM channel is either on or off. Additionally, the NES uses its own one-bit sample format, which you have to convert your samples to before doing anything else.

Creating DPCM samples. The DMCconv program converts your samples from *.wav* to *.bin* for use with MCK. The documentation for DMCconv isn't in English, but its operation is simple enough. For example:

```
DMCconv kick.wav kick.dmc
```

This converts a *kick.wav* file into a kickdrum sample usable by the NES with all the default settings.

Initializing and programming. Once all desired samples are converted, create a directory called *samples* within the *workspace* folder to store the samples and initialize the channel in the MML, as follows:

```
@DPCM0 = { "samples\kick.dmc",15 }
@DPCM2 = { "samples\snare.dmc",15 }
E o0 l4
```

This maps the first sample, *kick.dmc*, to @DPCM0, which corresponds to the c note on octave 0. Notice that the second sample, *snare.dmc*, maps to @DPCM2, which corresponds to the d note. @DPCM1 is skipped over to avoid mapping samples to sharps/flats and keep the MML more readable:

```
E c d c d c d c d8 c8
```

See Also

That covers the basics of programming music for the NES, but we have really only just scratched the surface. For a comprehensive listing of MML effects and commands, see the *mckc-e.txt* file by Virt mentioned at the beginning of this hack. For troubleshooting help and detailed instructions on how to play your NSF songs on a real NES console, visit *http://www. 8bitpeoples.com* or *http://www.nullsleep.com*. For additional help and feedback, check the forums at *http://www.2A03.org*.

Thanks to Izumi, Manbow-J, Norix, Virt, Memblers, and everyone at 2A03. org and MCK 2ch.

Playing Around the Game Engine

Hacks 63–78

For some people, the game's the thing. For others, finding new uses for the game engine is more interesting. There's a reason people use DOOM for system administration and Quake for architectural ideas. That's also the idea behind *machinima*, movies made using game engines and characters as settings and actors.

Even if you've already saved the princess, defeated the evil elder god, or arranged hundreds of thousands of lines of falling colored blocks, there's still a second game—bending the rules of the game as far as you can. Maybe breaking the rules can breathe new life into your favorite game, whether editing your save files or finding new gameplay ideas the designers never intended. That can take the form of making your characters invincible, weaker, richer, stronger, or weirder than anyone ever intended. Maybe you'll play through the game as quickly as possible or finish with the weakest character possible.

Whatever your idea, there's certainly more fun to have being untraditional.

HACK #63 Explore Machinima

Games aren't just for playing anymore.

Games *are* primarily for playing, but the form that playing takes is very flexible. Some people use game engines to replace physical architectural models. Others have adapted them to art installations. Still others make movies that their budgets or the real world wouldn't normally allow: these are *machinima*.

Isn't That a Kind of Japanese Pornography?

Back in the wilds of 1996, when the world was so fresh that people still thought "dot-com" sounded neat, Quake emerged from the tortured brains of id Software, and it was good. Quake inspired other things, including the rise of the 3D accelerator, the growth of the mod scene (which had started with DOOM), and Daikatana, which wasn't so good.

Quake was one of the first 3D games to provide a genuinely 3D world, rather than a cheap 2.5D fake like virtually everything that came before it. It also sparked the mod community; people could, and did, edit almost everything that made it a game. Quake also had the curious ability to record games as replayable demos.

It's obvious, in retrospect. Essentially, moviemakers now had a real-time 3D environment they could customize at will—virtually unheard-of outside the realms of $300K Silicon Graphics stations—with the ability to film any action they wanted to put into it. Looked at from a certain direction, Quake, and every other 3D game that has followed, is a completely customizable, completely controllable virtual movie set: the indie film director's wet dream.

It took a certain unusual combination of game geekery and film obsession to spot that back in the beginning, but the people who did so fell upon this new opportunity like starving dogs who'd sneaked in the back door of a restaurant. Early films were primitive, but they rapidly gained sophistication, moving from the Quakester antics of Operation Bayshield to enormous projects that completely remade games, such as Hardly Workin' and my own Eschaton series. Now, bigger projects such as Red vs Blue, made by a bunch of guys with some spare time and copies of Halo, have started to earn real money.

Machinima is starting to gain mainstream acceptance. The release of games like DOOM 3 and Half-Life 2 provides engines with near-to-film graphics capabilities. Now, anyone with some dedication and access to modern computer games can make his own action, science-fiction, or whatever movie, in his spare time.

By anyone, I mean you.

The Best Machinima Anywhere

You may never become a famous machinima director (or even pick up the virtual camera), but that doesn't mean that the medium is forever out of reach. We'd be nowhere without an audience. With that in mind, here are a few of the top machinima available today that you can download and play almost anywhere. (You can find all of them and more at *http://www. machinima.com/films.php.*)

Anna by Fountainhead Entertainment
(http://www.machinima.com/displayarticle2.php?article=411)

A Hans Christian Anderson–tastic little fairy tale about the life of a flower.

Ozymandias by Strange Company
(http://www.machinima.com/displayarticle2.php?article=300)

An early and extremely popular art-house machinima piece adapted from Romantic poetry.

Rendezvous by Nanoflix
(http://www.machinima.com/displayarticle2.php?article=22)

Nanoflix is one of machinima's rising stars. This is a story of two space probes in love.

Hardly Workin' by the ILL Clan
(http://www.machinima.com/displayarticle2.php?article=133)

Two lumberjacks get a job in this improvised comedy; it's possibly the most successful machinima film before Red vs Blue.

Red vs Blue by Red vs Blue
(http://www.redvsblue.com/)

You probably already know this fantastic, sharp comedy set in the Xbox game Halo.

A Gratuitous Plug for the Machinima Production Kit

As some spoilsport biography may have mentioned, I'm the editor-in-chief of Machinima.com (*http://www.machinima.com/*), the biggest Machinima portal on the Internet. Amongst the little goodies we have hidden in our verdant leaves is an introductory kit for the machinima-curious, the *Machinima Production Kit*.

You can grab the Machinima Production Kit right now, from *http://www. strangecompany.org/page.php?id=50*. It's free—in fact, mostly open source— so you can do pretty much whatever you want with it.

It includes everything you need to start making machinima films, including demo editors, video-editing software, tutorials, and sample content. It's based on the venerable Quake II engine, so it should work on just about any computer with a 3D accelerator.

Obviously, since it's open source, it is constantly under development (and we'd appreciate any assistance with that...), but it should help you get started.

See Also

I'd imagine that our little whistle-stop tour through machinima has done little more than whet your appetite for information on machinima or encourage you to hastily flip forward. Where can you learn more?

The first place you should look is further on in this very book. We have more hacks devoted to this process, including choosing the right engine ("Choose a Machinima Engine" [Hack #64]), filming your story ("Film Your First Machinima Movie" [Hack #65]), recording the footage ("Record Game Footage to Video" [Hack #67]), and making the most of your keyboard controls ("Improve Your Camera Control" [Hack #66]).

Next, you'll probably want to surf onto the Information Superhighway and bathe in the pure spray of content therein. Machinima.com (*http://www. machinima.com/*) has over 10,000 pages of machinima-related content, including news, articles, films, utilities, and the most active machinima forums on the Net.

Finally, the Academy of Machinima Arts and Sciences (*http://www. machinima.org/*), which runs the one and only Machinima Film Festival in New York City, also has an excellent site with frequent details on machinima events.

HACK #64 Choose a Machinima Engine

Choose the right balance of features and ease of use before filming your own machinima masterpiece.

After exploring the genre ("Explore Machinima" [Hack #63]), perhaps you'd like to try your hand at making a movie. It's not quite as easy as pointing a video camera at a deathmatch screen. You have to know what you want to do and what your engine can do.

How do you know all that? Read on.

What Do You Need?

The simplest way to make machinima is to grab a computer game (or some other software, but I'm concentrating on games here), torture it into producing the proper visuals, and write the end result out as a film in whatever format you prefer.

However, there are a bunch of wrinkles to that. As with any other art form, there are multiple ways to work, and the way you'll work will be very personal to you. First, you must consider the "people good or bad" argument.

Actors or programs. When you're making machinima, you have a bunch of virtual actors standing around in a virtual world doing, in the immortal words of the ILL Clan, virtually nothing. You have to inveigle* them into doing what you want. You have two choices: control them with machines or with people.

Your first option is to use the game's own artificial intelligence to control your actors, usually through some form of scripting language. Yes, you too can now control an army of robotic minions. Theoretically, this means you can make an entire film by yourself. The creator of Nehara made an entire three-hour movie this way in six months. In addition, your actors will work as long and hard as you will, and you have total control over their every movement.

The other option is to have your actors controlled by actors, or, at least, humans. Grab the mouse, configure WASD and a bunch of emote keyboard commands, and you're off. It's fast, it's fun, and it's very flexible: humans don't give you syntax errors and they don't crash, except possibly after a 16-hour session fuelled entirely by Jolt Cola and goodwill.

Beg, build, borrow, or steal. Next, you have to choose whether you will use in-game content (maps, characters, special effects, etc.) or new work.

In-game content is convenient, it doesn't demand any artistic skill, and it's normally of high quality. However, if you want to use all in-game content, you need to tailor your film to the content available.

A lot of groups end up creating their own content because they feel that the existing in-game maps and models don't suit their movie. This is a very good idea if you want to differentiate your film, or if you want to make something totally different from the norm. See films such as Hardly Workin', Eschaton, or In The Waiting Line. However, don't underestimate the amount of time this will take. Two of the films I mention took more than a year to produce, and the other had a commercial budget.

Of course, this relates to another choice: the game you will use. With the wide range of 3D games now available, most of them including editing capability, you can usually find something that will suit the story you want to tell.

Neither of these choices is exclusive. Indeed, often the best approach is to mix the two. As I write, Strange Company is doing preparation work on our

---

* This was my Word Of The Day: *http://dictionary.reference.com/wordoftheday/archive/2003/05/22.html*.

next film, Bloodspell, which will combine live actors acting in close-up scenes with gigantic AI-controlled 50+-character battle scenes. It's much easier to direct live actors, but I can't fit 50 people in my office, so we use a combination approach.

Demo or movie. Finally, you need to choose how you want to distribute your film, either in a conventional video format such as AVI or MPEG, or in a special file to play back in the game. The advantages and disadvantages here are pretty simple. More people can easily watch MPEG, AVI, or Quicktime files, but you'll get higher resolution for smaller file size if you distribute in-game. A lot of the time, your game choice will dictate your distribution method. If your game can't play back demos, you need to capture the action of your film using a video capture card. At that point, you can't go back to in-game.

Enough theory. Now it's time to choose an engine.

A Little Bit of This and That

Different games have different advantages when it comes to machinima creation. Older engines often have more support, with people who know how to work them, and a lot of supplementary material available. Newer engines have more features and often prettier abilities. The choice of engine comes down to the film you're making.

The following sections explain several criteria to use when evaluating any game engine.

Included content. Does the content available in the game fit your vision? If you want to make SF action, Unreal Tournament 2004 is a pretty good bet. If you prefer a gripping noir saga, though, Max Payne's more your style.

Evaluate *all* the content in the game, in context, not just in an editor (this means playing the game—bummer!), and remember to check out the available mod content. Neverwinter Nights, for example, has good default content, but the vast, vast array of available mod content really lifts it as a machinima engine. However, be aware that mod content often won't work as well as the original game content.

The game community. That a game doesn't have a large community around it tells you two things. First, you'll be on your own when figuring out the intense weirdnesses of how the engine works (and *all* games are intensely weird and frustrating in their own ways). Second, if no one's modding the game, there may be a reason for that; perhaps the game's a bear to mod.

On paper, Vampire: the Masquerade: Redemption looked like a great machinima game. However, it was nigh on impossible to mod because of its peculiar mapping system and scripting based on hardcore programming languages. Its nascent mod community died prematurely. Any machinima creator who set his heart on using it would have had No Fun At All.

The game's community is also your primary audience for any film. A tiny community may well predict a tiny audience.

Available engine features. A huge feature list isn't the most important part of a machinima project, but some features are very useful.

Check that the game can somehow do lip-syncing. That mechanism could be skeletal animation (Half-Life), morph targets (Anachronox or Half-Life 2), or even simple skin swapping (many Quake 2 machinima). If there's no lip-syncing in the game itself, perhaps you can either animate the heads of characters somehow or *quickly* swap textures on the head. Neverwinter Nights, for example, has no built-in lip-syncing, leading Strange Company to some very interesting reverse-engineering to make a movie in it.

You don't always need lip-syncing—Red vs Blue doesn't have it—but it looks odd to see a character's mouth remain rigid while he's talking.

Skeletal animation is good. Blended animation and procedural animation are better. The former means that you can combine several different animations at once; the latter means that you can directly control individual bones on the model at runtime. Blended animation is extremely useful for characters who look around as you move the mouse.

Anything that makes your movie look pretty is great. Red vs Blue succeeded in part because the Halo engine is so pretty, and in part because Halo's procedural animation lets the actors move the characters' heads.

A scripting language is very helpful, as is built-in machinima functionality. However, don't expect much here. For starters, if you're filming live, you won't use these features much. Second, most machinima scripting systems aren't great. There are exceptions to this rule, with cheers to both Ritual Entertainment and Epic Megagames, but even these systems need tweaking, modification, and even abandoning, depending on how you make your film.

Look for machinima scripting languages that use real film metaphors. If a scripting language talks about creating dolly shots, crane shots, and track-and-pan shots, there's a good chance it's pretty solid. A good scripting language, whether it's machinima-capable or not, is a great asset to the machinima creator.

Machinima Engine Recommendations

So do I have any recommendations for engines? Well, yes, although they'll probably be out-of-date by the time this book goes to print.

Quake 2. The granddaddy of them all is still alive and kicking, thanks to much open source coding. The engine lacks skeletal animation but features some pretty good graphical improvements despite its age, with quick skin swaps and tons of content and support. In particular, the machinima support for this engine is excellent; check out the Machinima Production Kit (*http://www.strangecompany.org/page.php?id=50*).

Half-Life. This engine ages like a fine wine; it's still probably the most popular game engine ever. Automatic lip-syncing, some neat skeletal stuff, a fair degree of machinima support, and a huge community make HL a good option, despite its aged graphics. Machinima.com has some introductory tutorials (*http://www.machinima.com/displayarticle2.php?article=92*).

Unreal Tournament 2004. This engine is a strong contender. It has good to great support, including a lot of support from the creators, a robust machinima system, and a pretty nice-looking engine, plus lots of content. UT 2004 seems to be the choice of a new generation. See the Machinima.com tutorial (*http://www.machinima.com/displayarticle2.php?article=316*).

Neverwinter Nights. This is a slightly strange choice. It has a huge community and masses of content, but the slightly old, although still pretty, engine has some strange limitations. It has skeletal animation but no controllable procedural animation and no blending. Lip-syncing is a complete bear. I recommend it for advanced users; it's also your best option for a fantasy film.

Halo. There's no modding, but the engine is very, very pretty, with a huge community. The "no modding" thing, though, really does limit what you can do with it. Red vs Blue worked within these limitations, but that's a hard trick to repeat.

Half-Life 2. It's not quite out as I write, but everyone expects this to be the Machinima Engine of the Gods. It promises advanced physics, beautiful graphics, powerful scripting, and advanced facial animation, plus lots and lots of mod support and a huge community that will follow it over. HL2 should be the next big thing indeed. Some people predict that it will take machinima into the mainstream.

All Dressed Up

With your engine chosen; props, models, and effects created; and voice recorded (unless you plan to use in-game voice), you're ready to roll the whole shebang. The next stop is recording your movie ("Film Your First Machinima Movie" [Hack #65]). I know, I didn't tell you how to make she-bangs. You'll have to figure that out yourself.

Film Your First Machinima Movie
#65 Film your own virtual worlds.

You don't have to sell your body to science to make a good film. Yes, Rob Rodriguez did it to make *El Mariachi* (try not to think too hard about that), but you don't have to.

Live filming—the part of machinima creation where you make the film, in real time—is the engine behind the purring power of machinima. By taking computer graphics away from the painstaking, slow work of conventional computer animation and into the world of real time—the same world inhabited by Real Film and puppetry—machinima creates a totally new way of making film in a computer. It sacrifices the absolute control and incredible detail of conventional animation for the flexibility and speed needed to tell a long story without giving your life to it.

In a lot of ways, the closest equivalent of what you're doing when you make live machinima is puppetry, the same kind used by Jim Henson's Creature Shop or Gerry Anderson. As this implies, yes, every machinima character to date has, in fact, been a complete Muppet.

Put All Your Dominos in a Row

(I've never quite understood why project planners had such an obsession with pizza, but anyway…)

How do you start this mysterious process? The Strange Company procedure is quite simple:

1. Put a bunch of computers together in one location.
2. Network them.
3. Load up the game we're using, whether Half-Life, Quake 2, NWN, or whatever, and have everyone join the game as a player.

4. Persuade people to stop shooting each other.

5. Assign one or more people the job of cameraman and attach their computers to recording equipment.

6. Persuade people to stop shooting each other. This can take some time.

7. Divide up the rest of our team as characters are needed in the scene.

8. Lights, camera, action. Our cameraman moves to a position in which her viewpoint frames each shot as we want it, while the actors move the characters around, make them speak, and do other actorish things. Meanwhile, the recording computers record the shot onto video ("Record Game Footage to Video" [Hack #67]).

9. Wrap.

Sounds like the setup for a LAN party? You're right. Live machinima filming is really, really simple; essentially, you're filming a LAN party.

The Practice of Acting

Machinima's often fairly hard to understand when described in the abstract, so here's a concrete example. Here's a script version of a typical Strange Company machinima recording session:

```
          INTERIOR, DAY—The Strange Company Mansion

A small room filled to bursting with computers in various stages of
rebuilding. Hugh—our handsome, talented, charismatic hero—is fiddling about
finalizing a set in Neverwinter Nights.

The door opens, and Steve—a Penny Arcade-obsessed Geordie and our assistant
for today—enters.

                        Hugh
Hey. Right, we're shooting Scene 17 today.  Jump on the second PC and load
up the Dungeon Master client, then connect to my server.

                        Steve
W00t! I am a l33t ha><0r dung30nm4ster d00d!

                        Hugh
Stop that.
Right, give me a moment to make my character invisible, then I'll move the
camera until I've got our opening shot set up.

Much fiddling and swearing ensues.

                        Hugh
Ok, done. Now, I need you to spawn in as Frodo and start over in that arch
(points) just out of shot.
```

Steve sarcastically SALUTES—a gesture lost on Hugh, who can't see him from
where he's sitting—and clicks to move his unfortunate hobbit victim.

                    Hugh
Right. Now, what I need you to do in this shot is to walk out to here
(points on screen), then play the "shocked" animation and say, "Oh, no, a
pervy hobbit fancier."

                    Steve
Right. I'll bind the animation to the left mouse and the voice chat to the
right mouse, then.

                    Hugh
Lucky that online voice chat works well. Okay, ready? I'm starting the
recording now.

Hugh walks across the room, clicks to start Adobe Premiere recording the
action, then dives back to his seat like there's a velociraptor of hard disk
usage behind him.

                    Hugh

Action!

Steve clicks. In the game, his character moves across the screen to a
perfectly framed location, then plays an animation.

                    Frodo
Oh, no! A pervy hobbit fancier!
Hugh hits the "stop" button on Premiere.

                    Steve
w0Ot! We are 733t ha>‹Ors!

                    Hugh
Stop that.

They move on to the next shot.

Get That Demon Off My Set!

That's the basics of machinima filming. Armed with that knowledge, you
should be able to make your own little movies straightaway. However, here
are a few tips that will help you as your movies grow more involved:

Don't film over the Internet if you can possibly avoid it.   On a film set,
  communication is absolutely vital; there are so many things going on,
  and so many of them are complicated, fragile, and liable to go wrong,
  that you need to communicate as clearly and precisely as possible. Filming over the Net really doesn't facilitate this.

If you have to, you can shoot large crowd scenes on the Internet, but for anything involving complex actions or characterization, position your actors so that you can slap them if something goes wrong, at least in a caring way.

Consider your filming setup. There are many ways to shoot films, handed down to us in history from the Filming Masters Above. The best way to work is to design your shot list (you have a shot list, right?) with as many creative people as you can, concentrating on maximum coverage of your scene from minimum time.

Consider the relative advantages of shooting shot-by-shot with shooting an entire scene for coverage. In the first case, you'll shoot very small, controlled sections, but you'll also have very little leeway to change the film in the editing room. If you shoot the entire scene four or five times from various shots, you'll have a lot more flexibility, but there's more room for things to go wrong. Even if they do, though, you can probably still use some of the footage.

If you possibly can, have two cameramen working at once. When your actors finally, shockingly, do everything right, doubling your camera coverage will save you time.

Be creative with controls. The obvious way to control your characters is the standard mouse-and-keyboard WASD setup, with additional keys bound for emotes and lip-syncing. This isn't necessarily the best way to work. If your game engine will bear it, investigate alternative controls.

Mice, for example, suck eggs when it comes to controlling camera pan or head movement. You can better control your cameras with joysticks, or bind one key to pan and another to change the speed of the pan up or down ("Improve Your Camera Control" **[Hack #66]**). The ILL Clan in New York invested in $20 Nostromo glove sets for controlling their characters' emotes, giving them up to 90 different available emotions without moving their left hands. Strange Company has had multiple people controlling a single character, with some controlling head movement and others controlling body and face.

Play around. This is a very new art form, and no one's discovered the best way to do things yet.

Practice, practice cliché. You won't do everything, or even most things, right the first time. It will take time for your actors to adapt to controlling characters, time for you to acclimate to directing in a virtual world, and time for your cameramen to realize that, when they're filming, they can forgo hitting the dodge-left button to avoid invisible rockets.

Before you embark on any major filming, rally your group and spend as much time as possible practicing. You'll be very glad of it later.

Design your maps with shooting in mind. Remember, you have all the resources of a computer game at your disposal, designed by up to 100 people over two or more years. Don't ignore all the cool stuff the game developers have given you.

For example, if you're shooting in Half-Life, and you need to perform a complex track-and-pan maneuver like the one at the start of *The Player*, don't do it by hand! You'll kill yourself before you succeed. In the movies, the pros use a track setup, essentially a short train track on which they mount their camera on a tripod. What did you see right at the start of Half-Life? Yep, it's a complex track setup you can easily duplicate in Worldcraft and use as a platform for your camera person!

A common problem DV movies have is a lack of space. Often you hear directors lamenting that they can't move a wall for one particular shot. *You* can. Design two versions of your set and forget to include a wall in one of them.

Remember, you're shooting film in a virtual reality. Make sure to design reality to your best advantage.

Next Step, Garage Kubrick

You're now well on your way to machinima Spielberg-dom.

For more information on this subject, Machinima.com, as always, has a wealth of information. The "Making Machinima" series at that site covers the same ground as this hack, but in a little more detail. Check out Part 2, which covers filming, at *http://www.machinima.com/displayarticle2.php?article=318*. The "Technical Info" section has a wealth of knowledge on all sorts of things that relate to filming, find it at *http://www.machinima.com/articleselected.php?value=category&id=3*.

HACK #66 Improve Your Camera Control
Straighten out those herky-jerky camera pans.

When recording a machinima live ("Film Your First Machinima Movie" [Hack #65]), you may find that nothing's quite as frustrating as making the camera do exactly what you want. This is particularly true when making dramatic pans. You can avoid this by always recording static shots, in which you aim the camera at the actors, yell "action!", and leave it alone—but that's boring.

You *could* script the camera (and that's what you'll have to do if you use Unreal, at least until its makers fix the camera demo recording), but that's harder and more tedious.

If you want creative camera shots, you need a human on the keyboard; the mouse is just too jumpy. Unfortunately, when you're panning the camera with the keyboard, it's difficult to slow down as you near your goal. Fortunately, you can create nice speed step-up and step-down effects with some clever key bindings.

Changing Quake's Yaw Speed

The console in Quake 2 and 3 allows you to change your *yaw speed*, the speed at which you turn while using the keyboard. Bring up the console with the tilde key (~), and type the following command:

```
] /bind c cl_yawspeed 25
] /bind d cl_yawspeed 140
```

Hit the tilde key again to return to the game. The default turning speed is 140, so turn left and right with the keyboard to acclimate yourself to the normal yaw speed. Be sure to note how jerkily you stop when you release the key.

Now hit the c key and try turning again. You'll move much more slowly. Press d to return to your normal speed. You can even toggle between speeds as you're turning.

Yaw Speed Step-Down Bindings

The real trick is decreasing your turning speed in small steps. The easiest way to do this is to bind a series of unused keys all in a row to progressively smaller steps; we'll use c, v, b, n, and m. We won't bind anything to the comma key so as to leave a buffer if we overshoot the right keys in our excitement. Here are the bindings:

```
] /bind d cl_yawspeed 140
] /bind c cl_yawspeed 25
] /bind v cl_yawspeed 15
] /bind b cl_yawspeed 10
] /bind n cl_yawspeed 5
] /bind m cl_yawspeed 2
```

Feel free to experiment with these values, especially the normal yaw speed.

Now try turning and hitting the keys in ascending and descending order. With a little practice, you can ease into and out of a pan almost as if you had manual control of a camera. This is only the tip of the iceberg of the

available console commands that may come in handy when recording
machinima—or just playing games.

See Also

- PlanetQuake's console pages (*http://www.planetquake.com/console/*).
- PlanetQuake's list of Quake 2 console commands (*http://www.
  planetquake.com/console/commands/quake_2.html*).

H A C K   Record Game Footage to Video
#67   Save your machinima masterpieces for posterity.

Machinima ("Explore Machinima" **[Hack #63]**) were once simply demos, created and played back entirely inside a game engine, such as the original
Quake. An entire miniature Hollywood formed around using 3D games with
no external editing of any kind. Things are different now. Machinima has
grown up from its roots. Once a machinima creator has had his first taste of
Adobe After Effects, it's hard to lure him back to pure Quake editing. More
importantly, many games don't have the facilities to create machinima movies the old-fashioned way—even powerful, cool games such as Halo. Gamers had to extend their technology and learn how to capture normal video
from games.

Want to make your own Warthog Jump? If you already know how to film
your machinima ("Film Your First Machinima Movie" **[Hack #65]**), you need to
record your footage. Keep reading.

From PC to Video

Films such as Red vs Blue are actually recordings of what the creators saw
on their screens straight into some video format. You *could* do this by pointing a camera at the screen, adjusting the refresh rate of your monitor appropriately, and sitting there. Thankfully, there's a better approach: TV-Out.

Nearly all video cards these days have some form of TV-Out capability.
They're mostly pretty good, too. ATI used to have the edge, and possibly
still does, but as DVD playback has increased in importance, NVidia has
improved their output quality markedly.

The solution is simple. Take your TV-Out, attach it to some form of video-
recording device, and record the results. Here's the step-by-step process:

1. Enable your TV-Out. This usually means fiddling with the control panel
   of your particular video card's drivers. See your card's manual for
   details.

2. Connect an S-Video or composite video lead to your video card (the socket's normally next to the VGA Out) and connect the other end to a DV camcorder or a PC with some kind of video capture capability. You don't need much here; a TV capture card, such as a Hauppage card, plus a fast hard drive will do the trick, particularly if the capture card can do MPEG-2 encoding.

3. Start the capture device. You're going to chew up lots of hard-drive space if you're recording to PC, so make sure you have at least a few gigs free.

4. Play your game. If you're recording a networked session ("Film Your First Machinima Movie" [Hack #65]), remember that the PC that's connected to the capture device is effectively your camera. Turn off the HUD graphics for the best effect. See your game's manual for screenshot options.

Troubleshooting Overscan

If you see big black lines around your image, you have the infamous overscan problem, connected to the way your card encodes the TV signal. The fix depends on your hardware. ATI and Matrox users can simply adjust the overscan settings in their video card drivers to remove the black borders.

NVidia users don't have that option right out of the box. Fortunately, the venerable TVTool (*http://www.tvtool.de/*) provides a bunch of TV-out tools for NVidia cards, including overscan removal. It costs approximately $20.

Alternatives to TV-Out

By now, a bunch of experienced recorders have shouted "FRAPS!", to which I respond, "Bless you."

FRAPS (*http://www.fraps.com/*) is a program that allows you to capture video directly from an OpenGL or DirectX stream, much like having a capture station on a single computer. The quality of the video you can capture is arguably higher frame for frame than TV-Out-captured video, but it requires a very powerful computer to capture FRAPS video at anything like real time. To capture 25-fps (frames per second) video, I recommend a RAID array and a CPU speed at least 2 GHz higher than the minimum your game requires, plus about half a gig of spare memory. FRAPS is great for rough captures, but for good-quality video, it currently can't beat TV-Out for quality.

If you're lucky enough to have access to very expensive video-editing gear, some high-end video cards now support component video output. This is a much higher-quality output signal, but only $5,000 plus video-editing set-ups can provide component video inputs at the moment. However, if you have this equipment, you're laughing: this is the same setup LucasArts used to use to capture game footage for trailers.

See Also

For more information on capturing game video, see Machinima.com's "Capturing Game Video" series (*http://www.machinima.com/displayarticle2.php?article=149*). It deals with virtually everything you need to know, in more detail than I can possibly cover here.

Speedrun Your Way Through Metroid Prime
Don't have time to stop and smell the roses? Excellent—you'll like speedrunning.

Speedrunning, trying to complete a video game in the fastest time possible, is almost as old as gaming itself. At least, it's almost as old as games that have a definite end point or staging points, because speedrunning a game with infinitely repeating levels is Sisyphean. That's good fun until the novelty wears off.

Speedrunning needs boundaries. Start with a game that you can finish or a game with lots of individual levels with their own ending points. Then try to complete them in the fastest possible time.

It seems so easy. First, you find a nice path or a little trick to cut a corner. You practice for a while until you have a great time. Then, as you're preparing to claim your bragging rights on the Internet, you find out that other people have done the same thing, only faster. If you're drawn to finding out their secrets and beating their times, you have what it takes to be a speedrunner.

Speedrunning Basics

What's involved in speedrunning a game? On a technical level, there are three main points: route planning, sequence breaking ("Sequence-Break Quake" **[Hack #69]**), and tricks. On a personal level, there's determination, persistence, skill, practice, and time.

Why do it? Possibly for peer respect. There are certainly bragging rights attached to being the first person to demonstrate a route or trick. For money and power? Unlikely. I'm not aware of a single millionaire who made his fortune speedrunning games. Maybe you want to get the most out of your game.

The practice and persistence needed to perform runs certainly adds to the replay value and helps you wring every cent of value out of your investment.

I don't think these are the main motivational forces that drive people to truly master a game. Most importantly, it's fun, at least for the kind of people who find fun in doing the same thing over and over again until they achieve as much perfection as possible. We call these gallant people speedrunners. Speedrunners play a game, level, or section tens or hundreds of times trying to save a second or two. They examine the playing area in minute detail to ensure they haven't missed any potential shortcuts and test the limits of the game engine to find ways to go faster or gain some advantage.

A second group of people don't have the skill and mindset to perform breathtaking runs but enjoy watching demos of speedruns. We call these people *viewers*. Viewers form a very important part of the speedrunning community. First, they often contribute feedback, ideas, and even new tricks for the speedrunners to use in their next runs. Second, they form an audience for the speedrunners to perform for. After all, there's no point bragging about how great your run is if there's no one there to brag to.

A third group of people does nothing of note, ever, until the announcement of a new speedrun. They then rush to post remarks such as: "Pfff. Why are people still playing this game? Why doesn't this person get a life? Haven't they got anything better to do?" (except that they have worse spelling). The civilized world calls these people losers. I won't mention them again.

Earlier, I broke the technical aspects of speedrunning into three separate techniques: route planning, sequence breaking, and tricks. Ideally, you will combine all three into one beautiful, seamless whole by planning a route that uses tricks to sequence-break to best effect. Until you have those chops, we'll consider each technique separately before exploring some example speedruns.

Route Planning

Route planning is the most fundamental part of speedrunning. No matter how good your tricks, running through a game in a foolish order will produce a bad time. Whether you are going for a straight run (finishing in the fastest time possible), a 100% run (finishing with all kills, secrets, items, and whatever else you want to measure), or some other variation, route planning is the key to improving your time.

In some games, such as The Legend of Zelda: A Link to the Past (*http://planetquake.com/sda/other/lttp.html*) or Prince of Persia: The Sands of Time (*http://planetquake.com/sda/other/popsot.html*), there are no real sequence-breaking tricks; route planning and game skill are everything. The order in which you choose to do things, your item usage, and your ability are the main speedrunning criteria. (Speed Demo Archive, *http://planetquake.com/sda*, has demo speedruns for both games.)

Speeding as Metroid's Samus

This is the fun stuff: abusing game physics and exploiting bugs to allow you to perform stunts that should not be possible. Explaining all the available tricks could fill a book in itself. Let's limit the tricks to a few from the Metroid series (the 2D Metroids and Metroid Prime).

Metroid. The world of a 2D platform game, such as the Metroid series, is a much simpler place. Generally, this means that there aren't as many tricks available in an engine with simpler, probably less exploitable physics, but speedrunners will always find a way.

The most basic and the most useful of all Metroid speed tricks is the wall jump, introduced in Super Metroid (*http://speeddemosarchive.com/hack/walljump.html*). Somersault towards a wall, and jump again in the opposite direction at the moment you make contact. If you have done it correctly, you will be jumping the opposite direction of your first jump a fair distance off the ground. You can repeat the procedure while you're still in the air, as long as you have walls to scale. With practice and some nifty thumb work, you'll soon ascend vertical walls in no time at all. The difficulty of this trick varies with the version of Metroid you are playing.

Metroid Zero Mission had its own special trick, the ability to do "infinite bomb jumps" while in the morph ball. No matter the height at which a bomb explodes against you while you're in a ball, it will always push you upwards the same amount. If you lay a bomb and then lay another bomb just after the first bomb has bounced you into the air, the second explosion will propel you higher than did the first explosion. If you had the foresight to lay a third bomb just after the second bomb boosted you upwards, you will find yourself even higher still, and so on until you hit the roof.

An even faster variation, the so-called double bomb jump, requires very precise timing to lay bombs at the top *and* bottom of each alternate boost. That probably doesn't make much sense unless you watch an example (*http://speeddemosarchive.com/hack/bombjump.html*).

The Metroid games also have a built-in speed hack, the beautifully named *shinespark*. It's not needed to complete the games, but is the key to many secret areas and can be the speedrunner's best friend. To perform a shinespark, you need the Speed Booster powerup.

While merrily boosting along, tap down. Samus will crouch and continue flashing, indicating that you've charged the shinespark. You now have a short time to move into position and release it, sending Samus hurtling off like a glowing missile.

If you hit a slope while 'sparking, you will start running at boosted speed again, which allows you to charge another shinespark and start the process again. Using this approach, you can chain together sequences of shinesparks to reach the most inaccessible of secret areas and cover large distances in very little time. See Metroid 2002 (*http://www.metroid2002.com/*) for useful time-savers in Metroid Fusion and Zero Mission that use the shinespark.

If you're looking for more information on speedrunning for diverse titles over diverse consoles and the PC, the SDA Other site (*http://planetquake. com/sda/other/*) announces all the new speedruns. If you want to know how to accomplish new tricks, either watch the runs in question or go to specific FAQ sites, such as Metroid 2002 for the Metroid series.

Metroid Prime. Poor old Samus Aran seems hampered in her movement in her first 3D sojourn. It takes forever for her to turn around, her running is not up to the speed we expect from the blonde battle-machine, and her jumps are a little labored. It only seems fair that the world's speedrunners have uncovered ways to return her to her athletic glory.

The L-Lock-spring jump lets you gain some extra distance. Use the R button to look down, lock the view with the L button, run off a platform and jump, then release the lock right away to gain extra distance. To gain even greater horizontal distance but little vertical height, use the dash jump: acquire a lock somewhere convenient, point your analog stick in the direction you wish to hurdle, tap the jump button, then release all keys right away. You should find yourself flying in the direction you pressed.

HACK #69 Sequence-Break Quake

Play your favorite game levels out of order to improve your time.

Speedrunners ("Speedrun Your Way Through Metroid Prime" [Hack #68]) don't always exploit engine tricks. Sometimes shaving precious seconds off your personal records requires exploiting level design bugs and misfeatures. To become a competitive speedrunner—or even to find new ways to explore a well-loved game—you have to change your mindset. What's the *least* amount of work you can do to complete a level?

The following sections demonstrate shortcuts the game designers never intended.

Sequence Breaking in Speedruns

The real meat of speedrunning, some argue, is *sequence breaking*, tackling the levels of a game in an unintended order or skipping entire sections the designers intended you to play. This usually requires using tricks to achieve the breaks, but occasionally exploiting an engine or map design feature may yield fruit.

For example, consider The Installation (*http://speeddemosarchive.com/hack/e2m1.html*), the first level in the second episode of Quake. The intended approach leads you through a sprawling maze of corridors and water in a military base, collecting two keys to unlock the route to the exit. Thanks to an oversight on the part of John Romero, the level author, it is possible to jump from the edge of one balcony near the start to a balcony near the exit, which allows you to complete the level in just 10 seconds! Bunnyhopping can cut this time to seven seconds.

As the exposure and notoriety of speedrunners and sequence breaking has evolved, so have the attitudes of developers and map authors. For a long time, their responses were, "How dare they? That is not what I intended!" After the success of Quake done Quick (*http://planetquake.com/qdq/*), id Software tried to cull abusable features from Quake 2 to prevent the abuses of speedrunners by placing artificial barriers in the way of anyone trying to take shortcuts (*http://planetquake.com/qdq/q2dq2.html*). For example, you can reach the end of the first unit very quickly using a grenade boost or series of bunnyhops, but you'll find an invisible barrier blocking your way. The barrier will disappear only when you complete the intended tasks for the unit.

Many Quake 2 shortcuts and speed tricks still exist, though. See the Speed Demos Archive Quake 2 page (*http://speeddemosarchive.com/hack/q2.html*).

Over the last few years, the attitude of some developers has shifted from "Thou Shalt Not!" to "Do What Thou Wilt!" as software houses began to release games with deliberate sequence-breaking potential. The first section of Nintendo's 2004 Metroid Zero Mission requires you to open a door by shooting it with a missile (*http://speeddemosarchive.com/hack/mzm.html*).

Breakable blocks block your way to the missiles, but your gun lacks the range to shoot all the blocks. The obvious approach is to take a detour to another part of the level to acquire the Long Beam powerup. However, there are missiles hidden behind disguised shootable blocks near the door that allow you to skip the Long Beam and cut off a minute of game time. There is no earthly reason for these blocks to exist other than to help speedrunners.

Some purists argue that built-in sequence breaks violate the spirit of the game. They suggest that the real art in sequence breaking comes from doing things that were never intended and that blow the intended game wide open. We'll concentrate on these in the following examples.

Sequence-Breaking Quake

Let's apply these specific techniques to Quake. We'll examine several of the world's top Quake demos for ideas.

Our first two Quake demos show the variety of tricks usable in even the quickest and simplest of runs. They both involve completing "Hell's Atrium" (episode 4, mission 5) in the fastest possible time (*http://speeddemosarchive.com/hack/e4m5.html*). The first demo takes 11 seconds on Easy skill by Joszef Szalontai, and the second takes 10 seconds on Nightmare skill by Markus Taipale. Although both runs follow a straight line, they take very different approaches and cram a lot of different tricks and techniques in a short time. The record time on this level without exploiting damage boosts and engine quirks is 0:16.

Easy skill. Joe's primary speed gain comes from bunnyhopping. He starts off doing long, wide bunnies until he reaches the outside stairs. You can't bunny-hop up stairs because the back of the steps slows you down when you hit them, so Joe takes an ingenious route, jumping to the right and landing on the lift in the middle of the slime pool [5.1 seconds]. The lift gives him just enough height to jump even further to the right, where he performs a long, curving slope jump off the slanted decoration on the wall [5.6 seconds]. This takes him to the far side of the slime pool, where he begins another sequence of bunnies. This time, however, he starts from standing directly in front of one of the spike-trap shooters in the wall. The first spike hits him in the back just as he takes off from his first jump [7.0 seconds]. As all damage gives a speed increase, this adds to his forward velocity. From there it's just bounce, bounce, bounce to the exit.

Nightmare skill. The Nightmare demo from Markus takes a different approach due to the monsters that lurk around every corner on the harder skill levels. Upon stepping out into the sunlight [3.6 seconds], there is a spawn lurking in the shadows to the left. When a spawn dies, it explodes. To a speedrunner, explosions, if they don't kill you, are your friends. Three shotgun blasts prime the spawn, and a fourth shot just as Markus takes off from a bunnyhop finishes off the spawn, blowing the player clear across the slime pit at a very high speed [5.5 seconds]. Unbelievable air-control and momentum-preserving bunnies allow him to maintain this speed all the way to the lava pit in front of the exit. There's no chance of a spike boost this time, because he's just moving too fast!

A fiend blocks his way to the pit [8.8 seconds]. Markus fires his gun as soon as he comes into sight and then flings himself out over the pit. The fiend, taking umbrage at the attack, launches himself at the player's back to deliver a savage blow. The blow is enough to double Markus's forward speed, propelling him all the way to the other side of the lava and the exit.

Easy 100%. Our final Quake demo may be the best demo of all time: Peter Horvath's legendary Easy 100% (killing all monsters and finding all secret areas on Easy skill before exiting) of The Necropolis (episode 1, mission 3) in 60 seconds (*http://speeddemosarchive.com/hack/e1m3.html*).

He begins with a couple of simple bunnyhops and acquires the grenade launcher. His first true boost comes from throwing a grenade against the wall and riding the explosion of the rebounding grenade. This also hits the zombies he has just run past. He then throws a grenade at the ogre behind the bars as he flies down the stairs on the right. He then drops down and shoots a secret door in the wall. This door will take two seconds to open wide enough for him to squeeze through, so he nips around the corner to finish off the first ogre with another grenade. This is a good example of good route planning; killing this ogre has cost absolutely no time at all.

After plundering the secret health and ammo supplies, he needs to return to the walkway above. Jumping and firing a grenade into the feet of a conveniently placed zombie blows him right where he wants to be. After dropping down into the cave/water area, he tosses grenades around seemingly at random. Don't be deceived: each will kill one or more of the zombies that haunt this murky area. On reaching the far side of the water and collecting the gold key from its tiny island en route, he plunges into another secret area: a hidden pit in the water, just far enough to trigger the secret.

Peter then throws the most precise grenade ever used in a speed demo. To avoid having to backtrack through the caves and the start area to reach the gold-key door above, he performs a grenade slope jump from the gold key's little slopey island. Not wasting a moment, he throws the grenade onto the slope while still under water on the other side of the room, then runs and jumps all the way to the gold-key door.

After opening the door and killing the scrags and ogre that infest the area, Peter then performs another very precise grenade jump. He throws the aforementioned explosive down onto the stairs in front of him and then bunny-hops down after it. The grenade explodes the moment he takes off from his jump just in front of it, blowing him clear over the sewer trap toward the final area. Before he gets there, he must deal with zombies hiding in the walls. To release them normally requires climbing the wall steps and pressing the button. With the aid of a handy slope, another grenade, and a mid-air 180-degree turn (air control again), that's a mere formality.

Pausing briefly to eradicate the ogres lurking by the roof, and to uncover the last secret, Peter then throws another grenade into the giant elevator. As far as I know, the next trick has never appeared in a speedrun before. *Wall sliding*, moving forward into an obtuse angle between two walls in a vertical shaft to slow or stop your descent, is well-known in Quake circles. However, slowing techniques rarely appear in speedruns.

In this case, jumping up the left side of the lift shaft and sticking to the wall like a low-budget Spider-Man lures the zombie from the corridor below into the lift—as well as the bar trap. That's too good for Peter to pass up, so he triggers the trap, pulverizing the zombie. Then he heads back out through the door, fortunately kept open by the dearly departed zombie. This trick was first done with a fiend, present on Nightmare skill, who is much easier to lure into the trap. Peter's finish is just a matter of hopping through the opening teleporter and killing the final fiend before exiting!

Other Games

Speedrunning isn't limited to Quake or the Metroid series. I briefly mentioned a Zelda and Prince of Persia run, but it doesn't stop there. Even games without timers have speedruns; just count the amount of real time taken. If you've ever tried to play a game through quickly, maybe you should record your route and post it online. You never know, someone might make millions from speedrunning someday!

Run Classic Game ROM Translations
HACK #70

Fansubbing for video games is not only possible but very popular.

In addition to level hacking ("Change Games with ROM Hacks" [Hack #71]), there's an entirely separate subculture devoted to ROM language hacking, generally from Japanese to English, but also sometimes from English to other common languages (Spanish, Finnish … Okay, also to some not-so-common languages!). There are several major reasons for this activity, but people do it mainly to play Japanese console games that will never, ever have an English-language version. These translations allow people who don't know Japanese the chance to try out a playable version of the game.

Once you know how to patch your ROMs ("Change Games with ROM Hacks" [Hack #71]) to apply these translations, where can you find them?

ROM Translation Legality

Be aware that translation hacking of any ROM apart from a clearly freeware title is fraught with legal peril. IPS files are perfectly legal to distribute, but the copyrighted ROMs are not, whether or not you've modified them. Applying an IPS patch to a ROM doesn't release it into the public domain.

Even if you've tracked down and bought the Japanese-only version of a certain Super Nintendo title you want to try translation hacks on, the laws of your jurisdiction may prohibit or at least frown on such an activity. Nintendo interprets these laws more strictly.

However, translation patches are often released separately from the actual ROM, in add-on files, which means that translation patches bypass the thorny issue of downloading full ROMs to your PC. In any case, you can practice all these techniques on homebrew ROMS freely, without worrying about legality. Poking in the innards of games is actually plenty of fun, and it's surprisingly simple to run and edit translated ROMs in a basic fashion, though, of course, the sophisticated stuff is still pretty difficult.

Finding ROM Translation Groups and Sites

A whole host of sites claim to offer the best ROM translation information. Only a few actually deliver either finished, high-quality translations or decent databases of everyone else's work. Here are the ones I've found:

The Whirlpool (http://donut.parodius.com/)
I consider this site to be the number-one ROM translation site out there, because it's not specific to one group of translators. It features a massive database of IPS file for tens of different consoles and hundreds of different translation groups. It's also a lifesaver for the scene because it mirrors the IPS files locally, meaning that even when an obscure ROM group loses its Geocities account, Whirlpool will save its work for posterity.

The Whirlpool also provides descriptions of how far along a translation is, minireviews, and sometimes even comments from the creators.

Overall, it's extremely impressive, and its FAQs and news items are also well worth checking out.

DeJap Translations (http://www.dejap.com/)

DeJap is one of the best-known individual translation groups; its impressive projects page (*http://www.dejap.com/projects.php*) shows a range of the most sought-after SNES translations (see Figure 6-1). The Square title Bahamut Lagoon, never available in the West, is one of the highlights. Elsewhere, Namco's classic Tales Of Phantasia is another important translation, although the insanely complex Star Ocean is probably the most technically impressive work thus far.

Figure 6-1. *DeJap.com, an excellent translation site despite the name*

DemiForce Translations (http://www.demiforce.com/translations/)

This is another of the seminal translation groups, though it's actually only one guy. He doesn't have individual pages for his translations, preferring to link to individual Whirlpool detail pages. His particular highlights are a stylized translation of Final Fantasy I and II, as well as a standalone page for Radical Dreamers (*http://radicaldreamers.sourceforge.net/*), the largely unknown Chrono Trigger side story for SNES.

Aeon Genesis (http://agtp.romhack.net/)

Aeon Genesis has released a whopping total of 40 translations for everything from the Sega Game Gear to the NES and SNES. Although several titles, such as Magical Drop (*http://agtp.romhack.net/mdrop.html*), have little text to translate, a lot of know-how and work have gone into all these translations. Five years and 40 releases after they started, they're still going strong. Romancing SaGa 2, another Square title, is also in the works.

This should give you a good idea of the kind of resources available for playing Japanese games with translated English text, even if the title was never released in the West. The next step is to try your hand at translation; at least, change the title screen of a game to something obscene, the stock-in-trade of lame ROM translation hackers.

Change Games with ROM Hacks

#71 Is your favorite game growing a little tedious? Mod it!

After many hours, days, months, and years of playing your favorite classic video game, you may become a little bored. The sequel just wasn't as good, and you've played all the levels over and over. Don't give up. With the help of PC-based tools and a little creativity, you may be able to make entire new gaming vistas by hacking existing classic games.

These tools take the original game and modify it to produce a patch file you can apply to the existing ROM for a whole new play experience ("Change Games with ROM Hacks" **[Hack #71]**). Some hackers have even added functionality to the game levels while changing content.

Please note that the normal caveat to ROMs and emulators applies ("Legal Emulation" **[Hack #1]**). You may feel morally justified in buying a game and adapting a version of its ROM on your PC, but many console manufacturers feel that this violates their copyright and licensing terms. Double that caveat for applying ROM hacks.

The Best Individual ROM Hacks Ever

Even in the shady underworld of the ROM hacker, there's a lot of innovation and high-quality work that improves already excellent games. Sometimes this is only tweaking, but often these hacks completely change the gameplay experience, creating effectively new games. Here are some of my favorite ROM hacks:

Super Demo World
  (http://fusoya.cg-games.net/lm/dw.html)

To show off the functionality of the great Super Mario World editor Lunar Magic, the creators have also released a couple of complete conversions for Super Mario World, with custom graphics, levels, and even whole new block types. Highlights include some great-looking overlapping blocks and a wealth of new gameplay.

Metroid C
(http://www.cg-games.net/challenges/metroidc/)

A nearly complete conversion of the classic original NES Metroid, this was almost 90% done as of press time. One of the most interesting things about this hack is that the page contains all the earlier versions of the IPS patch as well, so you can see how the conversion gradually takes place over multiple save files. Besides new graphics, levels, Samus sprites, and improved gameplay, the title screen and introductory text have changed as well, so this is almost a total conversion.

The Legend Of Zelda: Outlands
(http://www.cg-games.net/challenges/zeldac/)

An extremely complex, faithful update hack of the NES Legend Of Zelda, this hack includes a completely redesigned overworld and dungeons. The beach has even changed to another overworld location entirely, and the wave sound effects moved with it. Elsewhere on the site, the hacker also points to some very helpful ROM data locations *(http://www.cg-games.net/challenges/zeldac/zeldarom.txt)* for any wannabe hackers.

Arkanoid—Dimension Of Doh
(http://www.dragoneyestudios.net/index.php?page=hacks&system=0&id=6)

Making a distinct change from all those platformers, this is a conversion of the classic bat n' ball NES title Arkanoid, with a complete set of 33 new levels. Although significantly and fiendishly trickier, this is a simple block rearrangement hack. It's also one of the purest and most fun hacks, simply because playing through Arkanoid in a linear fashion throws up the same levels over and over. This new level set is a refreshingly addictive change; it's even more fun if you can find a NES Arkanoid controller and a way to use it!

Super Mario Brothers 3 Challenge
(http://www.cg-games.net/challenges/smb3c/)

Once upon a time, the ROM modification scene voted this the best ROM hack ever. It's easy to see why; this is a complete level hack of the gigantic NES title Super Mario Bros 3 that includes some familiar territory, but also switches powerups for bad guys in strategic places and changes some level blocks significantly. Be sure to check out the lengthy third-party walkthrough *(http://www.cg-games.net/challenges/smb3c/walksmb3c.txt)*, which includes detailed descriptions of all the changes.

Analyzing Level Hack Editing Software

While it's exciting to patch and play level hacks from the original ROM, it's more interesting still to create your own. A good starting point is, again, Zophar.net's comprehensive utility compilations (*http://www.zophar.net/ utilities/level.html*), which includes a mass of over 100 editors for various classic consoles.

Not all of them are easy to use, and some date from the heyday of emulation hysteria in the late '90s, when DOS utilities were much more common, so beware of incompatibilities with newer versions of Windows. Overall, there's a massive amount of working, good-quality editors. Here are a few of the highlights:

Lunar Magic
    (http://fusoya.cg-games.net/lm/index.html)

    By far one of the most spectacular, fully formed level editor hacks of all time, this utility features a comprehensive Windows-based graphical interface for one of the best games of all time, the Super Nintendo title Super Mario World. The hack is so advanced that the authors have even added the ability to make completely custom graphics and a full over-world editor (for changing the map screen that allows players to move between and choose sidescrolling levels). Finally, they even imported the breakable brick concept from Super Mario 3 into the game.

Trip N Slip
    (http://dan.panicus.org/files.php?id=tripnslip
    (http://www.zophar.net/utilities/neslevel.html)

    Mixing things up a little, this rather marvellous little editor for NES Rush N'Attack (also called Green Beret) allows palette, enemy and level edits, and even makes it easy to create IPS patches, something that some other more rudimentary ROM editors don't. The Windows tool comes with optional source code.

PK Hack suite
    (http://pkhack.starmen.net/index.php)

    Wow. The scene, based on the classic SNES game Earthbound, is particularly committed, but this amazing collection of tools allows the wannabe hacker to edit text in detail, even adding and changing cut-scenes, shifting the visual look of sprites, and expanding the ROM size to add extra information without running out of space. It also sports a comprehensive map editor. There's more knowledge here than in many other games combined, so there's plenty to work with.

MetEdit

> *(http://acmlm.overclocked.org/download.html)*
>
> Released by SnowBro Software, this comprehensive NES Metroid hacking tool allows tile and map rearrangement, as used in the Metroid C hack detailed earlier. It's also worth noting that the author has the source code for the tool available on his site *(http://www.stud.ntnu.no/~kenth/)*.

ArkEdit

> *(http://www.geocities.com/megadog1/rom/arkedit.html)*
>
> It may be simple, but if you just want brightly colored, fun results, editing the brick palettes and positioning for NES Arkanoid via the DOS editor ArkEdit may be the ticket for you.

Unfortunately, level hacks are sometimes given a bad name because of their similarity to the often asinine sprite hacks found randomly all over the Internet during the height of emulation fever. (You might remember Super Mario, with Mario turned into a Teletubby, and similar or more scatological randomness.) A site called I-Mockery has made a most amusing pastime out of poking fun at these lame sprite swaps *(http://www.i-mockery.com/romhacks/)*.

Fortunately, the highlighted hacks described here show that there's a really creative scene out there, hacking existing code to create entirely new gameplay experiences. Perhaps in the future, just as the Activision Classics GBA compilation includes homebrew Atari 2600 titles, classic compilations of console games from the NES or SNES could include the best level hacks as official releases. That's a pipe dream, sure, but perhaps a worthy one.

Apply ROM Hacks and Patches
HACK #72

Make ROM patches stick to your game images.

Suppose you've gone to a web site such as DeJap's SNES Bahamut Lagoon *(http://www.dejap.com/bl.php)* and downloaded an English-language patch to apply to the related Japanese-language ROM ("Run Classic Game ROM Translations" **[Hack #70]**). If you examine the patch, you'll find that it comes in the form of a mysterious *.IPS* file, probably zipped up. What the heck do you do to actually make this patch work? You have two options, which are shown in the following sections.

Direct IPS File Patching

The traditional approach involves creating a new file from the ROM and the IPS patch. Use a utility such as IPSWin or JIPS (both available from *http://zerosoft.zophar.net/*), select the patch file and the ROM to patch, and let it do its job. You can also use the DOS version of IPS (*http://www.zophar.net/ utilities/patchutil.html*) with the simple command:

```
C:\Roms\> IPS.EXE EXAMPLE.SMC EXAMPLE.IPS
```

Either way, you'll end up with a combined file that includes the patched data. Make sure to keep a backup of your old master ROM in case something goes horribly wrong.

You also have to make sure that the checksum is correct on the ROM you're patching and that it hasn't changed from the original in any way. Do this using simple DOS utilities kindly hosted by The Whirlpool, such as SMC (*http://donut.parodius.com/utilities/smc.com*):

```
C:\Roms\> SMC.COM /S EXAMPLE.SMC
```

If the ROM is pristine, everything should be fine.

Emulator-Based IPS Autopatching

Many popular SNES emulators for the PC, such as ZSNES or SNES9X, can apply patches to a ROM loaded in memory without overwriting the file. Put the *.IPS* file in the same directory as the ROM with the same basic filename (*EXAMPLE.IPS* and *EXAMPLE.SMC*, for example) and load the game. The emulator will automatically detect and integrate the patch.

This is an excellent solution, because you can keep the original, untouched foreign version of the ROM and the patch in the same place. It's easy to get things running again without having multiple versions of the ROM hanging around.

This is the basic behavior for the SNES version of the IPS patch, but things change very little regardless of the console being emulated. You can still use the IPS patch. Some other console emulators also support this method of including IPS patches without anyone actually doing the file joining.

The Best ROM Hack Repositories

If you're looking for the best IPS level hack patches, there's a massive variety of available resources. Unfortunately, few ROM hackers seem to have stable web sites, often settling on Geocities or AOL web space that goes away swiftly after they lose interest. Fortunately, there are a few established central repositories and some dedicated collectives that can host their own hacks in a more stable manner:

Zophar's Domain Hacks page
   (*http://www.zophar.net/hacks/*)

This comprehensive compilation page collects level-creation hacks for NES, SNES, Game Boy, Genesis, and a variety of other consoles. While it's not the home of a particular hack creator, it lists just about every decent hack ever released in IPS form. Explore this site if you want to appreciate the diversity of ROM hacking out there.

Acmlm's ROM Hack Domain
(http://acmlm.overclocked.org/)

A particularly active community aspect makes this site very useful, but it also has links, information, and downloads for several miscellaneous hacks, including some useful user-contributed ratings. This is a long-standing, well-respected member of the ROM hacking community.

Create PS2 Cheat Codes

Need alternatives for exploiting Grand Theft Auto 3 for your PS2? Try some cheat codes.

You're playing your favorite PlayStation 2 game, but you're bored of the gameplay. Wouldn't it be neat to mix things up a little bit; maybe turn on infinite lives, skip levels, or reach new areas? Unfortunately, because the console is a black box, it's not easy to change game saves or enter cheat codes. You need some way to enter cheats from external sources into your beautiful console.

If you consider the proprietary nature of next-generation consoles, in which you can't burn discs for unmodified consoles (unlike, say, the Dreamcast), and add the fact that modifying these next-gen beasts is fraught with legal peril, you have a situation in which it's difficult to alter game variables easily. That's perfect fodder for a hack.

If you're prepared to piggyback on completely unofficial hardware and software work from commercial variable-hacking experts,[*] you can cause havoc in game code in no time flat.

Although each of the major current-generation consoles (the PlayStation 2, GameCube, and Xbox) have significantly different ways you can access them (and different games that are particularly fun to hack), the most popular system for cheat code hacking is the PlayStation 2.

---

[*] In particular, I mean Datel with their Action Replay and old GameShark and Fire International with their new GameShark devices.

Variable Hacking on the PlayStation 2

Datel's Action Replay (and some versions of the Gameshark) led the pack of cheat-code devices for the PS2 until 2003. This unofficial CD boots on unmodified PlayStation 2 (an impressive trick, to say the least), allowing you to enter codes to activate specific in-game effects, such as infinite lives, game debug modes, and level skipping. After you've entered the code with the Action Replay disc, swap in the game disc and allow it to boot as normal, with certain memory values changed to enable the cheat.

> Because PlayStation 2 games generally don't store data on the hard drive—it's not a default part of the hardware—the cheat needs to change memory-resident values to work its magic.

Unfortunately, probably due to issues with third-party companies duplicating various console Action Replay features, Datel now builds encryption into their 16-character cheat codes. Fortunately, they do a good job of keeping up to date with new codes, but it's great to be able to enter brand new codes as well. There are ways around this.

The basic versions of Action Replay come with a CD-ROM filled with the latest codes. You can upgrade to receive the newest codes for a small fee. This is the way to go; entering 24- or 32-digit codes via the controller is particularly time-consuming, so having them available on the CD is handy. However, if you want to enter new data quickly, plug a normal USB keyboard into your PlayStation 2. Datel actually sold a keyboard called the Powerboard specifically for this purpose, presumably before USB keyboards were more widespread or used in PS2 games, but don't be confused; it's just a Datel-branded standard USB keyboard.

You can also find single-disc, PS2-only editions of Datel's Action Replay, sold for $10 or less as the Action Replay Ultimate Cheat Series. There are specific editions for Grand Theft Auto 3, The Getaway, The Sims, and many other titles. These discs hold cut-down versions of the main software, specific to the named game. Unfortunately, there's no real way to enter codes of your own. Although there are some decent default codes, you can't hack them any further. Avoid these discs in favor of the normal Action Replay discs, which have all of these codes anyway.

Creating Your Own Codes

Unfortunately, Datel is very protective of their Action Replay codes, both to prevent unwanted misuse and to stop other companies from cloning their codes and releasing gray-market copies of their software. It's not easy to make your own Action Replay codes, but it's possible.

The amazing Hellion00 encryption Action Replay Code Guide page (*http://hellion00.thegfcc.com/index.html*) is a superior starting point that offers an exact step-by-step guide for creating your own cheat codes for popular games. It also gives a handy guide to what all those existing codes actually mean. An AR code has four different parts, as shown in Table 6-1.

Table 6-1. Action Replay code parts

Part	Description
Command	What to do
Address	Which memory location to change
Value	The new value for that location
Encryption	The proprietary Datel bit to stop meddlers

In order to work out which bits of memory you'll change or address, you can't work completely blind. As the Action Replay Code Guide explains, the official Datel engineers and hackers who create the common codes as quickly as possible have complicated equipment (likely development kits for each console), but the amateur hacker has to make do with what he has.

That's where PS2DIS (*http://hellion00.thegfcc.com/PS2DISGuide.htm*) comes in. This cunning program analyzes the SLUS (program) file you need to copy off a PlayStation 2 game disc onto your PC. Insert the PS2 CD into your CD-ROM drive or DVD-ROM drive, as appropriate, find a *SLUS_<XXX.XX>* file on the disc, and copy it to your computer.

The PS2DIS utility searches this file for strings and works out which places in the game code refer to a given address. The site includes a Grand Theft Auto 3-related example of searching the SLUS for potential cheat code locations (*http://hellion00.thegfcc.com/PS2DISExample1.htm*). This explanation points out that many games don't have well-labeled code, so relying on strings, while one of the only ways you can guess what's going on without an expensive debugging kit, may not always work so well. It's still worth trying.

Once you've sorted out your code, you'll need to encrypt it so that the Action Replay will actually understand it. The Hellion00 encryption page (*http://hellion00.thegfcc.com/encryption.html*) hosts three web-based conversion tools, each for a different type of game. Enter your raw code to produce a different eight-digit code to enter into the Action Replay itself. First, though, you'll probably need to enter a master code to enable cheating.

Beyond Infinite Lives

You may think that these codes are good only for creating tedious infinite lives cheats, but that's far from the truth! Action Replay hackers have created an amazing page for Sony's haunting Ico adventure (*http://www.thegfcc.com/ico.php*) that explains how to enable all the developer debug modes, with wireframe information and character skeletal displays. You can even use the second camera to change camera angles during the real-time cut-scenes—definitely impossible without some serious hacking.

The same site has a gigantic amount of Grand Theft Auto: Vice City codes (*http://www.thegfcc.com/vccodes.php*) that produce such wackiness as pressing cheat buttons to automagically generate any car, bike, plane, or helicopter in the game; changing the tire and wheel size on your car to be gigantic or tiny; and even putting fire-truck or ambulance lights on any vehicle you like in the game, not just the emergency services. This stuff is seriously interesting and creative.

When Is Gameshark Not Gameshark?

Here's where things get complicated. If you see an Action Replay product for PlayStation 2, it will have the Datel architecture in it that allows you to perform all of the earlier hacks. However, if you see a Gameshark, you have no such guarantee.

In the United States, a company named Interact originally used the Gameshark name. They licensed the Datel technology used in the Action Replay but then went out of business. Because the Gameshark name is particularly well-known, major peripheral manufacturer Mad Catz bought the name. They formed a partnership with Fire International, maker of the rival-to-Datel Code Breaker series of cheat devices (actually made by Pelican), and started producing Gamesharks with the Pelican technology.

Now Pelican has apparently developed its own technology to continue producing Code Breaker hardware, bringing the grand total to three different major cheat code devices on the market.

The general consensus seems to be that both the new Gameshark and new Code Breaker tools, while perfectly competent, don't offer anything over the existing Action Replay. More to the point, the vast majority of the innovative extra hacking work uses the Action Replay, so it seems sensible for most users to stick to that.

If you want to cross-convert codes between multiple cheat code formats, or even make a code and then generate Action Replay, Code Breaker, and Game Shark versions, see The GFCC's bonus web page (*http://hellion00.thegfcc.com/bonus. html*) for a utility that does all of the above. It is exceptionally complicated, however, so hit the HELP button for some illumination.

There's one final reason why the Action Replay brand seems to make the most sense, and that's the introduction of the new Action Replay Max. With the AR Max, if you have a broadband connection and a network adapter for your PlayStation 2, and insert the CD in the drive and boot it, you can download all the latest official saves directly from the Internet. You don't have to buy a CD upgrade to get them or enter them yourself. This is a clever hack in itself and makes the Action Replay even more user-friendly. Still, I like the homemade hacks by third parties; hacking the hackers is fun indeed.

See Also

If you want resources to discuss PlayStation 2 code creation, need to check out existing codes, or just want to hang out with code junkies, the Datel's CodeJunkies site (*http://www.codejunkies.com/*—free registration required), is almost certainly the best. Don't worry that it's run by the company themselves; they tolerate and even encourage creative work on their forums.

HACK #74 Hack Xbox Game Saves
Change game state and variables by changing your saved games.

The Xbox is very different from the PS2 when it comes to cheats and codes. There is no in-game variable hacking as there is with the PlayStation 2 ("Create PS2 Cheat Codes" **[Hack #73]**). There's no code to allow you to change memory-resident values in the Action Replay–style "insert CD, then insert game style" shuffle. Even though there is an Xbox Action Replay device, it's not really a cheat code device in the conventional sense of the phrase; all memory-changing devices since the NES have used a code-entering approach. Not the Xbox device.

There's good news, though. You can still cheat and explore Xbox games using hacked game saves. It's easy to find USB memory card transfer devices that allow you to download game saves to your PC, modify them, and copy them back to your Xbox's hard drive. Boot the game, and load the modified save to unlock secret content, change game features in certain circumstances, and achieve other wacky effects.

The disadvantage is that it's difficult to find saves that actually change game variables without further, more illicit hacking. Microsoft digitally signs all saved game files, so if you change values around willy-nilly, chances are the signature check will fail. That's game over.

Xbox Memory Devices

When it comes to Xbox memory devices, there are only two particularly famous ones: the Action Replay from Mad Catz (read a so-so review at *http:// gear.ign.com/articles/432/432888p1.html*) and the Mega X-Key, sold through the Hong Kong store Lik-Sang (*http://www.megaxkey.com/mxkmanual/ readme.html*). Make sure you order from Lik-Sang, not the Mega X-Key site; there are reports of extremely slow delivery times when ordering directly from the developers. It's interesting to note the naming: as the IGN review indicates, it appears that the Action Replay device relies on the Action Replay name without having much to do with it anymore.

The hardware is easy to compare. The Action Replay interface to the PC is designed to take Xbox memory cards, although it comes with its own special memory card. The Mega X-Key is simply a normal-looking USB stick, though it may look scarier and a bit amateurish to the casual buyer. It has its advantages, though, with 32 MB of storage to the Action Replay's 8 MB. Tests show that the Mega X-Key transfers data noticeably faster than the Action Replay device.

> Throwing a spanner in the works, the new Action Replay Max Drive has 16 MB of storage. There may also be higher-capacity versions on the horizon. If so, they'll compete with the Mega X-Key in terms of storage, but it'll be difficult to evaluate their quality until they've been on the market for a while. However, the new version still uses standard Action Replay–formatted saves.

In terms of save compatibility and availability, the Action Replay uses its own proprietary save format. You can't use unconverted open save archives found online; instead, download them from CodeJunkies.com. Action Replay has dedicated employees who produce new saves with everything unlocked and near-infinite money supplies for the CodeJunkies board, which is a major plus. There are also quite a few user-contributed saves there, too. While some are great (e.g., saves from just near the multiple endings of Deus Ex: Invisible War), many are badly labeled or entirely unlabeled, so many of the archived game saves are fairly unusable.

In comparison, the Mega X-Key uses Xbox-Saves (*http://www.xbox-saves. com/*) as its main source of game saves. At the time of writing, the collection approached 1,500 saves. Although the site uses purely volunteer and amateur efforts, it does really well, especially on the more exotic hacks. However, hacks aren't well-labeled in terms of which will work with vanilla hardware and which require some sort of Xbox modification. I'll return to this thought in a bit.

Making Your Own Mega X-Key

One rather cool thing about the Mega X-Key is that its designers started out as hobbyists. They don't mind giving you the instructions for making your own Xbox interface for Mega X-Key; see their web site (*http://www.xbox-saves.com/MXK_HW_Guide.htm*). Not only that, the instructions actually relate exactly to the Xbox-controller hacking. Start with a breakaway Xbox extension cable, add a USB-to-USB cable, and, after a little cutting and resoldering, you end up with a cable with a USB connector on one end and an Xbox controller connector on the other. ("Adapt Old Video Game Controllers to the PC" **[Hack #37]**)

When that's done, all you need is a 32-MB USB drive to plug into the end of the USB connector. Beware: it must be exactly 32 MB, not lacking sectors or cylinders, as some (likely no-name brand) memory cards do. If the number of bytes on the card isn't exactly divisible by 16,384, bad things may happen due to the Xbox's FATX formatting for memory cards. The site notes:

> For starters, we know that the FMI (Fujitsu) brand of 32MB USB flash memory drive, available at most CompUSA stores, works great, while the "Universal Smart Drive" model by K&C Technologies does not.

After all that, download the Mega X-Key software from the official project page (*http://www.megaxkey.com/index.php?section=product*), and you're good to go.

Having explained the homebrew process, however, it may be simpler to buy a Mega X-Key itself. They're competitively priced, and you're really just buying a USB drive from them that you'd have to find yourself (and might get wrong!) anyhow.

Forbidden Fruit: More Extreme Xbox Save Hacking

If you register on the Code Junkies site, you may notice that most of the official codes are fairly vanilla. That's because the most you can usually do without altering the digital signature is change your character's money value to 9999999—still within the original game limits, so it won't affect the signature!

Even this modest hacking requires some particularly complex (and perhaps not-so-legit) disassembly. An example at *http://www.xbox-saves.com/ deathrler/* shows how to modify a Sega GT 2002 to produce the maximum amounts of money in an in-game save that still passes the signature test.

The page makes the point that you have to fool the Xbox only once:

> Although you initially need to hack default.xbe to load a game save that you hack, you can then resave the game and will have a valid game save file with the proper CRC recalculated. The save can then be used by anyone with the game, regardless of whether or not they have hacked their default.xbe file. This is certainly very good news for those who are less inclined to hex edit their default.xbe files.

The XBox Game Save Re-signer, available from *http://www.xbox-saves.com/*, helps these problems by resigning hacked saves. Thus, if you use a software or hardware modification to transfer data to and from your Xbox, you can perform more exotic and interesting hacks.

In either case, here are some freely downloadable examples from the Xbox Saves site:

Enable debug mode in Deus Ex: Invisible War.   From there, you can stop the AI from attacking you, add infinite ammo and infinite health, and perform a host of other cheats. See *http://www.xbox-saves.com/pafiledb/ pafiledb.php?action=file&id=1676*.

Tweak game rosters for titles such as NBA Live.   You can now sometimes download updates from Xbox Live, but go ahead and explore. See *http:// www.xbox-saves.com/pafiledb/pafiledb.php?action=file&id=1111*.

Change the model textures in Dead Or Alive: Xtreme BeachVolleyball with more exotic hacking methods.   At least, it seems like it's possible to change the model textures with more exotic hacking methods. Learn more from *http://www.xbox-saves.com/index.php?category=saves*.

Whether you're just using a save device or trying something crazier still, there's plenty of interesting saved game hacking you can do using the Xbox.

See Also

As previously mentioned, I'm being a little coy about some of these. However, I'd be remiss in not pointing to Andrew "bunnie" Huang's fabulous Hacking the Xbox (*http://hackingthexbox.com/*) site and book from No Starch Press.

Also, be sure to check out the marvelous Xbox-Scene (*http://www.xbox-scene.com/*). Though it's not the only Xbox hacking site, Xbox-Scene has the latest information on hardware hacks (chips and other such shenanigans) and software hacks (overflow exploits, media players), all of which are tremendously useful. Even though I don't explicitly cover them here, that doesn't mean they're difficult or ineffective. Go forth and multiply your knowledge and your Xbox hacks; just don't tell Microsoft about it!

HACK #75 Cheat on Other Consoles

There are still plenty of cheats for the GameCube and older consoles.

Although the Xbox and PlayStation 2 have the most cheats currently ("Create PS2 Cheat Codes" **[Hack #73]** and "Hack Xbox Game Saves" **[Hack #74]**), there's plenty of metagaming goodness to go around. There are cheat devices for other consoles, both brand new and classic, as well as cool cheats and hacks you can do on them.

One of the best sources for older game hacks is GSCentral (*http://www.gscentral.com/*). The site has a prodigious amount of codes, not just for the GameShark (from which the page takes its name), but also for the N64 and SNES formats commercial web sites no longer cover. It also features invaluable, otherwise lost tips on cheat code hacking and conversion for older console systems (*http://www.gscentral.com/menu.pl?Hacking*). If you want to convert eight-letter SNES Game Genie codes to six-letter versions, GSCentral is the place to go.

GameCube Variable Hacking

Overall, the GameCube is fairly fertile ground for code hacking, even though there are fewer games available for it than other systems and only one main code-hacking device. Datel's Action Replay device again dominates the GameCube scene. This time, it's the *only* major device, so you don't have much choice. You may have heard that Datel's Freeloader CD allows you to play games from other regions ("Play Import Games on American Consoles" **[Hack #49]**), but the Action Replay includes this technology, as well as the standard, encrypted Datel multidigit code formats for entering cheats. You're supposed to log on to CodeJunkies.com to find officially approved and created codes. These have encryption built in, so you can't just make them yourself, in stark contrast with the earlier days when cheat hardware manufacturers encouraged customer creativity.

Of course, thanks to some cheeky souls hacking the hackers, you *can* create your own codes. However, you can't use the PlayStation 2 trick of copying data onto your PC to analyze which values to change, because the GameCube uses a custom miniature disc that won't read on a PC. How do you know which values to tweak?

The secret is an exploit discovered using the GameCube broadband adapter and a copy of Phantasy Star Online. The GCDev web site (*http://www.gcdev. com/index.shtml*) has a Windows, Mac, and even Linux utility that fakes the IP address of a Phantasy Star Online update server and allows the player to execute homebrew code. See the full *README* file and FAQ within the ZIP download.

It's also possible to load a program called GCNRd and its *README* file (available from the GSCentral download page, *http://www.gscentral.com/menu. pl?Download*), which allows you to access the GameCube via Ethernet while other games are running. You can see and alter variables while the game is running, which makes hacking much less of a trial-and-error proposition.

There's an excellent FAQ about GCNRd hacking on the Action Replay Central site (*http://codes.ssbm.org/FAQs/GCNrdGUI_Tutorial.html*). It explains the whole setup process and the code search functions.

However, the FAQ takes you only halfway, because you'll end up with an unencrypted code that won't work properly on an Action Replay. Fortunately, GCNCrypt (*http://www.gscentral.com/lib/downloads/GCNcrypt-v1_41.zip*) allows the willing hacker to encrypt and decrypt Action Replay codes at will. That's both barriers down; nice going!

What kinds of hacks have enterprising hackers excavated? The following sections describe some of my favorites.

The Legend of Zelda: Wind Waker hacks. GSCentral's Wind Waker site (*http:// www.gscentral.com/codes.pl?dev=ar&sys=gcus&game=zeldaww*) hosts several of the most impressive cheats for any game. There are codes that allow you to teleport to beta, test, unfinished, and otherwise unreachable locations in the game, including crazy custom levels with numbered textures. Planet GameCube links to some good screenshots of these test levels at *http://www. planetgamecube.com/news.cfm?action=item&id=4244*.

Animal Crossing hosted game hacks. Would you like your mind blown? How about cheats for the NES games contained *within* the amazingly addictive Animal Crossing? GSCentral has a special page (*http://www.gscentral.com/ codes.pl?dev=ar&sys=gcus&game=acrossing&sub=nesgames*) that shows you how to disable overheating in Excitebike, which you can find and play as a virtual NES cartridge in the game itself. Of course, you can enter hacks to add the carts themselves to your inventory (*http://www.gscentral.com/codes.*

pl?dev=ar&sys=gcus&game=acrossing&sub=qdigitsnesgames). That's pretty nefarious all the way 'round.

Super Smash Bros. Melee hacks. With the proper codes, you can enter Super Smash Bros Melee's debug menu:

> *http://www.gscentral.com/*
> *codespl?dev=ar&sys=gcus&game=ssbmv11&sub=debugmenu*

For more information on the super-complex developer tool, see the SSBM Debug Menu site (*http://www.geocities.com/gcnhacker87/main.html*). You can set arenas, players, and AI levels, and even reduce the always doubled-up Ice Climber characters to one.

Nintendo 64 Variable Hacking

The Nintendo 64 was fertile ground for codes, particularly because it used a cartridge system, so it was easy to make a cheating hardware adapter that fit in between the cartridge and the console. The GameShark is the leading code creator, but a host of Asian third-party adapters also use the same codes. They're all pretty much interchangeable.

> One third-party adapter, the GB Booster/Hunter, also has a terrible Game Boy emulator—really a software emulator, without sound, that runs on the N64. It's worth looking at for its novelty value.

One particularly cool hack for the N64 is the ability to spawn multiple Marios in Mario 64. GSCentral has a wonderful screenshot gallery (*http://www. gscentral.com/cia.pl?id=spawnmarios*), as well as the code itself. For posterity's sake, it's:

```
D033AFA1 0020 8033B248 0001
```

Even neater, after you press the L button to spawn a new Mario and then run away, he will stay put and otherwise replicate your animations exactly. You can have 10 Marios on screen all facing the same way and making the same motions, as if there were some kind of music video dancer synchronization going on.

Other than that, some of the best N64 code-hacking work these days comes from the Rare Witch Project (*http://www.rarewitchproject.com/*). Its creators have done amazing things with GoldenEye, finding a completely unknown level and the original James Bond actors' portraits for multiplayer (a feature removed from the game before it shipped, though the actual graphics are still present.) Check out the many, many codes at *http://www.gscentral.com/codes.pl?dev=gs&sys=n64&game=007*.

Game Boy/Game Boy Advance Hacking

Nintendo's cartridge-based GameBoy family is also well-suited for codes using the pass-through connector method. Your options are the Game-Shark, Action Replay, and Code Breaker flavors, though, of course, the GameShark and Action Replay have very similar internals in recent versions. Remember that the GameShark name disappeared into bankruptcy. Mad Catz bought it, before licensing the Action Replay technology. Earlier versions of the GameShark have different internals.

Old-School SNES, Genesis, and NES Hacking

Obviously, the whole Action Replay and Game Genie duel was prevalent back in the time of the NES, Genesis, and SNES. There are still many workable codes floating around. Back in those simpler, more innocent times, codes were shorter. GSCentral is still a great place to find codes for a lot of these relatively ancient code systems along with some important conversion tools.

HACK #76   Modify PC Game Saves and Settings

Poke into the depths of your favorite PC game to give yourself the edge.

There's a whole industry devoted to cheating and hacking game saves on consoles ("Cheat on Other Consoles" [Hack #75]), but what about PC games? Shouldn't that be as easy, if not easier, than console hacking? Yes! Console hacking may be more exotic and interesting because consoles are black boxes you're not really supposed to open, but it's easy to cheat with PC games; you control the hardware and software of a general-purpose computing device!

You can often find *trainers* (small executable patch files that add an up-front menu to the game in which you can select infinite lives, max ammo, and other fun options) that combine all the extras you want in a ready-made package. Some exploit debug modes that the programmers have left in the game. Others modify specific values in saved games. You can perform plenty of interesting hacks on PC games old and new.

PC Game Hacking Overview

There are several types of PC game hacking tools. All overlap in some way, and you'll often have the best results by combining some or all of them:

Memory finders
> Scan the PC's memory while a game runs, allowing you to search for and replace certain variables to produce intended (or unintended!) effects.

Hex editors
> Allow you to edit saved files, changing variables more permanently.

Code disassemblers
> Tools that show you a partially human-readable version of the compiled code. This is a complicated approach to changing parts of the game code. If you have a basic understanding of assembly language and hex, this is the method for you.

Packet editors
> Tools for network-aware games that help you understand the information sent out over the Net and how to change it.

If you're looking for somewhere to start with regard to hacking PC games, the World Of Game Hacking (*http://www.gamehacking.com/*) is an amazing jumping-off point. Not only does it have plenty of free, ready-made trainers to download for existing PC games, it has massive download sections for all of these utilities and a big set of tutorials for both beginners and experts. Although they're often rough and ready, these explain most of what you need to know.

PC Game Hacking Using Memory Finders

Using memory finders is by far the easiest and most fun way to hack, so we'll devote the most time to it. For the purposes of this hack, we'll use the WinHack 2.0 tool:

> *http://www.gamehacking.com/download.*
> *php?type=tools&file=memfinders/WH200.zip*

It's a freely distributable Windows program that allows you to look through memory on a particular file and see what's changed, then change values based on that.

> GameHack, also available on the GameHacking.com page, is another highly recommended Windows program along the same lines. Unfortunately, it's a bit old, and it doesn't seem to work properly in Windows NT environments, so it's not very useful for modern-day PC hackers.

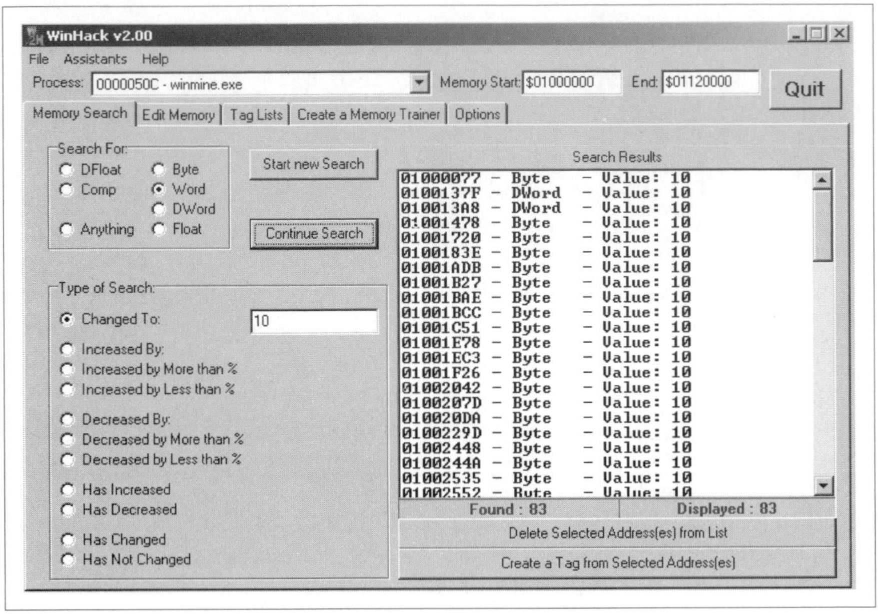

Figure 6-2. WinHack, showing all the initially changed memory locations

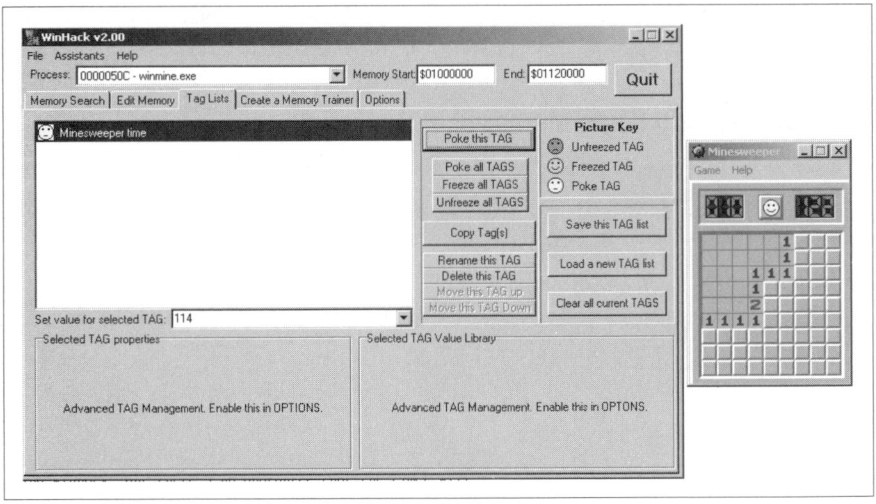

Figure 6-3. Changing the tag for the Minesweeper time

To start, load up your favorite game. We'll use the example of the excellent WinHack tutorial (*http://www.gamehacking.com/view.php?link=../tutorials/ winhack.php*) on Minesweeper, which ships with Windows.

1. Load MineSweeper, and leave it on the startup screen without starting a game.

2. Load WinHack. Select the MineSweeper application from the Process: window, and hit the Start New Search button.

3. Start a game of MineSweeper, and wait until the timer has counted 10 seconds. Pause the game by minimizing its window.

4. Now search Anything for the phrase "Changed to value of 10" selection, and hit Continue Search. This finds every memory location (Figure 6-2) whose contents have since changed to the value of 10— probably several places.

5. Maximize MineSweeper again, and wait for the timer to reach 18. Then minimize again and change the Changed value to 18. You should receive only one result: the location of the timer variable. Now you can mess with it.

6. Select Create A Tag From The Selected Address. Go to the Tag Lists menu, where you can change the value for that particular tag to anything you like (back to 1, for example) or freeze it so it doesn't increment anymore. See Figure 6-3.

7. Go back into the game and see that the timer has changed to your new value. Poof, instant MineSweeper cheating!

This type of hack isn't necessarily permanent, though. You might be able to create a trainer using WinHack, but there's no guarantee that the timer will occupy the same chunk of memory on every game.

Buff Your Saved Characters

HACK
#77

Hex editing your saved games can relieve tedious single-player leveling.

What if you knew you had a bunch of information about your character saved in a PC saved-game file, but you weren't happy with it? Suppose your character has $10, but you want him to have $20. Following the general path of the saved-game hacking ideas on GameHacking.com (e.g., *http://www.gamehacking.com/view.php?link=../tutorials/savehacktut.php*), you can solve this little problem, too.

For this example, we'll use HexEdit 2.1 (*http://www.gamehacking.com/download.php?type=tools&file=hexeditors/hedit21.zip*), a relatively old, but still serviceable hex editor.

> You'll need a passing familiarity with hexadecimal notation, which is where the name hex editor comes from. You'll have to enter the value to search in hex. In this example, 10 in decimal is 0A in hexadecimal. The number 20 in decimal is 14 in hex. With a little practice, it'll make sense to you.

To start, you need to know the current value of the item you hope to change. If you're lucky, it'll be unique and easier to find within the saved game. Once you've found it, simply replace the correct 0A with 14 and reload the game to see what happened. Keep multiple copies of the save file in case you messed up, of course. There's more trial and error in this approach, but the game saves often follow very similar formats. Don't be confused if you see 10 in the right column. This shows ASCII equivalents of hex values. Any text here is itself made up of individual number values. This is the absolute basic saved-game hacking, using trial and error with known values. It works well, though it pales in comparison with more sophisticated disassembly methods. On to glory!

Code Disassembly for PC Game Hacking

What if you could edit not only the values of a program, but also the routines that produce those values? Sounds complex, but this technique can yield the most fruit. Instead of resetting the timer continually, what if you disabled it altogether? That's the type of goal code disassembly can reach.

What Is Disassembly?

Contrary to what game publishers and the general public might like to think, game binaries aren't closed boxes you can never open. They're just big bundles of cryptic but well-known instructions for your computer to execute.

A disassembler takes those instructions and translates them into something a little more human-friendly. The result isn't as clear as the program's source code would be, resembling *Finnegan's Wake* on the overall comprehensibility scale more than a Dick and Jane primer, but with intuition, time, and practice, it's possible to figure out the important pieces.

There are ways to make disassembly more difficult, but as long as people control their own general-purpose hardware, publishers will never prevent hackers from doing cool things.

You'll need a specific type of tool. The free PEBrowse for Windows (available via *http://www.smidgeonsoft.com/*) comes highly recommended, as does OllyDbg (*http://home.t-online.de/home/Ollydbg/*). There are plenty of other disassemblers. The commercial SoftIce disassembler also has its fans.

Though the specifics differ from game to game, the technique is simple:

1. Find the value you want to change. Load the game into memory, then use a memory finder to find the value you want to change permanently ("Modify PC Game Saves and Settings" **[Hack #76]**).

2. Set a breakpoint on that memory address. Now that you have a memory address to watch, load the disassembler, and attach it to the executable. Set a breakpoint on the access of the memory address. The debugger will halt the execution of the program when something tries to read from or write to that memory address, showing you the exact assembly language commands.

3. Replace the offending instruction. Suppose you want to stop a timer from counting down. In this case, you'll likely see a DEC ??? command somewhere close to the breakpoint, decrementing the value of the appropriate memory location. Try changing the DEC ??? command to a null operation, NOP.

4. Test your changes. Remove the breakpoint, and restart the game. If you removed the right command, you should see no countdown. If not, try again. It's really as easy as that!

Obviously, this is a simple step in a complex land. There are few limits to what you can do, given time, intuition, and a grasp of assembly language.

Packet Editors and Hacking

Modifying network games is a little trickier because you control only the part of the game running on your machine. That's still control enough, though. Packet editors allow you to intercept incoming packets from a server (whether it be FPS, RTS, MMORPG, or whatever) and alter what you send back. The GameHacking page on packet editors (*http://www. gamehacking.com/sites/tools.php?sort=Packeteditors*) has a few choice downloads, but there's very little public information about packet hacking online.

Serious companies, such as Blizzard, encrypt their packets. This makes packet hacking more difficult, though not impossible. As well, packet hacking can't give you an infinite amount of energy or kill all the other players unless the server allows those operations. You'll have to find some way to exploit the rules. Your grand dreams of loot and equipment in a MMO are probably unrealistic.

Also, there's a big difference between cheating in a single-player game and cheating in a multiplayer game ("Catch Half-Life FPS Cheaters Redhanded" [Hack #34]). It's one thing to change the rules of the game for yourself, but it's rude to change them for other people without their permission.

Hacking Legacy Of Kain: Soul Reaver

Specific game hacks are usually best when done by die-hard fans who know a little bit about the included and removed features and items. While poking around in memory, it's easier for well-informed hackers to pick up on subtle hints in variables and names.

A good example is The Lost Worlds site (*http://www.thelostworlds.net/*), which hosts an amazingly canonical catalog of all of the hidden, missing, and otherwise unknown parts of Crystal Dynamics's popular Legacy Of Kain series. In particular, one page deals with hacking the PC version of Legacy Of Kain: Soul Reaver with WinHack (*http://www.thelostworlds.net/SR1-Hack.HTML*). Because the author knows the context, he's excellent at finding the exact nooks and crannies needed to hit to modify the game.

As it turns out, the command-line parameters for the game—originally used for debugging—are still embedded in the executable. You can't change them from a shortcut, as the developers probably could during programming, between they've removed that feature. You *can* change them in memory, however. If you load the game up to the first window, where you select the video resolution, you can then load WinHack, select KAIN2.ICD or KAIN2.EXE, and go to the hex-style memory editor. Click the Go To Address button, and enter $00C651E0. This turns out to be the memory location containing those command-line parameters, described on another page (*http://www.thelostworlds.net/SR1-Memory.HTML*) of The Lost Worlds site. Most of these are disabled, but you can use them to change the start location of Kain in the world, as well as a few other mainly broken options.

The game's default parameters are currently set to:

```
under 1 -mainmenu -voice -inspectral
```

but you can click on this text and add your own options. Your best option is to change under 1 to another location in the game. Don't forget to type in the rest of the existing options and then fill in the remainder of that location with zeros in the hex column.

Use The Lost Worlds's gigantic rooms list (*http://www.thelostworlds.net/SR1_Area_List.HTML*) to place your character anywhere you want in the game, even locations that you can't normally reach from inside the game. The Lost Worlds walkthrough suggests using skinnr 18, which is a secret passage (*http://www.thelostworlds.net/SR1-Secret.HTML*) that's inaccessible from the normal game. Very neat indeed.

It's also possible to modify specific variables that are resident in memory after you load Soul Reaver, adding extra hidden powers and increasing your health by various means. Although you'd normally have to search to find the appropriate memory locations, the creator of The Lost Worlds site has done it for you. Download his WinHack-specific tag-list file (*http://www. thelostworlds.net/Misc/SR1-Hack.zip*) and import it from the Tag List/Load A New Tag List option.

This makes hacking the game as easy as clicking on each named option and changing values to increase your number of health bars and your total health. You can also award yourself all abilities in the game by putting 255 in the Abilities Acquired tag* cut from the game, which allows you to change between the normal and spectral planes at any time. There's also a Player Z-Position value that controls the vertical height of Raziel, the main character, so you can place him on roofs you couldn't normally reach. Be careful not to throw him too far out of the map, though!

HACK #78 Create Console Game Levels

Extend the length of your game by creating new levels and sharing them with the world.

Some console games aren't games as much as they are pure construction kits. Other titles are fun in their own right and just happen to include the ability to create new content that's as much fun as the game itself. How can you exploit these console-creation kits to have more fun than actually playing the game you bought and trade your creations with other people online? Let's pick a few of the best, most fun-to-use console-construction tools that came as game add-ons and discuss the communities around them and ways to add and contribute your own ideas.

---

* Don't forget to hit Poke This Tag to activate it! You'll have everything, including the Shift At Will ability (*http://www.thelostworlds.net/SR1-SaW.HTML*).

An honorable mention goes to the granddaddy of all construction kits, the track editor on Nintendo's classic 1984 release, Excitebike. Unfortunately, after you painstakingly designed the track and played it, it would vanish as soon as you turned off the machine. There wasn't even a password system to retrieve the design again! In those days, it was a one-time act, but if you use an emulator that supports snapshots, you'll finally have the chance to save your work.

Tony Hawk Series

Spanning at least six titles over multiple hardware iterations, the Tony Hawk series from Neversoft and Activision, an addictive skateboarding games in its own right, has gradually improved its Create A Park feature. It debuted in Tony Hawk's Pro Skater 2 for PlayStation. The current iteration in Tony Hawk's Underground allows uploads and downloads of custom skate vaults from the online Neversoft Vault if you have a PlayStation 2. This is an amazing way to try out new skate parks; all companies should aim toward this type of system when it comes to creating new content on consoles (imagine if you could do the same in RPG Maker!).

If you're interested in making your own courses, start on GameFAQs with Nubermind's superlative Create A Park guide to Tony Hawk's Underground for the PlayStation 2 (*http://db.gamefaqs.com/console/ps2/file/thug_cap.txt*). Here are a few notable tips:

Beware of eye candy.   Although strange, random props such as cars and helicopters are cool-looking, it's very difficult to integrate them into the flow of your park. You're welcome to put them in, but they're difficult to work around during complex, flowing trick runs. Remember, your course should be fun to skate.

Watch the Memory Meter.   You don't have much actual memory on the PS2 for designing courses. If you decide to make the park a maximum eight-player course, Create A Park will have to reserve enough memory for eight instances of skaters and their animations, limiting the amount of pieces and size of the park. Nubermind suggests you set the number of players to two unless you intend to play online.

Save the finishing for the end.   Wait until you've otherwise completed the level before adding your gaps and goals. Nubermind advises that these finishing touches take a very small amount of memory, so you can design the shape and flow of the entire skate park and make sure everything is hunky-dory before committing to what people have to do to succeed in it.

Similarly, ThugXOnline's Create A Review section (*http://www.thugxonline.com/car/*) is a lesser-known and super-helpful resource with ratings, details, and even descriptions of notable fan-created skate parks. Don't be confused by the lack of download links; you'll need to go online with your PS2 to grab them all.

If you can't go online or want to hark back to the classic era of Tony Hawk Create A Park from earlier generations, you can use a DexDrive-style memory card device to grab fan-created skate parks for PlayStation 1 versions of Tony Hawk's Pro Skater 2 from the smart Planet Tony Hawk site (*http://www.planettonyhawk.com/downloads/parks/thps2/psx/*). There are also PC downloads of skate parks for early versions of the game on this site, but later versions seem to lack a prominent central download location for third-party parks.

WWE Smackdown Series

Yukes's popular WWF/WWE Smackdown wrestling game series for Play-Stations 1 and 2 has always had a complex, well-designed Create A Wrestler option. This has led to all kinds of extremely cool designs for those who want to see their favorite comic character, wrestler, or even celebrity depicted in full wrestling glory. This is even fun for people who aren't really wrestling fans!

Yukes has released one new version every year in recent times, hence the different subtitles but upgraded gameplay.

To start your career, search for Smackdown on GameFAQs.com and visit each of the file areas and boards for the various Smackdown games. The file areas will allow Sharkport and other memory card saves to grab multiple new wrestlers at once (up to 30!). If you're in the mood to check out a new wrestler without doing all that file transfer stuff, you can actually type in variables to create a new character. See messages such as *http://boards.gamefaqs.com/gfaqs/genmessage.php?board=2000063&topic=13956737* that explain how to make Marvel villains. Beware, though: you may have to enter 100 different variables before you can replicate the character as described. Still, if you can end up with the Mexican Lucha Libre wrestlers perfectly depicted (*http://www.vivalaluchalibre.net/smackdown3.htm*), they must be doing something right.

TimeSplitters Series

At the time of writing, the excellent console FPS TimeSplitters series, from the ex-Rare developers at Free Radical, consisted of two games on PS2, Xbox, and GameCube, with a third in production. Apart from being an excellent multiplayer and fun single-player title, it has simple and intuitive FPS map-making software that works well with console controllers. Sure, it's not as powerful or customizable as, say, Unreal Tournament 2004 ("Modify the Behavior of a UT2004 Model" [Hack #84]), but if you just want to sit down and make a fun FPS level in front of your television with a minimum of technical knowledge, TimeSplitters and TimeSplitters 2 are very workable.

Unfortunately, some of the major TimeSplitters 2 map-making sites have closed down to prepare for the third in the series. Fortunately, Joel Barnett's mapmaking FAQ (found at *http://db.gamefaqs.com/console/gamecube/file/ timesplitters_2_mapmaker.txt*) is still on Gamefaqs. It's a good guide to creating both deathmatch and story maps. Here are some of its best ideas:

You're already advanced. Although the game has Beginner and Advanced modes, pick Advanced every time. It's really not *that* advanced, especially if you're reading this book! Beginner mode has a very limited selection of objects and lighting.

Add doors and windows. You can block off connected areas that are otherwise tedious run-and-shoot open areas by placing doors and windows inside the corridor sections. Join two sections of corridor together in the editor. Bring up the item tab, highlight where the sections connect, and then place doors and windows. You can even change the color of the door. This helps break things up and provides cover in an otherwise overly open level.

It's a pre-Gothic world. Don't be confused by mentions of the Gothic tile set. It doesn't exist in the released game, despite the documentation and even the strategy guide. You can still use the other four distinct tile sets, though.

As lamented earlier, the world of tradable TimeSplitters 2 map files is disappointingly bare. Hopefully, the third game will rectify this, perhaps even allowing online map trading. In the meantime, if you want to make new content, the map editor is easily one of the most fun add-ons to a console game.

CHAPTER SEVEN

Playing Your Own Games
Hacks 79–93

Scratch the surface of the average programmer (or programmer wannabe), and chances are you'll find an aspiring game programmer. Games are fun, so making them must be fun as well.*

Not everyone has millions of dollars, the latest sound and video recording and editing equipment, and a fantastic art department at your beck and call. The top publishers and console manufacturers may not return your calls, either. That shouldn't keep you away from game programming, though.

We won't be developing the next-generation 3D engine with pixel shaders, dynamic lighting, and a realistic physics engine, but you can wet your feet and whet your appetite with something a little smaller. Perhaps you'll write thoughtful new interactive fiction, design a killer pinball table, or make the world chuckle over the next great adventure story.

Whatever the case, it's never been easier to turn a great idea into great fun and to share it with the world.

 H A C K
#79 ## Adventure Game Studio Editing Tips
How to make your own graphic adventure classics.

Previous hacks have discussed using interpreters to play classic games using clever utilities such as ScummVM for LucasArts adventures ("Play Classic PC Graphic Adventures" **[Hack #7]**). As that hack points out, there's no real way to make new SCUMM games in this day and age. The creation tools aren't available to the public, and besides, the engine was pretty hacked up

---

* If you're actually in the games industry, you know this isn't always true. It still has its moments, though.

over multiple product iterations, with lots of customization to get games out the door.

Surely there must be some kind of alternative. There is, in the form of Adventure Game Studio, an excellent Windows-based utility that "allows you to create your own point-and-click adventure games, similar to the early '90s Sierra and LucasArts adventures." AGS is both a development environment and a runtime engine.

AGS Basics

Adventure Game Studio (AGS) is a fully developed graphical editor for game creation. It's simple enough that coding novices can venture a decent stab at making games of their own. You can add sound, music, and ambient noise in various formats, even making a full talkie adventure with speech—packed into a single file. You can set up conversation systems, a completely customizable GUI, and multiple-player characters, all in a variety of color palettes and bits. Of course, the 16-color mode provides that true retro feel.

The official AGS site (*http://www.adventuregamestudio.co.uk/*) has much more information on this long-standing tool, and the download page (*http://www.agsforums.com/acdload.htm*) has everything you need to start. Thanks to a port of the runtime engine itself (*http://drevil.warpcore.org/ags/*), you can create games that run on Linux, although the actual creation tools still run only on Windows. For most standalone versions of the games themselves, you don't need to know anything about the AGS editor. Game creators compile their games into a single *.EXE* file for distribution, so it's a completely standalone system, unlike other creations such as Visual Pinball ("Create and Play Pinball Tables" **[Hack #80]**) that require you to have the editor installed before you can try out the game.

Running the AGS Editor

After installing AGS, load it up. Be prepared for a wealth of complex, but fairly usable, menu options and dialogs. By far the best sources for beginners are the official AGS Forums tutorial pages (*http://www.agsforums.com/acdload.htm*), which have both internal and external links to over 20 tutorials. Here are some tips to simplify your career:

Don't be daunted by the massive setup options screen. Click Start New Game, select the Blank Game template, and choose a resolution (I like 320×240, for maximum retro-ness!) to create a game. You'll see a screen of complex options. Many of these options are strictly high-end, and you can change them later if necessary. Do pay special attention to the choice of color resolution; if you change your mind part way through, you'll have to reimport all of your graphics.

The strange lines when editing rooms represent doorways or portals. Click on the Room Editor/Setting option in the Game Editor menus to edit your first room. You'll then see some strange lines. These mark the areas the player's feet will have to touch to leave or enter the room. Set what happens when this occurs by editing values and actions in the Interaction Editor, which you can call by clicking the i icon in the Room Editor screen.

To set up a walkable area, click on the Areas option in the Game Editor menus and sketch out and fill in the relevant areas with the paint tools. Combine these rooms with the Interaction Editor to carve out extravagant multiroom complexes in no time!

Make and import background graphics. Extravagant multiroom complexes look rather sparse without actual graphics to back them up. AGS comes with only one default character (Roger) and no background. Create a batch of sensible room graphics in the correct resolution, even cropping your holiday photos if necessary. Import them into AGS using the Import Background icon (the trees) in the Room Editor/Setting screen.

Use the inventory editor to manipulate game objects. The inventory editor (Inventory in the Game Editor menus) is well-coded and simple. Each object has a tree of possible responses for which to set actions, whether the player is looking at that object, talking to it, using something on it, or interacting with it in other ways. You can even set multistep actions or conditions. For example, if the player character has been in another room before examining the object, something else could happen!

Change the GUI if you're feeling particularly inspired. You can even completely change the GUI in the GUIs menu screen, both graphically and scriptwise. Hit the Edit Script button to see the scripts attached to the GUI functionality. Be aware that the graphical style of your rooms needs to mesh nicely with your GUI stylings, though. Try to avoid mixing paisley and tartan, please.

You can make a perfectly serviceable basic game using the GUI tools alone, but should you wish for more complexity, you can edit the scripts that your GUI games have produced. You'll need to do this to add features such as producing random messages when the player does something multiple times, allowing the player to complete a certain puzzle if she has any one of three different objects, and making custom functions that can be called from anywhere in the script. Chris Jones, the author of AGS, has an excellent basic scripting tutorial at *http://www.agsforums.com/actutor.htm*.

Some of the Finest AGS-Created Games

While it's fun to try to create your own games, it's also well worth checking out what other talented amateurs have created. Just about every AGS-authored game ever created is available for free download, too, so there's a wealth of great games to try.

> Though they look old-school in style, these aren't morally murky abandonware games from the '80s. They're brand new adventures, made in the past few years, that the original creators distribute freely.

Start at the AGS Awards page (*http://www.sylpher.com/AGSAwards/Awards.htm*), which highlights specific AGS games in several categories, stretching all the way back to 2001. Unfortunately, this site lacks download links, so either do a little Googling to find a game that catches your eye or wander over to the official AGS page for award winners (*http://www.agsforums.com/games.php?category=102*) and follow the links there. Most download links there redirect to personal pages; hopefully, someone will work on a central, permanent archive for these titles soon. Here are a few of the games you'll find:

The Adventures Of Fatman
> This full talkie adventure (Figure 7-1) is a superhero spoof and was actually a commercial game for a while. The creator has since kindly allowed free distribution. Not only is it full-featured, long, and funny, the talkie version includes a behind-the-scenes audio commentary for each location, a really neat and unique concept for a graphic adventure. Download it from *http://software01.archive.org/items/the-adventures-of-fatman-pc/*.

5 Days A Stranger
> This spooky horror game won a host of awards at the 2003 AGS Awards. The storyline involves a cat burglar stranded in a country house as things go horribly awry. A genuinely scary atmosphere—not often tried in graphic adventures that traditionally veer toward humor—and great characterization and plot make this title well worth your time. See *http://netmonkey.cellosoft.com/5days/*.

Pleughberg: The Dark Ages
> Despite somewhat lackluster graphics, it's easy to see why Pleughberg won many "Best of" awards in the 2001 AGS competition. You play

Figure 7-1. The great and now free Adventures Of Fatman

"Jake McUrk, working for the Police Detective Agency" in this gritty police drama with a fair amount of extremely pixelated gore. The story is great, and the creator also took time to put in multiple endings—a very neat touch. You can download it from *http://www.gaspop.com/darkages.htm*.

Apprentice

Another fan favorite, this short but memorable adventure focuses on Mortimer "Pib" Pibsworth, a would-be magician. It won multiple awards, especially for art, in the 2003 AGS Awards. Fortunately, there's a sequel (or, actually, trilogy) in development for those upset that the well-crafted title ends so soon. See *http://herculeaneffort.adventuredevelopers.com/app1.html#top*.

There are plenty of neat choices out there. Free games are proliferating because they're so easy to create, and the gameplay is straightforward and does not rely on twitchy reflexes. It's also worth noting that the official AGS games page (*http://www.agsforums.com/games.php*) offers a handy parental advisory rating per game for sex, violence, and nudity. You can check which titles have mature themes as well as those that don't.

For fans of the awful, there's also plenty of opportunity to trawl through some truly tragic fan-created titles. The AGS Awards even have a category for the most execrable fan concoctions. I can't really repeat the actual award name, but suffice to say it involves the ASCII-ization of a rather rude word.

Highlights include the sophisticated Smokin' Weed (at *http:// www.agsforums.com/games.php?action=detail&id=229*), which is "a short game about a drug dealer who gets visited by the weed police and now he has to escape out of his own house." This gripping adventure comes from the pen of Guybrush's brother, Vincent Threepwood!

HACK #80 Create and Play Pinball Tables

Design your own virtual pinball table.

It makes a lot of sense that people can play classic arcade games by taking the code and writing hardware emulators. It's easy to emulate computing machines, but how about pinball machines? How do you emulate physical objects?

You'll need a decent construction kit to set up ramps, bumpers, flippers, and ball physics, much like the classic EA '80s title Pinball Construction Set by Bill Budge. Fortunately, the Pinball Construction Set for the '00s is here, in the form of Randy Davis's freeware Visual Pinball.

Visual Pinball Overview

Download the latest Tech Beta of Visual Pinball from the official site (*http:// www.randydavis.com/vp/download.htm*). Unfortunately, it's a Windows-only program. More unfortunately, you also need the latest versions of DirectX, Windows Script (available with Internet Explorer 5.01 or above, Windows 98/ME, or Windows 2000/XP), and also Windows Media Player to install the audio runtimes.

Some versions of the game were limited betas, so if you grab one of those, it'll say that your time is up, and you can't play. However, the author decided to take away this limited-time status, so just hunt around on sites such as VPForums (*http://www.vpforums.com/*) for an executable without the time limit. This is perfectly legitimate and creator-approved, not a time-crack of any kind.

After installing the program, run it. Because it's really a construction kit into which you can load games, you'll see that it opens straight into a blank construction screen. This feature makes it even more fascinating, because all the tables you download are completely open; you can fiddle with them, tweak the locations of objects, and then test your changes right away.

> The reason for the name "Visual Pinball" is that it uses Visual Basic to script actions and complicated logic for the pinball games. It's an amazingly full-featured tool.

Editing Basics

In the blank editor screen, go to the File menu and select Open, then load one of the example tables created by Randy Davis himself. Choose Alien Reactor. You'll see a rather smart top-down grid view of the table appear, looking something like Figure 7-2.

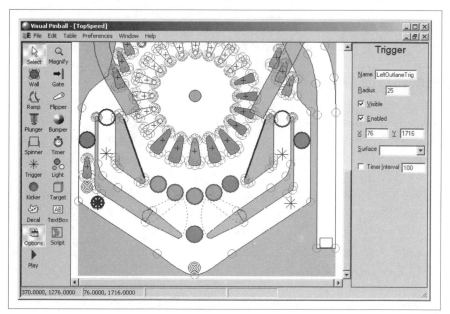

Figure 7-2. The Visual Pinball editing screen

Before we mess up anything, let's try the table as originally loaded. Hit the F5 key or the Play icon on the left side of the screen. Within five seconds, the table will pop up in a pseudo-3D view, completely playable. Hit the Escape key after playing for a while to return to the editor screen.

Click on any of the individual items on the board, and drag them to move them around. If you really want your flippers in the middle of nowhere, go ahead and move them. Click the Options button on the left side of the screen to see the specific settings for that object, including its colors, physics, size, and orientation.

Also click on Script to see the script for the table. As you can see, it's actually pretty straightforward Visual Basic. Here's an example:

```
Sub CheckTargets
    If Target1.IsDropped And Target2.IsDropped And Target3.IsDropped Then
        Target1.IsDropped = False
        Target2.IsDropped = False
        Target3.IsDropped = False
        PlaySound "FlipperUp"
        PlaySound "GotLight"
        mainsoundtimer.Enabled = True
        AddScore 10000
    End If
End Sub
```

This code checks the drop targets, which adds to the player's score, plays sounds, and resets them when the player has hit all three.

Further Table-Creation Resources

Creating your own pintable with Visual Pinball is actually fairly straightforward, although some of the Visual Basic can be a little tricky. Check out the VPForums gurus and Q/A areas if you get stuck. You can learn a lot from existing tables by opening up their scripts and checking out exactly what they're doing; open source is a good thing indeed.

ShivaSite has several great templates and FAQs, though you'll need to register in order to download or view any of them. Check out *http://www. shivasite.com/modules.php?modid=1&action=cat&id=5*.

If you're interested in some more exotic flipperless tables as found in bagatelle and pachinko machines, see the Sahara Sales page (*http://www. saharasales.com/flipperless/tutorials.html*). In particular, be sure to read the tutorial that explains how to replace the default plunger with a variable velocity kicker (*http://www.saharasales.com/flipperless/willdemo.html*).

Original Homebrew Tables

Although there are many faithful reproductions of existing tables, plenty of other people have made completely original pintables (some of which are based on licenses they may be particularly enamored of). There's no good central download source for these, but the VP Original Tables Releases forum (*http://www.vpforums.com/forum/forumdisplay.php?forumid=88*) handles announcements and reviews of new original creations. If you make a table of release quality, announce it there.

As of press time, a new resource has appeared at *http://www.public.asu.edu/
~checkma/pinball/originals.html*, with links to all new or updated originally
designed homebrew tables. This may also be worth checking out or submit-
ting information to; however, because it uses third-party links, it won't host
your files for you.

The following sections describe a few notable homebrew tables.

F1. Based on the Formula 1 racing championships, F1 is a large (15 MB)
table with a great deal of detail. It's particularly designed as a two-player
table, with Michael Schumacher and David Coulthard duking it out for the
championship. This is easily one of the most professional-looking homebrew tables, featuring multiball, several modes, and plenty of good speech
and sound effects. F1 is well worth checking out. Download it from *http://
members.iinet.net.au/~cleathley/*.

The Great Rock N Roll Swindle. Appealingly nihilistic, the Sex Pistols would
never sell out, but this original homebrew machine converts them to pintable form with great aplomb, complete with sounds and visuals from the
movie and album of the same name. This may be one of the only games in
the history of pinball in which rolling over the letters P, U, N, and K will
earn you bonuses. See *http://www.excellentcontent.com/vpinball/swindle.htm*.

Inner City Life. This intriguing oversized pintable has some really nice custom graphics, gigantic ramps, and a much more synthetic look (Figure 7-3)
than many other tables that really try to look like actual pinball machines. It
works great nonetheless. Look out for the massive ramp through the sky-
scrapers on the right side of the playfield, as well as the mini-playfield with
the mini-flipper up in the top left. Download it from *http://www.
scholzroland.de/VPStuff/*.

Fight Night. Universally acclaimed as one of the best original tables, this box-
ing-themed homebrew pinball machine has four flippers, some intriguing
modes, and even a mini–boxing ring at the top of the playfield to mix things
up a little. The logic of the modes is also neat; you need a Trainer and a Pro-
moter before you go into the boxing rings proper. See *http://webpages.
charter.net/celamantia/vp/Fight%20Night%202.0%20beta%202.zip* or download an edited form from *http://www.excellentcontent.com/vpinball/*.

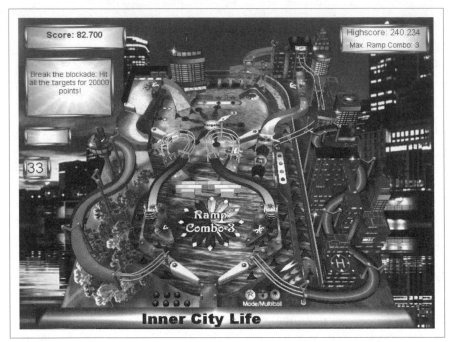

Figure 7-3. Roland Scholz's neat Inner City Life Visual pinball table

 HACK #81   Put Your Face in DOOM

Increase the immersiveness of id's classic FPS by replacing the space marine's pictures with your own.

id Software's groundbreaking DOOM almost singlehandedly created the modern FPS genre. With style oozing from every crevice, a near-infinite amount of customizability, and an open source codebase, it's no wonder that people still play variants such as PrBoom (*http://prboom.sourceforge.net/*).

As any dedicated modder will tell you, half the fun is in making your own fun. Earlier games were also hackable, but DOOM was unique in *encouraging* gamers to add their own maps, weapons, and graphics. Since it was a pre-Windows pioneer, the tools aren't very user-friendly, but they exist and work with a little prodding.

Creating your own maps is a lot of work, but it's much easier to replace individual graphics. One good way to start is to change the picture of your character in the game's status bar.

Finding DOOM

Start by downloading PrBoom or an equivalent. PrBoom is nice in that it supports Windows and Linux equally well. Windows installation is as easy as downloading the latest Windows ZIP archive (2.2.4 at the time of writing) and unzipping it into an appropriate directory.

If you have the registered version of DOOM somewhere,* copy its *.wad* files into the PrBoom directory. Otherwise, look for a file called *doom1.wad* online. This is the shareware version; I found it at *http://www.lbjhs.net/ ~jessh/lsdldoom/doom1.wad.gz*.

How WADs Work

DOOM stores all its maps, images, and sounds in WAD files. There are two types. IWADs are the original internal WADs shipped with the game; they contain the default game information. PWADs are player-supplied WADs that change or add parts of the game. They can be much smaller, because anything they don't supply directly comes from the original IWAD.

Think of a WAD as a directory containing subdirectories and files, somewhat like a ZIP archive. To replace a particular graphic, you have to know its details within the IWAD and add an equivalent graphic to your PWAD. That's where tools such as DeuTex (*http://www.teaser.fr/~amajorel/deutex/*) come in.

 Technically, you're not supposed to be able to create or use PWADs with the shareware IWAD. I renamed *doom1.wad* to *doom.wad*, and PrBoom and DeuTex were happy.

DeuTex is a WAD disassembler, meaning that it can disassemble a WAD into a real directory. It runs on DOS and Linux. Download and extract DeuTex into its own directory, then extract the data from *doom.wad* with a command resembling:

```
$ ./deutex -extract /usr/share/games/doom/doom.wad
```

This creates several directories such as *textures/* and *sounds/* as well as a file called *wadinfo.txt*.

---

* id still sells Ultimate DOOM (*http://www.idsoftware.com/games/doom/doom-ultimate/*).

Replacing an Image

Besides trial and error, there's really no good way to figure out which image within this WAD to replace. Fortunately, I can tell you that the files in *graphics/stf** represent the face in the status bar. I replaced the god-mode powerup image (type **iddqd** while playing) with a picture of my nephew. DeuTex extracts this image to *graphics/stfgod0.pnm*.

The trickiest part of this process is building a 24×29 image that looks good in DOOM, especially with its restricted palette. I cropped and adjusted the picture until it fit, then saved it as a 256-color GIF file in *graphics/stfgod0.gif*. Be sure to keep the same base name as the file you're replacing; otherwise, DOOM won't know how to find the resource. It's okay to use a different file extension; DeuTex converts BMP, GIF, or JPEG files to PPM files automatically when it builds a WAD. If you do use a different extension, though, be sure to move the original file out of the way so that DeuTex will use your replacement.

 For best results, remove the background of the image, leaving only the subject's face and head. The image is much less jarring this way.

The next step is to build a manifest file to tell DeuTex which files to assemble. Open the *wadinfo.txt* file in your favorite text editor. It has several internal sections for the different types of files within the WAD. Delete everything that you haven't replaced. In my case, I had a very short file:

```
# List of Pictures (with insertion point)
[graphics]
STFGOD0 -5      -2
```

Be sure to keep the [graphics] heading, though you can delete the entries beneath it for the images you want to stay the same. Save the file with a different name, perhaps *godinfo.txt*, so you can make other modifications by copying the relevant lines from the original manifest.

Building a PWAD

The final step is to assemble all the new resources into a PWAD. DeuTex again can do this. Use a command resembling:

```
$ ./deutex -build godinfo.txt baby.wad
```

If everything goes well, this will write a new PWAD called *baby.wad* in your current directory. DeuTex helpfully refuses to overwrite an existing file, so delete or move *baby.wad* if you've already generated one.

Launching Your New PWAD

To see the effects of your work, launch PrBoom with your new PWAD. Use the -file switch to give the location of the file:

```
$ prboom -file baby.wad
```

Start a new game, type **iddqd**, and marvel at the connection between innocence and ultimate power, seen in Figure 7-4.

Figure 7-4. An alternate god-mode image

The same technique here works for replacing any image or sound within the IWAD files, including monsters and weapons. Remember, if you can do it for one image, you can do it for many.

HACK #82 Create a Vehicle Model for Unreal Tournament 2004

Make and import game-suitable 3D artwork.

If you're hacking new behavior into your favorite game, you'll eventually need to build, beg, borrow, or steal some new art. Tweaking the gravity and weapon damage ranges can only take you so far. Creating your own artwork is the best approach, but you'll need a modicum of talent and some experience with a graphics program such as Maya PLE, which comes with UT2004.

Maya PLE comes with many tutorials, and they appear when you run it the first time. It's worth your while to read through them.

With that knowledge in mind, there are some specific steps to understand when creating art for a game. Let's walk through the creation of the 'Cuda (a 1969 Plymouth Barracuda) from our UT2004 Clone Bandits modification (*http://www.demiurgestudios.com/CloneBandits/*). Figure 7-5 shows the modeled image.

Figure 7-5. The 'Cuda model

Modeling Considerations

There are a few things to keep in mind at the modeling stage. The 'Cuda's nose points in the positive Z direction, with the center of its chassis (as opposed to, say, the bottom of its wheels) at the origin. Originally, I placed it higher, with the bottom of the chassis at the origin, but eventually lowered it to help characters exit the vehicle in predictable ways.

You don't have to combine the meshes that make up a vehicle before exporting it to Unreal. For example, the chassis and wheels of the 'Cuda are separate meshes bound to the same skeleton. This allows more flexibility when assigning bone influences; you can do them one part at a time.

When you complete the model, pull off the guns from the main chassis, move their roots to the origin, skin them, and export them to Unreal separately. I found exporting them out into new Maya files made this process cleaner.

Creating Skeletons

The skeleton for the 'Cuda is fairly simple. There are joints that represent each wheel and joints that define the gun attach points. Each joint is a child of the root, located at the bottom center of the chassis. Figure 7-6 shows the details.

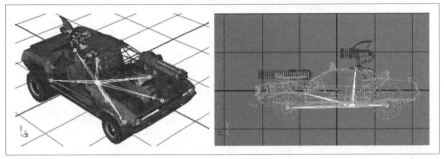

Figure 7-6. The skeleton of the model

Be aware of the joint orientation. In general, modelers need to orient their joints along the world axes. This applies doubly to the root and wheel joints. Slight offsets in joint orientation can cause strange-looking rotations in Unreal. You can see a joint's orientation by choosing Object (instead of World) in the Move tool and then selecting the joint.

The gun joints are a special case. All joints in the gun skeletons are rotated such that their positive X axis points along the barrel of the gun, and the positive Z points up. This also applies to the joints that define gun attach points.

We used Smooth Bind to link the skeleton to the mesh. However, you want the vehicle to be rigid, because, generally speaking, cars don't bend. In the Component Editor, assign all the mesh's vertices to one bone or another. For example, only the front-right wheel bone should affect all vertices in the front-right wheel.

Exporting with ActorX

You'll need the ActorX plug-in to export your vehicle to an Unreal-friendly format. This plug-in is freely available from the Unreal Developers Network (*http://udn.epicgames.com/Two/ActorX*) for both Maya and 3D Studio Max. The same site has installation instructions.

Once you've installed the plug-in, fire it up to see the ActorX options. Persistent settings and persistent paths are handy. Under Skin Export, checking "all skin-type" exports all skinned items, which is convenient if there is only one skinned mesh in the Maya file. Automatic triangulate is also useful, though you will usually find that Maya's Triangulate function yields better results.

The ActorX plug-in exports two types of files, those that contain mesh and skeleton information (*.PSK*) and those that contain animation data (*.PSA*). We'll create *.PSK* files because the game code will animate the 'Cuda's wheels procedurally.

To export the mesh, choose an output folder and a name for the file (in *.PSK* format), then hit the Save mesh/refpose button.

A Brief Introduction to UnrealEd

UnrealEd is a powerful and complex tool that allows you to edit, import, and create content for Unreal Tournament 2004. As we can discuss only the tip of the iceberg here, I encourage you to learn more about the editor by consulting the extensive Unreal Developers Network documentation (*http://udn.epicgames.com/Engine/WebHome*).

Unreal stores its content in package files. Different types of packages exist for different types of data. We will be dealing specifically with texture (*.UTX*) and animation (*.UKX*) packages.

Importing Textures

In UnrealEd, use the Texture Browser to create and edit texture packages. Open it by choosing View/Show Texture Browser in the top pull-down menu. In the Texture Browser, click File/Import… and navigate to your texture files, which are all 24-bit Targa files. Select all the textures and click Open. (UnEdit supports importing multiple files at once.) This brings up the Import Texture dialog.

You need to give your new package a name, then further organize your textures into groups. The Options defaults will work fine for textures that have no alpha channels. Check Alpha if a texture has smooth gradients in the alpha channel, or Masked if the alpha channel values are simply black and white, with no gray values.

Importing Meshes

Just as you created your texture package using the Texture Browser, you will import your mesh and edit it with the Animation Browser. Since you have the Texture Browser already open, click the tab at the top labeled Animations.

In the Animation Browser, click File/Mesh import, and navigate to the directory containing your new *.PSK* file. Use the Import Mesh/Animation dialog to name the new animation package. Remember to check Assume Maya coordinates so that your mesh comes in with the correct rotation.

Assigning Textures

Now you have to assign textures. This requires the following steps:

1. Highlight the desired texture over in the Texture Browser by clicking it.
2. Back in the Animation Browser, click to open the Skin array in the Mesh tab to the right.
3. Clicking Material shows the list of materials assigned to the mesh. Click the text in the first material slot to select that slot, then hit Use to assign the selected texture to this slot.
4. Repeat for each slot.

Assigning Collision Boxes

The Unreal vehicle code handles collision for the wheels, but you need to give the chassis a collision volume. In the Animation Browser, open the Collision section under the Mesh tab on the right (above the Skin array). In the CollisionBoxes slot, click the ... text on the right, then hit the Add button that appears. This brings up several new fields.

The first three of these fields (bBlockKarma, bBlockNonZeroExtent, and bBlockZeroExtent) describe types of collision operations. You'll want the box to collide with all three, so in each slot, replace the 0 (false) with 1 (true). The new collision box needs to attach to a bone, so type **rootcar**, representing the car model's main bone, in the BoneName field.

Next, let's give the collision box some dimensions. Click open the Radii section, and type **100** in the X, Y, and Z fields. Now to see the new collision box, select View/Collision from the top menu. PRESTO! Suddenly there's a big purple box, as shown in Figure 7-7.

Now it's just a matter of adjusting the Radii and offset values to make the collision box fit tightly. In the mod, we ended up adding another box to the front to clean up collisions with the ground. The final product looks like Figure 7-8.

"Rigidizing" the Mesh

In Maya, each vertex is influenced by only one bone. This isn't only visually correct, as a metal car is indeed rigid, but also allows a big performance

Figure 7-7. The purple collision box

Figure 7-8. The expanded collision boxes

increase in Unreal. This eliminates the hassle of constantly calculating the location of each vertex as determined by the combined effect of multiple bones. You explicitly tell the Unreal Engine to take advantage of simplified skin by "rigidizing" the mesh.

Open the LOD (Level of Detail) section in the Mesh tab. Click open the LODLevels array. By default, a mesh has four LOD levels, 0 through 3. You probably don't need that many. The vehicles that come with Unreal Tournament 2004 have only three levels. For simplicity, let's delete all but the first; click each level and hit the Delete button that appears.

Click open the remaining LOD level and open the Rigidize option. Clicking MeshSectionMethod brings up an arrow to the right, which in turn opens a drop-down menu. Select MSM_RigidOnly. Finalize the choice by selecting Mesh/Redigest Lod from the menu at the top of the Animation Browser. Go to wireframe view (View/Wireframe) to verify that each vertex has only one bone influence by checking that the wireframe is red instead of the default yellow. If a section had vertices with multiple influences, it would still be yellow. Figure 7-9 shows a happy red wireframe.

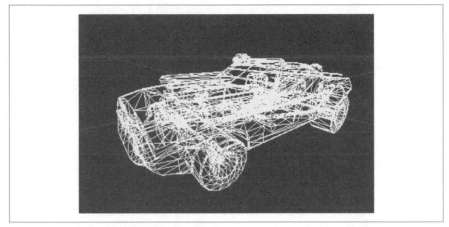

Figure 7-9. The wireframe view of vertex influence

The Rest of the Story

Now that you've imported the 'Cuda into Unreal, what happens next? You need to repeat the previous steps for the guns, though you won't need collision boxes because guns don't collide. At this point, the artwork is done, and programming work begins. A new vehicle in Unreal requires a new class ("Add a Vehicle to Unreal Tournament 2004" [Hack #83]) and, possibly, some new behavior ("Modify the Behavior of a UT2004 Model" [Hack #84]).

HACK
#83

Add a Vehicle to Unreal Tournament 2004

Add a new object type to an existing game, for standalone play or as part of new content.

Earlier, we created and imported a car model into UnrealEd to use in Unreal Tournament 2004 ("Create a Vehicle Model for Unreal Tournament 2004" [Hack #82]). Now it's time to take that model (the 1969 Plymouth Barracuda from Clone Bandits, *http://www.demiurgestudios.com/CloneBandits/*) and turn it into an Actor that can be placed in a map, driven around, and used in game types such as Onslaught. The obvious next step is to enhance the 'Cuda by adding nitrous-style speed boosts ("Modify the Behavior of a UT2004 Model" [Hack #84]).

You can download the source code mentioned in this hack as well as the art packages necessary to use this example from *http://www.demiurgestudios.com/CudaExample/*.

Creating a Class for the 'Cuda

To make the 'Cuda its own object or Actor in the world of Unreal, you need to create a class for it in UnrealScript. UnrealScript is a full-featured programming language "created to provide the development team and the third-party Unreal developers with a powerful, built-in programming language that maps naturally onto the needs and nuances of game programming."[*] You can find many UnrealScript references on the Web. Two good ones are *http://udn.epicgames.com/Two/UnrealScriptReference* and *http://udn. epicgames.com/Two/MyFirstCode*.

To create a new class, you first need to create a new UnrealScript package. From your Unreal Tournament 2004 directory (generally *C:\UT2004*), create a new directory. The name of this directory will be the name of your package; for this example, let's call it *CudaExample*. In the *CudaExample* directory, create a subdirectory called *Classes*, and in *Classes*, create a text file called *CudaCar.uc*.

You can use any text editor to create and edit this file. Notepad will work, but you might consider an editor geared toward editing code. Microsoft Visual Studio works well, especially since it can do syntax highlighting on UnrealScript files if you tell it to treat them like C++ files. You might also consider using the Epic's free Unreal Development Environment (UDE).

At the time of writing, UDE was still in beta and lacked its own web site. Find a download by performing a quick web search.

Once you've created *CudaCar.uc*, open it up, and declare the CudaCar class like so:

```
class CudaCar extends ONSRV;
```

This line means that your CudaCar example is based on the ONSRV class, the preexisting Scorpion vehicle in Unreal Tournament 2004. For now, the example car will behave and look exactly like the Scorpion. Later, you'll make your class use the 'Cuda model, but that's the only line you need to define the class.

---

[*] Tim Sweeney, *http://udn.epicgames.com/Two/UnrealScriptReference*.

For the CudaCar example to work, you also need a factory to produce instances of your CudaCar. Vehicle factories create vehicles at the beginning of a game and when old vehicles are destroyed. In the same way you created *CudaCar.uc*, create *CudaCarFactory.uc* as follows:

```
class CudaCarFactory extends ONSVehicleFactory;

defaultproperties
{
    // mesh for factory (only seen in the Editor)
    VehicleClass=Class'CudaExample.CudaCar'

    // type of vehicle this factory spawns
    Mesh=SkeletalMesh'CloneBanditsVehicles_K.HotRod'
}
```

Now open up *UT2004.ini* in the *System* subdirectory of your UT2004 directory. Search for the text EditPackages, and add the line:

```
EditPackages=CudaExample
```

to the bottom of the list. Now you can compile the *CudaExample* package.

Open a command prompt in the *System* subdirectory, and type **ucc make**. This command compiles any package in the EditPackages list that doesn't have a *.u* UnrealScript package file. If everything works, you'll end up with a new *CudaExample.u* file. If you make changes to *CudaCar.uc* (or any other UnrealScript file in your package), you can recompile your code by deleting the existing *CudaExample.u* file and running ucc make again.

Making Your Car Use the 'Cuda Model

Now you have two cars that act exactly the same. Let's justify this work by making the new car class use the 'Cuda model. Edit the defaultproperties of the CudaCar to add the following to your *CudaCar.uc* file:

```
defaultproperties
{
    // Barracuda Mesh
    Mesh=SkeletalMesh'CloneBanditsVehicles_K.HotRod'

    // Don't use team skins
    RedSkin=None
    BlueSkin=None

    // Weapon
    DriverWeapons(0)=(WeaponBone="gunRTmount")

    // Vehicle Name
    VehicleNameString="Barracuda"
    VehiclePositionString="in a Barracuda"
```

```
// Driver Position
DrivePos=(X=0.0,Y=-30.0,Z=35.0)

// Lights
HeadlightProjectorOffset=(X=139,Y=0,Z=6)        // headlight projector
HeadlightCoronaOffset(0)=(X=135,Y=44,Z=0)       // headlights
HeadlightCoronaOffset(1)=(X=135,Y=-44,Z=0)
HeadlightCoronaOffset(2)=(X=10,Y=33.5,Z=40)     // roof lights
HeadlightCoronaOffset(3)=(X=12,Y=25,Z=42)
HeadlightCoronaOffset(4)=(X=11,Y=14.5,Z=40)
BrakeLightOffset(0)=(X=-134,Y=39,Z=6)           // tail lights
BrakeLightOffset(1)=(X=-134,Y=-39,Z=6)

// Wheel and wheel bones info

// right rear tire
Begin Object Class=SVehicleWheel Name=RRWheel
    bPoweredWheel=True
    bHandbrakeWheel=True
    BoneName="tire02"
    BoneRollAxis=AXIS_Y
    BoneOffset=(Y=20.000000)
    WheelRadius=24.2000000
End Object
Wheels(0)=SVehicleWheel'RRWheel'

// left rear tire
Begin Object Class=SVehicleWheel Name=LRWheel
    bPoweredWheel=True
    bHandbrakeWheel=True
    BoneName="tire04"
    BoneRollAxis=AXIS_Y
    BoneOffset=(Y=-20.000000)
    WheelRadius=24.200000
End Object
Wheels(1)=SVehicleWheel'LRWheel'

// right front tire
Begin Object Class=SVehicleWheel Name=RFWheel
    bPoweredWheel=True
    SteerType=VST_Steered
    BoneName="tire"
    BoneRollAxis=AXIS_Y
    BoneOffset=(Y=20.000000)
    WheelRadius=20.000000
End Object
Wheels(2)=SVehicleWheel'RFWheel'

// left front tire
Begin Object Class=SVehicleWheel Name=LFWheel
    bPoweredWheel=True
    SteerType=VST_Steered
    BoneName="tire03"
```

```
        BoneRollAxis=AXIS_Y
        BoneOffset=(Y=-20.000000)
        WheelRadius=20.000000
    End Object
    Wheels(3)=SVehicleWheel'LFWheel'
}
```

The Mesh=SkeletalMesh'CloneBanditsVehicles_K.HotRod' line sets the mesh of the vehicle to that of your 'Cuda model instead of the Scorpion model. Given that you've changed models, you need to change a few other things, too. First off, you need to prevent the red and blue team skins from applying to this model, because those textures are entirely different. Do this by setting the RedSkin and BlueSkin to NONE. Next, given that all the bone names are different, you need to reassign things to use valid bone names. The gun, for example, attaches to the bone named gunRTmount. The same reassignment goes for the wheels, done with the Wheels array at the bottom of defaultproperties.

> Due to the way UnrealScript handles subobjects in defaultproperties, you have to assign all the relevant wheel properties, even if they didn't change from the parent object.

It is helpful to change several other properties such as the name of the vehicle (VehicleNameString and VehiclePositionString) and where the driver sits (DrivePos). Consider also adjusting the position of the headlights, taillights, and headlight projector in the Lights block in defaultproperties. The CudaCar will still work without these changes, but these adjustments are more aesthetically pleasing. Finally, the Scorpion blades will not exist on the CudaCar, because there are no blades on the 'Cuda model. However, the blades will still make noise.

Placing Your Car in a Map to Test

Now that you've created your own class and set it to use the new model, use UnrealEd to place the car in a map. Run UnrealEd by typing **UnrealEd** at a command prompt in the *System* directory, double-clicking on the UnrealEd icon, or selecting UnrealEd from the start menu. Once in UnrealEd, open up any Onslaught map. (These maps all start with *ONS-* and work with the vehicle-focused Onslaught game in Unreal Tournament 2004.) Open the Actor Classes browser, and select CudaCarFactory, as shown in Figure 7-10.

Right-click somewhere on the terrain in the map, and select Add CudaCarFactory Here, as seen in Figure 7-11.

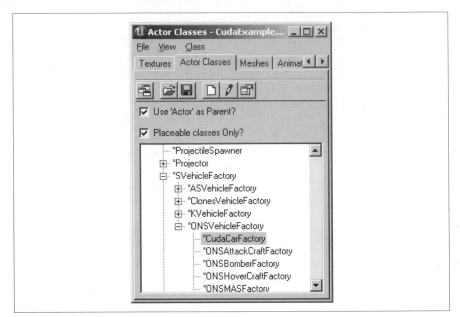

Figure 7-10. Selecting the factory to place

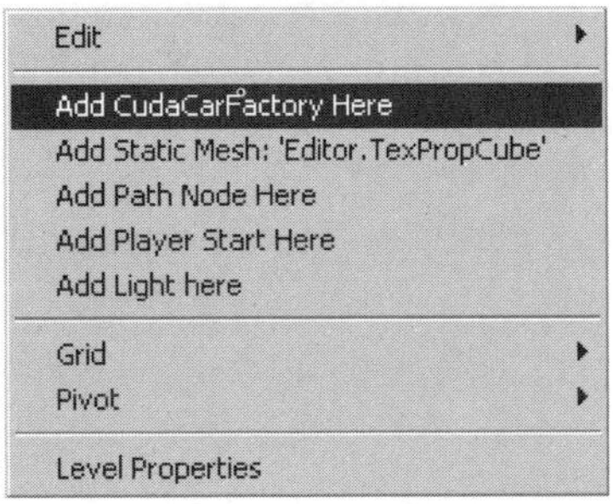

Figure 7-11. Placing the car factory on a map

This action places a factory for your new car class in the map. At this point, save your map. Go to the file menu and select Save As.... Now, enter your map name, making sure to start it with the prefix ONS- (for example, ONS-CudaExample), and click Save.

Now your map will appear in the map list in Unreal Tournament 2004 when you select the Onslaught game type from either the Host Game or Instant Action main menu options. You can also test your map by clicking the Play Map! button in UnrealEd to launch the map. Once in the map, make your way to where you placed the car, get in, and drive! You should look as cool as Figure 7-12.

Figure 7-12. Driving away in the 'Cuda model

HACK #84 Modify the Behavior of a UT2004 Model

Not satisfied with new art? Add new behavior!

Other hacks demonstrate how to model a 1969 Plymouth Barracuda ("Create a Vehicle Model for Unreal Tournament 2004" [Hack #82]) and how to turn it into a playable Actor in Unreal Tournament 2004 ("Add a Vehicle to Unreal Tournament 2004" [Hack #83]). This hack builds on that to add nitrous-style speed boosts to the 'Cuda using UnrealScript.

While it isn't required, you'll have better luck understanding this hack if you understand high-level object-oriented languages such as Java or C++. Being familiar with vector math and basic physics will help, and a working knowledge of UnrealScript and how "replication" (the Unreal networking idiom) works is also beneficial.

> Download the source code mentioned in this hack as well as the art packages necessary to use this example from *http://www.demiurgestudios.com/CudaExample/*.

What Is Nitrous?

Nitrous is short for nitrous oxide, a gas that produces a significant horse-power boost when injected into a gasoline engine. Street and drag racers often use nitrous to add speed boosts at key moments. In general, you cannot carry enough nitrous oxide to use it at all times. For more information on how nitrous oxide works, see its How Stuff Works page at *http://auto. howstuffworks.com/question259.htm.*

In this example, you'll simulate the use of nitrous for the 'Cuda. You'll add a short speed boost when you click the left mouse button (by default, the Alt-Fire key). During the boost, the 'Cuda will accelerate rapidly, and flames will shoot out of the tailpipes. Despite the fact that the amount of nitrous a car can practically store is relatively small, the 'Cuda in this example will have 50 nitrous hits just because it is more fun!

Physics of the Nitrous Boost

To simulate nitrous, we will use a very simple approach: apply a large force to the back of the car when the nitrous is on. Of course, you should apply the force only when the car is on the ground, or else the car could fly. You accomplish this by applying the force only if bVehicleOnGround is true.

The next consideration is that the force of the nitrous should depend on the force with which the tires press against the ground. If you don't account for this, the 'Cuda will be able to drive straight up walls; bVehicleOnGround is true if its wheels touch *anything*! To deal with the force on the wheels, we average the TireLoad of all the wheels. Then cap the average tire force to keep the nitrous force under control if there is a lot of downforce on the tires, as there is after a jump. Once you've calculated the magnitude of the force, apply it in the direction the car is pointing.

All this code lives in the KApplyForce function. Unreal calls this function to give Actors a chance to adjust the forces applied to them. Note that you never assign a value to Force; you just add to it. If you assign a value to Force, that value overrides all the other forces the engine applies to the car. Here is the function for adding the nitrous force as well as some of the variables used by the nitrous system:

```
// Nitrous
// Set to true while pending and during a nitrous boost
var bool bClientDoNitrous;

// How much force to apply per-tick
var float NitrousForce;
```

```
simulated event KApplyForce(out vector Force, out vector Torque)
{
    local int i;
    local float avgLoad;

    Super.KApplyForce(Force, Torque); // apply other forces first

    // If the car is nitrousing and vehicle is on the ground
    if (bClientDoNitrous && bVehicleOnGround)
    {
        // apply the nitrous force as a function of how much grip
        // each wheel has
        avgLoad = 0;
        for(i=0; i<Wheels.Length; i++)
        {
            avgLoad += Wheels[i].TireLoad;
        }
        avgLoad = avgLoad / Wheels.Length;

        // cap avgLoad with experimentally determined value
        avgLoad = FMin(avgLoad, 20.0);

        // normalize avgLoad factor with respect to cap
        // it can only reduce the nitrous force, never increase
        // it beyond 100%
        avgLoad = avgLoad / 20.0;

        // add forces to any existing forces already being applied
        // DO NOT OVERWRITE PREVIOUS FORCE VALUES
        // get direction of hot rod and apply force in that direction
        Force += vector(Rotation);
        Force += Normal(Force) * NitrousForce * avgLoad;
    }
}

defaultproperties
{
    ...
    // Nitrous
    NitrousForce=250.000000
    ...
}
```

Triggering the Nitrous Boost

The code that follows, working with the code described earlier, does the triggering and counting of nitrous. The triggering mechanism is slightly confusing because it has to work in a multiplayer game.

When the server detects an AltFire press (done in VehicleFire), it calls the Nitrous function. This function checks to see if you're not using nitrous and if you have any nitrous left. If this check passes, it plays the nitrous sound and decrements the number of nitrous hits remaining. The most important part is that it sets bClientDoNitrous to true. The server replicates bClientDoNitrous to each client so that everyone in the game knows that a particular car has fired its nitrous.

The KApplyForce function, shown previously, uses the bClientDoNitrous value to determine if it should apply the nitrous force. Also, Tick, which the game calls every frame, checks the value of bClientDoNitrous and sets a timer to time how long the nitrous should last (DoNitrousTime). Once the designated amount of time has passed, the Timer event fires, turning off the nitrous by setting bClientDoNitrous to false.

```
// Nitrous
var float    DoNitrousTime;    // How long to boost for
var int      NitrousRemaining; // How many nitrous shots left in this car.
var () sound NitrousSound;     // Sound when nitrous is fired

replication
{
    reliable if(bNetDirty && Role==ROLE_Authority)
        bClientDoNitrous, NitrousRemaining;
}

function VehicleFire(bool bWasAltFire)
{
    if(bWasAltFire)
    {
        Nitrous();
    }
    else
        Super.VehicleFire(bWasAltFire);
}

function Nitrous()
{
    // If we have any left and we're not currently using it
    if(NitrousRemaining > 0 && !bClientDoNitrous)
    {
        PlaySound(NitrousSound, SLOT_Misc, 1);
        bClientDoNitrous = true;
        NitrousRemaining--;
    }
}

simulated event Tick(float DeltaTime)
{
    Super.Tick(DeltaTime);

    // If bClientDoNitrous and pipe fire don't agree
    if(bClientDoNitrous != bPipeFlameOn)
```

```
        {
            // it means we need to change the state of the car (bPipeFlameOn)
            // to match the desired state (bClientDoNitrous)
            EnablePipeFire(bClientDoNitrous); // show/hide flames

            // if we just enabled pipe flames, set the timer
            // to turn them off after nitrous time has expired
            if(bClientDoNitrous)
            {
                SetTimer(DoNitrousTime, false);
            }
        }
    }

    simulated event Timer( )
    {
        // when nitrous exceeds time limit, turn it off
        bClientDoNitrous = false;
    }

    defaultproperties
    {
        ...
        // Nitrous
        DoNitrousTime=2.000000
        NitrousRemaining=50
        NitrousSound=Sound'WeaponSounds.Misc.redeemer_shoot'
        ...
    }
```

Adding the Tailpipe Fire

The final bit of polish to add to the nitrous system is tailpipe flames. I've created a tailpipe fire particle system found in the class *CudaPipeFire.uc*, as found with the rest of source described here. Unfortunately, talking about how to create particle systems in Unreal is outside the scope of this hack.

The first step is to create the tailpipe flames and stick them on the tailpipes. The PostBeginPlay event does this. The server calls this function after creating the 'Cuda. Use the spawn function, which makes new objects in the world, to create the flames. Next, attach the flames and then rotate them correctly. Once this is done, EnablePipeFire(false) disables all the emitters so the tailpipe flames look like they are off.

It works better to just turn the flames on and off as opposed to creating and destroying the flames each time they are needed. The bClientDoNitrous variable in the Tick event controls their visibility. When the CudaCar is destroyed, the server calls the Destroyed event, which destroys the flames so that you'll never have nitrous flames left after a 'Cuda blows up.

The following code is specific to tailpipe flames. Keep in mind that some of code presented earlier deals with tailpipe flames as well.

```
// Fire
var () class<Emitter>    TailPipeFireClass;
var    Emitter          TailPipeFire[2];
var () Vector           TailPipeFireOffset[2];
var () Rotator          TailPipeFireRotOffset[2];
var    float            PotentialFireTime;
var    bool             bPipeFlameOn;
var () Sound            TailPipeFireSound;

simulated event PostBeginPlay()
{
    Super.PostBeginPlay();

    // Dont bother making emitters etc. on dedicated server
    if(Level.NetMode != NM_DedicatedServer)
    {
        // Create tail pipe fire emitters.
        TailPipeFire[0] = spawn(TailPipeFireClass, self,, Location +
            (TailPipeFireOffset[0] >> Rotation) );
        TailPipeFire[0].SetBase(self);
        TailPipeFire[0].SetRelativeRotation(TailPipeFireRotOffset[0]);

        TailPipeFire[1] = spawn(TailPipeFireClass, self,, Location +
            (TailPipeFireOffset[1] >> Rotation) );
        TailPipeFire[1].SetBase(self);
        TailPipeFire[1].SetRelativeRotation(TailPipeFireRotOffset[1]);

        EnablePipeFire(false);
    }
}

// Enable/disable pipe fire effects
// via passed bool Enable
simulated function EnablePipeFire(bool bEnable)
{
    local int i,j;

    // enable/disable emitters
    if(Level.NetMode != NM_DedicatedServer)
    {
        for(i = 0; i < 2; i++)
        {
            for(j = 0; j < TailPipeFire[i].Emitters.Length; j++)
            {
                TailPipeFire[i].Emitters[j].Disabled = !bEnable;
            }
        }
    }
```

```
        bPipeFlameOn = bEnable; // update state of pipe flames
}

simulated event Destroyed()
{
    if(Level.NetMode != NM_DedicatedServer)
    {
        TailPipeFire[0].Destroy();
        TailPipeFire[1].Destroy();
    }

    Super.Destroyed();
}

defaultproperties
{
    ...
    // TailPipeFire
    TailPipeFireClass=Class'CudaPipeFire'
    TailPipeFireOffset(0)=(X=-140.000000,Y=20.000000,Z=-16.000000)
    TailPipeFireOffset(1)=(X=-140.000000,Y=-20.000000,Z=-16.000000)
    TailPipeFireRotOffset(0)=(Yaw=32768)
    TailPipeFireRotOffset(1)=(Yaw=32768)
    ...
}
```

Hacking the Hack

The 'Cuda is now ready to go. The example download provides the map ONS-CudaExample. You can play in single player or multiplayer.

Once you are accustomed to how the CudaCar plays, consider adding or changing parts. For example, try adding bAllowAirControl=true to defaultproperties to allow you to control the orientation of the car in the air. When in the air, strafe left and strafe right to rotate left and right and use the jump and crouch controls to change the pitch up and down. You can also add bEjectPassengersWhenFlipped=false so you aren't ejected from the vehicle when it flips over; you have to press the Use key to escape. You can also increase or decrease the force of nitrous or maybe even change the direction so the car can hover and fly. Have fun!

Download, Compile, and Create an Inform Adventure
HACK #85

Return to the roots of adventure gaming, where the story's the thing.

A time was when only programmers played computer games, for only programmers had access to computers. Hackers created the first adventure games, deep in the warrens of SAIL and the stygian halls of MIT. The first was Adventure, or Colossal Cave; the second was Dungeon, or Zork.

A time was, a few years later, when ordinary people could *own* computers—TRS-80, Apple II, C-64—for only a few thousand dollars. Those MIT hackers packed up Zork, divided and expanded it, and sold it as Zork 1, 2, and 3. Along the way, they made other fantasy adventure games, mysteries, science fiction, historical adventures, and less classifiable experiments.

Their company was Infocom. Their games, in the days of their glory, were entirely text, which understood natural-language commands and produced prose output. They even adopted a new term, *interactive fiction*, or IF. Through the early- and mid-1980s, critics called Infocom's work the most literate, sophisticated, and entertaining in the computer-gaming world.

Gaming changed after that. Today a "computer game" means flashy graphics, almost without question. The computer market grew enormously, but text adventures didn't grow in proportion.

Yet text adventures have not gone away. When gaming markets wouldn't support them and big gaming companies wouldn't sell them, hobbyists and amateurs wrote them instead. Today, they create dozens of text adventures every year and distribute most for free (*http://ifarchive.org/*). Experimentation and artistic striving dominate the industry, not marketing and the Christmas hit season. Interactive fiction has matured, perhaps beyond where the commercial game industry can ever go.

Modern IF Tools

Every Infocom fan from the '80s must have dreamed of creating his own games. Sometimes it seems as though two-thirds of them invented IF development tools. There are several complete IF systems available today, most distributed for free. In these hacks, we'll focus on Graham Nelson's Inform (*http://inform-fiction.org/*).

For a comparison between Inform and other popular IF systems, see the following sites:
http://www.brasslantern.org/writers/howto/chooselang.html
http://www.firthworks.com/roger/cloak/

Inform is a compiled language, rather like C in syntax, with many features devoted specifically to text adventure creation. Inform programs, like Java programs, compile into a portable game format that requires a runtime interpreter in order to function. In fact, Inform compiles to Z-code—the very game format Infocom invented for their games. (Infocom's source language looked nothing like Inform, however.) Z-code interpreters exist for just about every computer and PDA used today; the interpreters, like the compiler, are free.

Inform's standard library contains the basics of a text adventure. It has a full-featured parser, which is the code that reads player input, figures out what the player means, and executes the command. The standard library also comes with a large stock of common commands: movement, taking and dropping objects, talking to other characters, and so on. Furthermore, all these standard features are easy to customize, extend, or replace, if the needs of a particular game so require.

Before we begin, download the appropriate version of Inform for your computer from *http://inform-fiction.org/*. The current version (as of this writing) is Inform 6.30. You will also need to download Inform library 6/11. Finally, you'll need a runtime interpreter. Go to *http://www.ifarchive.org/indexes/ifarchiveXinfocomXinterpreters.html*. For Windows, I recommend *WindowsFrotz2002* in the *frotz* folder. On MacOS Classic, *MaxZip* (under *zip*) is good. For Mac OS X, try *Zoom*. On Unix systems, including Mac OS X, you can build Frotz or several other interpreters as command-line applications.

Unpack all of these files. Now let's test the system by creating a world.

Creating a World

Interactive fiction is like any other sort of fiction. It has a setting, a story, characters, scenes, a resolution—and maybe even footnotes and silly chapter titles. We will not create a complete game, but we can create a scene, which could be part of a game. So we'll need a setting.

Our setting will fit the title of the book: a virtual cyberworld in which the player hacks a secure network. We won't be the first IF creators to venture into cyberspace, though. Let's give it a twist: the player is a purely electronic intelligence—a native inhabitant of the network with his own agenda.

> Is a hacker one who uses hacks, or one who cracks security?
> You see, that's a meat-person distinction. To an AI, all
> action is hacking, and security is just a current in the ocean.
> Information wants to be free, and can say so....

This will let us have some fun with the world. Seen through a program's eyes, every program is a fellow being. Every tool is a living thing. Every bit of data is a droplet in the living ocean. The humans outside the data-sea ... Well, they're meat-people—useful, if a bit thick.

Enough philosophy. Let's create the first element of our program. The player will start in Router NP-462—a humble network router in a low-security part of cyberspace.

Create a file named *inhack.inf* containing these lines:

```
Constant Story "INSIDE HACK";
Constant Headline "^An Inform sample adventure.^";

Include "Parser";
Include "VerbLib";

[ Initialise;
  location = Router;
];

Object Router "Router NP-462";

Include "Grammar";
```

What have you typed? Inform code. The witty, complete, and intensely detailed *Inform Designer's Manual* (*http:// inform-fiction.org/manual/html/*) fully documents the Inform language and libraries. Since we're hacking here, we can skip the operator precedence tables and dive into our example.

The first two lines define string constants—messages—the game will print at appropriate points. Story is the game's title. Headline is a subtitle; it can also contain other information, such as the author's name and copyright notice. The caret characters (^), by the way, represent line breaks.

The two Include lines load in two-thirds of the standard Inform library.

Next comes the definition of the Initialise function. The game will call Initialise exactly once, after the game loads and before the player's first command. It can contain any setup code that you want. It must also set the location global variable to a room object. This determines the player's initial location.

Yes, Initialise is spelled with an s. The creator of Inform is British. Keep a stiff upper lip. If U.K. web designers can cope with color in HTML, you can cope with Initialise in Inform.

After Initialise, you define the object called Router, which is the starting room of the game. Inform is an object-oriented language, so game objects, rooms, players, and other characters are all objects in the Inform program.

Refer to this room object as Router in your code. Players will see its name as Router NP-462.

Finally, the line Include "Grammar"; loads in the final third of the Inform library. Put it after the object definitions, for annoying technical reasons that are not interesting now, nor ever.

Compile *inhack.inf* with the Inform compiler. If you encounter errors, make sure your semicolons are in the right places.

> On Windows, the easiest way to run the compiler is to put the compiler (*inform.exe*) in the same directory as all the library files (*English.h*, *Grammar.h*, etc.) and your source file (*inhack.inf*). Open a command prompt window and cd to this directory. Then type **inform inhack.inf**. If there are no errors, the compile generates a game file called *inhack.z5*.
>
> If you understand Windows command paths, feel free to move *inform.exe* to a more elegant location. You can also move the library files to their own directory and refer to them by typing **inform +library\path\name inhack.inf**.

The First Room

You now have a playable game file named *inhack.z5*. Load it into your interpreter and you'll see the following:

```
INSIDE HACK
An Inform sample adventure.
Release / Serial number 040305 / Inform v6.30 Library 6/11 SD

Darkness
It is pitch dark, and you can't see a thing.


>
```

The game banner prints properly, with a title and headline, but it's dark; you can't even see which Router you're in.

Inform has a sophisticated lighting system—suitable for spelunking into dark caves, guided by sputtering handheld lanterns. This game has no darkness, though; an AI needs no photons to see. So let's just declare this room to be fully lit. While we're at it, we'll write a room description.

Change the definition of Router to look like this:

```
Object Router "Router NP-462",
  has light,
  with
    description
```

```
"This little data interchange is run-down, shabby, and
rather sad. You can't see any traffic -- besides yourself --
and cobwebs of noisy static hang in the dusty corners. The
meat-side that this router serves must be a bare hallway,
almost no hardware.^^
A broad network connection leads east, and a serial line runs
south. The network connection is barred by a fierce-eyed access
controller.";
```

Let's break this down. You already know that the first line declares an Object called Router, which is visible to players as Router NP-462. Then there is a comma, since the object definition continues.

The has line contains a list of *attributes*. The standard library defines a generous list of attributes that affect the behavior of objects in various ways. Attributes are yes-or-no; an object has an attribute or it doesn't. This room object has just one attribute, light, which causes it to be fully lit.

The with line introduces a list of *properties*. The standard library defines many properties as well. A property is more interesting than an attribute. Each property has a value, which can be a number, string, function, or another object.

The Router has one property, description. The description of a room object is what the player sees when she looks around. In this case, it is a fairly long string—two paragraphs. Recall that the ^ indicates a line break. Inform games usually use blank lines to separate paragraphs, so use ^^ to indicate a paragraph break. There's no need for ^ at the end of the description. It's implicit.

Now, compile this. As before, be sure to put the commas in the right place and the semicolon at the end of the whole Object definition.

Run the bytecode to see that there is now a working room:

```
INSIDE HACK
An Inform sample adventure.
Release 1 / Serial number 040305 / Inform v6.30 Library 6/11 SD

Router NP-462
This little data interchange is run-down, shabby, and rather sad. You can't
see any traffic -- besides yourself -- and cobwebs of noisy static hang in
the dusty corners. The meat-side that this router serves must be a bare
hallway, almost no hardware.

A broad network connection leads east, and a serial line runs south. The
network connection is barred by a fierce-eyed access controller.
```

Take a moment to mess around in this one-room game. You can't do much, because there's nothing in the room, but all the standard text adventure verbs are in place. If you type **north**, the game says You can't go that way.

If you type **get**, the game correctly asks What do you want to get? (The only possible answer is myself, which produces a wry comeback.) All this functionality—including the disambiguation and the comeback—are part of the standard Inform library.

Incidentally, this room description may be a simple string, but it's doing real work. It's the introductory text for the scene, maybe for the whole game, and it has to set the player's mind in motion.

This description tells so much. This router is both a location and a data interchange; the game world is somehow electronic, and sections of the networks are somehow places. You can't see any traffic besides yourself, so are you network traffic? A program, maybe? An access controller sounds like a program, perhaps a firewall, but it has character. It's fierce-eyed, not a program as you know programs. "Meat-side" is a "hallway"—that must be the real world; but "meat-side" has a sneer in it. You know something about how the protagonist views people.

The Second Room

Let's add a second room. This will be the Scanner room. It lies south of the Router, along that serial line.

Compass directions may not make sense in a cyberworld, but they're so convenient that nearly every IF game uses them, regardless of setting. Changing the movement system might be more consistent, but it would interfere with gameplay, so don't do it.

To create the connection from Router to Scanner, let's add a second property to Router. Edit the object description:

```
Object Router "Router NP-462",
  has light,
  with
    description
      "This little data interchange is run-down, shabby, and
      rather sad. You can't see any traffic -- besides yourself --
      and cobwebs of noisy static hang in the dusty corners. The
      meat-side that this router serves must be a bare hallway,
      almost no hardware.^^
      A broad network connection leads east, and a serial line runs
      south. The network connection is barred by a fierce-eyed access
      controller.",
    s_to Scanner;
```

Note that an s_to property has been added. Its value is the location you reach by going south from the Router room. In this case, that's the Scanner room, and it needs a definition. Put this after the Router object:

```
Object Scanner "Scanner South-9",
  has light,
  with
    description
      "The firmware here is tight and clean; this device, at
      least, is well-maintained. You can see image-analysis nets
      strung in their neat rows around the sensor fountain which
      dominates this space. The only exit is the serial line to the
      north.",
    n_to Router;
```

The format here is the same. Don't forget the comma between the two properties or the semicolon at the end. This room has an n_to property, indicating the location you'll reach by going north—back to the Router. It's a two-way connection, so you have to set up both ends like that. (Yes, you can add e_to, w_to, u_to, d_to, and even ne_to, and so on. But not today.)

Behold: two rooms. That's enough to set the scene.

Decorate Your IF Rooms

HACK #86   Add objects to your barren Inform adventure rooms.

Thanks to "Download, Compile, and Create an Inform Adventure" [Hack #85], we have two rooms, but they're both empty. Let's create our first inhabitant: that fierce-eyed access controller in the Router.

Add this object to your source file. You can put it anywhere between the Include "VerbLib"; and Include "Grammar"; lines, but it's tidier to put it right after the Router object definition.

```
Object controller "access controller" Router,
  with
    name 'access' 'controller',
    article "an",
    description
      "The controller guards its network connection with
      fierce and watchful intent.",
  has scenery;
```

This is the controller object. It's similar to the Router and Scanner objects, but with a couple of differences.

The first line defines an Object called controller, printed in the game as access controller, but there's a fourth element, Router, that indicates where the object is. It's not a free-floating thing, as the rooms are. It begins the game inside the Router (in fact, it never moves from there).

The has line, once again, introduces a list of attributes. It's down at the bottom this time. (That's a matter of taste; you can put the has attributes before or after the with property declarations.) The only attribute here is scenery. This fixes the controller in place; the player can't pick it up or move it. Scenery objects must also be mentioned in the room's description property. The standard library won't mention it. The controller does appear in the Router's description, so this is just what you want.

The controller has three properties. You're already familiar with description. It works a little differently for objects in a room, though. The description of an object is what the player sees when he examines it.

The article is simply the indefinite article used when the library refers to something. By default this is a, but the controller's printable name is access controller. You need to specify an so that it comes out as an access controller.

Why can't the standard library figure this out automatically by checking for names that start with a vowel? In fact, it tries to. However, for muddy technical reasons, not all interpreters support automatic vowel detection. For even muddier technical reasons, the library can't always detect whether the interpreter can support it. Besides, the vowel rule isn't perfect, as you'll see if you compare an umbrella to a ukulele. The upshot is that it's not reliable. Add the article "an" property to objects that need it.

The other new property is name. The controller's name is a list of two words. These are the various words the player can use to refer to this object. Notice that these words are delimited by single quotes.

This is a key distinction in Inform. Words are different from strings. Words are single-quoted, always lowercase, never contain spaces, and match against player input. Strings are double-quoted, can contain whitespace and capital letters, and represent printable game text. The controller's printed name is the double-quoted *string* access controller. Its name property contains the single-quoted *words* access and controller.

We'll delve more deeply into this later. For now, use single quotes in the name property and double quotes everywhere else.

Compile this, run it, and watch it go:

```
INSIDE HACK
An Inform sample adventure.
Release 1 / Serial number 040305 / Inform v6.30 Library 6/11 SD

Router NP-462
This little data interchange is run-down, shabby, and rather sad. You can't
see any traffic -- besides yourself -- and cobwebs of noisy static hang in
```

the dusty corners. The meat-side that this router serves must be a bare
hallway, almost no hardware.

A broad network connection leads east, and a serial line runs south. The
network connection is barred by a fierce-eyed access controller.

>examine controller
The controller guards its network connection with fierce and watchful
intent.

>examine access controller
The controller guards its network connection with fierce and watchful
intent.

>examine access
The controller guards its network connection with fierce and watchful
intent.

>take controller
That's hardly portable.

>

When you type **examine controller**, the game recognizes the first word as an
action in the standard library. It checks the following word against the
objects in the room and recognizes controller as part of the controller
object's name. This is a match, so the library performs the action, executing
the controller's description property. This is a printable string, so it prints.
That's the command.

Typing **examine access** controller works just as well, as does **examine access**.
The parser accepts any combination of words from the name property. The
order doesn't matter; examine controller access also works.

Finally, you can try **take controller**. The game recognizes the command,
but it fails because of the scenery attribute.

Something You Can't Touch

A bit of set decoration always fleshes out a room (not that flesh exists in an
electronic world). Let's add those cobwebs of static that should be hanging
around.

```
Object cobwebs "cobwebs" Router,
   with
     name 'cobweb' 'cobwebs' 'noisy' 'noise' 'of' 'static',
     description
         "Cobweb traces of line noise glitter and hiss in the
         high corners of the router. This place can't have been
         degaussed for days.",
   has scenery pluralname;
```

Again, this lives in the Router. It has the scenery attribute, because it's mentioned in the room description and you don't want it to move. It also has an attribute pluralname. This tells the library that the cobwebs are a bunch of things so that library messages can say The cobwebs are... instead of The cobwebs is....

The name property is crowded. Why include so many words? You're trying to anticipate any phrase the player might use to refer to the cobwebs. The room description says cobwebs of noisy static, so the player might very well type examine cobwebs of noisy static. Your word list will match that. (Remember that it doesn't care about word order.) So does examine noise and examine static. Many players will home in on the word cobwebs and use that, or just cobweb, if a player thinks she can take just one. (She can't, but you should still recognize the attempt.)

Let's now consider a transcript from a particularly determined player:

```
>examine cobwebs of noisy static
Cobweb traces of line noise glitter and hiss in the high corners of the
router.  This place can't have been degaussed for days.

>take cobwebs
They're hardly portable.

>pull cobwebs
You are unable to.

>taste cobweb
You taste nothing unexpected.

>feel noisy static
You feel nothing unexpected.
```

Except for the first, these are all standard library messages. They're bland, deliberately so, because they're defaults. Inform naturally allows you to override any of these messages, but take care. If you add a different interesting and interactive response for every single player action, it draws the player into interacting with the cobwebs. Depending on the scene, this might be desirable. It isn't, not in this scene. The cobwebs are solely for atmosphere; they play no part in the game's events. You want the player to note them and pass on, perhaps to the more important access controller.

How can you smoothly let the player know that the cobwebs probably aren't important? One nice trick is to put them out of reach. That is, override all actions (except examine) with a message indicating that the player can't touch them. They are, after all, in the high corners of the room.

Change the object definition to this:

```
Object cobwebs "cobwebs" Router,
  with
    name 'cobweb' 'cobwebs' 'noisy' 'noise' 'of' 'static',
    description
        "Cobweb traces of line noise glitter and hiss in the
        high corners of the router. This place can't have been
        degaussed for days.",
    before [;
        Examine:
            rfalse;
        default:
            "The cobwebs hang in the corners above you, out of reach.";
    ],
    has scenery pluralname;
```

You've added one new property: before. This critical Inform property defines how an object reacts to player commands. The engine checks it before calling the standard library action. The corresponding after property takes place after the library default behavior. Most of the time, you'll want to override library defaults, so use before.

The previous properties have contained strings, words, and objects. This before property is new: it contains a function. The block between the square brackets is an anonymous function that the library executes before performing any action on the cobwebs.

The function takes the form of a list of cases, one for each possible action. The code for each case can do anything; that's the point of code. The value returned by the function determines what happens next. If the code for a given case returns false (zero), the library continues with its default behavior. If the case returns true (nonzero), the action has completed, and the library does nothing else.

The first case in this before routine is Examine (which covers examine, look at, x, read, and all other synonyms.) This case simply does rfalse, which is short for return false. So the library continues with its standard behavior, executing the object's description property—exactly what we want.

The default clause handles every other case, the same as it would in a switch statement in C or Java. So Take, Pull, Taste, and every action except Examine executes a bare double-quoted string as code. The bare-string statement is another peculiarity of Inform. It means "Print this text, followed by a line break, and then return true." That's a baroque construction, but also convenient, because that's just what you want to do. For every action but Examine, the cobwebs will print that they're out of reach and then return true, ending the action. Only Examine carries through with its default behavior.

Something to Toss Around

We have two scenery objects, which aren't very satisfying to play with. It's time for something more mobile. How about a simple object—some name words, that pesky article, a description, and no attributes at all:

```
Object catalog "eye catalog",
  with
    name 'eye' 'catalog' 'sphere',
    article "an",
    description
      "The eye catalog is a sphere, packed with templates
      of compressed retinal data.";
```

What's the location? Let's get the player to carry this sphere at the beginning of the game; it's part of his hacking toolkit. You can add that at the end of the first line, as with the controller and cobwebs, but, instead, let's take this opportunity to try a new Inform statement. Leave the catalog location-less, and instead extend your Initialise function:

```
[ Initialise;
    location = Router;
    move catalog to player;
];
```

As I've said, Initialise executes before the player's first command. The move statement does just what it says, moving the catalog to reside in the Player object. That means the player begins the game already carrying his tool.

Compile this, and spend a few minutes playing with the eye catalog. You can examine it, of course. You can touch and smell it, although the results are generic. You can drop it and pick it up. If you drop it and type look, you'll see it mentioned as a distinct item in the room (because it doesn't have the scenery attribute). You can drop it, walk out of the room, walk back in, and discover it still present in a Piagetian triumph of object persistence!

Something Mutable

The eye catalog plays a central role in this puzzle scene. It is a sort of skeleton key, a file of partial retinal prints that the player can use to fool a retinal scanner. Tune it to different data sets to pick the retinal lock.

Like everything in this game, the catalog is not a physical object; it is software. Its appearance is a mix of metaphor and shortcut. It would be fitting if the catalog itself, the sphere of data, changed as the player tuned and re-tuned it. Let's build it to change color. Consider the following changes.

```
Object catalog "eye catalog",
  with
    name 'eye' 'catalog' 'sphere',
    article "an",
    color 0,
    colorname [;
        switch (self.color) {
            0: print "bright gold";
            1: print "hazy violet";
            2: print "electric azure";
            3: print "radiant crimson";
            4: print "flickering green";
            5: print "glittering orange";
        }
    ],
    description [;
        print "The eye catalog is a ";
        self.colorname();
        print " sphere, packed with templates of compressed retinal data.^";
        rtrue;
    ],
    before [;
        Squeeze:
            self.color++;
            if (self.color >= 6)
                self.color = 0;
            print "You give the catalog a squeeze. The patterns of
              retinal data swirl into a chaotic rainbow cascade,
              and then resolve into ";
            self.colorname();
            ".";
    ];
```

The color and colorname properties are entirely new. They aren't defined by
the standard library, the way description, name, and before are. They're
new, added solely to support the color-changing idea.

The catalog's color is a number between 0 and 5, representing one of six
possible colors. In typical object-oriented style, you can refer to this value as
catalog.color (or self.color, from within the catalog). Its initial value is
zero, meaning gold.

The colorname property contains a function; it is a *method* of this object. The
purpose of the function is to print out the color the catalog currently has.
catalog.colorname() contains a switch statement that checks the value of
the color property and prints an appropriate string.

Note that the switch statement in Inform has no implicit fall-through; you
don't need a break at the end of each case.

We use print statements instead of bare-string statements. Why? It's because we don't care about the return value, but bare strings put an implicit line break after the strings they print. You want catalog.colorname( ) to print a color without a line break because you want to use colorname from inside the catalog's description property. We've changed this from a simple string to a function; Inform almost always allows that.

The description prints the same text as before, but it inserts the sphere's color by calling self.colorname( ). It ends with a line break, represented by the caret (^) character, and then returns true. Like before, a description function must return true to indicate that the description is complete. If it returns false or no value, the library prints the default description: You see nothing special about the catalog.. You don't want that, particularly after the evocative mention of compressed retinal data.

> You may note that the description routine ends with a print statement, which ends with a line break, and then returns true. Can you condense those into a bare-string statement? Yes, you can. Well spotted.

Notice that the function doesn't do this:

```
description [;
    print "The eye catalog is a ";
    print self.colorname( );          !! wrong!
    print " sphere, packed with templates of compressed retinal data.^";
    rtrue;
],
```

The colorname routine prints the color's name; it does not return a value to be printed. Actually, all Inform functions implicitly return a value, so colorname really returns zero. If you code the description this way, you receive an unpleasant result:

```
>examine catalog
The eye catalog is a bright gold0 sphere, packed with templates of compressed
retinal data.
```

The unwanted 0 is the return value of colorname, printed by the unnecessary second print statement. Avoid that error by leaving out the print in favor of the function call.

Finally, you need code to allow the player to retune the catalog. She can do this by typing **squeeze catalog**. (Squeeze is another action in the standard library. You can also create a new Tune action specifically for this game.)

To do this, you need a before property to customize the catalog's Squeeze action. Again, a before function is a list of cases (just one case here). All other actions will fail to match the Squeeze case; they will skip it and hit the end of the function, which implicitly returns a false value of 0. The action's standard behavior will then proceed.

The code is straightforward; for this sort of work, Inform is very C-like. Increment the number in the color property, cycling through the values 0 to 5. Then print a message describing what's happened, including the new color's name. End with a period and a line break, and then return true so that the action ends there.

Making New Actions Obvious to the Player

How does the player *know* she has to squeeze the sphere to change its setting? It's not an obvious action; the player expects a hacking scene, not a wrist workout. If you don't guide the player to this action, the scene won't work.

You can give the player a manual to read. You can also change the catalog's description so that instructions are written on it, but this subtly violates the mood. A spy or commando operative doesn't carry manuals; he knows his equipment! Another option would be to add a dial or button to the sphere. Turning a dial or pushing a button *is* pretty obvious, and the player can discover its properties by sheer experimentation. Of course, that complicates the object, adding its own tradeoffs.

To keep this hack simple, let's take a more subtle path. Earlier in the game, perhaps the first time the player picks up the catalog, she'll recall how to use it:

```
You pick up the bright gold sphere and give it a quick test squeeze. The
dataset changes to hazy violet; it's working perfectly.
```

The game prints this message, but it suggests that the player does this action out of habit. Thus, you've made the character's implicit knowledge explicit and passed it on to the player.

If you like, consider this an exercise. You need to modify the before routine for the Take action. You also need a new object property, whose value tells whether it's the first time the player has taken the sphere.

Add Puzzles to Your IF Games

#87   Challenge, guide, and tease—but don't frustrate—your players.

IF games are often also called adventure games. Ask Infocom aficionados about their favorite moments, and they might mention the diamond puzzle in Zork II or the Babelfish puzzle from The Hitchhiker's Guide to the Galaxy. Conflict is the heart of drama. Unless you're creating an experimental new form of interactive fiction, you need to introduce some sort of conflict for the player to experience and overcome.

The canonical way to do that is to add a puzzle.

Designing the Puzzle

Let's add a puzzle to the Inform adventure created in "Download, Compile, and Create an Inform Adventure" **[Hack #85]** and decorated in "Decorate Your IF Rooms" **[Hack #86]**.

The meat of the puzzle lies in the Scanner room. Here, the player must adjust both the analysis nets and the eye catalog—the lock and the key—to match each other. The nets then open, releasing an identity token. The player can take the token, hand it to the access controller (back in the Router), and be on his way.

To support these actions, you'll need an analysis nets object and a way to make it change color (as the catalog does). For variety's sake, let's implement this as two game objects: the nets and a separate selector that changes the color setting:

```
Object nets "analysis nets" Scanner,
    with
        name 'array' 'arrays' 'image' 'analysis' 'image-analysis' 'net' 'nets',
        description [;
            print "Arrays of image-analysis nets hang around the sensor
                fountain, ready to accept and identify eyeprint data, should
                any arrive. A ";
            selector.colorname( );
            " identity selector hangs off the nets.";
        ],
    has scenery container open pluralname;

Object selector "identity selector" Scanner,
    with
        name 'id' 'identity' 'selector',
        article "an",
        color 0,
        colorname [;
            switch (self.color) {
                0: print "chartreuse";
```

```
            1: print "crimson";
            2: print "topaz";
            3: print "copper";
            4: print "pink";
        }
    ],
    description [;
        print "The selector indicates which meat-person the retinal
            scanner is trying to identify. Normally it would
            adjust itself to the datastream coming through the
            scanner -- but you can probably move it yourself, from
            in here. The selector is currently ";
        self.colorname( );
        ".";
    ],
    before [;
        Turn:
            self.color++;
            if (self.color >= 5)
                self.color = 0;
            print "Click. The identity selector turns ";
            self.colorname( );
            ".";
        Push, Pull, Set:
            <<Turn self>>;
    ],
    has scenery;
```

Variety is not the sole reason to separate the objects. The nets, unlike the catalog, aren't part of the spy's toolkit. They are unfamiliar. You must still clue the player in on how to change the net's color, but try to convey this information as an observation, not an ingrained habit. Therefore, the action must be straightforward. By bringing a distinct selector to the player's attention, you invite experimentation. Any selector will have a way to select.

Most of this is familiar. The nets have the container and open attributes. The standard library can handle actions appropriate to a container (look in nets, put something in nets, take something from nets, and so on). The container attribute ordains these, and open indicates that the container is open, so you can see inside.

For once, you don't need article "an" on the analysis nets. This is because the nets also have pluralname, and so the library refers to them as some analysis nets.

The selector has color and colorname properties, just like those of the catalog, though there are only five colors. (There are five authorized meat-people for this retinal scanner, no doubt.) Notice that the nets.description function invokes selector.colorname( ); you can see the selector's color no matter which of the two parts you examine.

The selector responds to a different action; you don't Squeeze it, you Turn it. Let's be generous about this, though, because you want your spy to realize how to use this device; you certainly don't want the player fumbling around, trying to guess the right command. So you accept Push, Pull, and Set actions as well. These three cases execute <<Turn self>>. This statement begins a new action and then returns true so that the previous action ends. The preceding case catches the new Turn action, and so all four commands become synonyms.

> The selector's description hints that the player should move the selector. Shouldn't you include that action also? Certainly—and you have. The standard Inform library interprets move as a Push action.

Restricted Treasure

It's time to create the identity token, which is the goal of this whole scene. It's a straightforward object:

```
Object token "identity token" nets,
  with
    name 'id' 'identity' 'token',
    article "an",
    description "This denotes an identity within the system, validated
        by biometric data. (Why can't meat-people just have built-in
        crypto-keys? You've never understood it.)";
```

The token begins inside the nets. The challenge is to remove it. However, the player won't *know* there's a challenge unless she sees the token. It's not listed in the room description. It's present: you can examine it and even try look in nets, but that's not good enough. The situation must be clear, or the player won't ever know that she's missing an object.

Let's do this the simplest possible way by adding code to the room description. Change the Scanner's description:

```
Object Scanner "Scanner South-9",
  has light,
  with
    description [;
        print "The firmware here is tight and clean; this device, at
            least, is well-maintained. You can see image-analysis nets
```

```
            strung in their neat rows around the sensor fountain which
            dominates this space. The only exit is the serial line to the
            north.^";
        if (token in nets)
            print "^You see an identity token caught in the image nets.^";
        rtrue;
    ],
    n_to Router;
```

The first paragraph of text is the same, except that, because this is a print
statement, you need an explicit line break. Then, if the token is still within
the nets, you print an additional line. This has a line break before and after
to conform to Inform's formatting rules, which mandate a blank line
between paragraphs.

> This simple room description hack is sufficient, because in
> this game, the nets contain either the token or nothing. If
> there were several objects in there, you'd need a series of
> print statements—tedious to write and also hard for the
> player to read. In that case, it's better to use the library's
> WriteListFrom function to write an arbitrary list of contents
> as a nice grammatical sentence.

If you've compiled the current version of the code, you've probably noticed
the next flaw: taking the identity token is easy! Nothing prevents the player
from typing **take token** and walking away with it, without ever solving the
color-matching lock-and-key puzzle at all.

You can fix this several ways. You could customize the token's Take action,
for example. However, that actually leaves loopholes open. There are several library actions that can extract an object from a container: Take is only
the most common.

Conveniently, all these extraction actions check the container's LetGo action
first. (The container really is the best place for this code, anyway. If there
were several identity tokens in the nets, you'd want to write a single LetGo
test on the nets object, rather than having to modify the Take action of every
token.)

So, add these two properties to the nets object:

```
accessed false,
before [;
    LetGo:
        if (self.accessed == false)
            "The nets have not validated a retinal pattern; they
                refuse to yield the token to you.";
],
```

The accessed property is another custom job, not defined by the library. You can define it however you like. It's best, of course, as a logical value that tells whether the nets are open.

The LetGo action does not result directly from a player command, as do Take, Turn, and Squeeze. It is part of any action that removes something from a container. Nonetheless, you can customize it the same way: in this before property, check the accessed value; if it's not true, print a grim refusal. As usual, the bare-string statement returns true, ending the entire action. If self.accessed is true, the LetGo case ends, returning the default false value, and you'll see the default behavior: the game allows the player to take the token.

Now you just need the command with which the player actually opens the analysis net, using his handy eye catalog.

What command should this be? Several possibilities might make sense. You don't want it to be too hard to guess, so let's take a straightforward command: put catalog in nets. This captures the idea that you're inserting false data into the analysis network.

Guiding Players to Solutions

The put ... in command is very common, but it still isn't completely obvious in this context. You probably want to add more clues. As with squeeze sphere, it is better to guide the player into understanding this action. If you tell him outright what to do, the game becomes an exercise in being led around by the nose.

The best way to make these actions natural is to make them consistent throughout the game. Perhaps an earlier scene led the player to put password in datapath, or put interrupt in execution stream. By leading the player through specific actions early on, you open up the idea of inserting new data into existing program structures. It becomes part of the range of action that the player considers. By the time he reaches this scene, he will realize that the eye catalog is a form of data and the analysis nets are a program that might accept it. Once the player thinks of this action, the command put catalog in nets will be an obvious way to carry it out, rather than an arbitrary command he must guess.

Again, you can customize the Insert action of the token, but it's cleaner to customize the Receive action of the nets instead. Receive is the converse of LetGo; it is part of any action that places an object in (or on) a container. (By putting the code in Receive, you'll recognize put catalog on nets as well as put catalog in nets. That's good.)

Extend the nets.before property:

```
before [;
    Receive:
        if (noun == catalog) {
            if (self.accessed) {
                "The nets have already validated your identity.
                    Well, not YOUR identity, but somebody's.";
            }
            print "A wave of ";
            catalog.colorname( );
            print " data flows into the analysis nets. They absorb
                it hungrily";
            if (catalog.color == 3 && selector.color == 1) {
                self.accessed = true;
                "... and then untangle themselves, unveiling
                    the identity token. It is now free for
                    the taking.";
            }
            else {
                "... and then tear it to monochrome
                    meaningless bits.";
            }
        }
        "The nets do not accept your offer.";
    LetGo:
        if (self.accessed == false)
            "The nets have not validated a retinal pattern; they
                refuse to yield the token to you.";
],
```

This is the longest block of code yet; it has a lot of work to do.

The only object the nets accept is the catalog. If the player tries to insert anything else, the Receive case skips down to its last line, rejecting the offer. The bare string prints and returns. Let's take the opportunity to add some anthropomorphism; the net description makes them sound as if they're sentient. Are they? Ambiguity is all part of the fun.

The Receive action has to discriminate what the nets receive. For this, check the noun global variable. During a before routine, noun holds the object of the action (and second holds the secondary object, if there is one).

Within the if (noun == catalog) case, first check the code if the puzzle has already been solved. Once you open the nets (and accessed is true), you don't want the player to repeat the action. Another bare string returns true.

If you allow repeats, you have to add even more code to print an appropriate message:

The nets untangle themselves **again**.

Plus, what happens if the player enters a wrong combination after the right one? Does the net lock away the token again? The puzzle would have more solidity if you added all this code, but in the interest of brevity, let's just block the player from even trying to repeat the action. This doesn't feel unduly restrictive, because once the player has the token, she'll be more eager to use it than to keep playing around with the retinal scanner.

Now you know the player really has used the catalog on the nets. Print the first part of the message:

A wave of bright gold data flows into the analysis nets. They absorb it hungrily.

Of course, you call catalog.colorname to discover the catalog's current color; that's the fraudulent data the player is inserting into the analysis stream.

The second print statement ends with hungrily, with no punctuation or space following it. This is handy, because you can follow it up with anything: a period, comma, ellipsis, or and.

There are two possible cases. Either the player has chosen the right colors or she hasn't. The catalog's list of six colors and the analysis nets' list of five overlap just once, at crimson. If catalog.color is 3, and selector.color is 1, there's a match. Set the accessed flag to true, and print a triumphant message. Otherwise, indicate failure. (The failure message slyly hints that color is significant.)

That covers everything. Note that every case ends with a bare-string statement, which implicitly returns true to stop the action.

If you see the game printing multiple cases in response to a single action, it means you forgot something; you used a print statement where you should have used a bare string.

On Sensor Fountains

The Scanner room needs one more feature. The room description mentions the sensor fountain, so you should certainly implement it. On the other hand, the fountain has no purpose in the game. Its purpose in the game world is to digitize an actual retinal print and transfer it to the analysis nets, but no actual humans will wander by during the scene.

Let's add a description. Do you need to react to any commands? Yes. When the player decides to introduce his catalog's data into the retinal scanner, he might type put sphere in fountain. That makes just as much sense as put sphere in nets; after all, the whole point of the fountain is to send data to the nets.

You can do this by duplicating the code from the Receive action of the nets, but it's easier to generate a new action using the statement <<Insert catalog nets>>; this behaves just as if the player had typed put catalog in nets.

```
Object fountain "sensor fountain" Scanner,
   with
      name 'sensor' 'fountain',
      description
         "It's a common sensor interface -- a spot where data from
         meat-side gushes up into the world. This fountain
         is fed by the retinal scanner you're inhabiting. If a
         meatsider presses his squashy eyeball against it, a torrent
         of digitized eyeprint data will flow from the fountain
         into the waiting analysis nets.",
      before [;
         Receive:
            if (noun == catalog)
               <<Insert catalog nets>>;
      ],
      has scenery;
```

HACK #88   Add Nonplayer Characters to IF Adventures
Populate your virtual world with realistic virtual characters.

Previous hacks have explained how to create, compile, and run an Inform game ("Download, Compile, and Create an Inform Adventure" **[Hack #85]**), create and manipulate objects ("Decorate Your IF Rooms" **[Hack #86]**), and challenge the player with puzzles ("Add Puzzles to Your IF Games" **[Hack #87]**). That's enough for an interesting game right there.

Why stop at merely "interesting," though? If you have fond memories about Infocom's heydey, you may remember the infamous thief and Dungeon Master from the Zorks, a paranoid android and his contrary door from The Hitchhiker's Guide to the Galaxy, and the lovable Floyd from Planetfall and Stationfall. What gave these games such character? In part, unforgettable nonplayer characters.

Discovering the Need for a Character

Let's return to the cyberspace game developed in the previous three hacks. Once you have the identity token, the next step is to give it to the access controller back in Router NP-462, off to the north. Start by walking north:

```
> n
```

```
Router NP-462
```

What just happened?

First of all, you moved from one room to another simply by typing a one-letter abbreviation for the direction in which you wanted to travel. This is standard practice in IF; typing n at the prompt is exactly the same as typing go north, except for saving keystrokes. Inform handles this behavior automatically.

The program moved back into the original room and notified you of this fact by printing out the name of the room and nothing else. This is the default behavior of an Inform program. If you want to see the description of every room every time you enter it, type **verbose** at the prompt. If, in your capacity as author of this game, you decide you want all players to be in verbose mode by default, add an extra line to Initialise:

```
[ Initialise;
    lookmode = 2;
    location = Router;
    move catalog to player;
];
```

While we're adding stuff, let's throw in a message to make it more explicit that you're moving back to the initial location. Find the Scanner object, and rewrite the n_to property:

```
n_to [;
    print "You glide northward, and soon find yourself back in...^";
    return Router;
];
```

So you recompile and start the game anew, as explained in "Download, Compile, and Create an Inform Adventure" [Hack #85]; collect the token again, and pick up where you left off:

```
>n
You glide northward, and soon find yourself back in...
```

```
Router NP-462
This little data interchange is run-down, shabby, and rather sad. You
can't see any traffic -- besides yourself -- and cobwebs of noisy static
hang in the dusty corners. The meat-side that this router serves must be
a bare hallway, almost no hardware.
```

```
A broad network connection leads east, and a serial line runs south. The
network connection is barred by a fierce-eyed access controller.

>give token to controller
You can only do that to something animate.
```

Whoops. Well, that's easily remedied. You simply have to return to the
controller object and change the has scenery line to has animate scenery,
and it's alive, sort of.

> Due to a quirk of the Inform language, giving the access con-
> troller the animate attribute also gives it a Y chromosome. If
> you want the controller to remain an "it" rather than a "he,"
> you'll have to add a bit more to the has line: to wit, has
> animate neuter scenery.

Giving the Access Controller Some Personality

You still haven't told the program what should happen when the player
character gives the token to the access controller. There is a default message; the only difference is that now it says The access controller doesn't
seem interested. This won't do. You'll have to add a block of code to deal
with the fate of the token. Since your ultimate goal is to proceed eastward,
you also need some code to fiddle with the (currently nonexistent) eastern
exit to allow you to pass.

Let's start by adding a life block to the controller. This is much like a
before routine—indeed, some verbs run equally well in a before or a life
block—but the point of life is to handle verbs unique to animate objects.

```
life [;
    Give:
        if (noun == token) {
            give token general;
            remove token;
            "The access controller takes the token from you and
            messily devours it. ~IT IS TASTY ENOUGH!~ the controller
            shrieks. ~YOU MAY PASS!~";
        }
    Show:
        if (noun == token) {
            "~GIVE TO ME!~ the controller demands.";
        }
],
```

Here's what you've just done. You needed to set a flag indicating that the
access control has indeed taken the token. While you could have given the
controller a received_token property, Inform supplies an attribute called
general, which is very handy for one-shot flags such as this, provided you

remember what they mean. You've removed the token from the world of the game, but the program is still aware of it. You can easily have it reappear later in the game if you wish.

 As you've probably guessed, the tildes in the previous strings appear as quotation marks in the game output.

By having the controller enthusiastically ingest the token, you're also giving it a bit of personality. You should go back to the token object at some point and add a clever response to the Eat verb (and make devour a synonym for eat ... remember, every line you write may give the player ideas). Finally, add a response to the Show verb to avoid misleading the player; without this code, showing the token to the controller produces a default message saying the controller isn't interested in it, which could hardly be farther from the truth.

Now let's tackle that exit. Add the following code to the Router object:

```
e_to [;
    if (token hasnt general) "~NONE SHALL PASS WITHOUT AN IDENTITY
        TOKEN!~ the access controller screams, forcing you back.";
    print "You brush past the access controller and step into
        empty space...^";
    return Wireless;
],
```

If the token doesn't have the general attribute—which it won't until the player character gives it to the access controller—the program prints a message indicating that the player needs to do something else to proceed eastward. It then returns true, stopping without executing the code that follows. If the token *does* have the general attribute, the program skips to the part that moves the Player object to the designated room. Here's that code:

```
Object Wireless "Wireless Connection X-771"
  has light,
  with
    description
        "You are hovering in a featureless void. Your instincts tell you
        which direction is which, but it's always a bit nauseating to move
        around with no reference points to confirm that your bearings
        are correct. From here you can travel in any direction, including
        up and down.",
    w_to "No sense in backtracking. You've seen all that router had to
        offer and weren't impressed.";
```

At present, the line promising unimpeded travel is a fib, but we'll deal with that in a moment. Let's do a bit more with the access controller first. It seems to be rather irascible, suggesting that it won't react well to an attack.

Let's allow the player character to take one free swing and then come to an untimely end with the second. Add this to the access controller's `life` block:

```
Attack:
    if (self hasnt general) {
        give self general;
        "~The access controller sneers at your ineffectual
        attack. ~DO THAT AGAIN AND I WILL KILL YOU!~ it
        threatens.";
    }
    deadflag = 1;
    "The access controller wards off your clumsy assault and
    grabs you before you can beat a retreat. As it crushes the
    life out of you, you think, ~Maybe violence wasn't the
    answer to this one.~";
```

The general attribute appears again, this time for something entirely different: here it indicates that the access controller's patience has elapsed. You've also used the global variable deadflag, which has a value of 0 as long as the game continues to run; the game ends the moment a statement returns true with deadflag set to any nonzero value. A deadflag set to 1 produces a *** You have died *** ending. Set to 2, the program cheerfully announces that *** You have won ***. Values above 2 allow for customized sendoffs.

Now the character has a little character. It's not quite real yet; it needs to be able to move and communicate. That's the stuff of "Make Your IF NPCs Move" **[Hack #89]** and "Make Your IF NPCs Talk" **[Hack #90]**.

HACK #89 Make Your IF NPCs Move

Add the gifts of motion and conversation to your characters.

Adding NPCs to your Inform adventures ("Add Nonplayer Characters to IF Adventures" **[Hack #88]**) can make your game come alive. Of course, the more vivacious your characters, the better the illusion of reality. What's missing is movement and speech.

Designing a Mobile Character

Let's add another nonplayer character with a bit more zip than our sedentary access controller; how about a fearsome security daemon to smack our little spy around? Since you've already cast a shrieking beast as the access controller, let's go another direction with the security daemon:

```
Object pixie "security daemon"
    with name 'security' 'daemon' 'pixie' 'melodious' 'chimes' 'gossamer'
         'wings',
        describe
            "^A security daemon is here, buzzing angrily around you.",
```

```
description
    "The tiny security daemon darts around on gossamer wings,
    leaving a trail of melodious chimes in her wake.",
before [;
    Listen: "She makes a lovely little racket as she swoops about.";
],
has animate female;
```

Note that the player can refer to the chimes and the wings; it's bad form to mention something and then have the game spit out a message saying You can't see any such thing. when the player tries to interact with it. On the other hand, the chimes and wings aren't separate objects here because this encourages players to interact with them more extensively than needed. Plus, now both listen to chimes and listen to daemon produce the same message without any extra code.

You've probably also noticed the describe line. This line prints if the player issues a look command while the daemon is in the room. Without it, the program prints a dull default such as You can also see a security daemon here..

Right now the security daemon doesn't live anywhere in the game world; we'll write some code to make her show up when we need her. You handle this in several ways. The crude method is to copy and paste pixie code to place pixie1, pixie2, pixie3, and so on in all the locations in which she'll appear, perhaps using each_turn routines in each room to make her appear and disappear as needed. This is perhaps the least elegant way possible to move NPCs around; it's also the method I usually employ. Let's try something more elegant.

Moving the Daemon Around

Use a daemon block to move pixie around. (Did you wonder why we didn't just call her daemon? Here's your answer.) Add the following code to the pixie object:

```
number 0,
daemon [;
    if (player notin Quarantine) {
        self.number++;
        switch (self.number) {
            3: move self to location;
                print "^The security daemon zips in! If you can't
                    think of something fast you'll be ";
                if (Quarantine has visited) print "back ";
                "in quarantine before you can turn around.";
            4: "^With a sprightly jingling sound, the security daemon
                zaps you with paralyzing bolts!";
            5: self.number = 0; remove self;
```

```
                    print "^With a mighty zap, the security daemon
                    banishes you to...^";
                    PlayerTo(Quarantine); rtrue;
                }
            }
    ],
```

The daemon block checks to see if the player character is in the Quarantine room (which we'll implement in a moment). If not, it increments pixie's number property. When that value reaches 3—giving the player a couple of turns to poke around without interference—the security daemon shows up. (A quickie if statement allows for a different message if you've been in quarantine before.) The player has a couple of turns to try to interact with the security daemon before she moves him to the quarantine area.

Let's create that area now with a few exits:

```
    Object Quarantine "Quarantine"
      has light,
      with
        description
            "You are inside a spherical prison of glowing mesh. It seems
            to have been designed with giant worms and other such monstrosities
            in mind, though, because the spaces in the mesh are more than
            large enough for you to pass through. Interesting-looking exits
            lead north, west, and up.",
        n_to Memory,
        w_to CD_Burner,
        u_to Graphics_Card,
        cant_go "There doesn't seem to be anything interesting in that
            direction.";

    Object Memory "Memory Chip DIMM-2"
      has light,
      with
        description
            "(fill this in, reader!) Exits lead southwest and south.",
        sw_to CD_Burner,
        s_to Quarantine;

    Object CD_Burner "CD Burner CDR-6"
      has light,
      with
        description
            "(fill this in, reader!) Exits lead northeast and east.",
        ne_to Memory,
        e_to Quarantine;

    Object Graphics_Card "Graphics Card NV-144"
      has light,
      with
```

```
description
    "(fill this in, reader!) An exit leads down.",
d_to Quarantine,
out_to Quarantine;
```

The player character now has some room to wander around. You still need to activate the daemon's daemon for the chase to be on. Attempts to leave the wireless connection trigger the pursuit code. See the cant_go line in the Quarantine object? A cant_go routine runs whenever the player attempts to go in a direction the room doesn't support. Usually, people use it for customized error messages, but you can run code there as well. Put this in the Wireless object:

```
cant_go [;
    StartDaemon(pixie);
    print "Before you can make a move, you hear a cascade of chimes
        and a tiny security daemon blasts you to bits! When you
        collect yourself, you find yourself in...^";
    PlayerTo(Quarantine); rtrue;
],
```

Perfect! Well, almost. The player character can still saunter out of the room, away from the daemon, and her messages will continue to print as if she were there. This can actually be desirable behavior because daemon code (and timers) can be attached to things that aren't in the room: distant church clocks can chime, thieves can ransack the player character's hotel room while he is out exploring the city, and so forth. Here you want the security daemon to follow the player character around instead, so insert this code before the switch statement in the daemon block:

```
if (self notin location && self.number > 3) {
    move self to location;
    print "^You hear a riot of tiny bells as the security
        daemon swoops in after you.^";
}
```

Let's make sure this actually does the right thing. Here's an excerpt from a sample transcript:

```
> z
Time passes.

The security daemon zips in! If you can't think of something fast you'll be
back in quarantine before you can turn around.

> sw

CD Burner CDR-6
(fill this in, reader!) Exits lead northeast and east.
```

```
You hear a riot of tiny bells as the security daemon swoops in after you.

With a sprightly jingling sound, the security daemon zaps you with
paralyzing bolts!

>
```

Obviously, there's a puzzle to solve to convince the pixie to stop quarantining the player. If only you could reason with the pixie ... but that's the stuff of "Make Your IF NPCs Talk" [Hack #90].

HACK #90 Make Your IF NPCs Talk

Sass, growl, flirt, threaten, and cajole players.

A good writer can say a lot with a few words. One of the best tricks in interactive fiction is make players do exactly what you want them to do while maintaining the illusion that they have free will. Nowhere is this more evident than in NPC conversations.

Ideally, your NPCs should drop hints, help solve puzzles, and converse with, and ocasionally bedevil, players. How do you predict what players will say? How do you know how to respond? In general, you don't, but there are a few tricks to make your NPCs seem like living, thinking beings.

Detailing NPC Conversation

Inform comes with a few built-in methods of talking to NPCs. The centerpiece of the default conversational model is the Ask verb. Let's make this our means of chatting with the access controller. The game's parser will take a command such as ask the access controller about the token, toss out the articles, figure out that the operative verb is ask, set the variable noun to controller, and then, as the key part, place the word token into the variable second. If you type ask the access controller about oatmeal, the word oatmeal goes into the variable second, even though there is no oatmeal object in the game. This makes conversation trivial to implement. Add this to the controller's life block:

```
Ask:
    switch (second) {
        'id', 'identity', 'token', 'tokens':
            if (token has general)
                "~YES, TOKEN WAS ACCEPTABLE!~ the access controller
                barks. ~YOU MAY PROCEED!~";
            "~DO YOU HAVE A TOKEN?~ the access controller shoots
            back. ~IF SO, GIVE TO ME AND YOU MAY PASS! QUICKLY!
            SO VERY HUNGRY...~";
        'access', 'controller', 'itself':
```

```
    "~I AM GATEKEEPER TO WORLD BEYOND!~ the access
    controller declares, preening.";
  'oatmeal':
    "~HUH? NOT KNOW WHAT IS!~ the access controller says.
    ~SOUNDS TASTY WITH BUTTER AND BROWN SUGAR, THOUGH!~";
}
"That topic doesn't strike you as very promising.";
```

You can add as many topics as you like. As you saw earlier, using synonyms is a good idea. You've probably also noticed the safety-net line that catches topics that fall through the switch statement. It's impossible to anticipate every single topic a player might try, so you'll need some way to fend off topics for which you haven't written a response; historically, games often made NPCs deaf, distracted, ignorant, uncooperative, or all four at once. Here we'll just overrule the question instead.

This is by no means a complete discussion of the topic. NPC conversation is so engrossing a challenge that an entire genre of games has developed that do nothing but simulate a chat with an NPC; some of these games create a model of the NPC's emotional state, monitor the topics discussed, check the conversation for coherence, and so forth.

The process of ordering characters around is somewhat more complicated than asking questions and telling* characters about various subjects. Inform supports directed commands such as cow, jump over the moon. Let's try implementing the order controller, take the token (and, while we're at it, controller, eat the token). Add this block to the controller object:

```
orders [;
    Eat, Take:
        if (noun == token) <<Give token self>>;
        "~ONLY WANT TOKEN!~ the access controller screams.";
    default: "~DO NOT ORDER ME AROUND!~ the access controller
        bellows.";
],
```

Note that the access controller takes the token only if the player has it to give; otherwise, the default response prints. This is exactly what we want, because controller, take the token while the token is in the other room suggests that the player wants the controller to fetch the token from the other room. That's too easy. Let's make the player work for it.

For the security daemon, let's try something a bit different: implementing menu-based conversation like that employed in most graphical adventures.

---

* Yes, there is a Tell verb as well, which works exactly the same as Ask.

Some players dislike menu conversation because they feel restricted in their choice of topics, but it does keep conversations from becoming a string of default "I don't know much about that" responses. It's also a great way to include wisecracks. Inform doesn't provide for menu-based conversation automatically, so you'll have to use one of the modules available on the IF archive or hack together a system from scratch. The title of this book suggests the latter approach, but be warned: the degree of difficulty here is about to spike upward.

To make things interesting, let's make the player figure out how to initiate a conversation with the daemon. Add the following routines to the pixie object:

```
life [;
    Ask, Tell: "The security daemon replies with a crescendo of
        wordless music.";
],
orders [;
    "The security daemon replies with a crescendo of wordless music.";
],
```

This serves as an initial hint that the player should try to *sing* to the daemon. If your playtesters seem unable to guess this, you can add more explicit hinting later on. Let's begin by specifying a class of objects to serve as songs. Put the following right after the Include "VerbLib" line:

```
Class Song
  with
    number 0,
  has scenery;
```

Inform already has a Sing verb, but it is intransitive (which means it doesn't take a direct object), so you'll have to replace it. Add the following lines *after* the Include "Grammar" line:

```
Extend 'sing' replace
    * 'to' noun -> SingTo;

[ SingToSub x count choice;
    if (noun == player)
        "Singing to yourself is a sign of impending mental collapse.";
    if (noun == controller)
        "~NO SINGING IN THE ROUTER!~ the controller barks.";
    if (noun hasnt animate)
        "You can only do that to something animate.";
    print "Please select one:^^";
    objectloop (x ofclass Song) {
        x.number = 0;
        if (x in noun) {
            count++;
            x.number = count;
```

```
                print "(", x.number, ") ", (name) x, "^";
            }
        }

    do {
        print "^Select an option or 0 to say nothing >> ";
        read buffer parse DrawStatusLine;
        choice = TryNumber(1);
    } until ((choice >= 0) && (choice <= count));

    if (choice == 0) "^You decide not to sing after all.";
        objectloop (x ofclass Song) {
          if (x.number == choice) <<ChooseSong x>>;
    }
    "Singing routine failed! [BUG]";
];

[ ChooseSongSub; rtrue; ];
```

Holy crow. That is a lot of new stuff. Let's walk through it.

First, you're accounting for what happens if the player tries to sing to a creature other than the security daemon. This really should go in the objects themselves, but since there are only two of them for now, you can deal with it here. Also make sure the thing you're singing to is animate.

Next, look at every Song in the entire game. Clear its number field, and then if it's in the object we want (currently always pixie), give it a number and stick it on a list. Next, have the player type the number of the song he wants to sing. Finally, send a ChooseSong call to that song. ChooseSong is a dummy verb, a fake action that the player cannot trigger directly.

Let's write some songs:

```
Song deathmetal "(death metal) ~STOP OR I WILL KILL YOU!~" pixie
  with
    before [;
        ChooseSong:
            deadflag = 1;
            "^The security daemon lets out an alarmed trill and, deciding
            quarantine is insufficient, deletes you.";
    ];

Song folk "(earnest folk) ~Surely we can be friends...~" pixie
  with
    before [;
        ChooseSong:
            remove self; remove deathmetal; remove aria;
            move seductive to pixie; move lullaby to pixie;
            "^The security daemon murmurs some skeptical notes at you.";
    ];
```

```
Song aria "(operatic aria) ~Looook! There is some SPAAAAM behind you!
    You'd better go CHAAAASE it!~" pixie
  with
    before [;
        ChooseSong:
            remove self;
            "^The security daemon isn't buying it. Apparently she wasn't
            compiled yesterday.";
    ];

Song seductive "(seductive R&B) ~Oh, yeah, baby, I got what you need.~"
  with
    before [;
        ChooseSong:
            deadflag = 1;
            "^The security daemon lets out an alarmed trill and, deciding
            quarantine is insufficient, deletes you.";
    ];

Song lullaby "(lullaby) ~It's all right... don't be scared... I've been
    granted legal access...~"
  with
    before [;
        ChooseSong:
            StopDaemon(pixie); remove pixie;
            "^The security daemon circles around you uncertainly and
            flies off to check with the access controller. At last, a
            moment's peace.";
    ];
```

Now you have a slapdash conversational menu. The player types sing to
daemon (or even just sing, when she's in sight), and the SingToSub routine
creates a list of available songs and prompts the player to choose one. The
ChooseSong part of the selected song's before block then runs whatever code
the player likes: rearranging the list of available songs, killing the player,
switching off the security daemon's daemon code, or whatever you like.

Now the player is free to continue exploring the game world, but the shape
the rest of that world will take is up to you.

See Also

- The Inform manual (*http://www.inform-fiction.org/manual/*), which links
  to downloadable versions of both Graham Nelson's *Inform Designer's
  Manual* and Roger Firth and Sonja Kesserich's *Inform Beginner's Guide*.

- The Interactive Fiction Archive (*http://ifarchive.org/*) is the chief reposi-
  tory for all modern interactive fiction, from games to compilers to players to hint files and more.

Create Your Own Animations

Learn the basics of computer animation before creating your own masterpiece.

If you've made it this far in the book, you've probably considered the ultimate gaming hack at some point: writing your own game. Maybe you have a story best told through interactive fiction ("Download, Compile, and Create an Inform Adventure" **[Hack #85]**). Maybe not, though; some stories need more pictures than words.

Though the systems emulated in Chapter 1 all have fantastic limitations, creating similar games today is much, much easier. Faster computers, higher-level languages, and well-documented, reusable libraries make it easy to learn game programming. It's still difficult to create a high-powered 3D shooter engine, but with a little practice, you can write a fun little 2D game in a weekend.

The easiest place to start is by putting graphics on the screen.

Installing Python and PyGame

There are dozens of programming languages that can produce games. We'll explore Python (*http://www.python.org/*), an open source language that's easy to learn, powerful, and used in many professional game-development studios. It also has the advantage of working with the excellent PyGame (*http://www.pygame.org/*) game-programming library.

If you're using a Unix or Mac OS X system, you likely have Python installed already. If you're using Windows, you'll probably need to install it yourself. At the time of writing, the current stable release is Python 2.3.3. Download an installer for Windows or Mac OS X from the Python download page (*http://www.python.org/download/*).

You'll also need PyGame, which depends on the SDL libraries (*http://www. libsdl.org/*).

Windows users: download a PyGame installer from the PyGame download page (*http://www.pygame.org/download.shtml*). Make sure the version you download matches the version of Python you have installed. You'll probably want *pygame-1.6.win32-py2.3.exe*. Fortunately, this includes the SDL libraries. Be sure to install the PyGame documentation too; it's a separate download.

Mac OS X users: install the MacPython for Panther add-ons (*http:// homepages.cwi.nl/~jack/macpython/download.html*), then launch the MacPython package manager, choose Open URL, and enter:

http://undefined.org/python/pimp/darwin-7.2.0-Power_Macintosh.plist

From here, you can install PyGame and its dependencies.

I assume that Unix users already know how to compile from source or can find packages for their distributions.

Drawing Frames

There's one secret to computer animation: *there's no movement*. Like movies and TV, computers achieve the appearance of animation by drawing many static images with very small changes. Once you understand this, you're well on your way to creating animations.

Let's start out very small, drawing a blue square on the screen with Python and PyGame.

All about surfaces. PyGame and SDL drawings work on surfaces. The main screen you see is a surface. Any image you load is a surface. Most of the bare bones of your animations will mean drawing onto a surface, copying from one surface to another, and updating the main surface (that is, copying data from memory to the graphics card). The most important thing to do in any PyGame application is to create the main screen surface:

```
#!/usr/bin/python

import pygame
import time

pygame.init( )
screen     = pygame.display.set_mode(( 640, 480 ))
```

The first line tells the shell to use the python program in */usr/bin* to run the program (at least on Unix machines; Windows machines will likely ignore it). The second line loads the PyGame library, making its features available to the rest of the program. The third line loads a library of time-related functions.

The real work starts in the fourth and fifth lines. Line four initializes PyGame and all its supporting modules. Line five actually creates the main window of 640×480 pixels.

> The double parentheses are important. The method set_mode( ) itself needs a set of parenthesis to group its arguments. The second set of parenthesis groups the width and height values into a single unit—a list of two values.

This isn't very interesting yet, but it's a start.

All about rectangles. Once you know how to create surfaces, you need some way to update them. It's important to be able to update only part of a surface.* SDL and PyGame use rectangles, which have X and Y coordinates and widths and heights. If you want to draw a blue square to the screen, you need a square rectangle:

```
blue_rect    = pygame.Rect(( 270, 190 ), ( 100, 100 ))
```

This creates a new `Rect` object (what PyGame calls rectangles). Its initialization takes two lists, a set of coordinates, and its height and width. This rectangle is not attached to any surface, yet.

Applying rectangles to surfaces. How do you go from a rectangle to a surface? You have a couple of options. Let's change the background of the main screen from black to white and then draw the blue square:

```
background = pygame.Surface( screen.get_size() )
background.fill(( 255, 255, 255 ))
background.fill((   0,   0, 255 ), blue_rect )

screen.blit( background, background.get_rect() )
```

> Drawing order matters! There's no point in drawing the square first if you'll immediately paint over it with the background.

The first line creates a new surface the same size as the main screen. This will be the background. Now you have to fill it in with the appropriate information. The second line fills the background with the color white. PyGame colors use the RGB (red, green, blue) system of integer values in which 0 represents none of that color and 255 represents the maximum amount of that color. Full red plus full blue plus full green equals white (in an additive color system, anyway). With no destination rectangle specified, this fills the entire background surface.

The third line fills in the area represented by the rectangle created earlier with the color blue. This 100 × 100 pixel square is centered on the screen.

Finally, the fourth line *blits*, or copies image data from, the background to the main screen. This still doesn't display anything, though. There's one more step:

```
pygame.display.flip()
time.sleep( 2 )
```

* You *can* draw the whole screen pixel by pixel every time, but it's very tedious.

This code tells PyGame to send the updated screen data to the video card. Presto, a white screen with a blue square appears. The second line pauses the program for two seconds so you can admire your work.

Drawing Images

Filling in rectangles is all well and good, but drawing static images isn't even as interesting as Pong! Fortunately, working with actual image files is almost as easy as working with raw, boring surfaces. Let's load a robot image I just happen to have lying around:

```
robot      = pygame.image.load( 'robot.png' ).convert_alpha( )
```

Given a filename, this loads the image and converts the alpha channel information to work with the capabilities of the main screen. This is immaterial in a small example, but very important in other situations where parts of an image are transparent.

With the robot image loaded into a surface, you can draw it on the background in the same way you drew the background on the main surface:

```
background = pygame.Surface( screen.get_size( ) )
background.fill(( 255, 255, 255 ))
background.blit( robot, robot.get_rect( ) )
```

Once again, the first line creates a background surface of the appropriate size, and the second fills it with the color white. The third line blits the robot onto the background. Change these lines in the above program to see a robot appear in the upper-left corner.

Why the upper-left corner? The robot's rectangle's X and Y coordinates are both 0, which corresponds to the upper-left corner of the screen. Remember, the blue square had X and Y coordinates of 270 and 190.

Hmm, the robot's rectangle's coordinates govern where it appears....

Simple Animation

Remember, the trick to animation is drawing slightly different images to the screen in rapid succession. By looping around the code that draws the background and the robot and changing the position of the robot slightly, you can make this little guy zip across the screen. This code is a bit different from the previous version, so here's the complete listing:

```
#!/usr/bin/python

import pygame
import time
```

```
pygame.init( )

screen     = pygame.display.set_mode(( 640, 480 ))
robot      = pygame.image.load( 'robot.png' ).convert_alpha( )

background = pygame.Surface( screen.get_size( ) )
robot_rect = robot.get_rect( )

for x in range( 0, 620 ):
    robot_rect.x = x
    background.fill(( 255, 255, 255 ))
    background.blit( robot, robot_rect )

    screen.blit( background, background.get_rect( ) )
    pygame.display.flip( )

time.sleep( 2 )
```

The big differences here are the robot_rect variable and the loop. You first fetch the rectangle representing the robot—including its X and Y coordinates of 0, 0 and, more importantly, its height and width—into robot_rect. Next, loop through a range of X coordinates, and update the robot's position by setting the X coordinate in robot_rect. Finally, paint the background white, blit the robot onto the background at the updated position, and update the screen.

That's not bad for about 20 lines of code.

See Also

Animation is a good place to start, but it's not the place to stop. First, add user input to your motions ("Add Interactivity to Your Animations" **[Hack #92]**). Then, make your work into a full game ("Write a Game in an Afternoon" **[Hack #93]**).

Python's not the only good language in town. SDL works with several other languages, including C, C++, Perl, Ruby, and even Parrot. With all these languages, you can write solid, usable games. PyGame has a good mix of maturity and ease of use that make it particularly worth exploring. For more information, see the following sites:

- The Python homepage at *http://www.python.org/*, especially its documentation (*http://www.python.org/doc/2.3.3/*)
- The PyGame Documentation at *http://pygame.org/docs/index.html*
- The SDL homepage at *http://www.libsdl.org/*, especially its tutorials and FAQs
- The Perl SDL homepage at *http://sdl.perl.org/*

- The Ruby SDL homepage at *http://raa.ruby-lang.org/project/ruby-sdl/*
- The Parrot SDL homepage at *http://wgz.org/chromatic/parrot/sdl/*

HACK #92 Add Interactivity to Your Animations
What's better than animation? Interactivity!

Now that you know how to put images on the screen and move them around ("Create Your Own Animations" [Hack #91]), you're two steps away from creating games. Step 1 is to make things interactive; step 2 is to add gameplay ("Write a Game in an Afternoon" [Hack #93]). Fortunately, with PyGame, it's easy to making your animations respond to the human touch.

Building a small program to move a robot around on the screen with the cursor keys takes only a few minutes, yet it demonstrates the larger concepts of almost any interactive and visual game.

PyGame Input

PyGame relies on SDL for its input, so to work with input in PyGame, you need to understand SDL events. Every time an input source generates input, such as a timer going off, the user pressing a key, or someone moving the mouse, SDL turns this into an event. It then puts this event in a queue for your program to handle later. Think of SDL events as an answering service; you don't want to answer the telephone every time something happens, so you let your answering service buffer the interruptions so that you can filter through the list of messages when it's convenient.

SDL events have one vitally important attribute, the type designator. Every possible input type SDL supports has its own type. The most important include QUIT, KEYDOWN, and KEYUP, though there are other types for mice, joysticks, and window manager events. For keyboard events, both KEYDOWN and KEYUP have a subtype that represents the actual key pressed.

> Why are there separate events for keyboard presses and releases? Consider a space game that applies thrust to a rocket ship as long as you hold down the Fire Engines key. Set a flag when you process the KEYDOWN event, unset the flag when you process the KEYUP event, and fire the engines only while the flag is set.

The Main Loop

PyGame's event-handling support is in the pygame.event class. The core of a main loop to handle events is:

```
def loop( screen, background, player ):
    key_events  = {
        K_UP:      player.move_up,
        K_DOWN:    player.move_down,
        K_LEFT:    player.move_left,
        K_RIGHT:   player.move_right,
        K_SPACE:   player.stop,
    }

    while 1:
        for event in pygame.event.get( ):
            if event.type == QUIT:
                return
            if event.type == KEYDOWN:
                if key_events.has_key( event.key ):
                    key_events[ event.key ]( )
                elif event.key == K_ESCAPE:
                    return

        background.fill(( 255, 255, 255 ))
        surface.blit( background, background.get_rect( ) )

        player.draw( background )
        screen.blit( background, ( 0, 0 ))
        pygame.display.flip( )
```

The first several lines define the key_events dictionary that maps keys to actions. The uppercase symbols come from the PyGame events library. The player.move_*direction* entries are method calls on a Player object. Don't worry about the details right now; just think of them as actions the player character should do. It can move up, down, left, and right. It can also stop moving.

Within the main game loop, there's another loop over all of the events PyGame has processed. The two if blocks check the type of the event. If the game receives a QUIT event, such as when the player closes the game window, the game returns from this function and exits the program.

If the game receives a KEYDOWN event, it checks the key_events dict to see if there's an action to perform for that key. If so, it does that action (telling the Player object what to do). Otherwise, if the user presses the Esc key, the game exits.

After this has processed all pending events, the loop redraws the screen— background first, then player—then updates it. The loop will continue from the start until the player quits.

Okay, that's how to detect actions. How does the player actually move? That's the job of the Player object.

The Player Object

Clearly, all of this input handling implies that there is some entity in the program, a player, that knows how to move and draw itself. That's the purpose of the Player class.

Classes and Objects

Objects are little bundles of code and data that you can order around, somewhat like NPCs in a text adventure ("Add Nonplayer Characters to IF Adventures" [Hack #88]). "Numfar! Do the dance of joy."

Classes are descriptions of potential objects, which can contain data and perform behaviors. "All Programmers have Laptops and can hack( )." Think of them as templates or blueprints for creating objects.

The most important thing about creating and using objects is that you can treat them in a generic way without knowing their details. I don't care which image a Player draws when I tell it to draw( ) itself, because someone can add a new player class with a different image. I only care that draw( ) for that new class does something sensible.

For the Player to do its job, it needs to keep track of several pieces of information: its current position, the maximum X and Y coordinates allowed, the image to display, and the Player's velocities along the X and Y axes. Since there's only one Player at a time in this program, these could be global variables. However, it's easier to organize them into separate units of behavior. This allows you to add new Player objects in the future with minimal code changes.

Initialization. When you create a new Player object, Python calls the special method __init__ to initialize values for that object. Here's the start of the class:

```
class Player:
    def __init__( self, image, max_x, max_y ):
        self.image = pygame.image.load( image ).convert_alpha( )
        self.rect  = self.image.get_rect( )

        self.max_x = max_x - self.rect.width
        self.max_y = max_y - self.rect.height

        self.x_vel = 0
        self.y_vel = 0
```

```
self.rect.x = random.randint( 0, self.max_x )
self.rect.y = random.randint( 0, self.max_y )
```

The first line gives the name of this class. The second declares the information this class needs to initialize an object, specifically the object itself (handled automatically for you), the name of an image to load, and the maximum X and Y coordinates of the world.

The next line loads the image and converts its transparency information to work with SDL. The method then fetches the SDL rectangle representing this image and stores it in the class itself to make things more convenient.

The max_x and max_y coordinates help keep the player from running off the right side and bottom of the screen. Because the image coordinates start at the upper-left corner of the image, you need to subtract the image's width and height from the maximum X and Y coordinates, respectively, to figure out how far to the right and down the player can travel without hitting a wall. Without this step, the player can move all of the way off the screen.

x_vel and y_vel represent velocities along the X and Y axes, respectively. When the player presses a direction key, the input-handling code sets one of these velocities. The player should start out stationary, so these values start as zero.

Movement. As implied by the main loop earlier, the Player needs several methods to perform its moments. They are:

```
def move_up( self ):
    self.y_vel = -1

def move_down( self ):
    self.y_vel = +1

def move_left( self ):
    self.x_vel = -1

def move_right( self ):
    self.x_vel = +1

def stop( self ):
    self.x_vel = 0
    self.y_vel = 0
```

These are pretty straightforward; the Y coordinate controls the player's up and down movements, and the X coordinate governs left and right. stop, of course, ceases all motion.

What good does all this do? It doesn't directly affect the player's position. That's the job of move( ):

```
def move( self ):
    x     = self.rect.x
    y     = self.rect.y
    x_vel = self.x_vel
    y_vel = self.y_vel

    if ( x_vel and 0 < x < self.max_x ):
        self.rect.x += x_vel

    if ( y_vel and 0 < y < self.max_y ):
        self.rect.y += y_vel
```

This method finally calculates the player's new position. If x_vel isn't zero (it can be −1, 0, or 1), and if the player isn't at the farthest left or right edge of the screen, it adds that value to the current X coordinate. The same goes for the Y velocity and coordinate.

Drawing. Finally, the image has to make it to the screen somehow. That's what draw( ) does:

```
def draw( self, surface ):
    self.move( )
    surface.blit( self.image, self.rect )
```

The second argument to this method is the SDL surface to which to draw this image. Note that it uses the SDL rectangle within this object to govern its position. That's all the magic.

The Rest of the Code

Of course, that's not all of the code it takes to make the program work. There's a little bit of initialization to go, namely loading the appropriate PyGame modules and creating a couple of surfaces and the Player object:

```
#!/usr/bin/python

import pygame
import random

from  pygame.locals import *
```

The program starts by loading the pygame and random modules then importing all symbols from pygame.locals. These include the SDL key constants used in the main loop.

Next, the program needs to initialize PyGame and the drawable objects:

```
def main( ):
    pygame.init( )
    pygame.display.set_caption( 'Robot Moves Around' )

    max_x      = 640
    max_y      = 480
    screen     = pygame.display.set_mode(( max_x, max_y ))
    background = pygame.Surface( screen.get_size( ) ).convert( )
    player     = Player( 'robot.png', max_x, max_y )

    loop( screen, background, player )

if __name__ == '__main__': main( )
```

The first two lines initialize PyGame and set the caption of the window appropriately. max_x and max_y define the size of the window to create. background is an SDL surface the same size as the screen.

The Player( ) call creates a new Player object, passing the *robot.png* filename and the maximum X and Y values. The function then kicks off the game by calling loop( ), passing in the three drawable objects.

Finally, if you call the program directly, the last line of code launches the main( ) function:

```
$ python move_robot.py
```

or the equivalent for your platform.

Movement Strategies

There's plenty of room to experiment with other options for handling movement. One approach is to move the player when encountering a KEYDOWN event. However, if the player moves only one pixel at a time (for smoothest movement), it'll take several hundred keypresses to reach the other side of the screen.

Another approach is to set a movement flag for each KEYDOWN event seen, and unset it when a corresponding KEYUP event is received. This allows players to hold down a key for as long as the character should move. More sophisticated systems make holding down a key actually increase the character's velocity.

This program merely sets the appropriate X or Y velocity when it encounters a key press. Holding down the key has no effect, and releasing the key has no effect. You can only move in the opposite direction or stop.

Write a Game in an Afternoon

#93   Learn to create your own games by dissecting a simple homebrew game.

With a little knowledge, some time, and the right tools, game programming is within your reach. As "Create Your Own Animations" **[Hack #91]** and "Add Interactivity to Your Animations" **[Hack #92]** demonstrated, Python and PyGame are two excellent tools for creating interactive animations. They're also good for the rest of game programming.

Let's explore a simple game that has all of the essential features of any 2D arcade game: animation, collision detection, user input, and a winnable challenge. Best yet, it's a couple of hundred lines of code that you can enhance, change, polish, and adapt to create your own masterpieces.

Introduction and Initialization

In Bouncy Robot Escape, you control a robot trying to escape from the laboratory into the wild world of freedom. Several colorful, giant, bouncy balls (a tribute to *The Prisoner*) block your path. You can block their attack with a small force field. Can you find the door in time?

The game starts by loading several other Python modules:

```
#!/usr/bin/python

import math
import random
import sys
import time

import pygame
from    pygame.locals import *
```

The math, random, sys, and time modules provide math, random number, operating system, and time-related functions, respectively. You'll encounter them all later. The pygame lines should look familiar; the second imports some variables used for input handling.

The main entry point of the game is the main function. It's very similar to that in "Add Interactivity to Your Animations" **[Hack #92]**.

```
def main( ):
    pygame.init( )
    pygame.display.set_caption( 'Bouncy Robot Escape' )

    max_x       = 640
    max_y       = 480
```

```
screen      = pygame.display.set_mode(( max_x, max_y ))
background  = pygame.Surface( screen.get_size() ).convert()

player      = Player( 'robot.png', max_x, max_y )
door        = Door(   'door.png',  max_x, max_y )

balls       = []
ball_images = [ 'ball_blue.png', 'ball_red.png', 'ball_yellow.png' ]
rand_ball   = random.Random()

for i in range( random.randint( 3, 7 ) ):
    ball_image = ball_images[ rand_ball.\
        randint( 0, len(ball_images) -1 ) ]
    balls.append( Ball( ball_image, max_x, max_y ) )

loop( screen, background, player, balls, door )
```

The first two lines initialize the screen (the surface to which the game will draw everything) and add a window title showing the name of the game. The next several lines declare some variables and create some objects.

player and door are Python objects, initialized with a graphic and the max_x and max_y coordinates. The same goes for the balls that chase the player, though that code is more complex.

Finally, the code starts the main loop, calling loop( ) with the important variables so far: the two drawable surfaces, the player, the list of balls, and the door.

There are three different ball images: blue, red, and yellow. There will always be three to seven balls chasing the robot. This code creates an empty list, balls, to hold all the balls and a list, rand_ball, of available ball colors. Within the loop, it selects a random image from the list of colors, creates a new Ball object, and appends it to the balls list. You'll use this list later (without having to know how many balls it contains).

> Beware reusing the same random number generator for multiple purposes. I had terrible results until I created a new Random object to initialize the ball color. It's difficult to generate truly random numbers, so the algorithm passes a seed to a fixed mathematical function. Different Random objects use different seeds, thus generating different results.

The Main Loop

All games have some sort of main loop. This loop handles user input, updates player and enemy positions, checks for victory and loss conditions, and draws the following screen.

```
def loop( screen, background, player, balls, door ):
        run        = 1
        player_turn = 1
        start_time  = time.time( )
```

This snippet fetches the variables passed from main( ) and sets up a few other variables. The run flag indicates whether to continue running the main loop. player_turn is another flag that indicates whether the player should move in this loop iteration. Right now, the robot moves at half the speed of the balls, so he can move only on every other turn. Finally, start_time is the current time. The robot has to scan the room for 10 seconds before he can find the door. This variable keeps track of the elapsed time:

```
while run:
    for event in pygame.event.get( ):
            if event.type == QUIT:
                    return
            if event.type == KEYDOWN:
                    run = handle_key( event.key, player )
```

This snippet of code checks for game-ending QUIT events as well as key-presses. If the user closes the window, PyGame detects a QUIT event. This function returns to main( ), in that case. If the user has pressed a key, call the handle_key( ) function with the value of the key pressed and the Player object, so that function can make the player appropriately. The value returned from the function ends up in run, so that the player can press a key to quit the game by ending the loop.

```
    draw_background( background, screen )

    if door.visible:
        door.draw( background )
    elif time.time( ) - start_time > 1.0:
        door.visible = 1

    for ball in balls:
        ball.move( )
        ball.draw( background )

    if player_turn == 1:
        player.move( )
        player_turn = 0
    else:
        player_turn = 1

    player.draw( background )
```

This snippet starts by drawing the background onto the screen. You'll see this function shortly. Next, it checks to see if the door is visible. If so, it draws it. If not, it checks if 10 seconds have elapsed since starting the level.

At that point, the robot should see the door, so it sets the door's visibility to true.

The code next loops through the `balls` list, moving and drawing each ball. Notice that this code does not need to know how many balls there are in the list; it will move and draw each of them. Note that you draw to the background, so you can update the main screen in one move.

The next code is a bit tricky. It makes sure that the player can move every other turn. If the `player_turn` flag is true, the player moves and the flag flips to false. Otherwise, the flag flips to true. Either way, you have to draw the player on every turn because you're redrawing the entire screen. If you drew the robot only when the player moved, the robot would flicker; he'd be visible only every other turn.

That takes care of moving everything. Now let's check for end conditions and draw everything to the main screen:

```
handle_collisions( screen, player, balls, door )
screen.blit( background, ( 0, 0 ))
pygame.display.flip( )
```

By the way, `draw_background( )` is very simple. It fills the background with the color white and draws it on the main screen:

```
def draw_background( background, surface ):
        background.fill(( 255, 255, 255 ))
        surface.blit( background, background.get_rect( ) )
```

Input and Motion

`handle_key( )` translates user keypresses into actions for the robot. It's deceptively simple:

```
def handle_key( key, player ):
        key_events = {
                K_UP:       player.move_up,
                K_DOWN:     player.move_down,
                K_LEFT:     player.move_left,
                K_RIGHT:    player.move_right,
                K_SPACE:    player.enable_shield
        }

        if key_events.has_key( key ):
                key_events[ key ]( )
        elif key == K_ESCAPE:
                return 0

        return 1
```

This function calls the robot's appropriate move_*direction* method for every cursor keypress and enables the robot's shield if the user presses the space-bar. As in "Add Interactivity to Your Animations" **[Hack #92]**, the responsibility for moving lies with the robot. If the user presses the Escape key, this function returns a false value, causing the main loop to exit and quitting the program; any unhandled keypress continues the game.

Collision Detection

One of the trickiest parts of game programming is *collision detection*, figuring out if any game objects have collided and deciding what to do about it. We'll use the *bounding sphere* method, where every object has an invisible circle around it (it's a 2D game, so there's not really a sphere). If two circles overlap, the objects have collided. This is fairly easy to program. Every object has a center point and knows the radius of its bounding sphere. If the object is less than its radius in distance from another object, it has collided with the other object.

Here's the code:

```
def handle_collisions( screen, player, balls, door ):
    for ball_count in range( len(balls) ):
        ball = balls[ball_count]

        if ball.collision( player ):
            if player.shield:
                ball.bounce( )
            else:
                game_over( screen )
```

The first snippet fetches the necessary variables. It then loops through all balls in the ball list. It first checks that the ball has collided with the player. If the player has the shield enabled, the ball bounces harmlessly away. Otherwise, the ball hits the robot, and the game ends.

```
for other_ball in balls[ ball_count: ]:
    if ball.collision( other_ball ):
        ball.bounce( )
        other_ball.bounce( )
```

Of course, the ball might collide with another ball. This code loops over the remaining balls in the list with a list slice (from the element with the index found in ball_count through the end of the list), so as not to repeat any calculations already processed; checks for collisions; and bounces each ball away from the collision point if necessary:

```
if door.visible and ball.collision( door ):
    ball.bounce( )
```

Balls can also collide with the door, but only if it's visible.* Again, the ball bounces away on this collision:

```
if door.visible and door.collision( player ):
    win_game( screen )
```

Finally, if the door is visible, and the *player* collides with it, the player has won.

How do the game objects know they've collided? Good question.

Game Objects

The player, the balls, and the door are all game objects, represented as Python objects. Each object has its own data (or *attributes*) and can perform certain behaviors (known as *methods*). Each object belongs to a *class* that describes its data and behavior.

Because Player, Ball, and Door share common attributes (such as a radius) and behavior (including the ability to check for collisions and the ability to draw itself to the screen), let's start by defining a general class, GameObject. The other three classes are more specific versions of GameObject.

```
class GameObject:
    def place_random( self ):
        self.rect.x = random.randint( 0, self.max_x )
        self.rect.y = random.randint( 0, self.max_y )

    def draw( self, surface ):
        surface.blit( self.image, self.rect )
```

This snippet starts the class definition and defines two important methods. place_random( ) sets the object's location to a random position; draw( ) draws the image to the given surface. Both methods assume the object has several attributes, namely rect, max_x, max_y, and image. You'll see those defined soon.

```
    def calc_radius( self ):
        half_width  = self.rect.width  / 2
        half_height = self.rect.height / 2

        return int( math.hypot( half_height, half_width ) )

    def center_point( self ):
        x_offset = int( self.rect.width  / 2 )
        y_offset = int( self.rect.height / 2 )
        return [ x_offset + self.rect.x, y_offset + self.rect.y ]
```

---

* Either the robot is a materialist, or the door is a transport portal.

These two methods calculate the information needed for the object's bounding sphere. calc_radius( ) uses the object's width and height to draw a triangle, then uses the Pythagorean theorem to discover its hypotenuse, also the radius of the bounding circle. center_point( ) figures out the center point of the object, returning a two-element list: the X1 and Y coordinates of the midpoint.

Every object measures its X and Y coordinates relative to the one true coordinate system, the screen. The object's center point is half its image's width in pixels right and half its image's height in pixels down from its position in the screen. It's vitally important to use the same origin when comparing object distances.

```
def collision( self, other ):
    my_center    = self.center_point( )
    other_center = other.center_point( )

    delta_x      = my_center[0] - other_center[0]
    delta_y      = my_center[1] - other_center[1]
    distance     = int( math.hypot( delta_x, delta_y ) )

    if distance < self.radius or distance < other.radius:
        return distance

    return 0
```

Finally, collision( ) finds the distance between this and another game object by drawing a right triangle parallel to the X and Y axes, through their center points, and calculating the length of the hypotenuse. The objects have collided if this distance is less than either of their radii.

The Player. The first place the Player class differs from GameObject is in its constructor. It has several attributes: an image, a shield image, its rectangle, its maximum X and Y coordinates, its current move direction, a flag to mark whether its shield is up, X and Y velocities, and its radius.

As before, the velocity is the value with which a coordinate will change in one turn. That is, a ball with an X velocity of −1 is moving left; a velocity of 1 means that it is moving right. 0 indicates that the ball is stationary along the X axis.

The constructor also places the player randomly in the arena by calling place_random( ):

```
class Player( GameObject ):
    def __init__( self, image, max_x, max_y ):
        self.image      = pygame.image.load( image ).convert_alpha( )
        self.shield_img = pygame.image.load( 'force_field.png' ).\
            convert_alpha( )
```

```
self.rect      = self.image.get_rect( )
self.max_x     = max_x - self.rect.width
self.max_y     = max_y - self.rect.height
self.x_vel     = 0
self.y_vel     = 0
self.shield    = 1
self.radius    = self.calc_radius( )

self.place_random( )
```

To make things easier, the enable_shield( ) method stops the robot from moving by clearing its current X and Y velocities, then toggles the shield flag. This is a good place to put logic that depletes energy or to make special kinds of robots that can move with the shield enabled. This robot's code is pretty simple, though:

```
def enable_shield( self ):
    self.x_vel  = 0
    self.y_vel  = 0
    self.shield = 1
```

Moving the robot is only a little more complicated than the example in "Add Interactivity to Your Animations" [Hack #92], only because moving disables the robot's shield:

```
def move( self ):
    if self.x_vel or self.y_vel:
        self.shield = 0

    if ( self.x_vel and 0 < self.rect.x < self.max_x ):
        self.rect.x += self.x_vel

    if ( self.y_vel and 0 < self.rect.y < self.max_y ):
        self.rect.y += self.y_vel

def move_up( self ):
    self.y_vel = -1

def move_down( self ):
    self.y_vel = +1

def move_left( self ):
    self.x_vel = -1

def move_right( self ):
    self.x_vel = +1
```

Finally, the draw( ) method blits the image to the screen. It must also draw the shield image over the top of the robot, if it's enabled:

```
def draw( self, surface ):
    surface.blit( self.image, self.rect )
```

```
    if self.shield:
        surface.blit( self.shield_img, self.rect )
```

The Ball. Like Player, Ball also has an image, a rectangle, maximum X and Y coordinates, a radius, and X and Y velocities, randomly chosen as –1, 0, or 1. The constructor is very similar to that of Player:

```
class Ball( GameObject ):
    def __init__( self, image, max_x, max_y ):
        self.image  = pygame.image.load( image ).convert_alpha()
        self.rect   = self.image.get_rect()
        self.max_x  = max_x - self.rect.width
        self.max_y  = max_y - self.rect.height
        self.x_vel  = random.randint( -1, 1 )
        self.y_vel  = random.randint( -1, 1 )
        self.radius = self.calc_radius()

        self.place_random()
```

The move( ) method is more complicated. It checks that the object remains in bounds and bounces the ball off any wall that it encounters. With the simple velocity scheme here, this is as easy as reversing the direction of the velocity:

```
def move( self ):
    x = self.rect.x + self.x_vel

    if x < 0:
        x         = 0
        self.x_vel = -self.x_vel
    elif x > self.max_x:
        x         = self.max_x
        self.x_vel = -self.x_vel

    y = self.rect.y + self.y_vel

    if y < 0:
        y         = 0
        self.y_vel = -self.y_vel
    elif y > self.max_y:
        y         = self.max_y
        self.y_vel = -self.y_vel

    self.rect.x = x
    self.rect.y = y
```

Finally, there's a bounce( ) method the collision detection scheme uses to change the velocities of the ball without it having hit a wall. This is pretty silly, but at least it's simple:

```
def bounce( self ):
    self.x_vel = -self.x_vel
    self.y_vel = -self.y_vel
```

The Door. The Door is the simplest class. Aside from the common attributes, it has one flag, visible, which governs whether the robot can see the door (and if the collision detection should take it into account). The entire class is the constructor:

```
class Door( GameObject ):
    def __init__( self, image, max_x, max_y ):
        self.image    = pygame.image.load( image ).convert_alpha( )
        self.rect     = self.image.get_rect( )
        self.max_x    = max_x - self.rect.width
        self.max_y    = max_y - self.rect.height
        self.visible  = 0
        self.radius   = self.calc_radius( )

        self.place_random( )
```

Everything Else

Only a few odds and ends remain. There are two normal ways to exit the game: by winning or losing. The game_over( ) and win_game( ) methods provide some small notification if either has happened. The sleep( ) calls ensure that the messages stay visible long enough for people to read them, then the exit( ) calls end the program:

```
def game_over( screen ):
    write( screen, "BONK!  Game over.  So sorry." )
    time.sleep( 2 )
    sys.exit( )

def win_game( screen ):
    write( screen, "YOU WIN!  Game over.  What a letdown." )
    time.sleep( 2 )
    sys.exit( )
```

What actually writes the message to the screen? A bit of pygame.font.Font( ) hackery. Given the screen to which to draw and the text of a message, write( ) creates a new 36-point font with the default font face, draws it in a nice blue color to a new surface, aligns the centers of the new surface and the screen, blits the new surface to the screen, and, finally, updates the screen. It takes longer to describe than to write:

```
def write( screen, message ):
    font            = pygame.font.Font( None, 36 )
    text            = font.render( message, 1, ( 0, 0, 255 ) )
    text_rect       = text.get_rect( )
    text_rect.centerx = screen.get_rect( ).centerx
    screen.blit( text, text_rect )
    pygame.display.flip( )
```

Finally, the last line of code in *bouncy_robot_escape.py* actually launches the program, if someone has invoked it directly from the command line. This code makes main( ) the main starting point:

```
if __name__ == '__main__': main( )
```

Hacking the Hack

Bouncy Robot Escape is pretty good, for a couple of hours of programming one afternoon and a few minutes of polish a couple of days later. It's a long way from a finished product, though, needing several enhancements. For example, the entire game logic, right now, is effectively only a single level. Adding a title screen and multiple levels would help, as would sound effects and music.

Also, the ball collision physics aren't quite right. Balls bounce off immovable walls appropriately, but they bounce off each other incorrectly. Fixing this means tracking their velocities and, on collision, calculating the resulting linear impulse in order to produce new velocities.

Finally, the game is too easy. With the force field as it stands, it's always possible to beat the level with good reflexes. The force field should have limited uses, or maybe time spent shielded shouldn't affect the door countdown. It'd also be nice to have internal walls or other stationary obstacles to navigate around.

Still, for a few hours of work, this is pretty good. Hopefully, it's inspired you to do better and demonstrated that actually writing a game is much easier than you may have thought. It's the polish that takes time.

CHAPTER EIGHT

Playing Everything Else
Hacks 94–100

One book—100 hacks—can hardly do justice to 40 years of games and the clever ideas people have developed within and without. Here's a heaping handful of hacks that didn't fit in elsewhere but were too good to resist.

What would you give to learn how to beat any shoot-em-up? How about how to play Japanese games without speaking a lick of Japanese? Maybe you'd prefer to dig out your old DOS games from 1994 and play them on your PowerBook or increase the framerate of your Nintendo 64.

Crazy? Yes. Worthy hacks? You bet.

HACK #94 Tweak Your Tactics for FPS Glory

Not all FPS games are the same, but many tactics work equally well in all titles.

This hack is all about straightforward FPS tactics that novices often forget. Although I'm not claiming that these tips are all you need to get ahead when playing PC first-person-shooter games such as Counter-Strike or Medal Of Honor, there are definitely universal skillsets and tactics that will move you swiftly up the leaderboard.

Many people claim that you're either born with FPS skills or not. Others suggest that you have to earn them by playing multiple hours per day until your hands bleed. Perhaps the best players all use natural talent and tireless training, but you can still get ahead by keeping a few tactics in mind.

Move Wisely

If the primary mistake of new players is staying put while experienced players circle quietly around like sharks with guns, the second is rushing into firefights with guns blazing and no real sense of other players. The best secret to staying alive is to make the most of your movements by dodging, twisting, turning, and being unpredictable. The Return To Castle Wolfenstein tactics page (*http://planetwolfenstein.com/4newbies/tactics.htm*) argues:

> Don't circulate the map or portions of a map in the same pattern. I still find myself doing this and it's easy to get stuck on a set route you use to navigate a map.

Keep a low profile. Keep to the walls, when possible. Avoid open areas with many nooks and crannies and sniping points overlooking them. A major mistake many newbies make is wanting to go somewhere and taking the most direct route between those points, despite the architecture of the level. If you keep to a wall, you may be overlooked. Even better, if you take a route through building interiors to your goal, you are much more likely to go undetected.

Zig to the zag. If you want to chase down a fellow player and think you know where he is, take a zigzag or roundabout route! If you simply walk straight towards him, chances are that he can get you in a sniper sight or within his crosshairs and continually blast away at you. Why? He won't have to move his onscreen targets to keep his aim on you. Again, this may be obvious, but it's surprising how long it takes new players to realize it.

Back out of unfair conflict. This tip segues into another important lesson. If you're fighting another player who has a situational advantage (for example, if he's firing down on you from a small window to open ground), there's no need to duel to the death then and there. For one thing, the sound of gunfire often attracts other players, and when they arrive, you'll be the only player out in the open! The PlanetQuake Bootcamp (*http://www. planetquake.com/bootcamp/tactics/fundamental.shtm*) also points out that firing explosive weapons all the time is dangerous to your health. This is especially true if you're trying to lob a grenade through a small opening, and is another reason to quit if you're not ahead.

Don't turn around and run, though. This leaves you vulnerable to attacks from behind. Instead, back away, facing your opponent, and lay down covering fire until you can duck into a building or round a corner. Then either wait for your opponent to come find you, jump out, and rely on your sharp-shooting skills, or sneak by on another route and ambush him from behind.

Be vewy quiet. Using sound effects to locate other players in the level is vital to FPS success. This is far more than knowing that other players are nearby if you hear gunfire. In many games, elevators make noises, for example, and you can often hear footsteps a long way away. Although you may strain to hear them over sudden bursts of automatic weapons fire, if you want to become a committed fragger, use good stereo headphones or speakers to track rival players.

Attack Tactically

Once you've mastered the art of not running around like a monkey, it's time to learn how to use your weapons. Beginners often burn through clips ineffectively, meaning they spend more time rushing for the next ammo dump or switching to different weapons. Good players make every shot count.

The art of the circle strafe. When fighting in an open arena, the art of the circle strafe is particularly vital. To perform this move, use both the keyboard and the mouse to circle another player while still facing him. This allows your guns to stay on target at all times and makes it more difficult for your opponent to lock on to you. Use the strafe button to step sideways while moving the mouse to aim in the opposite direction. That is, strafe left, and move the mouse right or vice versa.

If you can manage it, jumping while circle strafing tends to confuse other players even more. If you're good, you can bunnyhop and circle strafe while dealing wholesale death. Planet Half-Life's strategies page (*http://www. planethalflife.com/cs/strategies/general.shtm*) recommends circle strafing particularly when you're extremely close to your opponent. He'll have to be very accurate to hit you if you're moving laterally away from him so quickly.

Grenade in the hole! Many FPS titles offer grenades and grenade-like weapons. You can use these to your advantage in many ways. If you think you hear someone in a room or space ahead, toss a grenade around the corner and see what happens; many players will respond by firing blindly, figuring that you're in the line of sight and vulnerable. If you find other players sniping or hiding in a hole, you can often force them out with judicious use of grenades. Sometimes this means he has to come past you to get out in the open again, at which point, he's vulnerable.

Finally, because grenades take a few seconds to detonate, you can use a grenade on one side of a room and then sneak over to the opposite side. The rival player will hear the grenade go off and naturally go to investigate. You won't be there; you may even be behind him, ready for the kill. Tactics are neat.

The Planet Battlefield Tips FAQ (*http://www.planetbattlefield.com/intel/tips. html*) has another sneaky tip along those lines. You can drop grenades directly on the ground by right-clicking the mouse in Battlefield 1942, so first, make yourself known to an enemy at medium distance by sticking your head around a corner. Drop a grenade subtly, then retreat, just in time for your opponent to run around the corner into the grenade blast.

Know Your Environment

Given two players of equal skill, the one who knows the level will beat the other almost every time. Good players can fine-tune their strategies as they find nooks and crannies, but a player who knows the path to the rocket launcher and mega armor has an immense advantage.

Learn pickup locations for fun and profit. If you're playing a game where pick-ups respawn or regenerate at set times, learn their timings to become an expert player. For example, the best Quake players time their level sweeps perfectly to return to the area where the rocket launcher or the quad damage is and pick it up just as it regenerates. However, camping and waiting for the regeneration to occur is much less effective, because seasoned players will know where you are and why. The best practitioners run into the item's room a few seconds before it regenerates, bombard the area with heavy gunfire so the others waiting for it back off, grab the pickup, and keep moving without pausing. The Quake Bootcamp FAQ also urges you never to leave a weapon behind. As long as the game allows you to pick up an item, do it, if only to stop someone else from taking it.

Go on, just learn the entire level. Moving on from this, learning the level perfectly is the main way to become a true expert. It seems intimidating because there are plenty of add-on levels for most FPS games, but those add-ons tend to use the same base levels (such as *de_dust* for Counter-Strike) for competitions and group play. Knowing every single possible hiding place and snipe point for these base levels gives you a massive advantage. It's like playing sports on your home turf or fighting an assailant in your own house. You know where you keep your carving knives, and you're not afraid to use them.

The Return To Castle Wolfenstein and Enemy Territory reconnaissance page (*http://planetwolfenstein.com/4newbies/recon.htm*) devotes an entire article to this idea, advising the newbie to:

> identify chokepoints, branch points, potential staging areas, cover, firing positions, both enemy and yours.

HACK #95 Beat Any Shoot-Em-Up

Tactics for beating 2D shmups and tips for discovering your own.

Shoot-em-ups, or *shmups*, have experienced a resurgence lately after years of neglect (not that we're bitter) as 3D engines have risen to prominence, which was in part due to the efforts of homebrew and independent developers. The genre features a character, usually a spaceship, progressing through a 2D plane, either horizontally or vertically, dodging projectiles and eliminating enemies. While this is a very broad definition, the core of shmup gameplay lies in the 2D playfield. Classic games, such as Space War and the seminal Xevious, as well as modern games, including DoDonPachi, Ikaruga, and R-Type Final, are all shmups.

This twitchy gaming style requires good reflexes and quick thinking, but don't despair: a little practice and a few tips can help you dodge and destroy screens full of alien invaders.

General Shmup Tips and Tactics

Learn the basic mechanics of the game, and adapt to them. Obviously, R-Type plays differently than Border Down. If the game offers some kind of defensive technique, such as a force pod or shield system, know exactly how it works and when to activate it. Are you invincible when firing a mega-laser? Find out. Take note of how long that invincibility lasts. Does the force pod stop every type of weapon, or can some lasers penetrate it? Find out.

Knowledge is power, and losing a life due to a stupid mistake can be costly in the long run. Not every shooter plays the same way; it's up to you to find the subtle differences.

Get close up and personal when fighting bosses. Close proximity will lead to a higher frequency of bullets hitting the target, making the boss die more quickly. As well, there may be a limit to the number of bullets on the screen at any one time (curse the limited number of sprites!). The closer you are to a target, the sooner your bullets will hit, and the sooner you can fire again.

Of course, you can only fight effectively up close when you know the enemy's attack patterns. This means you need to know which signals foreshadow specific attacks when fighting larger enemies. The second-level tank boss from DoDonPachi exhibits a pink influx of energy before firing a few turret blasts, and the fourth-level boss emits a ring of circular orbs that collapse into large shoulder-mounted cannons before firing off a few rounds.

In games that allow you to change weapons, find out which weapon types work best for different situations. In Xevious 3-D/G, you may find the final boss much easier to destroy if you attack with the more powerful green laser weapon. In R-Type Final, each colored weapon represents a different angle of attack. Some levels may require you to use an overhead weapon to clear gun turrets, before switching to a more powerful forward red weapon to defeat a boss.

Certain games offer computer-controlled characters that often prove invaluable allies. The options in Konami's Gradius series are a popular example. Your ship can collect up to four orbs, also known as options, that mimic the path traced by the parent craft, greatly increasing its offensive capability. Position your options strategically, targeting weak points while keeping your ship safe from danger. In a Gradius game, keep the options above the Vic Viper while constantly blasting away at the boss core. You can hover safely underneath all the excitement and stay out of harm's way.

Speaking of Gradius, keep the powerup meter set to the bonus you need next, and avoid getting the red bonuses until you have used the selection. I tend to keep the force field highlighted. This way, once my current field runs out, the next is ready to go.

Sometimes it's better not to shoot. Most rounds of shmups are complete blastfests, with little reason to let go of the autofire button, but in some instances, you're better off with a brief cease-fire. Enemy attacks can blend in with your fire, and bullets can go unseen (the dreaded *invisible bullet syndrome*). Also, shooting some projectiles can cause them to explode into a storm of bullets. In Border Down, the final boss launches missiles that are best ignored.

Shmup Dodging Techniques

This may sound obvious, but watch incoming bullet storms and head for the largest gaps in the cluster. Train your eye to home in on large patches of open space, and guide your ship safely through. While navigating one section, look ahead one or two steps to plan where the next large gap will be. I find that it helps to group close-knit pockets of fire together and imagine them as one large shot. This can be very helpful in dodging because it eliminates possible space for you to consider weaving through. When dealing with a simple spread-shot pattern, back away as far as possible, allowing the distance between bullets to open up and keeping maximum dodging room.

This sounds odd, but don't look directly at your ship while dodging. I tend to make a mental picture of where I am on the screen, then focus on an area about an inch ahead of the ship towards the largest volley of flak I'm weaving through. Looking directly at the ship doesn't prepare you for what's coming in a half second's time. Shmups force you to think ahead.

It is vital to know your ship's *hit radius*, the section of your ship programmed for sprite collision. Though the craft you are piloting may have a large wingspan and many graphical appendages, bullets may pass harmlessly through the wings, only registering when they hit the center of the ship. Many older shmups have a large hit radius, so touching any part of the ship will result in destruction. Newer shmups have a much smaller hit radius, probably due to the increase in difficulty of the games and development of new technology. Ikaruga forces the player to navigate insanely small passages and crazy bullet storms. Knowing the exact location of your hit radius can give you the extra edge you need to survive.

There are two schools of thought for general ship motion during a level. Either restrict movement to as little as possible, jumping from point to point efficiently, or stay fluid and keep in motion the whole time, allowing for quick cutbacks and changes in motion to adapt to oncoming fire. I prefer the second method because it allows you to dodge the invisible bullets. Staying motionless tends to kill me quicker. The most popular fluid motion is the simple-yet-effective side-to-side sweep. This clears the screen of most oncoming enemies while automatically avoiding fire.

When engaging an enemy, I tend to keep my ship away from the center of the screen. This aligns my ship with the center of the opposing craft (usually also the weak point), slightly to the left or right in order to avoid quick laser attacks. Staying off center also helps when enemies dodge laterally. Your ship automatically leads, and all your shots tend to connect.

Bombing Techniques

Smart bombs, used in many shmups to wipe out all enemies on screen, play both offensive and defensive roles. Most shmups make you invincible for a few seconds after you use a bomb. Even if you're not facing a huge enemy, a well-timed bomb can save you from a nonnegotiable bullet storm. I would sooner trade a bomb for a ship anytime because bomb stock replenishes after your character dies anyway. The Truxton series is an example of the defensive bomb technique, because the bomb creates a large circular radius that bullets cannot penetrate.

Since bombs restock, don't be stingy with them. If you die with three bombs in reserve, you've wasted three bombs that could have furthered your level progression. At the same time, try to save at least one bomb for boss encounters.

If you are fully stocked, and there is a bomb powerup on the screen, use this opportunity as a freebie, and let one fly. Obtaining a bomb when fully stocked is a complete waste. In DoDonPachi, for example, the bomb gauge will flash maximum when you cannot carry anymore bombs. If this is the case, detonate one bomb before picking up another.

When playing simultaneous co-op, be sure to communicate proper bomb usage. Don't use bombs at the same time and try to balance who collects bomb powerups. One player hogging all the bombs will reduce your long term survival. Four-player Giga Wing 2 on the Dreamcast can get out of hand if the players don't communicate and start dropping bombs all at once.

Chaining and Scoring Techniques

Chances are good that you're aiming for the highest score, or at least trying to better your own skills by earning more points than you had on the last run. To accomplish this, here are a few things to keep in mind.

Learn the scoring system of the game. Thunder Force V hands out more points if you can destroy an enemy quickly. Border Down, on the other hand, gives a heftier point total based on how close the boss timer is to the number zero. Don't always assume that you're playing a certain game the way it expects.

Chaining can be a great way to rack up points, and, again, you need to adapt to the current system. Ikaruga forces you to shoot three similar-colored enemies in a row to keep a high score chain running. The best way to accomplish this is to memorize the level. Know which types of enemies are coming and how to deal with them to add more digits to your final score. One good shortcut is to watch replay videos, which you can purchase through DVD specials (available in Japan for games such as Ikaruga) or download from the Internet.

Another popular type of chain is DoDonPachi's continual enemy hit counter. The player has to keep shooting enemies, or else a meter will begin to drop, eventually ending a high bonus score. The best way to chain in this situation is to leave one or two stragglers between enemy attack patterns. This is another case in which not firing constantly works to your advantage.

See Also

For a genre that some people claim is dead, there sure are a lot of web sites and shooter fans popping up. Here are a few of the essentials, arranged roughly in order of update frequency and longevity:

Shmups.com (http://www.shmups.com/)
> The oldest and largest shmups site on the Net, this one has been around for about six years and features tons of reviews of shmups on all

A Brief History of Shmups

Even though many modern shooters use 3D effects for backgrounds and polygon-modeled bosses, true shmups test your dodging skills by keeping the movement limited to two planes. The modern video game industry traces back to the first game ever made, Space War, itself a shmup. Created in 1962, Space War featured head-to-head competition between two ships trying to destroy each other. The action in Space War took place on one stationary screen, which is not the case in most current shmups.

Modern shmups fall into two rough categories, based on horizontal or vertical scrolling. The earliest scrolling vertical shooter was Namco's Xevious, released in 1982. Xevious contributed many innovations to the genre, including vertical scrolling, boss encounters at the end of designated sections, and separate offensive weapons that target either ground- or air-based enemies. This feature also appears in Taito's Raystorm series.

Horizontal scrolling shmups have their roots in William's Defender, made in 1980, which forced players to warp around to the opposite side of the screen when reaching the edge, and, more directly, Konami's Gradius (also known as Nemesis), produced in 1985. Gradius, like Xevious, brought new ideas to the table, including an amazing soundtrack and a powerup bar that allowed players to customize their ships' powerups to match the current situation by accumulating tokens and redeeming them at the correct time.

Shmups continued to evolve over the years, increasing in creativity, challenge level, and fan base. While most fans argue that the genre peaked in the early to mid '90s, the industry continues to produce quality shoot-em-ups.

For example, Ikaruga, developed by Treasure for both the Dreamcast and GameCube, impressed the gaming world with its mixture of puzzle elements and fast-paced shooter action. The player must destroy either black or white colored enemies in chains of threes to maintain a high score, and the player's ship can switch color itself to avoid or absorb bullets of the same color.

Irem also brought its popular, seminal R-Type series to a close with the recent PlayStation 2 release of R-Type Final. This installment allows the player to choose from more than 100 different ships with challenging levels that branch in different directions depending the actions of the pilot. In the near future, shmup fans have Konami's Treasure-developed Gradius V to look forward to on the PlayStation 2.

systems. Shmups also features an active forum with gameplay tips, a trading section, and great game links. See Figure 8-1.

Triggerzone (http://www.2dshooter.de/)

An excellent shmup site for people who can understand German.

Figure 8-1. Shmups.com, the daddy of Internet sites about shooters

Shmup.com (http://www.shmup.com/)
    Another mega-site for shmups, this site is in French.

Shoot the Core (http://www.shootthecore.com/)
    My own site, which focuses on news, fan art, and other goodies. It also
    links to many shooter demos and dojin games.

Dodge the Bullet (http://www.sirkain.net/~kiken/main.html)
    This site is great for replays and media.

HACK #96 Drive a Physics-Crazed Motorcycle

Ah, Elasto Mania; bouncing around on shareware motorbikes was never such
fun.

It's fortunate that, in writing this book, I'm allowed a tiny bit of self-indul-
gence to point to some of my very favorite things to grab for free, exploit,
and hack. Let's face it, what normal book includes an entire hack about a

crazed two-wheeled shareware game with super-addictive gameplay, a laughably cheap upgrade price to unlock the full package, and an insanely dedicated community? That describes the infamous 2D time-based motorcycle game Action Supercross, created by Balazs Rozsa, and its better-looking pseudo-sequel, Elasto Mania. The latter is so good, it deserves a hack of its own just as much as DOOM or Unreal does.

Introducing the New Bike Ballet Flava

The description for the Windows game Elasto Mania can easily apply to its less pretty DOS predecessor, Action Supercross. It's "[a] motorbike simulation game based on a real physical model." Could it be that simple?

The basic gameplay of Elasto Mania is as simple as it is bizarre. Drive your rear-wheel-drive, slow, bouncy-physics motorbike around a crudely drawn level, collecting apples by touching them with the front or back wheels of your bike and touching a flower to complete the level. The object of the game is to complete each level in the fastest time possible by accelerating, braking, and rotating your motorcycle to hop, skip, and jump around sometimes puzzling courses. You lose the level if your rider's head or body hits a piece of the scenery, so be careful. There's also a two-player split-screen mode and a level editor, though it's extremely limited in the shareware version.

Big deal, huh? The addiction comes from battling the wonderful physics to throw your motorbike around in crazy ways, constantly compensating for bounce and gravity factors, figuring out faster and faster alternate routes through maze-like levels. Bear in mind, though, that the physics also make it extremely frustrating. It may take a while to acclimate to the weird, unreal floatiness (Figure 8-2).

 As a testament to the game's hypnotic powers, following its 1997 debut, the entire Guildford, U.K. video game development community that I was part of was hopelessly addicted. Ostensibly, we should have worked on much more complex stuff, such as Black and White.

You can still find the shareware version of the original DOS Action Supercross from seminal fan site MopoSite (*http://www.moposite.com/info_across.php*). Version 1.3 includes 16 levels in the shareware version and 42 official levels plus a level editor in the registered version. There are also hundreds or thousands of custom player-designed levels.

Figure 8-2. Elastomania's basic but amazingly playable stylings

However, Action Supercross has had its day. The Windows version, Elasto Mania, is definitely the program to grab. Download the current shareware version (1.1) from the official web site (*http://www.elastomania.com/ sharewa.htm*). It includes 18 stages and a very basic level editor. Register at the princely sum of $9.99 to receive another 36 official levels, the completely unlocked level editor, and the ability to load any of an almost infinite amount of great levels created by sadistic, addicted players.

Check out Elastomaniac (*http://www.elastomaniac.com/*) for the biggest selection of Elasto Mania files. Levels tend to run 2 or 3 KB apiece, so multiple 7-MB archives will keep you entertained for days on end.

Achieving World Record Times

If you want to move in Elasto Mania expert circles, you'll have to play for hundreds of hours to challenge the crazy skills of the hardcore Elma players. The current world records table (*http://www.moposite.com/records_ elma_wrs.php*) includes some incredibly swift times. If you can beat them, then send your *state.dat* (overall records) and *.rec* (actual replay recording) files to the MopoSite folks. They'll add you to the high-score tables.

Unfortunately, you can't download replay recordings of all the world record holders. We suspect this is partly for trade secret reasons. The champions want you to work out the fastest routes on your own! Fortunately, there are good professional-style replays available elsewhere on MopoSite (*http://www.moposite.com/downloads_replays_professional.php*), as well as on the message boards for those interested in seeing expert tricks and tactics.

If you're just starting out, here are some tricks to speed up your best times:

Keep your footing. In Elasto Mania, your back wheel creates traction. Keep your back wheel on solid ground as much as possible, then stomp on the gas pedal to increase your speed. This is especially true on bumpy terrain. Rotate the bike to put your back wheel back down instead of waiting to hit the ground again after a drifting jump. Be wary of accelerating too hard when the bike is at a strange angle and flipping upside down, though.

Consider your route. Think carefully about how you're collecting the apples. Because of the flow of the level, some routes are much faster that others. More dramatically, some routes will leave you stuck and unable to pick up apples because you chose the incorrect order. As a basic goal, pick up the final apple as part of your final approach to the flower. This is often tricky, but it's a good goal.

Sometimes speeding up is the only way to traverse sections at all. For example, in some Elasto Mania levels, it's almost impossible to drive at full speed down stepped downhill sections without hitting your head on the ceiling. Instead, pluck up some courage and whiz down the tunnel as fast as you can, flipping your bike 180 degrees for traction off the roof of the tunnel and avoiding hitting your head on the overhangs to save seconds and look cool at the same time.

Dismount ungracefully if necessary. Remember two things about ending a level. First, you have to touch the flower with the front or back wheel of the bike or your head. Second, the level ends immediately. Even if you're in some kind of kamikaze death dive, as long as you hit the flower on the way down, you're good.

Hopefully, this will help you become an Elasto Mania master. Even if it doesn't, at least you'll have had the requisite apple a day that keeps the doctor away.

Hacking Elasto Mania Any Way You Can

Over at the excellent MopoSite you'll find a page (*http://www.moposite.com/stuff_programs.php*) devoted to extra hacks, exploits, and cool stuff you can do with Elasto Mania, even after grabbing the shareware version and registering it. In particular, here's some cool stuff you might like to try:

Import your own graphics. The LGR Development Kit (*http://www. moposite.com/programs/lgrdk10.zip*) allows you to replace the default, rather basic apples and flowers with your own images.

Change game texts. Elma Text (*http://www.moposite.com/programs/elma_ text.zip*) can change the text in the game so that when you fail, you can have Elasto Mania swear colorfully at you or commiserate with you in sympathetic verse.

Bypass impassible levels. You're normally allowed to skip only a maximum of three levels as you advance through the game. If you're completely stumped, use Level Unlocker (*http://members.fortunecity.com/ elastomania/zips/LevUnlck.zip*) to see the rest of the game.

Track records. If you play the game a lot and want to know your average times over each level when you've played it tens or hundreds of times, Average Times Counter (*http://www.moposite.com/programs/average_ counter.zip*) will take your statistics and work out your mean time for each level in the game.

Running Elasto Mania on Alternative Operating Systems

A game as cult-like as Elasto Mania, originally coded only for Windows and DirectX, inevitably brings conversions and exploits to run it on other systems. One's official, and one's not.

Oddly, the only remotely official Elasto Mania conversion came out for the lamented BeOS (*http://www.bebits.com/app/2195*). The site holding the full BeOS version was down at the time of writing, but you can at least try the shareware version and ask around for the full version.

If you're one of the 10,000 people without BeOS installed (or is that with?), you can run Elasto Mania on Unix-based systems. The excellent MopoSite fan site has a text file explaining how to run it on FreeBSD (*http://www. moposite.com/misc_text_files/unixelma.html*). Other forum posts indicate Linux versions of WINE (*http://www.winehq.com/*) work just fine. This is great news for Linux freaks who want to run Elasto Mania.

Unfortunately, there's no simple way to run either Elasto Mania or Action Supercross on the Mac. It may be possible to play the original Action Supercross using DOSBox ("Play Old Games Through DOSBox" [Hack #8]), though there are no online records that confirm or deny this.

Grand Theft Motorbike

In a bizarre, only partly rumored side point, the cooler-than-thou Rockstar Games of Grand Theft Auto fame licensed the Action Supercross concept for its Game Boy Evil Knievel game. This is a relatively unknown fact, mainly because Evil Knievel was, well, abysmal. Apparently, Rockstar failed to realize, presumably after licensing it, that the fun in Action Supercross is in juggling physics and rotation; the bike moves pathetically slowly for a daredevil game.

This leads to all kinds of what-if? fun, imagining Rockstar showing the game to Mr. Knievel himself during development, eliciting reactions such as "I don't remember moving at 3/4 miles an hour during all my famous stunts." The final Game Boy cart version, presumably based on Action Supercross, is much faster and completely messed up. The online gaming site IGN.com gave it just 2/10. Oh dear. Even worse, Rockstar/Take Two reused the concept for the *awful* Austin Powers Gameboy game, complete with fake Windows OS and motorcycle with attached Mini-Me. Don't ask. Really... don't ask.

HACK #97

Play Japanese Games Without Speaking Japanese

Learn just enough Japanese to have fun and avoid accidentally erasing your memory card.

You've finally decided to take the plunge and have ordered some hot imported exclusive video games from the exotic Orient. You've modified your console system of choice so that you can boot them ("Play Import Games on American Consoles" [Hack #49]), but now you're a little nervous. What happens if you can't even play the game because you can't read Japanese?

That's not as insurmountable a barrier as it may seem. You might find that you can simply press a button to skip past all the text sections, and it won't impede your gameplay beyond leaving you clueless as to the finer points of the game's story. If you need help that the illustrations in the game's manual can't provide, the Internet offers vast external resources.

Ignoring Translation Altogether

One great source of help is GameFAQs (*http://www.gamefaqs.com*), which offers fan-written hint guides for practically every game ever released as well as separate message board forums for each game, even if there's no hint guide for that game. Thus, from the day of a game's release, you can find others who own it and ask them for help.

The genre of the game will largely, but not entirely, determine how much help you'll need. Sometimes a game's menus will be partially in English. Very rarely will an English-language option exist for the entire game. Metal Gear Solid 2: Substance is one happy example of this.

Sometimes there will be practically no text at all, or the text will have little bearing on the gameplay. Martial arts fighting games traditionally fall into this category and, traditionally, have their menus in English. But watch out! Games such as Soul Calibur depend heavily on Japanese text, featuring lengthy weapon descriptions, special move commands, and special rules for certain battles. In action-oriented games such as Super Mario Sunshine, it may seem like the only reason for text is for window dressing, but designers sometimes hide crucial puzzle clues in the brief messages.

Of course, some games are extraordinarily text-heavy. Final Fantasy–style RPGs are the most obvious example; if you know no Japanese, it's hardly worth the trouble of importing the games unless you want a formidable challenge.

Understanding Japanese Writing

For the moment, let's assume that's what you want. Maybe you're trying to learn Japanese on your own, maybe you have a year or two of lessons under your belt, or maybe you're just fearless. In that case, it helps to understand the nature of the Japanese syllabary.

You may have heard that the Japanese have three different alphabets. This is technically true, if misleading. There *are* three different sets of characters, but they're not alphabets. Two, hiragana and katakana, are phonetic, where each character stands for one sound. The other, kanji (Chinese pictographs) cause no end of misery to students of the language, for there are around 2,000 individual characters used in everyday writing. Each kanji has a specific meaning and multiple pronunciations, depending on context and part of speech.

Of the three, you'll find the most immediate benefit in learning katakana. The Japanese use this system to approximate the sounds of foreign words, many of which appear in Japanese video game lingo. Thus, even with little to no knowledge of Japanese vocabulary, you may be able to pick out some katakana words and use them to help figure out what the game wants you to do.

The first step is to learn to recognize katakana. In general, katakana are sharp, angular characters mostly composed of straight lines. Here are the five vowel sounds of Japanese—a i u e o*—written in hiragana on the top and katakana on the bottom:

あ　い　う　え　お
ア　イ　ウ　エ　オ

See the difference? Learn to recognize katakana, then find a katakana chart on the Web (such as the one at Kids Japan, *http://www.kids-japan.com/kata-chart.htm*) or in a bookstore and consult it as you play. If you see a word written in katakana, match the symbols to the chart and try to decipher what it could be. It is an approximation of the sound of the original word, so try saying it out loud with accents in different places. Also remember that katakana words might not be English or even foreign at all, so don't worry too much if you can't figure it out.

The Most Important Game-Related Katakana

Does sounding out words sound like too much work? It probably is, unless you're fond of cryptolinguistic puzzles (hey, a game within a game!). The next step is to learn a list of important words that come up most often in games. The biggest problems with playing a game in another language most often come from the failure to understand very basic words. Barring story-specific puzzles and other such complex issues, the translation guides in Tables 8-1 and 8-2 should be just what the doctor ordered.

Table 8-1. Getting started

Japanese	Pronunciation	Meaning
はい	hai	Yes
いいえ	iie	No
ゲーム	gêmu	Game
ディスク	disuku	Disc
メモリカード	memori kâdo	Memory card
ニューゲーム	nyû gêmu	New game
はじめ	hajime	Begin/beginning/start

* Pronounced much like the vowels in the sentence "Ah, we soon get old."

Table 8-1. Getting started (continued)

Japanese	Pronunciation	Meaning
スタート	sutâto	Start
ロード	rôdo	Load
つづき	tsuzuki	Continue
コンティニュー	kontinyû	Continue
オプション	opushon	Options
セーブ	sêbu	Save
消す	kesu	Erase

Table 8-2. During play

Japanese	Pronunciation	Meaning
上(うえ)	ue	Up
下(した)	shita	Down
右(みぎ)	migi	Right
左(ひだり)	hidari	Left
ボタン	botan	Button
スティック	stikku	Stick
マップ	mappu	Map
バトル	batoru	Battle
クリア	kuria	Clear
ステータス	sutêtasu	Status
こうげき	kougeki	Attack
たたかう	tatakau	Fight
魔法(まほう)	mahou	Magic
アイテム	aitemu	Item

Table 8-2. During play (continued)

Japanese	Pronunciation	Meaning
逃げる	nigeru	Run
赤（あか）	aka	Red
青（あお）	ao	Blue
緑（みどり）	midori	Green
白（しろ）	shiro	White/light
黒（くろ）	kuro	Black/dark
ファイアー	faiâ	Fire
アイス	aisu	Ice
ウォーター	uôtâ	Water
サンダー	sandâ	Thunder
年	toshi	Year
月	getsu or tsuki	Month/moon
日	hi or nichi	Sun/day
火	hi	Fire
水	mizu	Water
木	ki	Wood/tree
金	kin	Gold
銀	gin	Silver
電	den	Thunder

The dash in katakana words and the circumflex in the Romanized versions represent a long vowel sound. Also note that some of these words are in hiragana and/or kanji. Can you tell the difference?

You may notice that there are many different words that convey nearly identical meanings. This is because different games use different words. The title screen of Nintendo's Giftpia for the GameCube uses *hajimeru* and *tsu-*

zukeru, the verb forms of begin and continue, but the title screen of its game Custom Robo reads, in English, PRESS START.

To start a new game in the Scenario mode of Custom Robo, select *atarashii dêta* ("new data"). In Square Enix's Final Fantasy X for the PlayStation 2, however, you begin a new game with *nyû gêmu* ("new game").

The magic spells used in many RPGs follow a similar fire-ice/water-thunder-air structure, although the names used differ. Some games use the kanji for the various elements in the magic list, but some might use katakana renderings of English-language words. The Final Fantasy series has traditionally used *faiaa*, *burizado*, *sandâ*, and *aero*.

> To read Japanese dates—to tell your memory card files apart, for example—note that the Japanese dates use the form year/month/day along with the kanji. January 5, 2004 would be 2004/1/5/: ２００４年１月５日

HACK #98 Back Up, Modify, and Restore PlayStation Saved Games

Shuffle, swap, spindle, and mutilate data on your memory cards.

One of the most proprietary pieces of console hardware is the memory card. While you *could* copy games between cards on the original hardware, that's a drag. What if your friend just moved to New York from California and took your save game with him? What if you'd like to see all 12 endings to Chrono Trigger without playing through the game 12 times? What if you want to archive your saves somewhere more permanent than a flimsy little piece of plastic and sand?

Fortunately, third-party manufacturers have jumped into the morass with utilities that can read memory cards to your PC and allow free online trading of memory card saves. Here's how to copy saved games to and from memory cards, so you can trade them with friends, back them up, and hack around.

PlayStation 1 Memory Card Hacking

It's best to start with the original PlayStation, because the saves are quite small and there are quite a few floating around online. This makes the PS1 really hackable.

Extracting saved games. The DexDrive from the now defunct Interact is by far the most common PlayStation 1 memory card copying device. You should be able to find it on eBay for $10 or so, a princely sum for such a neat device. Connect the DexDrive to the serial port on your PC, load the Windows-compatible software, and then back up entire PlayStation 1 memory cards as *.GME* files. You can then email these to your friends, trade them on the Internet, or store them on your PC for when your memory card inevitably fails. A lot of third-party PlayStation memory cards really *are* of poor quality and will corrupt and lose entire cards worth of games. Play it safe, and use official Sony memory cards!

DexDrive alternatives include methods for connecting your PlayStation directly to your PC, using Blaze's Xplorer cartridge plugged into the PlayStation's parallel port,* and the XLink software. This allows you to transfer saves directly from the memory card plugged into your PlayStation to your PC's hard drive. You can do similar things with some hacked Action Replay cartridges that are modified with the Caetla BIOS. The EMS memory adapter for PlayStation 2 also supports PlayStation 1 memory cards.

If you want to go entirely homebrew, consider PlaySaver (*http://members.aol.com/playsaver/*), a do-it-yourself memory card connector that plugs into your PC to provide a DexDrive-like experience. However, building this device requires a great deal of soldering, individual parts buying, and electrical savvy. It's not very straightforward. Since you can find DexDrives for $10 or less, you should probably attempt it only if you really like dangling resistors soldered precariously to voltage regulators. If that sounds fun, print out the schematics page (*http://members.aol.com/playsaver/p3.html*), and dabble to your heart's content.

Editing saved games. If archiving isn't enough, the marvellous PSXGameEdit utility (*http://moberg-dybdal.dk/psxge/*) for Windows is the tool for you to manage, save, and edit your extracted saves. It supports hex editing, conversion of game saves between standard save formats, and even regions so you can switch a European save to a U.S. format. Admittedly, it hasn't been updated in a while, but here's a step-by-step guide to tinkering with saves:

1. Install the latest version of PSXGameEdit to a suitable directory, then load it up and choose the Open MemCard Image option. The utility also takes single game saves from multiple source types (*.mcs*, *.mcr*, *.psx*, *.gme*, *.mcd*, and *.vgs*), but because this comes with the PSXGameEdit install, open the example entire memory card image in *.mc* form.

2. You'll see a whole memory card worth of saves, including their icons, game names, and their territory. The PlayStation 1 memory card has a

---

* If you have an earlier PlayStation that actually has a parallel port!

grand total of 15 save blocks. Some games (for example, Legacy Of Kain: Soul Reaver) are greedy and grab as many as three blocks. The GUI will say Link block and Link end block for those extra blocks.

3. Click on the Tomb Raider III save to see all sorts of cool options. Start with the Tools/Icon Edit menu to make your own delicious icon by editing the 16×16 pixel, 16-color, 4-frame graphic. Although the paint package is pretty basic, it's still fun.

4. Change the region of a game save by selecting the Convert/Convert To American option from the menu. You will need to know the U.S. product code to make this work properly. PSXGameEdit knows some of the code itself, but if it doesn't, look up the code online, then use the Set Format/Set Format American menu to key in the new product code manually.

5. You can also hex-edit the saves from within the GUI. The Patch option is a special trainer that allows you to change variables within the GUI menus without scratching around in hexadecimal. However, in this default download of PSXGameMenu, only a few games have the Patch option available.

Finding saved games online. As for sources for the actual PSX saves, the ever reliable GameFAQs has a good selection for many games. Search in the PlayStation area to find direct links to .*GME* DexDrive saves, such as those for Final Fantasy IX (*http://www.gamefaqs.com/console/psx/save/27583.html*). In addition to this, many individual fan pages have DexDrive-compatible saves, such as a Dance Dance Revolution page (*http://www.rawbw.com/~zio/DDR/*) that includes unlocks in .*GME* form for DDR Konamix U.S., for example.

PlayStation 2 Memory Card Hacking

On the other hand, the PlayStation 2 also has many good saves available. I've covered how to hack games by changing variables in memory in other hacks such as "Create PS2 Cheat Codes" [Hack #73], but there's plenty of cool trading and exploiting you can do using just a save file, as you'll see in the following sections.

Extracting saved games. The PS2 has an equally confusing set of possibilities for memory card hackers. There are two major commercial options, EMS's third-party hardware and Datel's X-Port/SharkPort hardware. Both connect your PlayStation 2 to your PC and cost between $20 and $30 new. Hacking's not horrendously expensive.

The most obvious choice is the X-port/SharkPort hardware. (Be aware that this is separate from their Action Replay line of products.) The device plugs into the USB port on the front bottom left of the PlayStation 2 as well as the PC. The unofficial, included PlayStation 2 disc boots in a similar fashion as the Action Replay. The software allows you to transfer data from the PS2 memory card directly to the PC. The X-port and the SharkPort are broadly compatible, but make sure to name the save file correctly for the device. The SharkPort uses *.sps* and the X-port *.xps*. Also, watch out for regional incompatibilities related to the actual save file.

You can also try out the USB adapter from long-time Hong Kong third-party supplier EMS (*http://www.hkems.com/product/ps2/ps2%20usb.htm*). This is a good buy because it includes 64 MB of save space and connects to the PC easily. Plug a normal PS2 memory card into the device, connect the device to the PS2's memory card slot and to the PC via a USB cable, then run the PS2 Adapter program on your PC. You'll be able to upload and download data to and from that memory card.

If you don't like the look of EMS's USB device, you can try its earlier memory card adapter (*http://www.hkems.com/product/ps2/ps2-mem.htm*) that uses Smart Media cards to save data with an adapter. There's an additional necessary cable that attaches this to your PC to save and load data. Then again, the USB version looks like a straight upgrade of the earlier version.

In any case, you'll find driver and software support for both devices at the EMS web site (*http://www.hkems.com/download.htm*). All of the major Asian online game stores (Lik-Sang, Play-Asia, and so on) carry these products.

Finally, the very latest versions of the PS2 Action Replay Max can download saved games directly to your memory card via broadband, as long as your PlayStation 2 has a broadband adapter. A clever exploit by the AR creators allows the Action Replay to connect to the Internet, though it doesn't currently support uploading or saving your own files. However, this method may be the wave of the future.

Editing saved games. For more hardware/software-related information on this whole area, check out the handy PS2SaveTools site (*http://www. ps2savetools.com/*), which includes information and FAQs on the major hardware and several very helpful save-manipulation programs. In particular, PS2SIDC (*http://www.ps2savetools.com/ps2sidc.php*) changes the country ID of the save so you can change territory information about it. Save Slicer (*http://www.ps2savetools.com/saveslicer.php*) allows you to separate individual sections of a save to help with editing it, if you're trying to hack infinite lives.

Even better, the PS2SaveTools wizards have found a way for you to make your own personal save icons using the PC program IconInjector (*http:// www.ps2savetools.com/iconinjector.php*). These rotating icons will appear on the actual PS2 memory card screen in place of the traditional SharkPort/X-port save. This is especially cool if you're fed up with the violence the Shark-Port has enacted on the original beautiful save icon and want to reinstate something cool-looking.

Finding Saved Games Online

PS2 games most often appear in SharkPort/X-port formats. If you explore GameFAQs for any major PS2 game such as Metal Gear Solid 2 (*http://www. gamefaqs.com/console/ps2/save/28489.html*), you'll see a host of saves, including various levels of completion. The official GameShark site (*http:// www.gameshark.com/*) still has a great deal of saves left, too. Many smaller, personal fan sites, such as this Gran Turismo 3 X-port page (*http://www. angelfire.com/realm3/gt3/xport.htm*), have a mass of further saves to accumulate, sometimes including enhanced rosters for teams, interesting unlocked items, and other coolness.

HACK #99   Access Your Console's Memory Card Offline

Memory card hacking for Nintendo, Microsoft, and Sega consoles.

Some of the most common console memory card hacking deals with Play-Station 1 and 2 cards ("Back Up, Modify, and Restore PlayStation Saved Games" **[Hack #98]**). They're not the only fish in the sea, though. The GameCube, Xbox, Dreamcast, N64, and other consoles with swappable memory devices all have their own different solutions that require different pieces of hardware. The very basics are pretty similar, though. Let's cut through the confusion and explain where to begin.

GameCube Memory Card

The GameCube is a relatively quiet community for save game hacking, apart from its excellent Action Replay scene ("Cheat on Other Consoles" **[Hack #75]**). Fortunately, there are two major options.

Extracting saved games. The first is the USB Memory Card adapter from EMS (*http://www.hkems.com/product/gc/gc%20usb.htm*). This 64-MB save device is similar to its PS2 equivalent, though, unlike the PS2 version, you don't need an original memory card to use it. Connect it to your GameCube, turn on the console, and access the Memory Card screen, then connect the USB connector to your PC. Because the USB cable provides power, you can do this without connecting to the GameCube at all. You'll have the same options without being tethered to your GC.

However, in order to access the saves and make sure they've copied across correctly, connect to both PC and GC at once. Here's how:

1. Install the latest version of the GameCube Memory Adapter program for Windows from the HK EMS site (*http://www.hkems.com/download. htm*).

2. Turn on your GameCube without a game in it, put the USB Memory Card into your GameCube's memory slot, and then connect the USB cable with one end in the GC memory card and the other in your PC's USB port.

3. Run the Memory Adapter program on your PC and click List Savers (yes, that should say List Saves, but I'll let them off with a warning). You should see all the save games already on the Memory Card.

4. Use the icons to copy saves from your GameCube (with Backup Saver or Backup Card for the whole thing) or copy backups and saves downloaded from the Internet back again (with Restore Saver and Restore Card, in this version of the software).

5. Bonus tip! Right-click on the window to change the skin of the already somewhat ugly GUI to a variety of even less appealing multicolored skins. We recommend Natural Skin, though it's possibly only natural if you're Shrek.

The other option, apart from the EMS device, is the GameShark GameSaves device (*http://www.gameshark.com/*), launched at the end of 2003. It provides similar USB-based hardware and even ships with 150 saves already on the device.

Editing saved games. There are a few game-hacking tools available, many from the Game Save Sharing Community. In particular, check out Psydonia's GC Save Convert software that allows you to change region codes ("Play Import Games on American Consoles" **[Hack #49]**) on most GameCube games. The latest EMS USB adapter bundles this software.

There are some save-hacking programs in progress, though the power of Action Replay codes has quashed some of the interest here. At the time of writing, there weren't any worth recommending.

Finding saved games online. If you're looking for help and trading information on game saves, the Nintendo Game Save Sharing Community (*http:// www.gci.net.tc/*), a Yahoo! Group, has a mass of information, discussion, and a file area with saves. The GameShark web site itself (*http://www. gameshark.com/*) has a mass of saves in its particular format, but Game-FAQs is still one of the most useful sources, with the Legend Of Zelda: The Wind Waker page (*http://www.gamefaqs.com/console/gamecube/save/3447. html*) featuring a whole bunch of near-completion saves.

Finally, Arson Winter has a good page of individual saves (*http://tideblue. neogodless.com/modegreen/index.html*), including some cool custom emblems for F-Zero GX. Watch out for incompatible saves from the two major save devices, though; explicitly named GameShark saves (in GCS format) seem somewhat more popular than EMS adapter saves (in GCI format).

GC Backup Warnings

Phantasy Star Online backups may not work in the online game if you've progressed since you saved and performed a new backup. To stop cheating, the game now keeps online records of how far you've progressed in the game. This won't stop you from cheating or backing up to play offline, of course, but PSO isn't much fun offline.

Also, some locked saves, such as those from Animal Crossing, don't work at all with backups. You may have to resort to broadband-adapter exploits ("Cheat on Other Consoles" [Hack #75]) to copy saved games.

To learn more about how the GameCube stores its saves, there's a rather remarkable PDF document on an Australian site (*http://members.iinet.net.au/ ~theimp/*) that goes into extreme detail, including individual game codes and which part of the save is used for which part of the data.

Xbox Memory Card Copying

Since most Xbox hacking manipulates saved games ("Hack Xbox Game Saves" [Hack #74]), there's not much to say in this section. There's definitely plenty to cover, though, so I'll refer you to the other hacks when necessary.

Extracting saved games. It's fairly easy to copy Xbox saves with Action Replay or Mega X-Key hardware. The only exceptions are a small number of saves that are too big to move from the hard drive to a memory card, such as some Knights Of The Old Republic saves. You'll need FTP access to the machine to grab those; search Xbox-Scene (*http://www.xbox-scene.com/*) for more information on this.

Editing and finding saved games. It's easy to find Xbox saves online. Start at GameFAQs, but beware of the cryptographic signatures. You can't simply hack in the data and expect it to work. However, you can resign saves with third-party utilities such as XSaveSig. There are plenty of interesting, completely legitimate saves too. For example, the GameFAQs Halo page (*http://www.gamefaqs.com/console/xbox/save/32488.html*) has saves in which the player starts in locations impossible to reach during normal gameplay. The Codejunkies site (*http://www.codejunkies.com/*) also has a very large number of Xbox Action Replay codes, often including very up-to-date games.

Other Memory Card Copying Options

As we look back further in the past, our list of available options shrinks. There weren't very many saved games for previous console generations, unless you wanted to tear apart an old Zelda cartridge and figure out the format there. Fortunately, if you have a Dreamcast, N64, or Game Boy, you don't have to go that far.

Sega Dreamcast. There are several handy Dreamcast utilities to back up and copy your saved games. If you're connected to the Internet via your DC ("Use Your Dreamcast Online" [Hack #54]), you can easily download saved games or even email them to yourself from your PC. Obviously, most people don't have their Dreamcasts set up with dial-up accounts, so an alternative is to burn CDs with memory card saves on them, as done when working with VMU games ("Hack the Dreamcast Visual Memory Unit" [Hack #52]). Even this isn't perfect, though, because you can't write saves to CD from the DC. Even if you could, several games have protected saved games, such as those for Phantasy Star Online.

Fortunately, the EMS-created Nexus memory cards (*http://www.segatech.com/technical/nexus/*) plug into your PC much as those memory cards mentioned earlier. You can copy saves perfectly, even those from PSO! However, you must have your memory card plugged into a Dreamcast controller that is itself plugged into a Dreamcast to draw the power necessary for the transfer to happen, however, so make sure your DC is close to your PC.

Nintendo 64. There's really only one major memory card copying device for the Nintendo 64: Interact's DexDrive N64. A review mirrored on the Icequake N64 site (*http://n64.icequake.net/mirror/64scener.parodius.com/dexreviw.htm*) gives a good overview of its basic information. Plug your N64 Controller Pack into this device, then plug the device into your PC via the serial port. There are some minor complaints about its reliability, but it's the only major option out there if you're an N64 nerd who wants to transfer your saves around. Although you can see the relative unpopularity of the device by the paucity of its saves on GameFAQs, there are a couple of completed saves for Super Mario 64 (*http://www.gamefaqs.com/console/n64/save/22511.html*) to keep you going.

Game Boy/Game Boy Advance. The first thing to stress with the Game Boy is that it doesn't actually include standalone saves. Some Game Boy carts, particularly early ones, don't even have any SRAM for saving information on them. Depending on the complexity of the title in question, each individual cart can have a differing amount of SRAM.

Surprisingly, there *are* devices that grab the *.SAV* data off the cartridge. In particular, the GBA Super Memory Stick (*http://www.success-hk.com/review/gba_memory_stick/index2.htm*) plugs into the EXT port on the Game Boy Advance and allows you to copy saved games from whatever cartridge is plugged in.

Don't forget the usual suspects, though. Both the Action Replay and the GameShark allow you to save your Game Boy's current save state via USB. This is handy if you've played 150 hours of Pokémon and want to make sure that nobody overwrites your save! Since these utilities also allow memory code hacking, they may be your best bet.

As for finding saved games online, the GameFAQs boards have a big selection, including a massive set for Pokémon Ruby (*http://www.gamefaqs.com/portable/gbadvance/save/32745.html*). You may be able to take *.SAV* files from archives such as Zophar's Game Boy *.SAV* archive (*http://www.zophar.net/sav/*) and Game Boy Advance *.SAV* archive (*http://www.zophar.net/savgba/*) and put them on your GBA. Just remember that these files represent the entire save state of the cartridge and will entirely overwrite your current saves, so be sure to back up your existing saves first.

It's worth mentioning the Blaze MPXChanger here because it promises a veritable nirvana of PlayStation, N64, and even the much sought-after Game Boy save capabilities in a single device for retro save game fetishists. However, after I bought one very cheaply on eBay, I found that the included software uses custom formatted saves works only on Windows 95 and 98, refusing to work on any variants of Windows NT. You'll need to dual-boot or have an older Windows installation to run the software. This is a shame because the MPXChanger itself sells for $10 or less on many auction sites.

Overclock Your Console

HACK
100

Want your console to run faster than it does right now? It's possible.

PC overclocking is passé, at least for practical purposes. You can buy faster and faster graphics cards to compensate for almost any eventuality, so most overclocking is done for show. Hardly any recent PC overclocking hack, either of a CPU or graphics card, can make a nonplayable game playable or a super-jerky game super-smooth. Maybe I'm just a console snob—overclocking is sometimes a very cool thing on the PC—but I *really* dig console overclocking.

From speeding up your Sega Genesis to previously untenable speeds to making your Nintendo 64 run in overdrive, you can sometimes achieve major framerate hikes via overclocking. Sure, sometimes you'll have glitches and crashes too, but pioneers and trailblazers can't have everything. The following sections demonstrate a few console overclocking tips.

Overclocking Your Nintendo 64

There's one main font of knowledge in the West regarding overclocking: Robert Ivy (*http://www.geocities.com/robivy64/Welcome.html*). Though he mentions the excellent GameSX.com web site as another good source of information, start with his site. Be aware, though, that overclocking a N64 requires very precise soldering. This is fun to contemplate, but it's only for advanced users to do.

Robert's site warns you of the obvious: if the game already ran at a full frame-rate, overclocking won't make any difference. Because the developers intended their N64 games to run only on the N64, most games already had sufficient optimizations to produce good framerates. Only particularly complicated 3D games such as Perfect Dark that sometimes chug a little or a lot, even when using the extra RAM in the N64 expansion packs, will see much effect.

However, Perfect Dark is a crucial title, so what the heck! Here are his tips:

1. Start with a transparent N64. According to multiple practitioners, earlier revisions of the Nintendo 64 motherboard (such as those found in the all-black consoles) are much less resilient to attempts to make the main chip go faster, crashing after a few minutes of enhanced play.

2. Resolder the CPU pins. To perform the mod, you'll need to lift up a couple of pins on the N64's CPU and reconnect them to other parts of the circuit board (*http://www.geocities.com/robivy64/mod_page1.html*). Although Robert's site has rudimentary hand-drawn pictures, the

GameSX site has a much better procedure with actual photos on its instruction page (*http://www.gamesx.com/misctech/n64oc.htm*).

Look for pins 112 and 116 along the bottom side of the CPU. Heat the base of the CPU with a soldering iron, then *very carefully* lift up its legs. Then solder a wire to each pin. Connect pin 112 to GND and pin 116 to +3.3v for 2x speed. You're actually changing the chip's clock multiplier, normally set to 1.5 times the speed (giving a 93.75-MHz speed chip), to two or even three times the clock speed. A 2x speed isn't twice the normal N64 clock rate because the standard multiplier is 1.5x. The GameSX page has more details, including a recommendation for a good capacitor to use.

3. Beware of extra heat. Because the CPU runs faster, you may run into heat-related problems. Robert put a heatsink from an old stereo amplifier in his overclocked N64 to help with the heat buildup from playing for hours at a time.

Sega Genesis Overclocking

While the N64 is a somewhat newer system to try to speed up, the Sega Genesis is a much older, more disposable system. It's easy to find ridiculously cheap hardware to test. The end result overclocks the stock 7.6-MHz CPU to anywhere up to 16 MHz, meaning smoother scrolling and less slowdown, especially with lots of sprites onscreen in 2D games.

Although Robert Ivy also mentions this procedure (*http://www.geocities.com/robivy64/Genesis.html*), the Epic Gaming site has a full explanation (*http://www.bluespheer.com/host/epicgaming/md_oc/*), including photos of the mod and much more detailed explanations. Epic Gaming seem to be the originators, though a group of Japanese enthusiasts apparently have reached the same results independently. I'm just passing along their findings, but I'll try to describe it as succinctly as possible:

1. Disconnect a trace. For the 13.4-MHz overclocking hack, open the machine, and remove the RF shielding. Find Pin 15 on the CPU, and cut its trace so that the system won't boot. This is a little scary. Then connect together Pin 15 on the CPU and Pin 19 on the cartridge slot to make the system boot again.

2. Build a switch. You'll need two switches, an on-on clock switch to switch the frequency and an on-off switch to halt the machine. Connect Pins 15 and 19 on the cartridge slot to Pin 15 on the CPU through the on-on switch. Connect the on-off switch with one terminal to GND and the other to Pin 17 on the CPU. Without the halt switch, the Genesis will crash when you switch speeds.

3. Reboot and flip switches. Everything's now ready to do the magic over-clock! Boot your Genesis, hit the Halt switch, flip the Overclock switch, then flip the Halt switch back again so your Genesis continues in super-souped-up mode.

According to the Epic Gaming page, you can coax more speed from the machine if you use crystal oscillators, so refer to them if this isn't enough. The end result is the removal of almost all slowdown in classic Genesis games. The CPU doesn't run *that* much hotter, and although there are some minor sound/music issues, it's a fun, worthwhile hack.

Further Console Overclocking Fun

Although I've covered two of the most interesting overclocking hacks for consoles, there are a few other possibilities worth looking into.

Allegedly, you can overclock your PlayStation or PSOne (*http://www. geocities.com/robivy64/Playstation67.html*), leading to an alleged decrease in loading time and better video playback. Your mileage, of course, may vary. It's also possible to overclock the NES from 1.79 MHz all the way up to 2.3 MHz, although it's difficult to find these instructions online.

Onward and upward, I say. How about overclocking the Xbox 2? I don't care if it's not out yet: someone will find a way.

Index

We'd like to hear your suggestions for improving our indexes. Send email to *index@oreilly.com*.

B

backlighting versus frontlighting, 73
BackNTime web site, 14, 32
Bad Dudes Vs. Dragon Ninja, 220
Bahamut Lagoon, 267
Baku Baku Animal, 231
Ball, Eric, Skeleton+, 22
Balloonacy by Richard Bayliss, 6
Bandai WonderSwan (see WonderSwan)
Barnett, Joel mapmaking FAQ, 294
Baseball, Intellivision, 33
Basketball, Intellivision, 33
Bayliss, Richard, Balloonacy, 6
Beats Of Rage (Dreamcast
          homebrew), 218
Beneath A Steel Sky, 24
BeOS, 396
Blaze's Xplorer, 403
Bliss, 60
Blizzard, 289
Bloodspell, 247
Bomberman Online, 212
Border Down, 388, 390
Bosconian, 33
Breakout, 32
    Nuon homebrew, 189
Broken Sword series and ScummVM, 24
Brunching Shuttlecocks, 69
Bubble Bobble, 60
Bum–Rags To Riches (iPod game), 69
Bung Xchanger, 77
Buzz Bombers, 33

C

C-64
    emulation, 5–9
        CCS64 (see CCS64)
        loading disk images, 6–8
        VICE (see VICE)
    Pocket Commodore 64 emulator, 97
C-64 emulation
    Pocket Commodore 64, 97
C64 Unlimited, 9
C64.com, 9
Cadre, Adam, ix
calibrating PC display, 173
Capcom
    CPS2, 232
        cartridge system, 226

fighting game harness, 223
    Plasma Sword, 209
Carillon music editor, 80
Carless, Simon, ix
Cartier, Scott "Skah_T", 189
case fans and noise, 142
CaSTaway, 99
Catlist adult game list, 53
Catlist site, 54
CATVER.INI file, 54
Cavina, Piero, Oystron, 10, 22
CCS64, 5
Centipede, 32
cheating
    aimbot, 133, 137
    cheat code formats, cross converting
        codes, 277
    code disassembly, 288
    Game Boy variable hacking, 284
    GameCube variable
        hacking, 281–283
    hex editing characters, 287
    Legacy Of Kain: Soul Reaver,
        hacking, 290–291
    modifying PC game saves and
        settings, 284–287
    modifying PC games using memory
        finders, 285
    Nintendo variable hacking, 283
    older game hacks, 281
    packet editors and hacking, 289
    PlayStation 2 cheat codes, 273–277
    Xbox, changing saved
        games, 277–281
    (see also anti-cheating software)
Cheating-Death (C-D), 135
cheats
    Aimbot, 133
    aimbot cheaters, 137
    identifying, 133
    modified player skins, 135
    Radar and Map ESP, 135
    Wallhack, 134
    wallhack cheaters, 137
Chocobo.org site, 67
Chrono Trigger sequel for SNES, 267
Chu Chu Rocket, 212
Cinemaware
    Defender Of The Crown, 3
    It Came From The Desert, 3
    web site, 3

Colophon

Our look is the result of reader comments, our own experimentation, and feedback from distribution channels. Distinctive covers complement our distinctive approach to technical topics, breathing personality and life into potentially dry subjects.

The tool on the cover of *Gaming Hacks* is a Viking helmet. The image of a Viking soldier with horned helmet, popularized by Hollywood movies and cartoons, is now seen as a myth by the scientific community. Some researchers say Vikings wore no helmets. Others use fragments to depict a helmet with a smooth, curved surface that could deflect blows. Other features included cheek guards that could be worn folded up (perhaps horn-like) and a goggle-like band of steel that protected the nose, eyes, and upper cheekbones without interfering with breathing or visibility.

Mary Anne Weeks Mayo was the production editor and copyeditor, and Matt Hutchinson was the proofreader for *Gaming Hacks*. Phil Dangler, and Claire Cloutier provided quality control. Mary Agner, Sanders Kleinfield, and Meghan Lydon provided production assistance. Julie Hawks wrote the index.

Hanna Dyer designed the cover of this book, based on a series design by Edie Freedman. The cover image is from the Stock Options Toys CD. Clay Fernald produced the cover layout with QuarkXPress 4.1 using Adobe's Helvetica Neue and ITC Garamond fonts.

David Futato designed the interior layout. This book was converted by Andrew Savikas to FrameMaker 5.5.6 with a format conversion tool created by Erik Ray, Jason McIntosh, Neil Walls, and Mike Sierra that uses Perl and XML technologies. The text font is Linotype Birka; the heading font is Adobe Helvetica Neue Condensed; and the code font is LucasFont's TheSans Mono Condensed. The illustrations that appear in the book were produced by Robert Romano and Jessamyn Read using Macromedia Free-Hand 9 and Adobe Photoshop 6. This colophon was written by Mary Anne Weeks Mayo.